THE
TEST
OF BATTLE

The American Expeditionary Forces in the
Meuse-Argonne Campaign

Paul F. Braim

 White Mane Books

This White Mane Books publication
was printed by
Beidel Printing House, Inc.
63 West Burd Street
Shippensburg, PA 17257-0152 USA

In respect for the scholarship contained herein, the acid-free paper used in this book meets the guidelines for permanence and durability of the Committee on Production Guidelines for Book Longevity of the Council on Library Resources.

For a complete list of available publications
please write
White Mane Books
Division of White Mane Publishing Company, Inc.
P.O. Box 152
Shippensburg, PA 17257-0152 USA

Library of Congress Cataloging-in-Publication Data

Braim, Paul F. , 1926–
    The test of battle : the American Expeditionary Forces in the
Meuse-Argonne campaign / Paul F. Braim
        p.   cm.
    Includes bibliographical references and index.
    ISBN 1-57249-085-3 (alk. paper)
    1. Argonne, Battle of the, 1918. 2. World War, 1914-1918-
-Campaigns--Meuse River Valley. 3. United States. Army. American
Expeditionary Forces--History--World War, 1914-1918. I. Title.
D545.A63B73   1998
940.4'34--dc21   97-46690
                                                            CIP

PRINTED IN THE UNITED STATES OF AMERICA

This book is reverently dedicated
to the memory of
DANA J. PYLE
who served in the First World War,
held the offices of National Commander,
National Quartermaster/Adjutant
and Region 3 Commander
of the Veterans of World War I
of the United States of America,
and served his nation well in
many civic and patriotic causes.
He has left this encampment
to join his comrades
in eternal rest.

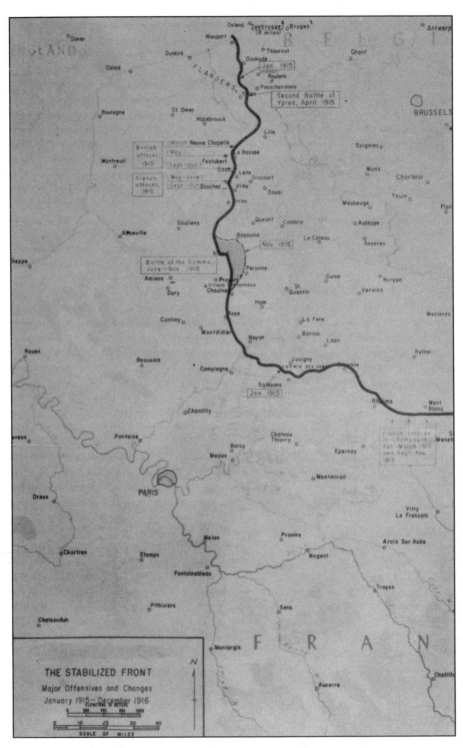

Map 1. The Stabilized Front, 1915–1917.
Department of History, United States Military Academy, map to
accompany interim text, *The Great War*. West Point: U.S.M.A., 1979.

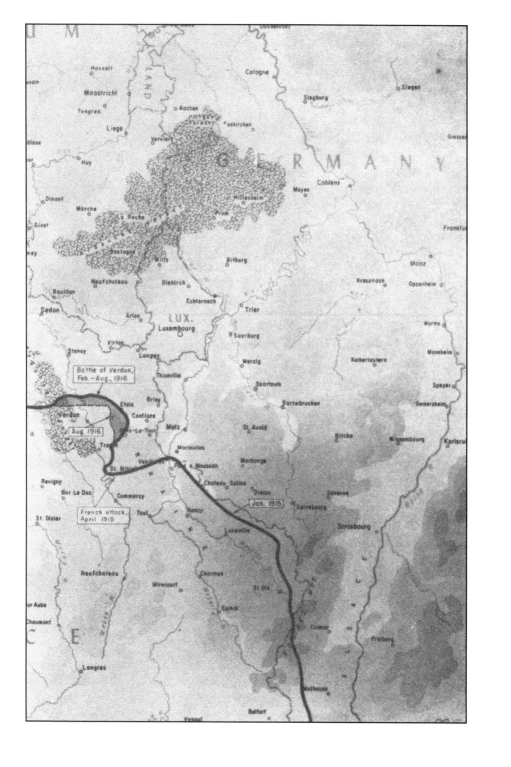

CONTENTS

FOREWORD

During the earliest months of American belligerency in 1917 the United States government had to answer a most important question: What military support should it contribute to the cause of the Allies? This decision had to be consistent with the larger political goals to which President Wilson had committed the nation. His aim was to create a situation in which both the Central Powers and the Entente Powers would have to agree to a peace settlement of American design. Wilson had in mind a peace that would not be much more acceptable to the principal leaders of the Allies than to those of the enemy coalition. He wanted to forge a new world order based on a league of nations—a far cry from the future envisioned in the competing collections of secret treaties that bound together the two European coalitions.

Whatever the outcome of peacemaking, the first task was to defeat the Central Powers; to achieve this end the United States had to make a significant contribution to the war on land as well as on the sea. If the Central Powers met defeat, particularly a truly catastrophic one, they would be unable to resist whatever was offered in the postwar settlement. Wilson calculated further that the war would have been so devastating that the victors would probably have suffered almost as much as the vanquished. Given the exhaustion of both European coalitions, the United States, reaching the apogee of its power as Europe reached its nadir, could reasonably expect to dominate a peace settlement however unpalatable in diverse ways to the Allies.

The problem for President Wilson was how to make a significant contribution to the defeat of the Central Powers on land, while at the same time maintaining broad freedom of action to proceed as he wished after the war came to an end. In essence, France and Britain wanted the United States to supply troops as individuals or in small units to serve as replacements for depleted European armies. The United States would ship personnel; the European armies would do the rest. This approach would ensure efficacious American assistance at the earliest possible moment and lead to the earliest possible decision.

To propositions of this nature the American military leaders returned a definitive rejection. They were fully prepared to concentrate American forces on the Western Front, because the decision was sure to take place in that theater and because the United States could exert maximum pressure more quickly and more effectively there than anywhere else, but the conception of "amalgamating" American soldiers into European armies never received serious consideration in Washington. The American people would never have permitted it; the army was unalterably opposed to any such course; and it might well have had deleterious consequences for Wilson's peace plans.

Instead of amalgamation the President chose to mobilize a strong independent army, one that would operate in its own sector of the Western Front, under its own commanders, according to its own doctrine, and with its own services of supply. Such an army, after making a considerable and perhaps even a decisive contribution to victory, would surely enhance the American bargaining position at the postwar peace congress.

The decision to field an independent American army entailed considerable risk. The situation in Europe was quite desperate. After all, the Germans had resumed unrestricted submarine warfare on the high seas against neutral and noncombatant shipping, although it would almost certainly lead to American belligerency, because they were convinced that they could force a decision before the unprepared Americans would exercise much influence on the outcome. Despite these portents the Americans did not diverge from the decision to mobilize and deploy an independent army. Given their low level of preparedness, in April 1917 the United States could not hope to undertake land operations on a truly independent basis until 1919, and perhaps not even until 1920. Nevertheless, even after the many reverses of 1917—the French defeat on the Western Front, the British failure to force a breakthrough on the Somme, the collapse of Russia, and the terrible rout of the Italian army at Caporetto—the United States unswervingly adhered to the concept of an independent army. It was an unavoidable concession to the exigencies of both the domestic political situation and the imperatives of the plan to create a league of nations.

A remarkable effort was made to begin the mobilization of a great independent army during 1917, but as 1918 began it was evident that the end of the process lay very far in the future. Only a few troops had been shipped to France, and it was obviously unfeasible to occupy an independent sector for many months.

Developments during the early months of 1918 thoroughly compromised the rational American plan to field an independent army. When Germany failed to win by using submarines in 1917, the German army was concentrated in France in the desperate hope of achieving a decision on land before the Americans could put in enough resources to ensure an ultimate victory for the Entente. The German assault began on 21 March 1918, and it did not cease until 18 July, when the Allies gained the initiative. During the emergency the United States agreed to ship only front-line troops, an expedient that militated against the early formation of an independent army because it cut off the flow of support units. Moreover, the Commander of the American Expeditionary Forces, General John J. Pershing, agreed to the temporary brigading of American divisions with French and British counterparts, under European command, to gain experience in quiet sectors, although some American divisions saw service during the defensive battles of March–July 1918. This process further disrupted training and activities essential to the creation of an independent army.

Although the massive German attacks bent the Allied front, it did not break, and General Ferdinand Foch, the generalissimo, assumed the offensive as soon as the German attacks were stopped. Shortly thereafter the impatient Pershing was allowed to form the American First Army, although it lacked many of the normal components of such an organization. It was quite a far cry from an independent force.

The First Army conducted its first operation, a kind of rehearsal for more difficult service, against a huge salient at St. Mihiel, near the right of the active front in a largely quiet area. Pershing intended not only to reduce the salient but to move north and east against vital rail lines, deemed essential to the continuing supply of the German units fighting all along the front. If these communications were interdicted, the First Army would make a vital contribution to the final decision—just what had been intended, even if the First Army was but a pale shadow of the force that had been contemplated earlier. Unfortunately Foch, now a marshal of France, decided to restrict the attack on the St. Mihiel salient. Pershing received orders to reduce the salient, but then break off the advance. He was then to move the First Army westward to the Meuse-Argonne sector, where it would cooperate with French units in attacks coordinated with those of the British and the Belgians to the north. The Franco-American elements would move northward and the British and Belgians eastward, displacing the entire German line.

The attack on the St. Mihiel salient, which took place on 14–16 September 1918, proved most successful, but in retrospect it does not appear as impressive as was claimed at the time. The German high command decided not to fight for the salient, but to withdraw, a means of shortening the line. This retrograde movement began just before the Americans jumped off. In effect the First Army simply speeded up the German evacuation. A more experienced force might have captured most of the retreating defenders, but they were able to escape with much of their equipment.

The stage was thus set for rapid deployment to the Meuse-Argonne sector. It had to be accomplished in a mere ten days, because the big push was scheduled for 26 September. Although the Americans would not encounter the better German divisions in France, they would have to fight in very difficult terrain that favored the defense. It would be a severe test indeed for the fledgling American troops—far from the degree of readiness for combat that had been envisioned earlier. This premature operation stemmed from the unexpected circumstances that materialized in 1918—first the German offensive and then the Allied counteroffensive. These events thoroughly disrupted Pershing's preparations to field an independent army and also forced extensive combat operations long before the Americans were fully prepared for them.

Although the American army ultimately gained its objectives in the Meuse-Argonne Campaign, the victory came only after ghastly losses in blood and treasure and agonizing delay. Shortly *afterwards* the German army collapsed completely, and diplomatic negotiations led swiftly to the Armistice of 11 November 1918. This outcome obscured much of the real history of the Meuse-Argonne Campaign. Certain Europeans on both sides of the conflict raised questions then and later about the effectiveness of the American operations, but these criticisms were either ignored or dismissed as sour grapes. Consequently military historians have never really provided a fully comprehensive and authoritative history of the campaign.

Colonel Paul F. Braim (U.S. Army Ret.) has set himself the task of preparing a detailed and objective campaign history of the Meuse-Argonne operations. To this task he brings broad experience as a career army officer and expertise in the methods of the professional historian. In his civilian guise he is Dr. Paul F. Braim; this study began as a doctoral dissertation at the University of Delaware. It moves well beyond the collection of myths, halftruths, and downright misconceptions that until now have colored our perceptions of this important event.

Perhaps Colonel Braim's principal accomplishment is to have asked the right questions and to have approached his task without debilitating preconceptions. Other scholars are bound to contest his findings, which of necessity constitute the beginning rather than the end of a full professional inquiry into the topic. They are nevertheless a crucial turning point; all future accounts must necessarily depart from this one, a pioneering enterprise. Colonel Braim has used scholarly techniques that greatly enhance the utility of his work. He has walked the terrain, applying the skills of an expert combat soldier in following the battles. He has made a diligent examination of many extant records. He has also consulted a panel of historians who have offered previous assessments of the American army's performance during 1918, allowing him to measure his results against prevailing viewpoints.

In conducting this investigation Colonel Braim always retains an awareness of the necessarily desperate conditions that obtained on the battlefield—those extraordinary pressures that manufacture "the fog of war." Awareness of the unexampled confusion that prevails on the modern battlefield greatly strengthens the cogency of this professional estimate.

For all these reasons it is a privilege to commend this volume to those concerned about the American participation in the Great War of 1914–1918. It moves well past previous authorities; it should exercise significant influence on future evaluations of the American Expeditionary Forces.

DAVID F. TRASK
Washington, D.C.

PREFACE TO THE FIRST EDITION

Sixty-seven years have passed since the guns fell silent on the Western Front in France. The "war to end all wars" halted—for a score of years—but did not end! The American Expeditionary Forces Headquarters wrote their after-action reports, and their operational directives and administrative papers were diligently correlated and stored in Washington, D.C. Most of the records and reports of the major Allied and Central Powers were likewise collected. Many of the senior commanders, both the victorious and the defeated, rushed from the battlefield into print, claiming, in their memoirs, credit for victory or giving excuse for defeat. Called the "Battle of the Memoirists," these literary struggles continued into the 1930s. The leaders of the victorious European armies generally downgraded the efforts of the United States on the Western Front, while the former American commanders jabbed at each other with ever more intense criticism. The defeated German military found solace in accusing their politicians of having given them a "stab in the back."

The issues of "The Great War" became obscured and relatively forgotten with the onset of World War II; subsequently, studies of the Second World War took precedence. The official narrative history of the First World War, which was being drafted by the Historical Division of the United States War Department, was canceled in 1948. A few scholars, however, continued to labor to record the events of World War I and to stress its relationship to contemporary world problems. They have called for additional studies of the accumulations of archival material that are resting in relative obscurity in the national libraries and archives of the former contesting powers.

This work attempts to summarize and analyze a portion of that material connected with the participation of the American

Expeditionary Forces (AEF) in the Meuse-Argonne Campaign, the greatest test of battle that the American army had undergone up to that time. The manner in which the Army of the United States rapidly expanded to twenty times its prewar strength and met the tremendous challenge of the Meuse-Argonne, provides an understanding of the capabilities and limits of a free society to fight a modern war with little preparation, and suggests some lessons of value regarding military preparedness and coalition warfare.

In undertaking this study, this author posed some basic questions: Why did the AEF undertake such a difficult task? Were the Americans sufficiently trained to meet the challenge? Was American military leadership as poor as some of our Allies charged, or as inspired as some participating officers claimed? How was the Meuse-Argonne Campaign planned and conducted? How did the campaign turn out? What was gained; was the hard-won success worth the cost? What failings, mistakes, and inadequacies are revealed, and what lessons can be derived from that campaign? Finally, was the campaign a decisive contribution to the Allied victory?

The archival material of the AEF, through which this author waded, contains a wealth of orders, reports, maps, records, diaries, letters and memorabilia to permit a researcher to gain an appreciation of the challenges that the AEF faced. Reconnoitering the restrictive terrain of the Meuse-Argonne, provided an empathy with those who fought there. New information and opinions were gained from a number of scholars who were knowledgeable about that campaign. Talking to veterans of the fighting, and reading their notes, letters, and memorabilia, provided a sense of communion with that event—that awful delight experienced by a historian as he lifts one corner of the shroud of time that obscures a great event.

During research, this author's opinions were forming on both sides of most of the questions posed earlier. It became apparent that there were wide variations in the experience, ability, and aggressiveness of the American military leaders. However, the opportunity to take aggressive action was not presented in the same way to each leader, and some military leaders were burdened by tremendous missions, which the resources they commanded could in no way fulfill. In assessing the plans, problems, successes, and failures of the AEF in the Meuse-Argonne, this author found no "Great Captains" in the American roster; nor were any fools or scoundrels found for condemnation—although some leaders had been condemned by being removed from their commands during the campaign. What was discovered was a hard-working group of relatively inexperienced leaders, struggling mightily with a most unique and challenging set of battlefield management requirements, which taxed their resources and capabilities to the limit. This story bears telling, and its lessons should be learned, for it was a noble struggle, the like of which the militarily unprepared society of the United States has been required to undertake again and again.

To relate the story of the Meuse-Argonne Campaign, it is necessary to refer to the annotated maps convenient to the narrative. Tabular data are provided in appendixes. Military abbreviations and symbols used are explained in Appendix 1. The opinions of veterans of the First World War were gained from interviews and from a review of the responses of World War I veterans to a Military Service Experiences Questionnaire issued by the Military History Institute (MHI) of the United States Army.

Thanks is due, in the first instance, to Dr. David F. Trask, Chief Historian of the United States Army's Military History Center, who suggested that the Meuse-Argonne Campaign needed further scholarly research, and offered guidance on unresolved matters related to it.

Eternal gratitude is also expressed to Dr. James M. Merrill, distinguished professor emeritus of the University of Delaware, whose unfailing support and encouragement were sustaining and inspiring during the long, often-interrupted work on this history. Deep appreciation is also sent to Doctors George F. Frick, Raymond C. Callahan, and Gerald M. Straka of the University of Delaware, who reviewed the manuscript and gave the author many hours of guidance, evaluation, and encouragement. Indebtedness is also acknowledged to Mr. Charles Shaunessey, who guided the author's research through the old army records of the National Archives. Scholarly guidance was provided by Colonel Harold M. Hannon and Major James W. Rainey of the Department of History, United States Military Academy. Colonel Donald P. Shaw and Colonel Rod Paschall, directors of the United States Army's Military History Institute, were most helpful, as was Dr. Richard J. Sommers, the institute's archivist, and Dr. Jay Luvaas, the Harold K. Johnson Visiting Professor of Military History. Captain Jonathan M. House of the Combat Studies Institute, United States Army Command and General Staff College, gave expert assistance. Mr. Peter Simkins of the British Imperial War Museum deserves much thanks for providing informed opinion on the British armies of the period. Mr. Norman Iorio, Superintendent of the United States Military Cemetery at Romagne, assisted in reconnaissance of the battle area. Colonel Joseph Whitehorne of the United States Army's Center of Military History also provided valuable planning assistance. Among the many scholars who provided information and informed opinion, this author cites Father Donald Smythe (SJ) of John Carroll

University. From his two-volume biography of General Pershing and from discussions with him, this author gained a deeper insight into the subject than gained from any other single source. Appreciation is offered here to all the scholars who gave of their time and expertise in responding to queries. Their names are in the bibliography, and their opinions are reflected throughout this book.

The text of this study was typed and proofread by the patient and skilled labors of Charles Cook; a thorough and very painful editorial "scrub" of the text was made by Harvey C. Fenimore, Jr., and Barbara R. Braim. To these, appreciation is offered. It must be said, however, that the responsibility for the material and conclusions presented herein is solely that of this author.

ACKNOWLEDGMENTS

Appreciation is expressed to the Head of the Department of History of the United States Military Academy, West Point, New York for permission to reproduce the maps from the U.S.M.A. text, *The Great War* (West Point: U.S.M.A., 1979).

Appreciation is also expressed to the director of the U.S. Army's Military History Institute, Carlisle Barracks, Pennsylvania for permission to reproduce selected photographs from the *Terrain Studies* of the American Battle Monuments Commission (Washington: GPO, 1931) held in the institute's archives.

INTRODUCTION

Ten years have passed since publication of *The Test of Battle*. During that period, scholarly interest in The Great War has increased, as has research and writing on that seminal human tragedy. In the interim, this author has gained new perspectives of the events and personalities of that war, as well as a deeper appreciation of the physical and cultural limitations within which its leaders struggled to achieve their objectives. The general result, reflected in this revision, is a more sympathetic assessment of the decisions of leaders at all levels in the Meuse-Argonne Campaign, and a less condemnatory analysis of the performance of the American Expeditionary Forces.

In addition to those persons to whom the author has expressed appreciation in the Preface, the following are deserving of recognition for their guidance and assistance: Father Donald Smythe (SJ), Dr. Anne Cipriano-Venzon, Dr. Richard R. Bobb, Dr. Martin K. Gordon, General Robert C. Kingston, Admiral Norman C. Venzke, and Lieutenant Colonel Roger Cirillo, all of whom provided professional guidance and editorial comment, and Marc Gardner and Gerry L. Wityk, who worked diligently to translate old typescript into computerized copy. The final text and supporting data remain, as with the original publication, the sole responsibility of the author.

1

EUROPE CHOOSES WAR

Europe went to war in 1914 with enthusiasm, self-confidence, and "righteousness" on both sides of the contest. Political leaders were nearly unanimous in their readiness to go to war to resolve power relationships; their military chiefs were equally ready to fight and certain of quick and relatively painless victory. That element of the citizenry which was politically aware—the educated, affluent intelligentsia—was "up" for a war, a war that would provide high adventure and fulfillment to their hopes for personal ennoblement. The lower classes of Europe, who would carry the terrible burden of the war on both sides, were less publicly articulate, but they were, in almost all European countries, gaining in political consciousness and developing nationalistic ideologies.[1] The approach of the "Age of the Common Citizen" was shaking all the monarchical systems of Europe, even as population growth produced pressures for geographic changes to reflect new power positions. Few political or military leaders, or savants, appreciated the destructive power that modern weaponry and an industrial society were even then able to deliver upon a fixed battlefield.[2]

Among the more significant improvements in the implements of war that were developed during the latter half of the nineteenth century was an effective breech-loading rifle with magazine feeding. This increased the average rate of fire of the rifleman from about four shots to thirty shots per minute. The rifling in the barrel and the precision manufacture of bullets markedly increased the killing range of the rifle under combat conditions. Smokeless powder came into general use late in the nineteenth century, as did the most effective mass killer, the machine gun, although the latter was only used as an "emergency" support weapon by most Western armies prior to the First World War. Lighter artillery pieces, with

1

improved breech mechanisms and a more lethal exploding shell, had been developed, which quintupled artillery effectiveness against troops in the open or in uncovered fortifications.[3]

Scientific developments in the civil arena also contributed to enhancing the efficiency of combat. The telephone improved command and control by allowing instantaneous communication between headquarters; it also permitted artillery to fire an indirect parabola from emplacements in the rear, directed by an observer with a telephone. The tremendous increase in railroad mileage allowed armies to move hundreds of miles in one day and provided munitions and sustenance for millions during periods of intense combat.[4] Colonel Trevor N. Dupuy, in his text *The Evolution of Weapons and Warfare,* graphically illustrated a tenfold increase in the lethality of weapons during this period.[5]

With regard to strategy and tactics in this era, Dr. Theodore Ropp in *War in the Modern World* has pointed out that there was very little change from the parade ground methods of past centuries.[6] The warning of amateur strategist Ivan Bloch, as early as 1898, that "war has become impossible except at the price of suicide" was heeded by few. Reports from military observers on the terrible effectiveness of modern weaponry during the Russo-Japanese War (1904–1905)—in which each side took one quarter million casualties—were also generally ignored.[7] The armies of "The Triple Entente" (to be called in this text the "Allies") were confident of the moral superiority of "l'offensive l'outrance" (offensive to the utmost). And they moved to war in varicolored uniforms, the better to be seen by their commanders—and, of course, by the enemy. The Germans, who directed the "Central Powers" (the Triple Alliance less Italy) in the war, had a better military system. They used the ground in attack and defense better than did their enemies, and they wore a dull field grey.[8]

A minor Balkan incident (the murder of the Austrian Archduke) precipitated a worldwide conflagration. The Great War was undertaken by the major powers of Europe with a verve and spirit almost romantic in character—a gladness to be about an exciting, important new crusade. Poets "sang" of the thrill of the contest, while even philosophers justified the commitment. The political crisis of the summer of 1914 also provoked a powerful momentum toward war: the massive mobilization and countermobilization of millions of men within the shrinking time-distances in Europe. Like a "genie" let out of a bottle, preparations for defense of the homeland quickly grew beyond human authority to prevent their spillover into a clash of arms.[9]

Six million men were mobilized in the heat of a very warm summer across the face of Europe. Germany deployed 1,500,000 against France, which moved 1,000,000 to her own eastern border. Britain readied over 100,000 men to deploy to the continent north of the French deployment. Russia called up 1,400,000; Germany sent 500,000 to the east to oppose them, while Austria moved 500,000 against the Serbs and the Russians.[10]

As has been noted, the armies of Europe, excepting only the German, were not trained or equipped, nor were their leaders prepared to fight and sustain their forces on a modern battlefield. The Germans, having been devastatingly victorious in their previous continental war (the Franco-Prussian War of 1870–1871), were enabled by their growing industrial and demographic might to adopt an expansionist foreign policy, which required a strong military force. The German general staff system, devised and dominated by Prussians, was the most efficient in the world, a superbly effective agency for directing modern armies. The appreciation of the effectiveness of the machine gun by the Germans, and their infusion of machine gun teams into the forward elements of their armies, gave them a considerable superiority in killing power over that of their enemies.[11]

All the armies of Europe had developed war plans based upon mobilization rates and, except for the British, on conscription. Each of the war plans of the European powers, including those of the minor European states, assumed the martial superiority of its forces; all plans consisted of a bold, short offensive thrust. None succeeded—though the Germans did come very close to victory. Called "The Schlieffen Plan," the German war plan was drawn up by Count Alfred von Schlieffen, Chief of the Great General Staff in 1905. It called for a wide turning movement on the Western Front, with the major force sweeping through the low countries and northern France to trap the French in a cul-de-sac.

The European war plans were developed by planners with some rudimentary knowledge of the plans of presumed enemies; however, all assumed the ability of their forces to delay or defeat enemy thrusts with minor forces, while their own offensives were striking decisive blows in their enemies' rear. The French strategic plan (Plan XVII) called for an offensive in Lorraine. It was, by chance, so complementary to that of the Germans as to have brought about near-fatal results to the French.[12]

One month after the murder of the Archduke, Austria-Hungary declared war on Serbia (28 July 1914). On 29 July Austria bombarded Belgrade. Russia began mobilizing on 30 July. Germany demanded that Russia cease mobilizing, then mobilized herself on 1 August. France did as well on that date. Germany then went to war with France and Russia. When Germany demanded free passage against Belgium, then moved into Belgium on 3 August, Britain declared war on Germany (4 August 1914). The other powers of the Triple Alliance and Triple Entente then exchanged formal declarations of war, except Italy, which voided her obligations to the Triple Alliance.

On the Western Front, the forces were nearly evenly matched: eighty-seven German divisions were opposed by sixty-two French, seven Belgian, and seven British divisions. The Infantry division, the standard independent fighting unit of all modern armies, numbered about eighteen thousand soldiers in European armies in 1914. Later attrition lowered this figure to twelve to fifteen thousand. A cavalry division had five thousand to six thousand troops. But, the Germans had more modern artillery, more and better automatic weapons with forward elements, better mobility and logistics, better discipline, and better commanders than their foes.

The German drive swept through Belgium and northwestern France like a great scythe. The momentum of the German strategic envelopment finally was attenuated, with the spearhead of the German advance only some forty miles from Paris. The French, and their British allies, countered this advance with a strategic penetration of their own, which forced the Germans back and brought about a stalemate.[13] Called the "Miracle of the Marne," the Allied victory was due more to luck than to martial skill and courage. Both sides were experiencing coordination problems. Subsequent attempts by each to envelop the flanks of the opposing forces caused a rapid surge of the battle line north to the English Channel near Dunkerque. This "race to the sea" was a tie, and resulted in a stabilized situation all along the front, from the channel to Switzerland. Frontal attacks by both sides were repeated throughout the remainder of 1914 with heavy losses, as each side made maximum use of artillery, barbed wire, and the very lethal machine gun. Modern weaponry had established the primacy of defense in war![14]

During 1915, the major European powers attempted to gain maneuverability in a strategic sense, by launching offensives in other theaters. The Germans launched a major offensive on the Russian Front and gained a momentous victory at Tannenberg, wiping out or capturing nearly one half the Russian army and expelling it from East Prussia.[15] The British attempted a bold amphibious operation in the Dardanelles, which failed because of inept execution, with heavy casualties. They gained some security for their Suez lifeline by the seizure of German colonies in Africa.[16]

In 1915, Italy entered the war on the side of the Allies; it bloodied its armies against the Austrians in the Isonzo region.[17] Along the Western Front, the Allies made a series of limited attacks in Artois and Champagne without causing much change in the line. "Attrition warfare" had become the accepted method for winning on the Western Front, as the leaders of both the Entente and Central Powers found themselves unable to devise techniques which would allow for extensive maneuvers in offensive operations.[18] The Allies, in particular, were experiencing coordination problems between their "cooperating" military forces.

1916 was the year the major powers of Europe sacrificed a whole generation of their young men in attempts to prevail over their enemies through sheer weight of explosive power. "God was," as Hanson Baldwin said, "on the side of the big factories as well as the big battalions."[19] Previously unimagined tonnages of artillery ammunition were poured on the opposing trenches, and massed armies of conscripts were thrown against barbed wire and machine guns. The Germans attempted to bleed the French white at Verdun, and they succeeded in killing more than half a million French, while suffering nearly half a million casualties of their own in failing to gain that vital area. Following the denouement of that battle, the British Expeditionary Force (BEF), with French assistance, launched their own major offensive in the area of the Somme River during the summer and fall of 1916. An immense artillery preparation of seven days' duration turned the battlefield into a wasteland of carnage and spoilage. Over the resulting rubble the British attacked in waves, "the men in each, almost shoulder to shoulder in symmetrical, well-dressed alignment . . . at a slow walk. . . ."[20] At the end of this Allied offensive, the Germans had lost 650,000 men, while British losses were 420,000 (60,000 in a single day) and French losses were 200,000. The end of the year 1916 found the fighting lines on the Western Front in practically the same positions as they had been at the beginning of the year. Map 1 (in the front matter) shows the trace of the battle line and the location of the campaigns in this period.[21]

On the sea, the British lost a unique opportunity to destroy the German High Seas Fleet at Jutland, largely because of their excessive caution. The British, however, forced the German fleet back into harbor, from which it never again emerged in force.[22] Meanwhile, submarine warfare was beginning to take a heavy toll on Allied shipping, while the Allied blockade was producing significant shortages of food in the homelands of the Central powers.[23] A Russian offensive in Eastern Europe in the spring and summer of 1916 resulted in temporary success, which was turned around by the Germans and Austrians, resulting in losses approximating a million men on each side of the line. On the Italian front, the fighting surged back and forth through the Isonzo and Trentino regions with no significant gains and with heavy losses being taken by both Italian and Austrian forces. By the end of the year, all the major contestants had reached a state of near exhaustion of their manpower, and food supplies at home were nearing critically low levels.[24]

Politicians and articulate persons of the bodies politic, on both sides, clamored in anguish and anger against the sterile tactics and the bloody operations that had taken place.[25] Writers, scholars, and other savants have since criticized the lack of strategic innovation on the Western Front during this period. It has been, and remains today, popular to condemn those responsible for prosecuting the Great War, because they were not able to do so in a less bloody fashion. Hanson Baldwin made the point, however, that millions of men fighting in a relatively small, confined area, using weapons of mass destruction are necessarily committed to the strategy of attrition. Trevor Dupuy has also excused the generals from full responsibility for the carnage that industrial society brought to the battlefield in 1914.[26] However, C. S. Forester, in his text, *The General,* incisively castigated the unimaginative, tradition-bound "Colonel Blimps," whose refusal to try new strategies caused the loss of the flower of the nations.[27] It was industrial technology that developed the weapons of mass destruction. It was also industrialization that sustained the large armies to replace those slaughtered.

In fact, there were tactical innovations made by both contestants. Lieutenant General Wilhelm Balck, a student of battle tactics who commanded on the Western Front in World War I, in his text, *The Development of Tactics—World War,* detailed the important changes that were being made by both sides during the stalemate.[28] The massing of artillery, which reached a density of one gun per four meters of front line, forced the development of a system of multiple connecting entrenchments by both sides. The trench line nearest the enemy was lightly occupied, often abandoned during enemy "drumfire." A second line of entrenchments, beyond the observed fire of the enemy, contained the major defensive force. A third line, out of artillery range, with deep, covered bunkers, housed the reserve. The area between these lines was defended by machine-gun pillboxes, camouflaged and mutually supporting. When the Allies attacked, the Germans surrendered the first trench, then contained the thrust by flanking fire from bypassed pillboxes and trench groupments, while the reserve moved along connecting trenches to swiftly attack the penetration, also in flank. The Allies, according to Balck, were less flexible, more inclined to fight for their sacred land, but their defenses gradually came to resemble those of the Germans.[29]

In his text *If Germany Attacks: The Battle in Depth in the West*, Captain Graeme C. Wynne (British Army) credited the German General Fritz von Lossberg with another defensive innovation in late 1915: Siting the second, the "main defensive line," on the reverse (rear) slope of ground to protect the soldiers in this line from the devastation of increasingly accurate direct-fire weapons of the enemy! Wynne also noted that the Germans learned in 1916–1917 to disperse their bunker locations and to move reserves out of deep entrenchments when under fire, as "these were only deathtraps."[30]

In the attack, both sides learned to move their infantry closely behind rolling barrages of artillery. By 1917, the Germans had begun relying on short-range attacks to avoid the disorganization which inevitably occurred when the attacking elements made a deep advance. After seizing a single trench system, German troops immediately assumed a defensive posture, dug in, reorganized, then moved again if no counterattack came. Balck said they learned that a deep penetration was often lost because attacking troops had become disorganized when the inevitable counterattack came. He charged the failure of the French offensive of 1917 to the attempt to make too deep a penetration—as well as to the fact that the Germans knew the attack was coming and were prepared for it. A technique to gain surprise in attack was learned late in 1917 by both contestants—and by the Americans in 1918: the use of short, violent artillery preparatory fires, rather than the long "drumfire" of the artillery defenders had come to expect.[31]

Despite these innovations, the stalemate and the carnage continued throughout 1917. The British strategist General Sir Frederick Maurice said of this stalemate: "It took the French and British four years to recover from the initial mistakes of (French) Plan XVII."[32] The long stalemate eventually led the Germans to develop bypass tactics, while the Allies turned to the tank to effect the rupture of enemy defenses.

2

1917—THE YEAR OF HOPE AND DESPAIR

When the embattled Europeans faced the dawn of 1917, the third year of total war, they saw yet another stalemate on most of the battlefronts of the world. On the map of Western Europe, a 376-mile trench system ran from the North Sea southeast to the border of Switzerland. Much of the area on both sides of this jagged scar was plowed and pockmarked from intensive shelling and equally feverish digging, and the earth had been poisoned by the carnage. Rain and mud were constant companions of the soldiers. After three heartbreaking years of a war of attrition, the armies on both sides were depleted and the civilian manpower pool exhausted. The great vulnerability of soldiers attacking across the battlefields was illustrated by the millions of dead lying "over the top," deaths incurred in driving the battle lines an insignificant distance east or west. Gas was regularly used, and the tank had made its appearance. The effectiveness of the internal combustion engine had not yet been fully realized on the battlefield, neither in tank operations nor in the air; but truck convoys were a regular feature of the extensive logistics systems, interspersed with animal and human carriers, delivering hundreds of thousands of tons of material and supplies to the front. Patrols and raids into "no man's land" were sporadic activities, designed to capture prisoners and to determine the location and nature of enemy activity. Preparations for offensives were usually easy to discover because they required the movement of masses of men and supplies forward preceding each operation.

The turn of the year was a time for the military and political leaders of both coalitions to revise their aims and strategies. The Germans made the decision to go on the defensive on the Western Front, to withdraw from vulnerable salients, and to attack in the east to eliminate Russia from the war. Following Russia's elimination, their plan was to concentrate all their forces for a swift victory in the west, before American power could make a significant difference in Allied strength. To aid in this plan, the Germans persuaded their Austrian allies to undertake another offensive, one designed to drive the Italians out of the war.[1]

In the Allied coalition, a "star" arose, promising early victory— the French General Robert Nivelle. A dynamic personality, Nivelle proclaimed that the philosophy of the pre-World War French armies would serve again as a model for success: offensive actions, carried out violently and without regard for the casualties incurred! Despite high-level objections and fears that this philosophy would produce even greater human carnage, Nivelle's spirit finally gained him the support of the new French War Minister, Paul Painleve. He (Nivelle) also convinced the new British Prime Minister, David Lloyd George, that a violent offensive would rupture the German lines and allow for a deep strategic penetration that would end the war.[2] This impending Allied offensive was widely discussed in Allied capitals and even in French newspapers; it was, thus, no surprise to the Germans. To strengthen their defenses, the Germans made a strategic withdrawal from 25 February to 5 April 1917, abandoning the Noyon salient and establishing the "Hindenburg Line," centered on strong defenses across the center of France from Arras south to the Aisne River. These actions also freed a large number of front-line divisions to provide a German reserve. In conducting their withdrawal, the Germans devastated the areas they left behind, destroying homes, railroads, and roads, even poisoning wells. While such actions were militarily sound, they further incensed the Allies, and even turned neutral opinion against the German cause.[3]

Refusing to admit that the German strategic withdrawal had made an Allied offensive less likely of success, Nivelle urged the British to conduct a "spoiling attack" with the intention of drawing reserves away from the Aisne area. On 9 April 1917, the British launched a series of attacks in the vicinity of Arras. The attacks had some initial success, but they gained little ground and caused scant shifting of German reserves. Furthermore, these attacks caused very high losses among the British and Canadian forces, already weakened by the mass casualties of 1916.[4]

On 16 April 1917, an unusually cold and snowy morning, Nivelle launched his grand offensive, labeled the "Second Battle of the Aisne."[5] (Map 1 shows the location of the Nivelle offensive of 1917.) Attacking with a force of 1,200,000 men supported by 7,000 artillery pieces, the French assaulted the Hindenburg Line along a forty-mile front between Soissons and Rheims; the main attack was aimed at the Chemin des Dames, a series of wooded, rocky ridges paralleling the front. After that objective was seized, the attackers were to conduct a deep exploitation drive. Just before the attack—unfortunate for the French—German aviators seized control of the sky from Allied aviation; the German airmen then helped to direct artillery fire, which played havoc with Allied columns of infantry, artillery, and tanks. The Allied artillery barrages rolled *forward* too fast for the advancing infantry, which found itself caught in well-laid German machine gun fire from the flanks. French gallantry in the face of murderous fire enabled the attackers to take the ridge of the Chemin des Dames, but the attack stopped after four days of fighting, and proceeded no further despite repeated assaults. The Germans, from their deep system of elastic defenses, launched strong counterattacks.

Result: The Nivelle Offensive was a colossal failure! The French lost approximately 190,000 men. German losses were considerably lighter. Although these losses were of no greater magnitude than those of previous years, the bold promise of success in this battle, of strategic penetration, and of victory—a promise so evidently unfulfilled—devastated French morale. Mutiny broke out and spread rapidly among French troops. Mutinous actions by relatively large groups occurred in at least fifty-four French divisions. The French line facing the Germans quickly became "combat ineffective." Their defenses uncovered, the French nation was in mortal danger. General Nivelle was replaced by General Henri Pétain. A cautious and wise campaigner, he first set about restoring the confidence of the "poilu" in the ranks. He listened to the soldiers' complaints, provided them with better living conditions, and had them remain on the defensive. Unique is the fact that the French were able to censor all public information on the mutiny, successfully withholding knowledge of it from the enemy—something they had never been able to do before and were seldom able to accomplish again.[6]

The French armies in disorder, it became the British lot to launch attacks with weary and weakened forces to prevent the Germans from taking advantage of the Allied turmoil. Despite parliamentary opposition, General Douglas Haig, Commander of the BEF, launched a strong drive in the alluvial mud of Flanders. In a strategic sense, it worked. The attention of General Erich Ludendorff, the German Quartermaster General and *de facto* commander of the armies of the Central Powers, was fully engaged by the resumption of offensive operations by the British. To facilitate this offensive from the Ypres Salient, the British Second Army was given the mission of seizing the dominating terrain, the Messines

Ridge complex. Careful preparations led to a successful, set-piece attack. After a seventeen-day artillery preparation, the Second Army, on 7 June 1917, detonated a mine containing one million pounds of explosives under the Messines Ridge and executed a well-planned attack. Surprise was complete, and the British gained the ridge position quickly. Casualties were relatively high (17,000 for the British and 25,000 for the Germans). Nonetheless, this clear-cut victory restored Allied morale; it was particularly cheered in Britain. On 31 July 1917, the BEF, accompanied by the French First Army, launched its main offensive in the vicinity of Ypres, following a thirteen-day intensive bombardment. The low ground in the Flanders area, sodden with rain, had become an almost impassable quagmire. The British forces struggled forward slowly in the mud from July through November, with high casualties. Then, another horror of war emerged: mustard gas was used by the Germans for the first time! German aircraft were also becoming very effective in strafing attacks, employing machine guns mounted on their airplanes. The taking of Passchendaele ridge on 6 November, with great casualties for the British, ended the offensive. The casualties from Passchendaele caused post-war British history books to depict the horror of offensive operations against entrenched troops—a horror that was to affect British political and military decisions throughout World War II. The Ypres offensive cost the British 300,000 casualties, while German losses were estimated at 260,000. The offensive gained a strip of ground five miles deep.[7]

Stubborn as ever, despite such losses, Haig continued to conduct small offensive operations through the rest of 1917, a series culminating in the very successful attack by massed tanks at Cambrai on 20 November 1917. This attack opened a five-mile salient into the German lines—a salient not exploited by the British, who were not prepared to follow up such a success. The salient was subsequently eliminated by German counterattacks. When the year ended on the Western Front, the battle lines remained little changed from their locations at the end of the previous year, despite huge intervening losses.[8]

On the Eastern Front, Russian operations in 1917 were severely hampered by political turmoil at home. In March, a revolution forced the abdication of the czar. That event was followed by an outbreak of street fighting, in which soldiers joined the rebellious workers. Soon the Russian armies, weakened by defections from their ranks and a lack of direction from headquarters, were retreating from the line of contact with the Germans on the Baltic.

The new Russian regime (the Provisional Government) pledged to continue to wage war against the Central Powers.[9] Under the leadership of Alexander Kerensky, the Russians gathered their forces for an offensive in the summer of 1917. The troops were led by the new Chief of Staff, Alexei Brusilov, the most capable general in the theater. Employing surprise, together with an unprecedented amount of advance planning, Brusilov's July offensive resulted in some initial success. But the heart was not in the Russian soldiers to fight. A German counterattack on 19 July 1917 resulted in the retaking of all the area previously gained southwest of Petrograd (St. Petersburg). The German offensive accelerated in the autumn; the opposing Russian forces were either in disarray or nonexistent. The Germans, attacking in the north toward Petrograd and as far south as the Pripet marshes, were only limited in their advances by their inability to supply their forces, which were moving great distances.[10] During this period, the German forces employed new tactics for swift penetration, for the bypassing of strong points, and for the coordination of infantry movements with artillery fire. Called "Hutier Tactics" for their inventor, General Oscar von Hutier, these shock assaults were the basis for the "Blitzkrieg tactics" of the Germans during World War II.[11]

In October 1917, the Kerensky government, in a state of near chaos, abandoned Petrograd for Moscow, and the Bolsheviks began to take over power in the major cities. The final revolution of 7 November 1917 established the Bolsheviks as the ruling power in Russia, under Vladimir Lenin and Leon Trotsky; that duo began dickering with the Germans for a peace treaty. On 15 December 1917, after Bolshevik delaying tactics failed to stop the advance of the German armies, an Armistice was agreed upon, effectively taking Russia out of the war.[12]

Meanwhile, the Italians had been driven backward in 1917 by an Austro-German offensive, which culminated in the battle of Caporetto during October and November of 1917. The Italian line was penetrated by means of the new Hutier Tactics. A disastrous withdrawal, followed all the way to the Piave River, the Italians suffering over 700,000 losses (including 400,000 desertions). The defeat caused the Allies to send eleven divisions to Italy from other theaters; it also forced them to form a Supreme War Council in an attempt to provide unity for the Allied military effort.[13]

The only significant military successes for the Allies that year were gained by the British in Palestine. Lloyd George, the British Prime Minister, gave his support for a British-led offensive in Palestine in 1917, by directing a significant diversion of manpower and munitions to that theater. In that British offensive, General Edmund Allenby drove the Turks back along the Mediterranean and entered Jerusalem in triumph on 9 December 1917.[14]

The other land theaters were of little significance to the Allied global situation.

In May 1917, the British instituted the "convoy system" to protect their shipping. Proposed by U.S. Admiral William Sims, supported by Lloyd George, and opposed by most of the British admiralty, the convoy system quickly ended excessive losses in Allied shipping, and considerably eased the Allied supply situation—at the front and at home.[15] The reinforcement of the Allied blockade by American warships, followed by raids on German bases, further reduced German supplies, and adversely affected morale on their home front. The entry of the United States into the war on 6 April 1917 had little effect on the fighting fronts, because United States forces were not engaged in significant land battles during 1917. The tremendous wealth and industrial power of the United States, however, brought an immediate reinforcement to the Allies' war efforts and to the sustenance of their people.[16]

3

AMERICA SENDS AN ARMY TO FRANCE

Some apologists for the German cause have argued that the United States was never "neutral in thought as well as action"—a condition of sentiment called for by President Wilson as the European war began in August 1914.[1] It is true that major American industries quickly turned to producing material of war for the Entente Powers. The Allies were also able to float huge loans in the United States, and foodstuffs from America assured the survival of their peoples. One could argue that the United States was trading with all customers who called for our goods; the Central Powers were unable to trade with us because of their location and the domination of the seas by Great Britain. It is also true that all American sentiment was not with the Entente Powers. In his text, *The Wars of America,* historian Robert Leckie says:

> Others who were of German descent naturally echoed the Kaiser's cry that Germany must have her place in the sun, while those of Irish blood, remembering Albion's crimes against Erin, prayed to see her humbled. The heartland of America, meanwhile, the home of isolationism and of the Progressive Movement, raised the banners of strict neutrality. . . . Immigrants to America, many of whom could be described as refugees from European militarism, turned their backs with a scornful "plague on both your houses," while Socialists and their sympathizers frankly rejoiced in the *Götterdämmerung* of the dynasties. . . . In all, the great bulk of the American people, especially the working men, were neutral.[2]

As the war in Europe entered its second year, ever closer association with the Entente markets, and with their propaganda, was causing Americans to identify emotionally with the Allies. It was

14

primarily the widely publicized sinking of merchant ships by German submarines, whose submarine crews made little or no attempt to rescue survivors, that was turning America against Germany. The sinking of the British passenger liner *Lusitania* on 7 May 1915, with the loss of 1,198 lives including those of 128 Americans, raised American anger against the "Hun" and ended her "neutrality in spirit." President Wilson's sharp note of protest only temporarily limited German submarine activities. Meanwhile German espionage operations in America were exposed in our press. On 7 December 1915, Wilson laid before the Congress a comprehensive plan for improving national defense; then the President toured the nation urging increased military preparedness. On 3 June 1916, Congress passed the National Defense Act. It provided for the immediate expansion of the Regular Army to 175,000 men, and, in increments, to 223,000 over a five-year period. For the Regular Army, seven infantry and two cavalry divisions were authorized. Each division was then provided with a signal battalion, an aero squadron, larger medical detachments, and administration and supply elements. The act also authorized a National Guard of 450,000 and established *a Reserve Officer* Training Corps at universities, colleges, and military encampments. It contained provisions for governmental assistance for industrial preparedness for the production of wartime materials.[3]

Woodrow Wilson was reelected in November 1916 by a slim margin; his party's slogan was, "He kept us out of war."[4] Although the victorious President called for a "peace without victory," two events turned him into a strong supporter of the Allies: While the German Chancellery talked of a peaceful settlement, Wilson learned that the Kaiser had secretly ordered the resumption of "unrestricted" submarine warfare on 1 February 1917. That same month, the British informed our government of the "Zimmerman Telegram," to Mexico from the German government offering generous terms for Mexico's going to war with the United States as an ally of Germany.[5] America's outrage thundered in the press and in civic halls, and a military "preparedness program" took to the streets on parade. When two American ships were torpedoed in March 1917, President Wilson sadly prepared his request to Congress for a declaration of war. War was declared on Germany on 6 April 1917.[6]

Despite the authorizations of the National Defense Act of 1916, most of which were awaiting implementation, the onset of the war found the United States, as in all previous wars, unprepared both politically and militarily. A host of difficult problems descended upon American leaders and their small staffs in Washington—problems that required immediate resolution by the Congress, and, in many cases, by executive directives. Although Abraham Lincoln had enacted economic regulations under his "war powers," there was no precedent for organizing the entire nation for war. Business and transportation had to be coordinated to supply the burgeoning army at home and abroad and to provide major war material and sustenance for America's allies. These requirements called for a significant increase in the authority of the executive branch of government, for bipartisanship in legislative affairs, and for the ability of civil and military leaders to organize and think in broad and bold terms for the effort to be made. It required civilians, appointed from industry and academe, to make decisions on politico-military matters, a field in which they were totally inexperienced. It required the promulgation of policies and directives that limited, severely, the constitutional rights of private citizens.[7]

The War Department Headquarters (which had been limited by act of Congress to a total of nineteen officers) was no more ready to direct the military build-up than were the civil agencies of the United States. Only a small contingency plan for military expansion existed. The staff of the Army War College at Fort McNair in Washington, D.C. had, in 1915, drawn up a "concept plan" for a million-man army. The plan had received little attention until the declaration of war; then it was seized upon by the War Department as the basis for a military build-up. This was the very thin reed on which the War Department had to lean for the expansion of the army![8]

In April 1917, the Regular Army of the United States totalled 133,000 enlisted men and 9,000 officers; an additional 67,000 National Guard troops had been federalized and were on active duty along the Mexican border. No units larger than a regiment (2,000 men) were active. One machine gun company, of six weapons, had become organic to each infantry regiment in 1916.[9]

On 18 May 1917, with the enthusiastic recommendation of the Congress of the United States, the President signed the Selective Service Act, making the entire manpower of the United States available to prosecute the war against the Central Powers. The act called for the immediate raising of the Regular Army and National Guard to the strengths authorized by the National Defense Act of 1916. On 3 July the President called the entire National Guard to federal service. The first draft registration, on 5 June 1917, registered ten million young men for service. Through subsequent registration acts, nearly half of our male population, or approximately twenty-six million, were registered for the draft. Of these, some 4,800,000 were called into the armed forces, the army receiving a total of four million inductees. The army's total strength at the highest point, the time of the Armistice, was 3,865,000, of which 200,000 were officers.[10]

The draft functioned very smoothly, with few protests and little difficulty in meeting the increasingly large calls made upon the system. It is worth noting that 69 percent of the men called up for induction were considered physically fit for service—a much higher percentage than that found acceptable in Allied countries. The United States could easily have fielded an army of ten million men without calling upon any of the deferred or exempted elements of our male population.[11]

Equipping a large, modern army was a far greater problem than manning it. Except for a stock of 600,000 magazine rifles (caliber .30, Model 1903, commonly called the "Springfield '03" because the rifle was made by the Springfield, Massachusetts armory), the army had no relatively modern weapons or equipment. For field artillery support, the army could only muster a total of 600 three-inch guns, subsequently discarded except for training purposes. Despite the tremendous expansion of the American armaments industry, only one hundred artillery pieces manufactured in the United States reached our troops in France before the Armistice. The American army adopted and puchased the French 75- and 155-millimeter artillery weapons. The prewar army had only a few tanks for testing purposes, and only 55 aircraft, most of which were considered unsafe for combat flying. Despite the tremendous expansion of America's industrial capacity, which had already occurred to support the Allied war effort, U.S. industry was unable to produce weapons for its deployed military forces, except in small numbers, by the end of the war. Major weapons were purchased or borrowed from the Allies.[12]

Lacking equipment, housing, and even officers, the selective service inductees moved to army posts and camps for training. To increase the Regular Army, infantry divisions (designated the 1st through the 20th) were organized, mostly at old army posts. The National Guard divisions called to the colors formed infantry divisions numbered 26 to 42. A National Army was created, consisting of volunteers, the majority of the drafted men, and newly commissioned officers. These were housed in sixteen new divisional camps, the divisions designated numbers 76 to 93 (some numbers were not used). Besides the divisional camps, many special camps were constructed for the training of officers and enlisted specialists in artillery, engineering, signal, tanks, aviation, and chemical warfare. Because most of the divisions (Regular, National Guard, and National Army) ultimately were filled by draftees, the army abolished divisional distinctions by the type of service in July 1918.

Fifty-five divisions were activated, of which forty-two served in France.[13]

The War Department plan called for six months of training for each new soldier at one of these home bases, generally the one nearest to his point of induction. That training was to be followed by two months of training in France, and one month of experience in a quiet sector of the front, before a serviceman entered into battle. As the build-up accelerated, however, training periods for a great many of the troops were much shorter.

England and France sent eight hundred officers and noncommissioned officers to the United States to assist in training the American army. These advisers were distributed to various divisional and special camps throughout the United States. They, and subsequent liaison groups and visiting Allied specialists, urged the adoption of their tactical concepts for the fighting of the war, whenever they were not pressing even more vigorously for the integration of American troops into Allied armies. Adding to the training pressures the Americans experienced through their allies was the belief expressed by British and French military and political leaders, until practically the end of the war, that the United States could never raise, equip, and sufficiently train an American army to take the field prior to the decisive time at which the tide of war would turn. The British and French also believed the American Officer Corps could not be expanded sufficiently, nor was its regular component capable of leading large forces in modern war.[14]

The pressure from the Allies in these regards paralleled the thinking of many American military and political leaders immediately prior to America's entry into the war. In response to French Marshal Joseph Joffre's suggestion that the Americans send a single division to France to bolster Allied morale, the War Department quickly announced a plan for gathering a division of twelve thousand men from existing regular units. The Department cautioned, however, against "the early dispatch of any expeditionary force to France," because of the lack of American training and capability in modern warfare.[15] This attitude, echoed throughout the army hierarchy, was based on the fear that poor performances by untrained masses of American soldiers would deplete Allied morale, while raising the morale of the Germans.[16]

There is little evidence that President Wilson even considered the commitment of an army force to the war in Europe prior to the last days of March 1917. This commitment appears to have been the last priority among his decisions. The U.S. was going to war primarily to ensure freedom of the seas: Wilson agreed we should send a naval force to cooperate with Britain to destroy the submarine menace. He also agreed with Walter Hines Page, United States Ambassador to Great Britain, that the U.S. must help the Allies with loans and supplies. But, in March 1917, he quickly rebuked the War Department staff for their eagerness to "get in" on plans for fighting the war.[17] As late as 19 March 1917, Colonel Edward M. House, President Wilson's "Adviser," wrote him on this matter: "No one looks with favor upon our raising a large army at the moment, believing it would be better if we permit volunteers to enlist in the Allied armies." House believed, as did others among Wilson's advisers, that the role for America would be primarily to provide industrial and economic aid, and that military aid should be provided only as needed by the Allies.[18]

Major James Rainey, who did a comprehensive study of the development and training of the American Expeditionary Forces (AEF), believed that President Wilson's tilt toward fielding the AEF came shortly after our entry into the war, as he (Wilson) realized that the weight of American political influence in the postwar world would likely be related to the degree of our participation in the fighting, the victory, and the sacrifice. Wilson may have been influenced in reaching this conclusion by another adviser, Herbert Hoover, who, as early as 13 February 1917, stated:

> Our terms of peace will probably run counter to most of the European proposals, and our weight in the accomplishment of our ideals will be greatly in proportion to the strength which we can throw into the scale.[19]

Wilson was certainly thinking of an American army in France in the late days of March. In his private discussions with *New York World* reporter Frank I. Cobb, the evening before his war message to Congress, Cobb remembers Wilson agonizing over the need for "illiberalism at home in order to support our men at the front."[20]

Certainly Wilson came around to wanting an American army in France upon calling for a declaration of war. Shortly after the approval of the declaration, he played an active role in selecting a Commander in Chief for the American Expeditionary Forces. Of the seven major generals on active duty in 1917, one, Major General Frederick Funston, died on 19 February.[21] Four generals were too old and relatively infirm. Another, Major General Leonard Wood, who was very popular with the American people and with Congress, was an active Republican who had criticized the administration's lack of courage in not standing up to the Germans. The remaining general, Major General John J. Pershing, was a fine commander who had carried out a difficult political-military task in Mexico. He was selected to head the AEF.

Major General John J. Pershing was a "regular" officer with thirty-one years of military service. A graduate of the United States Military Academy who had held the esteemed cadet rank of First Captain, Pershing had extensive small-unit combat experience pacifying Indians and Filipinos. His military nickname was "Black Jack," a reference to his early duties commanding black soldiers. A taciturn disciplinarian, he had commanded American army units on the Mexican border from 1915 to 1917, and had led the pursuit of the bandit Pancho Villa into Mexico. His service also included duty as military attaché in Tokyo during the Russo-Japanese War. He had been promoted by President Theodore Roosevelt from captain to brigadier general over 862 more senior officers. When selected to lead the AEF in May 1917, he was the junior of six major generals in the army, at age 56. Within three weeks, he was on his way to France, with orders, dated 27 May 1917, from Secretary of War Newton D. Baker to form, train, and commit to battle the AEF under his command. These orders had been approved by President Wilson. The key paragraph in these orders read:

> In military operations against the Imperial German Government you are directed to cooperate with the forces of the other countries employed against the enemy; but in so doing, the underlying idea must be kept in view that the forces of the United States are a separate and distinct component of the combined forces, the identity of which must be preserved. This fundamental rule is subject to such minor exceptions in particular circumstances as your judgment may approve.[22]

Pershing was "vested with all necessary authority to carry on the war vigorously in harmony with the spirit of these instructions and toward a victorious conclusion."[23] Such a charter "made Pershing almost czar" with respect to the American effort in France, according to one of Pershing's biographers, Frank Vandiver.[24] However, these simply stated instructions were challenged by the Allies—by means of diplomatic and, later, direct disagreements—and executing them was a greater personal struggle for Pershing than operating against the enemy.

On 14 June 1917, General Pershing and his small, hand-picked staff arrived in France, beginning the American commitment to the war on the Western Front.[25] Charged by the War Department with recommending an organization to fight the war in Europe, Pershing quickly shook off the enthusiastic welcoming and introductory celebrations, settled into his temporary headquarters in Paris, and put his staff to work. The units of the U.S. 1st Division began arriving on 26 June 1917, and moved to Gondrecourt to begin training.[26]

When General Pershing departed for France, the War Department Headquarters had formed no definite plans for the military effort required of America. After Pershing's planning staff studied the military situation in brief, Pershing cabled the War Department on 6 July 1917: "Plans should contemplate sending over at least one million men by next May."[27] However, the War Department had sent its own board of officers to Europe (the Baker Board) to study and recommend the size and organization of the force to be committed to Europe. Not to be upstaged by this group, Pershing directed the members of the War Department Board and his AEF staff to consider together the plans proposed by his (AEF) Operations Section. The picture (next page) shows General Pershing surrounded by the members of the AEF Staff and the Baker Board. Many of these officers would become commanders of major U.S. organizations as the war progressed.[28] The AEF plans were subsequently adopted. Known as the General Organization Project, the plan, dated 10 July 1917, stated:

> It is evident that a force of about a million is the smallest unit which in modern war will be a complete, well-balanced, and independent fighting organization. It is taken as the force which may be expected to reach France in time for offensive in 1918 and as a unit and basis of organizations. Plans for the future should be based, especially with reference to manufacture of material, artillery, and aviation on three times this force, that is, at least three million men. Such a program . . . should be completed within two years.[29]

The messages began a relationship between AEF Headquarters and the War Department, which, under the pressures of frequent program changes and lagging communications, grew more hostile by the month. One of Pershing's earliest recommendations, supported by reports from United States military missions, was to increase the size, firepower, and staying power (ability to absorb casualties) of the American division. The War Department Headquarters melded these recommendations into an organization called the "Square Division," larger than most corps had been in the Civil War and twice the size of contemporary British, French, and German divisions. It was composed of two infantry brigades (each with 8,500 personnel), one artillery brigade (one heavy artillery and two light artillery regiments with a total of seventy-two guns), a combat engineer regiment, three machine gun battalions, plus signal and administrative units. Totalling 28,000 personnel, the division was strong (260 machine guns), but unwieldy and slow in reaction, maneuver, and movement by foot.

General Pershing standing in center, with members of AEF staff and those of War Department Baker Board.

U.S. Army Signal Corps Photo, archives of U.S. Army Military History Institute, Carlisle Barracks, Pennsylvania.

Unable to produce enough Springfield rifles in a time for shipment of the projected total of American Expeditionary Forces (AEF), the military turned to other weapons. Since 1914, both Remington and Winchester companies had been making Enfield Rifles for the British; this model was quickly rechambered for the caliber .30 ammunition, and called the 1917 Enfield. It was this weapon with which the majority of the AEF was armed. It was as good a rifle as any on the battlefields of the Western Front.[30]

Because most of the machine guns were heavy and awkward for one man to carry, an automatic rifle was developed to allow a moving soldier to sweep enemy before him by automatic fire. The best automatic rifle was developed by John M. Browning, and became known as the U.S. Automatic Rifle, Caliber .30, or the Browning Automatic Rifle, more commonly called the BAR. A total of 80,000 were manufactured; most were issued to the AEF. The BAR provided moving infantry with a small-unit automatic weapon; however, it was rather heavy, at 18 pounds. It also tended to jam and to break down when fired at the maximum rate of 500 rounds per minute, because of excessive vibration. When fired, it also rose off target because of recoil, and it expended the ammunition in its small magazines rapidly, requiring frequent reloading.[31]

The AEF initially purchased the French Hotchkiss Machine Guns, Model 1914; however, this gas-operated weapon was very heavy, at 54 pounds, although it was reliable. The British Vickers Machine Gun, Model 1915, was also purchased for the AEF; it was a 38-pound water-cooled weapon, somewhat better for use with moving troops. The Vickers, in a lighter version, was the primary machine gun used in Allied aircraft. After the Browning Machine Gun, Model 1917, became available, it was preferred by the AEF. This gun was also water-cooled, and weighed 36 pounds; however, firing at 500 rounds per minute with minimum stoppages, it was somewhat more reliable than either the Hotchkiss or the Vickers.[32]

After these huge U.S. divisions were organized and into encampments, it was discovered that the great number of personnel in each unit provoked problems in command and control for their inexperienced leaders. Furthermore, reorganizing the National Guard and Regular Army divisions according to the new table of organization and equipment created extreme organizational turbulence at the very time that most organizations were being called to the colors.[33]

General Pershing's AEF staff met with the Baker Board on 11 July 1917 to discuss the type of artillery to be provided for the AEF. Disagreeing with the Baker Board's recommendations for a light general support weapon, the AEF staff argued for the French 155-millimeter (six-inch) gun. For direct support of maneuver units, the AEF desired the French 75-millimeter cannon. Their argument was that these weapons would provide the weight of firepower needed, and they could be made available from French sources much sooner than weapons produced in the United States. The artillery matter was settled as the AEF staff wished.[34]

As the pace of mobilization increased, the War Department Headquarters was quickly "swamped" in paperwork. A functional organization of the War Department Headquarters had been created in 1904, under the vigorous leadership of Secretary of War Elihu Root; however, the department still consisted of a very small staff supporting the Chief of Staff and a number of semi-independent bureaus (such as that of the Adjutant General). These bureaus were, theoretically, under the direction of the Chief of Staff; actually, they carried on direct relationships with Congress and with the executive agencies. The small War Department General Staff of nineteen officers was also involved in War College instruction; some staff officers had their offices at the War College at Fort McNair, across town from the War Department headquarters in the State, War, and Navy Building.[35] In rapid order, four officers held the titles of Chief of Staff or Acting Chief of Staff during 1917. The fourth one, Major General Peyton C. March, finally received the permanent appointment and the rank of full general (four stars) on 20 May 1918.[36] Prior to March's assumption of the duty of Acting Chief of Staff on 1 March 1918, the War Department continued its peacetime procedures at its leisurely pace, including an eight-hour day for most of its staff. Consequently, even after the declaration of war, papers and messages piled up in the Department's message center and in the halls outside departmental offices. The first series of complaints that Pershing and his staff registered was that their messages and requests were not refused—they just were not answered at all.[37]

The question of the number of men to be shipped to fill the AEF grew to become an increasingly difficult decision. The War Department staff could never catch up with the demands of the AEF for thousands more than the numbers previously scheduled— a problem exacerbated by the increasing demands of the Allies for American replacements. Allied requests often caused political agreements, at the highest U.S. executive levels, for the provision of numbers of American troops that the training and transport system could in no way provide. March's first cable to Pershing (in March 1918) stated that he would ensure that at least two divisions per month were sent to the AEF. This would mean a force of 56,000 men in divisional units and an additional 36,000 men as support troops per month. However, Pershing had already agreed with the British (in January 1918) to bring six additional divisions in British transport—these divisions were to be trained by the British and committed to the AEF after the completion of their training.[38]

Additional pressures came upon the War Department from the Congress. On 12 December 1917, the Senate Military Affairs Committee began hearings on the progress of American military preparations. Its Chairman, Senator Chamberlain (D/Oregon) announced, "The military establishment of America has fallen down." Secretary of War Newton D. Baker remained placid throughout the hearings, despite demands in the press for his resignation. But he and General March worked tirelessly to improve the quality and timeliness of departmental affairs.[39]

It was obvious to Secretary Baker and General March that the AEF Headquarters did not appreciate the problems with which the War Department was wrestling in matching limited resources to increasing demands. It was equally obvious to General Pershing that the War Department had failed to comprehend the enormity of his task—to organize a million-man theater of operations, while receiving, training, equipping, and sustaining those early arrivals who were to flesh out the basic organizational structure itself. On 15 March 1918, General March cabled Pershing suggesting a resolution to the attitudinal problem between their headquarters: an exchange of thirty officers between the two headquarters, to be followed by subsequent reassignment exchanges. The AEF staff was suspicious. Pershing's Chief of Staff, Brigadier General James G. Harbord, suggested that this offer was a prelude to March's taking over the AEF. Only one exchange was half-heartedly effected by the AEF.[40]

The heart of the problem was the degree of control over the AEF and its commander to be exercised by the Chief of Staff of the Army. Pershing was promoted to full general (four stars) on 6 October 1917. The Army Chief of Staff was still a two-star general. An early confrontation occurred on the matter of temporary promotions to general officer. In March 1918, General March requested Pershing's recommendations for such promotions. Pershing responded with ten names. The list sent by the War Department to the Senate for confirmation contained only half of Pershing's recommendations. It contained names of officers in the United States considered by March to be most deserving of promotion, and it contained names of a few officers in the AEF (such as Colonel Douglas MacArthur) not recommended by Pershing. Pershing exploded! In cables to March and Baker, he disapproved of the list and demanded that confirmation be withheld until he sent additional recommendations. March fired a cable in return: "There will be no change in the nominations already sent to the Senate." Pershing let the matter drop for the time, but bad relations continued between the two leaders and between their headquarters, and the problem resurfaced again and again.[41] Morale among the hard-working officers in the War Department was low; they were publicly called "slackers" by newsmen, who should have known better. Most hoped to escape to France, and many of the more capable succeeded.

Immediately after their arrival in France, Pershing and his small personal staff examined the organization of the British and French headquarters. Pershing approved a functional staff system for the AEF modeled primarily upon that of the French, with some attachments and sophistications based upon the fact that the American organization had to interact with the British and French forces as well as French civil departments and agencies. Initially, the AEF planning staff was divided into three sections: operations, intelligence, and administration. Upon moving to their permanent headquarters at Chaumont, a more operationally oriented staff organization was effected. This AEF Headquarters organization was based on a Chief of Staff, and a four-way division of staff responsibilities among assistant chiefs, according to function: that is, one staff agency was assigned responsibility for all matters having to do with Personnel (labeled G-1); one dealt with Intelligence (G-2); one with Operations and Training (G-3) (Training was later separated into its own staff function, G-5); and a final staff function dealt with Supply (G4). Technical organizations and staffs, such as Engineer and Medical, abounded in association with these four, later five, primary staff functions. As the staffs grew and their procedures became relatively standardized, the management of the war began to take on the appearance, for the American army, of a large business operation, as it had been for the Allies for the past three-and-a-half years.[42]

Keeping uppermost in his mind that the United States would field a separate military force on the Western Front, General Pershing gained the approval of the Allies for the Americans to develop that force and its support in the Lorraine Sector, generally the area southeast of Verdun to the Swiss border. After he opened his headquarters at Chaumont, Pershing worked to establish the organizational and structural foundations of the American Expeditionary Forces in France. The Lorraine sector was a relatively quiet portion of the defensive array. However, because of its location, close to German communication support complexes and resource areas, it could pose a tremendous threat to the entire German front—a great salient north and west of this area—if an American offensive were launched from there.

The area was also an excellent region for the establishment of the infrastructure necessary to support the AEF in field from the ports and bases in the rear. While the British were generally established in the north of France, close to the English Channel ports for their support, and the French were established athwart the center of the fighting line, their location protecting the bulk of their vital installations and the capital city of Paris, the area south of the French was relatively unencumbered by active Allied military installations. With improvements in the ports and throughput systems, it could function as an American operational area, based on the southwestern ports of France. It was upon this skein that Pershing and his growing staff built the complex organization of the American Expeditionary Forces in France.[43]

Out of supply activities an organization grew to manage the line of communications functions from the ports to the rear boundaries of the combat forces. This was initially called the "Services of the Rear." It was divided into nine Base Sections for the receipt of supplies (each with one or more port complexes), an Intermediate Section in the center of the area for storage, classification, and transshipment of supplies, and an Advance Section for the distribution of supplies to the combat forces in the zone of operations. Later this agency was called the "Services of Supply" (SOS). Organizing these logistical activities while coordinating the throughput of supplies and personnel with the French created many problems and bottlenecks. The organization became so large and its functions so complex as American divisions arrived in the country that suggestions were made to the Secretary of War, and ultimately to the President, that this agency be taken out from under General Pershing's personal supervision and made a separate organization, coequal with the AEF. This matter is taken up again in chapter 4.[44]

With respect to training for battle, Pershing and most of the regular officers of the "old army" believed in the efficacy of the well-trained soldier using his rifle and bayonet. The "Regulars" were certain that the mass citizen army, formed by conscription with little professional leavening, would require extensive training and experience prior to undertaking combat operations. Pershing saw this training requirement as being largely the responsibility of the War Department and of the continental training establishment in the United States.[45]

In his thesis on the training of the AEF, James Rainey incisively summarized the difficulties under which this training was undertaken and recorded the failure of the leadership to develop and coordinate an offensive doctrine that could have been translated into effective training for operations in France.[46] Rainey argued persuasively that the army's only experience with large-scale offensive operations came from Civil War days; this experience had faded from living memory and from the texts and regulations relating to contemporary military operations. He opined that the experience of the Regular Army was largely of small-unit operations and cantonment administration. This argument was reinforced by Pershing's own opinion of the army's residual capabilities, and the condition was further agreed upon by many of the "memoirists" who wrote their judgments immediately after the war.[47] On the other hand, Irving B. Holley, Professor of History at Duke University, argued that a good bit of preparation for the high command of major armies had been gained by the regular officers through the army school system; some of the regulars also had had the opportunity to observe foreign armies in "modern" operations.[48] It is true that most regular officers had gone to the line or staff school at Fort Leavenworth; fewer (only 4.7 percent) had attended the highest military school, the Army War College.[49] This schooling had prepared the few for high command and staff duties, but none had any such experience. Rainey's argument that the army had a "small unit mentality" that adversely affected its ability to develop a system of training for modern warfare appears to be a fair assessment of the regular officer establishment.[50]

While Pershing expected the War Department to provide training guidance and doctrine appropriate to the battlefields of World War I, the Department was unprepared for developing this doctrine, and clearly deferred to Pershing to provide recommendations in this regard. Pershing responded to their requests for guidance with a strong statement, the essence of which was that "the rifle and the bayonet remain the supreme weapons of the infantry soldier and . . . the ultimate success of the Army depends upon their proper use in open warfare."[51]

Pershing believed that the three years of trench warfare on the Western Front had established a "mind set" among the Allied commanders, which was defensive in nature, and accepted attrition in attack, without seeking alternatives that would accomplish the same military objectives with fewer casualties. He felt that the Allied generals had become accustomed to moving their troops directly from trench to trench, placing increasing amounts of heavy fire forward of their advancing soldiers to protect them, to destroy enemy positions, and to attenuate the enemy's strength. He believed that the Allies were too concerned with the defensive firepower of the machine gun, with absence of flanks that could be turned, and that aggressiveness in attack was no longer demanded by Allied commanders.[52] Pershing's observations convinced him that an "offensive spirit" was still the essential element necessary for victory on the Western Front. He was adamant that a self-confident individual soldier, skilled with the rifle and the bayonet, could advance against enemy positions with bold maneuvers and forward movements on the strongly defended modern battlefield. This philosophy he expressed in training guidance and in cables to the War Department.[53] War Department offensive doctrine was embodied largely in the Infantry Drill Regulations of 1911, as revised in 1914 and 1917. The 1911 edition and the later revisions contained the statement that:

> machine guns must be considered weapons of emergency . . . of great value at critical though infrequent periods of an engagement. . . . Machine guns should not be assigned to the firing line of an attack. When attacking a hostile armed with machine guns . . . infantry must silence them before it can advance. . . . An infantry command should concentrate a large number of rifles on each gun in turn, until it has silenced it.[54]

One could, perhaps, blame bureaucratic indolence for the Department's failure to change significantly the Infantry Drill Regulations, despite the tremendous increase in the amount and lethality of firepower (particularly of machine guns) that had been displayed during three years of the world war. It is more difficult to explain Pershing's insistence upon "Open Warfare" maneuver for attacking arrays of machine guns in a limited zone of advance without open flanks. His observations and those of his staff of the fighting in his front yard should have caused him to modify his precept, or to explain open warfare as a later stage of advance. Professor Russell Weigley of Temple University, author of several military histories and studies, has expressed amazement at Pershing's failure in this regard, and at his (Pershing's) apparent inability to change his prewar convictions in the light of his observations as commander in chief of the AEF.[55] The author David Kennedy, in his text *Over Here: The First World War and American Society*, has also criticized Pershing for having "overlooked" the firepower of machine guns and artillery in emphasizing maneuver over firepower. Rainey, however, stated that the problem was greater—that of defining an appropriate modern offensive doctrine, a problem which even the Allies had not solved. Some observers, even within Pershing's own staff, argued that the effects of modern firepower had reduced infantry maneuver to short movements from one covered position to another. The result, Rainey stated, "was that no clear and positive explication of the tactics of open warfare was ever published."[56]

The influence of Allied doctrine, which could be called "cautious offense," was considerable, especially upon American military missions and early liaison groups. After all, the Allies had had considerable combat experience in modern warfare, and the U.S. had none. Allied offensive doctrine was translated into War Department tactical instructions despite Pershing's insistence upon open warfare. The AEF staff then reproduced the War Department Instructions as their own guidance to AEF organizations, at the same time as AEF spokesmen were criticizing Allied tactics. Obviously, the AEF headquarters, which was becoming a large agency, was not functioning in harmony.[57]

With respect to the training given American units in France, AEF inspectors reported to Pershing that the training being presented by French instructors in the line and in AEF schools continued to emphasize defensive and trench warfare. On 4 July 1918, the AEF Chief of Training, Colonel Harold B. Fiske, reported that he had come into possession of a "secret" memorandum of the French General Headquarters instructing French commanders to impregnate American units with French methods and doctrine. The Fiske Report (enclosing the French secret memorandum) made the point that:

> The offensive spirit of the French and British armies has largely disappeared as a result of their severe losses. Close association with beaten forces lowers the morale of the best troops. Our young officers and men are prone to take the tone and tactics of those with whom they are associated. Whatever they are learning that is false or unsuited for us will be hard to eradicate later . . . The French do not like the rifle, do not know how to use it, and their Infantry is consequently too dependent upon powerful artillery support. Their infantry lacks aggressiveness and discipline. The British infantry lacks initiative and resource.

Colonel Fiske's report ends by recommending that American training in France be emancipated from Allied supervision. Pershing annotated the report with handwritten guidance to his Chief of Staff: "This is entirely my own view." He went on to direct that the AEF should work out a means by which American forces could be advised of the falseness, the "heresies" of French doctrine.[58]

There is evidence that, as the Americans gained direct combat experience in 1918, the AEF staff was gradually forming a new tactic for the offensive, which muted their "open warfare" ideal with an appreciation of the realities of the power of defensive weaponry. An example of a mutational approach to "open warfare" was revealed in a study by the AEF Deputy G-3, Lieutenant Colonel Hugh A. Drum: "Since, on the Western Front, open warfare will occur only in periods, followed by long periods of trench warfare, the ideal organization is that best suited for offensive trench warfare."[59] Such conclusions also led to a reconsideration of the square (heavy) division originally advocated by the AEF. Many commanders and staff officers felt that the heavy division (with two brigades, each of two regiments) was too large for offensive warfare. However, in the aforementioned study, Lieutenant Colonel Drum wrote that the war of mass and attrition would continue to require heavy divisions, since "the gaining of ground counts for little; it is the ruining of the enemy's main army that will end the struggle."[60] Major General Hunter Liggett, Commander of I Corps, and considered the most perceptive of AEF commanders, groped for a solution to the problem of applying open warfare to the Western Front. In a letter to Colonel Fox Connor (AEF G-3) on 9 April 1918, he wrote:

> I am enclosing a copy of a memo which I have drawn up . . . upon some practical line for open warfare offensive and defensive. I can find nothing in the mass of literature I have received which teaches this, to me, essential question.[61]

Some scholars who have studied Pershing's theories have concluded that his insistence upon "open warfare tactics," despite evidence that such tactics were more theoretical than practical, was an attempt to infuse and maintain an offensive spirit within the AEF.[62] It appears that even Pershing came to doubt his emphasis on open-warfare maneuver. On 7 August 1918, he instructed his Chief of Staff, Major General James McAndrews, to make a study of the whole question of attack against machine guns and artillery, opining that, "perhaps, we are losing too many men." The resulting study promulgated to the AEF on 5 September 1918 (just prior to the initiation of the St. Mihiel campaign) delineated the difference between "trench warfare" and "open warfare" in the following terms: Trench warfare is characterized by "regulation of space and time by higher command down to the smallest units . . . little initiative . . . by the individual soldier." Open warfare is "irregular formations, scouts preceding the assaulting waves, and a high degree of individual initiative. . . . Primary reliance upon the infantry's own firepower to enable it to get forward."[63] The reader of these instructions can only conclude that the emphasis upon open warfare was modified by the realization that strong supporting fire and slow movement may be necessary in assaulting well-defended fortifications, and that "open warfare" was a condition that occurs after the penetration of trench systems. Russell Weigley argued that

Pershing had concluded, by this time, that no real alternative remained except a strategy that aimed at destroying the German armies by grinding them into ruin."[64]

A greater training problem than that caused by uncertain tactics was the extreme personnel turbulence taking place within army units in the United States. Divisions forming and training were frequently stripped of thousands of their troops to fill units deploying according to an ever more accelerated schedule. These units were then refilled with new draftees. This turnover required the repetition of basic training in the affected units. It also "gutted" unit integrity and provided little time for subordinate commanders to get to know their men or to gain experience in leading their troops. Senior commanders and staff officers were absent, often on trips, attending boards, and busy with school details. In the build-up of the AEF, which increased in geometric progression to a three-million-man force, insufficient attention was given to the need for establishing supporting organizations, staffs, and housekeeping, and labor elements. Thus, when base-support requirements became imperative, combat units were further stripped of civil specialists and technically qualified personnel to perform such functions—functions necessary to the equipping, sustaining, and processing of the combat units overseas and toward the front.

The personnel chaos was compounded by an uneven flow of recruits from the draft levies. Adding to all this turmoil was the inadequacy of training facilities and the scarcity of weapons, equipment, and ammunition for training. Rainey characterized the turnover as "personnel rapes." He cited as an example the training experience of the 78th Division. In November 1917, this division was filled with personnel beginning training in the United States. Frequent personnel levies so reduced their numbers that by January 1918 the units were at one-third strength. The division was only at 50 percent strength in April, but by June 1918 it had been filled, largely with new recruits; it then sailed for Europe.[65]

The absence of modern weapons for training is well recorded in the 28th Division's "Official History":

> Rifles, automatic rifles, trench mortars, 37, 75, 155 millimeter guns used in combat were not secured until the Division reached France. We had one bayonet for every third man, which meant changing for drill. For several months we used improvised wooden guns for machine gun work. The one 37 millimeter gun in camp was a novelty. The Division had but few gas masks, which made training slow and difficult.[66]

The chart in Appendix 2 depicts the period of time that each of the 42 AEF divisions spent in the United States, in the rear of the line in France, in the battle line, and in combat. The graphics show that, except for divisions deployed in 1917, each had at least six months in the United States, adequate time to complete a four-month unit training program. The personnel turmoil described above, however, ensured that few had gained the requisite individual and unit training upon their arrival in France. Pershing was aware of the poor state of training of the divisions arriving in France in 1918. Earlier, he had encouraged the War Department to form a central training committee to manage all training and training facilities. His recommendation was rejected by the War Department, largely because of the pressure of combat branch and technical staff specialists, who argued for their traditional training and school prerogatives.[67] Rather than agree to the creation of a new training-management body, the War Department expanded the existing War College Division Training Committee. Major General John F. Morrison was recalled from duty in France at Pershing's recommendation, and was appointed to head this Training Committee as the Army Director of Training.[68] Although Morrison came from the AEF, Pershing was never satisfied with the War Department Training Committee's efforts to inculcate the tactics of "open warfare" into training in the United States. He later wrote in his memoirs, "Training continued defective, being usually limited to trench warfare."[69] Pershing's criticism also reflected the opinion of many in the AEF that the War Department was being influenced unduly by Allied officers and their theories. These suspicions were confirmed when French and British military attachés on duty in the United States were "attached" to the Training Committee of the War Department.[70]

Pershing had previously attempted to divide the training being given on both sides of the ocean, to offset the limited maneuvering area available in France, by tasking the War Department to concentrate on long-range marksmanship training and "open warfare" in training in the United States. This recommendation, which he had made on 19 October 1917, also involved Pershing's acceptance of the responsibility for providing "trench warfare" training in France. Using the trenches already available in France, American units could gain realistic acclimatization to the conditions of trench warfare.[71] The War Department accepted Pershing's recommendations; however, their later directives indicated that "trench warfare would be taught by division commanders in the United States under the special instruction of their British and French advisers. "Open warfare" was not neglected in training instructions, but it was only mentioned in general terms. Pershing protested this deficiency in War Department training guidance, and the War

Department promised to place greater emphasis on "open warfare" training.[72]

A major task for the new AEF Headquarters was the training of American forces in France. It was recognized that the divisions shipped to the combat zone would require area training and acclimatization to the theater of war and to the nature of the combat there. It was agreed between the AEF and the Allied headquarters that American divisions, on their arrival, would be placed in association with "veteran" French divisions—to be trained and to receive orientations, subsequently to take their place "in the line" as the final phase of their training.

The training was to be accomplished in three phases: The first phase was to consist of familiarization and retraining with the weapons being used in theater, followed by tactical exercises in the training areas up to the division level, where the terrain permitted. The second phase embraced a one-month tour by infantry battalions and like units of supporting arms in the trenches under French regimental command. During this phase, commanders were to be stationed with the French and British units to observe operations under fire. The third phase was to consist of division-level exercises by the combined arms of infantry, artillery, and aviation, operating as teams. Following these exercises, each division was to go into the line, under its own commanders, as part of a French corps.[73]

To supplement this divisional training, Pershing directed the establishment of a broad program of schooling for gunners, specialists, and officers in France. The program, developed by the Assistant Chief of Staff for Training (G-5) and approved by Pershing, would set up schools beginning at the corps level to serve the needs of the divisions and supporting troops for specialist training. Each corps would be assigned a training division to conduct its training. Each corps would also have a replacement division to process replacements forward and to reassign returnees. The training division would conduct the in-country training of troops received from the replacement division. This division would also train soldiers to become noncommissioned officers. Each corps would form an Infantry School to give tactical and weapons training to rifle company commanders, machine gun unit commanders, and commanders of mortar units. Each corps would also organize an Artillery School to instruct officers and enlisted men in artillery instrumentation, communications, firing, ranging, and targeting; an Engineer School to train engineer company and platoon commanders, sappers, and pioneers; a Cavalry School to train personnel in mounted service; a Gas School that would train all arms and services in the use of and defense against gas; a Signal School that would train communications NCOs and signal company and platoon commanders; a Corps Sanitary School that would train ambulance and field-hospital officers. The Corps Aeronautical School would have a Combat Aviation Course and a Combat Balloon Course. Finally, each corps would also have a Field Officers School that would train majors and lieutenant colonels—their training would include visits to all other schools of the corps.[74]

At the army level, schools would consist of a General Staff College, which would train officers for staff work. Army line schools would train company and battery commanders for infantry, artillery, engineer, and signal units. The line schools would also provide familiarization and refresher training for captains, majors, and lieutenant colonels of all arms of the service. An Officer Candidates School would be established to train soldiers to become officers. An Anti-Aircraft School would be opened to teach the employment of artillery and machine guns in an anti-aircraft role. The Army Artillery School would train officers and men in heavy artillery, trench artillery, and railroad artillery. The Army Signal School would train personnel in telephone and telegraph, radio, visual, and carrier pigeon communications. It would also train personnel in communication system operations. The Army Aeronautic School would train pilots and balloonists and would also train infantry and artillery observers for flying duties. The Army Sanitary School would give courses in greater depth (than those at the corps level) to hospital and medical personnel on health matters. The Army Engineer School would be designed to give courses in bridging, mining, searchlight employment, ranging, topography, camouflage, sapper (tunneling and mining), and pioneer (basic engineer) schooling—all at a higher level than that of the corps schools. The Army Infantry Specialists Center was also established to train personnel in conducting training in musketry, use of the bayonet, sniping, automatic weapons firing, throwing grenades, trench mortars, and 37 mm cannon firing. The Army Center of Information was to establish conferences and demonstrations for generals and colonels of all arms. The Army Tank School was designed to train tankers and tank commanders. The Army Gas School was established to provide training in chemical warfare and in defenses against chemical operations.

In addition, in each army corps, the replacement division would set up a training center to retrain infantrymen as cooks and bakers, clerks, mechanics, saddlers and horseshoers, stable sergeants, drivers and packers, chauffeurs, telephone operators and telegraph and radio operators—skills needed for services within the rear areas at the various headquarters.[75]

This great complex of schools was based on the extensive systems of the British and French. Its establishment was, for the most part, fully accomplished. Three of the corps established school systems; these were turned over to Army G-5 as the corps became involved in battle. All the planned army schools were opened and operational, except the Cavalry School; experience proved that it was not needed. In addition, an American Expeditionary Forces University and a Bandmasters School were founded. The initial cadre of instructors was almost entirely French, with a leavening of British officers, and few Americans. The irony in this situation is that the Americans were forced by shortages of qualified instructors to rely on the Allies, with whose training philosophies they disagreed.

It was Pershing's intention to make up for the deficiencies in knowledge of his officers and men and to achieve the "standards of West Point" in the AEF. He insisted that all commanders and their general staff officers attend the line or staff courses. Furthermore, he drove his trainers to establish his "open warfare" philosophy in the schools and to replace the Allied instructors as soon as possible. Even with minimum American staffing, the school system severely taxed the officer strength in theater. The initial instructor quota especially was a heavy cut in the officer strength of the 1st Division—the only one in country at the time of the activation of the school system. This drawdown of personnel was very detrimental to the division's preparations for imminent operations.[76]

By his insistence on training before combat and his inspections and reports, Pershing got his training and school systems. The drain on combat strength was criticized by division commanders, by the Allies, and even, finally, by Secretary of War Baker, who allowed that training could be shortened and still be effective in time of war, since proximity to the area of combat made troops eager to learn.[77] After the first sessions of the AEF school program, the quality of the students attending declined rapidly. Busy and harassed commanders preparing their units for combat quite naturally sent officers and men whom they could most afford to lose. A good man sent to school was lost at a critical time—and maybe lost forever, assigned to the school faculty or to a higher staff job.[78]

Deficiencies also existed in the instruction. AEF inspectors repeatedly noted that the schools were not presenting approved instruction in an informative manner, and especially that "open warfare" tactics were not being taught. The AEF staff was certain this was caused by the omnipresence of Allied officers on the faculties. James Rainey, however, showed that even senior American officers lecturing at the schools put emphasis on the attack and defense of fortified positions, and had little to say about "open warfare."[79] There is, on the other hand, ample evidence that the Allied officers maintained a patronizing attitude in conducting their instruction. The French high command provided this guidance to their officers who were detailed to instruct and act as liaison to the AEF: "Recognize the delicate nature of this association, but ensure correctness of instruction!" The American hierarchy was found, in many instances, to be in agreement with the French assessment of "correct" battlefield tactics.[80]

The AEF school system continued throughout the war, despite the intensity of combat. The General Staff College at Langres graduated 537 officers before the Armistice. Courses were three months in length. The Line (tactical) School, also at Langres, came to serve as a preparatory course for the Staff College, receiving officers of less military experience for a three-month, low-level tactical course. The line school had four sessions before the end of the war and graduated 488 officers. With respect to Officer Candidate Schools, these were organized at Langres, San Saumur, and Mailly. They were under pressure to produce officers because of the heavy losses of officers caused by the Meuse-Argonne fighting. Casualties among platoon and company commanders were particularly heavy. The total number of men commissioned from officer candidate schools in France was 6,895 infantry, 2,384 artillery, 1,332 engineers and 536 signal officers—all quickly absorbed into AEF units.

To meet the increasing demands for officers, several of the three-month courses had to be shortened. The schools established by three of the corps were deemed to be adequate for training all the officers and noncommissioned officers in the replacement system. These schools, altogether, graduated 15,916 officers and 21,330 noncommissioned officers for a total of 37,246. The courses at all of the schools were entirely too short for the nature of the training; under the circumstances, they constituted a reasonable compromise between the demand for haste and the compelling demand for the preparation of soldiers for battle.[81]

With respect to the organizational training of the deployed divisions, only the 1st Division (the first in France) went through the entire three-phase program, as prescribed by the AEF and as represcribed by Pershing after inspection of that division's training.[82] After coming out of the trenches in March 1918, the 1st Division underwent refresher training. Still, after nearly a year in training and in battle, this division was found to be too much "trench-oriented" by AEF G-5 inspectors. This was the premier division of the AEF, containing the greatest number of Regular Army officers and noncommissioned officers, showcased in training, and having the most experience on the fighting line. If it was judged at this stage to be minimally combat effective, then all the other divisions undergoing the AEF regimen would likely be less so. The main problem, as Rainey stated, was that "open warfare" training, as it was explained by the AEF, was inapplicable to the fighting conditions in France in 1918—at least as the 1st Division had seen these conditions.[83]

The training of the next three American divisions to arrive was directed according to the model of the 1st Division's training. The great German drive beginning on 21 March 1918, however, eliminated the third phase of the training of these divisions. Instead, they were committed to blunt the German drive; then they remained operationally committed, despite Pershing's desire to disengage them for more training. As the divisions gained combat experience, they modified, considerably, the AEF directives in their training guidance. Under the pressure of the circumstances that prevailed in April 1918 which demanded the early combat commitment of arriving divisions, Pershing himself shortened the division training to a four-week "first phase" program of individual and small-unit training.

As shown in the chart in Appendix 2, the twenty-nine divisions committed to battle averaged two months in France before entering the line; six had one-and-a-half months of preparation (the 5th, 6th, 35th, 81st, 82d, and 88th); and two (the 29th and 37th) entered the line after only one month overseas. Again, it must be noted that much of this "training" time was spent moving, reorganizing, drawing supplies, and performing routine camp duties and prescribed details. Since the divisions conducted their own training in accordance with a general army directive, it is understandable that little more was done than the firing of assigned weapons. A problem which impacted on large unit training was the fact that elements of a division were often billeted in small towns spread over a ten-mile area. Bringing them together for training was difficult and time consuming.[84] The divisions that were rushed over in British transports from January through March 1918 and were trained with the British suffered the additional problem of having been filled with recruits just before deployment. Their commanders were hard-pressed, as were their British trainers, to teach them even the rudiments of individual combat before they were moved into the trenches. AEF inspectors reported that the training given by the British was poor, fragmented, boring, and, as with that provided by the French, contrary to AEF offensive doctrine.[85] As a result, Pershing decided that divisions arriving in the summer of 1918 would be trained by the AEF itself. The need to commit the divisions arriving that summer to the ongoing battles made their training short and rudimentary, though the AEF Headquarters had planned otherwise.[86]

Because of Pershing's emphasis on and dissatisfaction with training, the AEF G-5 Staff became very large and powerful. This staff division took over production of training manuals, developing hundreds before the Armistice. The staff also organized and supervised the entire school system, conducted frequent training inspections, and published Notes on Recent Operations. By mid-1918, G-5 had one representative with each division, observing and correcting training and operations, and reporting back to Colonel (later Brigadier General) Harold B. Fiske, the Assistant Chief of Staff for Training (G-5). Fiske was a dour personality, intensely dedicated to his mission, who appeared by his manner to disapprove of everything he saw. His inspectors appeared to affect that manner when inspecting units in the field. The inspectors were generally dissatisfied with the quality of training observed. It should be noted that training was often deemed unsatisfactory by observers not connected with the command chain. Not only was it rushed, due to the chaotic changes in status of units taking training, it was also given little attention by commanders who were pressed with more immediate tasks.[87]

Most of the historians with whom this author corresponded thought the Americans were better trained than the Allies credited them to be, but none took the position that the AEF was well or properly trained. Russell Weigley supported Rainey's conclusion that the training emphasized was inappropriate to the combat the Americans faced.[88] Jay Luvaas, a noted military historian, agreed with them, and he added the opinion that time limitations precluded adequate training, whatever had been the emphasis, a view echoed by Theodore Ropp, Professor of History at Duke University.[89] General Theodore Conway, who served under World War I veteran officers, said those veterans believed training had been inadequate.[90] The British authors who responded to this author's queries all characterized American training as inappropriate even as they also criticized the United States for tarrying too long in a training mode in France.[91] Dr. James Stokesbury, a Canadian author, gave a more kindly but still critical opinion of the quality of American training.[92]

It seems logical to conclude that the chief problem was a lack of time to conduct training. The attempt to create the base of a three-million-man army in a few months caused such personnel turbulence that training had to be sacrificed to the more visible requirements of bringing troops into the line. Although AEF training/tactical guidance was unclear and inappropriate to the battlefield, it was not followed where it differed from combat requirements as perceived by those closest to the fighting. Pershing and his staff were aware of the uneven state of training in units committed to combat—they were forced to overlook the fact that some soldiers were not sufficiently trained to kill and defend themselves. Former Infantry Private Edmund Seiser, Headquarters Company, 316th Infantry Regiment, 79th Division, stated that he had not seen a rifle or a pistol until he reported to the 79th Division, and then, almost immediately, he was sent on to an outpost. Corporal William Sibley, Company B, 109th Infantry Regiment, 28th Infantry Division, in the Argonne Forest, stated that a few replacements arrived in the forest wearing white civilian shirts. They said they had had only two weeks in the army before they left the United States. Private Frank Groves, Company H, 28th Infantry Regiment, 1st Infantry Division, stated, "Our training did nothing to equip us to take care of ourselves in combat. Training in the U.S. was not realistic. Training in France was nonexistent." With regard to AEF schools, Lieutenant Colonel Merritt Pratt (who served as a junior officer in Company G, 131st Infantry Regiment of the 33rd Division in the Meuse-Argonne fighting) said that the AEF schools gave inadequate and uninteresting training.[93] Perhaps some of these comments can be discounted because of the long time that has elapsed since the experience. However, the training system which brought relatively untrained men to the front should be condemned. In Pershing's behalf, his frequent complaints to the War Department about the receipt of untrained or partially trained men should be noted. The AEF's training programs, however, did not take full advantage of the time available to make up training deficiencies. It appears that, in the rush of great events, the problems of receiving untrained men and officers were either forgotten, or that attempts to train these men were overtaken by more pressing business.

4

THE AMERICANS MOVE INTO THE LINE

When the representatives of the Allies met at Rapallo, Italy, in November 1917 to coordinate their future operations, it was agreed that the strategies and tactics they had employed previously had resulted in unacceptable losses, and that the societies supporting the conflict on the Allied side could not continue to sustain this kind of attrition. The French army was still unstable as a result of the mutinies of 1917, and that entire nation was in a defeatist mood. The British were strained, but they had borne their losses better. General Allenby's victory in Palestine had helped British morale. The tank and the airplane were just beginning to show some promise—and the Americans, young, exuberant, and physically larger than their European allies, were supposed to be arriving soon. It was decided that victory had to wait for the production of more tanks and the arrival of the Americans.[1]

Realizing, at that late hour, the need for better international coordination of their war efforts, the Allies formed a Supreme War Council. The purpose of the new body was to effect improved military coordination on the Western Front. It was to overwatch the general conduct of the war, approve war plans submitted by national military commanders, and make recommendations to the national governments for the conduct of the war. National military commanders were to remain responsible to their own governments. The Council was to consist of the prime minister and a member of the government of each of the great powers whose armies were on the Western Front. The Council proposed to meet at least monthly. One military representative from each of the great powers would form a committee of technical advisers to the Council. These would be in permanent, day-to-day session, to advise the Council. The permanent military representatives appointed to the Council were:

for France, General Ferdinand Foch; for Great Britain, General Sir Henry Wilson; and for Italy, General Luigi Cadorna. The question of American representation on the Council was a delicate one. The United States was in the war in a "cooperative status" with the Allies. The American government had no treaty of alliance, and it had made no pledges regarding Allied war aims.

The idea of a War Council as a policy and decision making body did not sit well with the Commander of the BEF, Douglas Haig, and a good many British political figures opposed it also. President Wilson, however, cabled his approval, strengthening the new Council's political status. The American President, with the advice of the Secretary of War, then appointed Major General Tasker M. Bliss, the Chief of Staff of the United States Army, as the permanent military representative on the Council. Ignoring Allied entreaties, President Wilson avoided the issue of appointing a political representative to the Council.[2]

The peril that all the Allies recognized was the likelihood that Russia would be forced out of the war shortly, and that the full weight of the Central Powers' forces could then be turned against the Western Front before the Americans arrived to balance the Central Powers' forces. On the other side of the line, the Central Powers were equally concerned with heavy losses. Acute food shortages had lowered morale at home. But their military leaders were confident that, by the rapid shifting of forces from the east to the Western Front, they could gather sufficient strength to gain a final victory before the Americans could arrive in sufficient numbers. In fact, Hindenburg and Ludendorff confidently promised the Kaiser that victory would come with one more gigantic offensive on the Western Front. By dint of good staff work, the Germans were able to pull some fifty-six of their divisions from the Eastern Front prior to the end of the war with Russia. These were then trained in the new "Hutier Tactics" in preparation for moving them as "shock troops" to the Western Front. Additional divisions were being readied for dispatch to the Western Front as Ludendorff, the virtual Commander of the forces of the Central Powers, prepared his "spring offensive."[3]

The Allies pressed the query: Where are the Americans? The 1st Division had completed its training in the rear, and had assumed a defensive position "in the Vosges," a quiet sector of the line, on 21 October 1917. On 3 November, a German raid caught them unprepared; three American soldiers were killed, five were wounded, and twelve captured—the first American casualties in the war.[4] By the end of 1917, four American divisions were in France;

two more were on the way over. A total of 9,804 officers and 165,080 men were assigned to the AEF. Pershing continued to emphasize training, and the organization of a balanced, self-sustaining force, including a sizable administrative and logistical support complex. The small number of American combat forces, compared to support forces, was very disappointing to the Allies. Their entreaties for assignment of individuals and small units of American infantrymen as fillers in their armies now took on more strident tones.[5]

The AEF staff was also reflecting the pressure on its commander. An AEF staff study, done in November 1917, indicated that the situation might become grave for the Allies if the bulk of the eighty German and Austrian divisions remaining on the Eastern Front were committed into battle in the west, adding to the strength of those in France. It was agreed at General Headquarters (GHQ) of the AEF (apparently, also by Pershing) that the situation might arise in which units of the AEF might have to be used to reinforce the armies of the Allies, as a last, desperate resort. But, the study concluded, the Allies should be able to stop the enemy without American reinforcement if "they held firm and secured unity of action." The situation and its prospects in no way justified curtailing plans to form an army under the American flag, the study concluded.[6]

Allied proposals for the integration of American troops into their armies were nothing new; they had begun in April 1917, as soon as it was apparent that America intended to field a ground force in France. The Joffre-Vivani visit to the United States in May 1917 was the occasion for Marshall Joseph Joffre (the former Commander-in-Chief of French forces) to suggest a French-American partnership, with the French acting as the seniors in leading the Americans in battle. (This proposal was never presented officially.) A British proposal to draft Americans into British battalions (presented by British Major General G. T. M. Bridges in April 1917) was quickly rejected by the American government.[7] Late in 1917, the Allies tried to gain "Yankee" reinforcements through General Bliss, the American member on the Supreme War Council; Bliss was sympathetic to their plight, but, nonetheless, supported a separate American army.[8]

In December, the British Ambassador to the United States, Lord Reading, carried a proposal to President Wilson's adviser, Colonel Edward House, for reconsideration of the "amalgamation" of American companies or battalions within British divisions. This appeal stressed the return of those units to American command, "if later desired." It had the personal support of Lloyd George. House queried Pershing, who emphatically rejected it as yet another attempt to subvert the build-up of an American army. House supported Pershing, but the political pressures continued. On 25 December 1917, the War Department cabled that both France and England were pressing for amalgamation. Pershing answered that "no emergency exists which would warrant putting our companies and battalions into British and French units."[9]

In January 1918, Pershing made two positive responses to this continuing pressure. Marshal Pétain and Pershing agreed that the program for moving American divisions into the line should be expedited. Pershing also agreed to a British plan to expedite the shipment of American troops to France for training and service with the British, using British ships. Pershing insisted that the units involved would be trained for major independent operations and that they be returned to the American command when called for. The agreement, concluded on 30 January 1918, involved six American divisions; it was called the "Six Division Plan." The British agreed on the ultimate return of American divisions, but their later complaints showed that they expected to employ these divisions indefinitely.[10]

The Allies increased their pressure on Pershing by means of the Supreme War Council's approval, on 12 January 1918, of Note #12, drafted by their military representatives. This note stated that France could only be successfully defended if "British and French forces are maintained at their present aggregate strength, and receive the expected reinforcement of not less than two American divisions per month."[11] Pershing chose the occasion of this memo to send a cable of bitter complaint to the Secretary of War regarding the failure of the War Department to provide even the numbers of personnel previously agreed upon. The winter of 1917–1918 being one of the coldest on record, he also castigated the War Department for its failure to provide the troops with adequate winter clothing.[12]

The increasing German threat eventually led to ever increasing American combat force commitments being made to the Allies. By recalling some divisions from Italy and more from the east, General Ludendorff assembled more than 3.5 million men on the Western Front by the spring of 1918. Approximately two hundred German divisions faced one hundred sixty-nine Allied division equivalents. The location of the front lines in 1918 and the offensives of 1918 may be followed on Map 10 (on pages 180–181). The Germans assembled sixty-two of their best divisions along the Somme. Their plan was to split the Allied forces at their juncture and to roll the British back against the English Channel, with the hope, thereby, of taking them out of the war. The principle on which Ludendorff's offensive was based was to defeat the British, the stronger force, first. Then, the less combat-effective force, the French, would fall easily to the might of German arms. The area of the juncture of the Allied armies, the Aisne-Marne region of France, was also viewed by the Allies as a point of great significance. They were not deceived about German intentions; in fact, all along the line it was known that a "spring offensive" was due, and, generally, it was appreciated that its purpose was to split the Allied forces from their cooperative but fragile union. Viewing the growing disparity between Allied forces and their reinforcing enemy (potentially, a disadvantage in numbers of two to one) the French prodded Pershing to put the other American divisions in France into the line.[13] On 19 January 1918, the 1st Division took over a sector north of Toul. By the agreement of Generals Pershing and Pétain, this sector was to be expanded to include an American corps, then the American army. The 26th United States Division ended its training and entered the line in the Chemin-des-Dames sector on 8 February 1918; on 21 February, the 42nd Division entered the French line near Luneville. The 2nd Division was brigaded with the French in the Verdun area on 18 March 1918.[14]

Despite the obvious threat to the juncture point of their combined forces, neither General Haig nor General Pétain would do more than give each other assurances that each would reinforce the other in the event of attack in his sector. The tendency to concentrate reserves, such as there were, near the center of the mass of each army was a natural command action. Thus, the area of the juncture, athwart the left flank of the Fifth French Army where it joined the Third British Army (the Amiens sector), was weakly manned, and, considering the manning that had been established in the trench warfare of the time, relatively overextended.

The Germans, having trained their troops to attack closely following a rolling barrage of artillery, struck on the morning of 21 March 1918, after a short but intensive artillery barrage that was heavy in gas and smoke. Aided also by a thick fog, small groups of highly trained "shock troops" rushed forward; bypassing centers of Allied resistance, they seized vital terrain. The swift movement of the "shock troops" surprised the defenders; the Germans drove through the positions of the Fifth French Army and the right wing of the BEF—gaining the banks of the Somme River in the first forty-eight hours. As he had promised, General Haig shifted British forces to reinforce his right flank, and he tardily dispatched two divisions to the command of the Fifth French Army. The German attack was temporarily halted, the result of elasticity of the Allied defenses, the shifting of their reserves, and the exhaustion of the leading German divisions.[15]

The Allies, however, were frightened by this attack. It was far more violent, more successful, and more strategically threatening than anything that had occurred since the Battle of the Frontiers in 1914. The Germans had advanced forty miles in eight days. They had taken 70,000 prisoners. Allied casualties exceeded 200,000. But German casualties were as high, and their "shock divisions" were decimated. The giant "Paris gun" began lobbing shells into Paris, while Lloyd George and his staff hurried over from London to consult with their counterparts about the new situation.[16] It was agreed by the British and French, and seconded by Pershing, that Marshal Ferdinand Foch would be given the role of "coordinator" of all Allied armies; he would be responsible for "strategic direction," controlling the general reserves of both forces and the commitment of those reserves. Pétain and Haig reluctantly surrendered control of their reserves; by so doing, they took another step toward a coalition command.[17]

On 9 April 1918, the Germans struck again, this time along the Lys River in the British sector of Flanders, north of their Amiens salient. Following an intensive bombardment, eight German divisions attacked along the south bank of the Lys, broke through a Portuguese division, and reached open country beyond the British trenches. Foch refused Haig reinforcements, sensing the British would hold. Haig gave his "backs to the wall" order, and the British held. The Germans held the Passchendaele Ridge, but little else of value. British losses were high—305,000; but German losses reached 350,000.[18] A third German offensive struck the French Fifth and Sixth Armies in the Aisne region, south of the first penetration. The drive broke through their defenses on the Chemin-des-Dames on 27 May and gained twenty miles the first day. Three days later, the German forces stood on the banks of the Marne River at Chateau-Thierry, less than fifty miles from Paris—a position that they had not been able to reach since the early days of 1914.

In this crisis, the Allies renewed their pressures for American replacements for their forces. On 27 March Lloyd George requested of President Wilson that three hundred thousand men be shipped at the earliest moment and that trained divisions in France be put into the line immediately. "We are at the crisis of the war," he cabled.[19] Wilson showed his mettle by refusing to throw "our troops in to stop up that hole." He passed Lloyd George's request on to Secretary Baker in Paris.[20] At the same time, the Supreme War Council was pressing Pershing to approve immediate, temporary amalgamation of his troops with those of the Allies. On 28 March, the permanent military representatives (including General Bliss) recommended to the Supreme War Council, meeting at Douellens, that all plans for the shipment of Americans to France be altered, and that for the foreseeable future, only infantry and machine gun units be shipped. This recommendation was approved and promulgated as Joint Note 18. Pershing, after remonstrating with General Bliss, gained Secretary Baker's approval of a message to President Wilson regarding Joint Note 18. They recommended that the President approve the shipment of only infantry and machine gun units in the emergency, with the following provisos:

> These units to be under the direction of the Commander in Chief of the AEF He will use these . . . to render the greatest military assistance . . . keeping in mind always the determination of this government to have its forces collected . . . into an American Army.[21]

The President approved this response.

Hearing that the Douellens conference had also appointed Foch as Coordinator of the Allied armies, Pershing (who considered Foch's position to be that of supreme commander) motored to Foch's headquarters and made a historic commitment: "Infantry, artillery, aviation; all that we have are yours. Use them as you wish!"[22] Pershing's agreement to provide all his forces meant, according to his memoirs, that he would provide the five divisions of the American forces then in France. This would have given the Allies the equivalent, as Pershing saw it, of ten of their own divisions. However, the Supreme War Council's requests for infantry and machine gun troops had resulted in the War Department's being directed to dispatch these troops without their accompanying support. Pershing's return cable stressed that:

> Americans must not lose sight of the purpose to build up divisions and corps of their own . . . must avoid the tendency to incorporate our infantry into British divisions where it will be used up and never relieved.[23]

Pershing recommended that the infantry in two divisions be sent by British shipping and that two be sent by American shipping, but that present plans should go no further than this shipment of infantry without supportive arms. By return message, Secretary Baker relayed the President's concurrence with Pershing's interpretation of the American commitment and restressed Pershing's authority to decide questions of American cooperation or replacement.[24] These agreements threw the War Department's plans, still in the stages of development and partial execution, into a "cocked hat." Infantry and machine gun personnel would have to be pulled out of four divisions, to be shipped in a relatively semi-trained or untrained state during April and May of 1918. Furthermore, the British government in the person of Lloyd George, chose to assume that the dispatch of infantry and machine gunners was to be continued for succeeding months. The terrible losses of the early spring, as the German army drove to the banks of the Marne for the second time in the war, also caused General Foch to appeal to French Prime Minister Clemenceau for his representation to the American President that additional infantry and machine gun personnel (at the rate of one hundred twenty thousand per month) be provided on a continuing basis. Accompanying this political pressure, great personal pressures were brought to bear upon General Pershing at a meeting of the Supreme War Council at Sarcus (General Foch's headquarters) on 27 April 1918. General Bliss also attended that meeting, representing the United States. Bliss was more inclined toward immediate support for the Allies, and less worried about the ultimate results of such action, than was Pershing.

In his *Memoirs*, Foch speaks of a ready accord regarding the need for the shipment of American infantry and machine gunners. Pershing's description (in his *Experiences)* records a bit more acrimony at that meeting, especially when he discovered that the British had apparently gained President Wilson's prior agreement to the shipment of only infantry and machine gun troops for an additional four months. (Pershing, himself, had been apprised of this presidential agreement only a few days before and he had hastened to object to the continuation of such shipments.) After much discussion, it was agreed to continue shipments of machine gunners only for the month of May, and to reconsider the matter later in the light of the Allied situation.[25] Pershing followed this agreement with a cable to the Secretary of War, requesting that plans be developed for a one-and-one-half-million-man U.S. army in France as soon as possible. The War Department replied that 1,500,000 was an impossible number of men to draft, because such large numbers of men could not be housed, trained, or shipped by any configuration of existing resources.[26]

At the meeting of the Supreme War Council on 1 and 2 May 1918 at Abbeville, the Allied leaders insisted on continuing the shipment of only infantry and machine gunners for the month of June. The French complained at that meeting that no provision had been made, thus far, for a diversion of those forces shipped by British tonnage to serve with the French army. French Premier Georges

Clemenceau made a strong statement protesting the fact that all of the infantry and machine gunners had gone thus far to the British, and he demanded that the French receive the same number (120,000) in June. Clemenceau also stated, "There are close to 400,000 Americans in France at present, but only five divisions, or about 125,000 men can be considered as combatants. This is not a satisfactory proportion."[27] Pershing responded that, in his opinion, the best way to help the Allied forces was by the quick formation of an American army. At this point, Foch asked, "You are willing to risk our being driven back to the Loire?"

Pershing said, "Yes, I am going to take that risk. Moreover, the time may come when the American army will have to stand the brunt of this war, and it is not wise to fritter away our resources in this manner." Pershing recorded that all five of the Allied party attacked him with all the force and prestige of their high positions. He finally stated, with the greatest possible emphasis, "Gentlemen, I have thought this problem over very deliberately and will not be coerced." Others present have claimed that Pershing accompanied this statement by pounding on the table. The council adjourned for the day to take up the matter of American reinforcements on 2 May.[28]

The next day at the Abbeville conference, Lloyd George made the strongest appeal yet propounded by the British:

> If the United States does not come to our aid, then perhaps the enemy's calculations will be correct. If France and Great Britain should have to yield, their defeat would be honourable for they would have fought to their last man, while the United States would have to stop without having put into the line more men than little Belgium.[29]

Pershing agreed to continue the shipment of one hundred twenty thousand American infantry and machine gunners for June and to reconsider the need for such shipment in July. He gained from this session the agreement of the Supreme War Council that an American army should be formed as early as possible, under its own commander and its own flag. It was also agreed that any tonnage over and above that necessary to ship the required numbers of infantry and machine gunners would be devoted to bringing over such other troops as the AEF commander would determine necessary. Pershing gained some flexibility in this commitment, allowing him additional personnel for in-theater support and administration.[30]

Pershing's commitment of the best American divisions to the Western Front at the Marne River helped sustain the fragile Allied defenses there. By the night of 31 May 1918, the motorized machine gun battalion of the United States' 3rd Division was dug in at Cha-teau-Thierry; it helped to hold that bridgehead over the Marne. The rest of the division also took up positions along that river. On 1 June, the 2nd Division took up positions north of the Marne, west of Chateau-Thierry, protecting the main route to Paris. Ludendorff, convinced that he was on the brink of a breakthrough, threw his reserves against the hastily deployed Americans. For the first days in June, the issue was in doubt at the highest headquarters—but not on the line. The Americans had stiffened the Allied defenses; their aggressiveness had inspired the wary French. Together, they stopped the German offensive cold!

Meanwhile, the 1st Division, in the first American offensive operation of the war, attacked on 28 May 1918 and seized Cantigny and commanding ground at the tip of the Amiens salient. Holding on desperately, despite furious counterattacks, they lost more than sixteen hundred men, but maintained the position. On 6 June, the 2nd Division attacked. "C'mon, you sonsabitches, do you want to live forever?" shouted Sergeant Daniel Daly, as he led his marines into Belleau Wood—and into the annals of Marine Corps history.[31]

The fighting was fierce in Belleau Wood, Boursches, and Vaux, but the Americans moved forward. The German offensive was stopped all along the line. Total casualties for the American debut were 11,384. While the United States' contribution resulted in only modest gains, they provided bloody affirmations of American com-bat capability both to skeptical Allies and the scornful enemy.[32] Although it was not known at the time, the German offensive had been virtually terminated. Many credit the infusion of the large American divisions with "tipping the balance," as the author John Toland has stated. He added, "The great spirit of our soldiers and marines was an inspiration to the tired French, and struck terror in the Germans. We attacked so recklessly."[33] The author Don Lawson agrees with Toland. "The entry of the Americans into the fighting was simply the straw that broke the German camel's back. Had the Americans not entered precisely when they did, the war might very well continued in a stalemate situation . . . followed by a forced political settlement."[34] Colonel William Griffiths, a devoted student and analyst of The Great War, adds: "The very size of the U.S. square division, reaching 28,000, compared to the 9,000 of the understrength European divisions, infused great strength to the Allies. The U.S. would play their trump—inexperi-enced but willing manpower. . . . They would succeed by manpower and enthusiasm.[35]

On 9 June 1918, Ludendorff tried to regain his momentum. Attacking westward from Soissons and southward from the Amiens salient, his armies attempted to merge the Amiens and Marne salients into one. But the French were ready, and the Germans were tired. By the fifth day, the attack had run its course, having gained only nine miles. A lull settled over the front. In June, Pershing created three corps. I Corps, under Major General Hunter Liggett, took over responsibility for the American divisions in the vicinity of Chateau-Thierry. II Corps, under Major General George W. Read, took responsibility for the 27th and 30th Divisions moving to fight with the British forces. III Corps, under Major General Robert L. Bullard, awaited assignment. On 4 July it was announced that one million Americans were in France; three hundred thousand were to arrive each month thereafter. Nine divisions had experienced some combat; two others were completing training, and eight had just arrived—totalling nineteen divisions in country.[36]

Back at the War Department Headquarters, manpower deployment agreements made in Europe, and changes thereto, arrived in fragmentary fashion. Often, departmental headquarters gained crucial information from the press before hearing of decisions from Pershing's own headquarters. Frequently, they also received more complete details of agreements, and even of changes in the fighting situation, from General Bliss at the Supreme War Council than they did from their counterparts in the AEF. This was the result of a very strict interpretation on the part of Pershing's headquarters of the need for and adherence to strict censorship, a series of restrictions to which the Army's Chief of Staff, General March, in particular, did not fully agree.[37]

A strict secrecy of plans, and particularly of schedules for troop shipment, was necessary because of the German submarine threat, and to prevent the enemy from knowing the full value and time-table of American reinforcements. However, censorship was an unpopular measure and newsmen used all sources, professional and personal, to gain and publish information of a sensitive nature. While many were restrained by their own sense of ethics and patriotism, much sensitive information was, in fact, published in the press, and as well much nonsensitive news was classified and withheld by staff officers overly concerned with secrecy.

These communications problems often made the discussion of routine disagreements blossom into major confrontations between the commands, which frustrated Pershing even though he normally won every contest over conflicting aims and objectives. In the meantime, the AEF formed its own staff coordination section, modeled on that of the War Department, and a veritable blizzard of paperwork began descending from these headquarters to all their agencies, providing guidance and directing action.[38]

All American problems were now increasing rapidly in scope. But the problem of shipping more and more men, as the historian Edward Coffman put it, became a nightmare of schedules and revisions, commitments and overcommitments for the War Department. The shipping program reached its peak during the summer of 1918. In the months of June, July, and August, a daily average of almost ninety-five hundred soldiers made the Atlantic crossing. Pershing, encouraged by the Allies, urged an even greater program.[39] On 1 June 1918, the three prime ministers, Lloyd George of Britain, Clemenceau of France, and Orlando of Italy, met as the Supreme War Council at Versailles. This meeting was primarily to determine the requirements for American reinforcement, as a follow-up to the conference held at Abbeville the month before. It was held at a time when remarkable German successes at the Marne had provoked great uncertainty as to the future of the Alliance. The following message was approved and sent to the President of the United States:

> We desire to express our warmest thanks to President Wilson for the remarkable promptness with which American aid was provided.... The crisis, however, still continues. General Foch has presented to us a statement of the utmost gravity which points out that the numerical superiority of the enemy in France (162 Allied divisions now oppose 200 German divisions) is very heavy, and, there is no possibility of the British and French increasing the number of their divisions . . . He, therefore, urges the utmost insistence that the maximum possible number of infantry and machine gunners . . . be shipped from America in the months of June and July. . . . He places the total American force required at no less than 100 divisions, and urges the continual raising of fresh American levies which, in his opinion, should be not less than 300,000 a month.

Signed: Clemenceau, Lloyd George, Orlando.[40]

After much animated discussion, Pershing agreed to the Allied proposal that had been sent to the President, provided that shipping would be allocated also for support troops to build up the AEF structure, as had been done for the previous month. His agreement, cabled to the War Department 10 June, read:

> The following agreement has been concluded between General Foch, Lord Milner, and myself in reference to the transportation of American troops in the months of June and July. The recommendations are made on the assumption that at

least 250,000 men can be transported in each of the months of June and July by the employment of combined British and American tonnage. We recommend: (a) For the month of June: First, absolute priority be given to the transportation of 170,000 combatant troops (viz. six divisions without artillery, ammunition trains, or supply trains, amounting to 126,000 men and 44,000 replacements for combat troops). Second, 25,400 men for the services of the railways, of which 13,400 have been asked for by the French Minister of Transportation. Third, the balance of the troops in categories to be determined by the Commander in Chief American Expeditionary Forces. (b) For the month of July: First, absolute priority for the shipment of 140,000 combatant troops of the nature defined above (four divisions minus artillery etc., amounting to 84,000 men, plus 56,000 replacements). Second, the balance of the 250,000 to consist of troops designated by the Commander in Chief American Expeditionary Forces. . . . (d) We recognize that the combat troops to be dispatched in July may have to include those which have had insufficient training, but consider this a temporary emergency such as to justify an exceptional departure of the United States from sound principles of training, especially as a similar course is being followed by France and Great Britain. Signed: Foch, Milner, Pershing.[41]

The upshot of the conference was that Pershing got another commitment from the Allies to help build up the AEF.

With respect to planning the American build-up, however, many problems had been created: Pershing had called for a sixty-six-division AEF in May 1918; now, on 10 June, he upped this figure to the round number of one hundred divisions. His cable reflected confidence that the War Department would be able to provide both troops and supplies with the help of Allied shipping and resources. One hundred American divisions would be equivalent to two hundred European divisions—a figure that would match the strength of the entire German force. The War Department general staff worked mightily to determine the feasibility of a hundred-division commitment. Finally, they set a figure between Pershing's first and his second request, a total of eighty divisions, to be the maximum that could be handled even by the straining of all resources. The eighty-division project would, the War Department estimated, require 3,335,000 Americans in France; to ship and sustain these would incur a cargo deficit of over 4,850,000 tons, utilizing American and projected Allied transport resources. The "eighty-division program," however, was the one upon which the War Department generally worked and around which they planned. Even this figure would require the reduction of all resources not absolutely necessary for operations in the field. Automatic resupply of food, ammunition, and other expendables for the theater was cut from fifty pounds per man per day to thirty pounds, in hopes of effecting this eighty-division program.[42]

Still another problem plagued planners at AEF and War Department Headquarters. By agreeing to an "eighty-division program," Pershing thought he had agreed to a total of eighty combat divisions, plus twenty divisions for training and replacement duties. The War Department considered that it had agreed to a grand total of eighty divisions. Thus, the numbers of men required for various categories of troops were always in disagreement.

These rapid changes in plans and programs were not fully coordinated with the military supply agencies and throughput facilities. Not only were there considerable problems within the continental United States (problems that saw the shipment to Europe of troops in a relatively untrained state, lacking items of uniform, weapons, and equipment), but there were also tremendous backlogs of supplies at the ports in Southern France and at the various support installations within the Services of Supply. The War Department considered one of the major problems to be the failure to evacuate material from the ports and docks, and the failure to turn around shipping for return to the United States. Accordingly, General March and Secretary Baker developed a plan for better management of the Services of Supply by separating them from Pershing's control. Under this plan, the Services of Supply would become a co-equal command in France under the command of Major General George W. Goethels, then Quartermaster for the War Department. This plan, which had apparently been approved in concept by President Wilson, was sent to Pershing for comment—it received his violent rejection! Pershing noted that it was a principle of war that all forces in a theater should be under one commander.

While Goethels was preparing for deployment overseas, Pershing appointed the former AEF Chief of Staff, Major General James G. Harbord, as the new commander of the Services of Supply, replacing General Francis Kernan. Pershing then made a whirlwind tour of the Services of Supply, together with Harbord, and he reported to the Secretary of War that his inspection, and his appointment of Harbord, had assured him that the Services of Supply were now capable of handling their difficult tasks without further action being needed on the part of the War Department.[43] This skirmish ended attempts on the part of the War Department to limit the scope of Pershing's responsibilities.

The confrontations between AEF Headquarters and the War Department Headquarters came to a head in August 1918. Pershing had complained forcefully in letters to the Secretary of War that the Army's Chief of Staff, General March, was assuming a curt and commanding tone in his cables. In the middle of August, Pershing wrote again to Baker telling him that the War Department general staff was poorly organized and functioning in a faulty manner. He also had the temerity to suggest that a change in the Chief of Staff of the army might be in order. (General March, with a date of rank of 20 May 1918, was junior to Pershing as a four-star general.) Baker stood by General March during this assault, and, to establish clearly March's authority over both the AEF and the War Department bureaus, Baker issued General Order No. 80 in late August, which stated that "the Chief of Staff is the immediate adviser of the Secretary of War . . . charged by the Secretary with the planning, development and execution of the Army program." The order provided that this officer would take rank and precedence over all officers of the army. This appeared to settle, at least in terms of ultimate responsibility, the problems between the War Department staff and the AEF.[44]

On the Western Front, the German forces, although physically close to Paris, were fading rapidly in strength as June turned into July. Foch still reported that Germans outnumbered the Allies in divisions, but the weight of numbers was fast swinging to the Allies. Foch himself was enthusiastically preparing a counteroffensive when the Germans launched their final offensive of the war.[45]

Ludendorff called it the *Friedensturm* (Peace Offensive). Its results did, indeed, hasten the coming of peace, but not as Ludendorff had intended. Massing a total of fifty-two divisions in two armies, the Germans drove one army southeast from the Marne salient, the other attacking south from the vicinity of Reims. The two forces were to meet on the Marne. But the French had recovered their Gallic "esprit," and no "heart" remained in the German forces. East of Reims, the French commander, apprised of the pending attack by aerial observation, withdrew his troops (including the American 42nd Division) from forward positions prior to the attack. During the German advance, their supporting fire beat down on empty trenches, while the French counterbattery fire decimated the advancing German ranks. Then the French and Americans repeated their withdrawal from their second (intermediate) zone; on the third line, they held.

To the west, a French division had been outflanked and folded rearward, leaving the American 3rd Division beset on three sides. Their steadfast defense (especially by the 38th Infantry Regiment) earned the division the title "The Rock of the Marne"! Going around the Americans, the driving Germans "forced" the Marne, and established a sizable bridgehead southwest of Reims; two Italian divisions were driven back. British divisions moved in and stopped that advance. French resistance around the Marne bridgehead anchored on the American 3rd Division. As early as 17 July, it was apparent to Ludendorff that the offensive had run its course. He terminated this operation and turned his attention to Flanders, moving his headquarters there. Although Ludendorff planned to make another great offensive (against the British in Flanders), the attacks in the Champagne-Marne in July were the last westward movement of the German army until 1940.[46]

It is to the credit of the spirit of General Foch that he was confidently planning an Allied counteroffensive before the German attacks ceased. Even as the Germans (and Austrians) were attacking in the Champagne-Marne area, Foch launched a limited counterattack on 18 July 1918 in the Soissons region to cut the highway from Soissons to Chateau-Thierry—the German supply route to the Marne salient. The 1st and 2nd United States Divisions led this attack, under the French Tenth and Sixth Armies, respectively. Some American units reached their attack positions on the run at "H hour" (the time for beginning the attack). Preceded by a short, heavy bombardment of artillery, in a rainstorm, the units jumped off at 0430 in the morning. The attack struck "trench" (second-rate) German divisions as a complete surprise. Assisted by French tanks, American and French divisions made gains of up to five miles the first day. This success caused the offensive to be extended to the east. When notified of the Allied gains, Ludendorff shifted reserves to Soissons, cancelled the attack on Reims, and, later, abandoned the planning for an offensive in Flanders. The U.S. 1st Division had performed credibly in this counteroffensive.

1st Division was the premier regular-army division of the U.S. It was created primarily from Regular Army organizations and units existing at the entry of the U.S. into the World War, and by assignment of Regular Army personnel to fill that division. Organized on 24 May 1917, it was shipped overseas beginning on 14 June, and the first units arrived in France on 26 June. The division completed its organization in France under command of Major General William L. Sibert; major units were trained in the Gondrecourt area. It entered the line for experience in Lorraine, under Major General Robert L. Bullard, and from January until April 1918, occupied defensive positions in the Ansauville Sector. Committed into the Cantigny sector in April, it recaptured Cantigny during a counter-offensive, then participated in the French Aisne-Marne Offensive in the Chateau-Thierry area, capturing six towns. The division was the showpiece of the AEF, repeatedly referred to by Pershing as exemplifying the standard for all other divisions to follow.[47]

The American 3rd, 4th, 26th, and 28th Divisions also took part in the Allied drive east and northeast; the American I and III Corps began actively directing the advance in their sectors, joined by the American 32nd, 42nd, and 77th Divisions. On 19 July, the German resistance stiffened; then Ludendorff directed a phased withdrawal from the Marne salient to the line of the Aisne and Vesle Rivers, covered by "stay-behind" machine gun teams and artillery barrages. The Allied counteroffensive halted at the new German positions on 6 August 1918.[48]

Eight American divisions had performed creditably in the offensive. In his postwar report to the Secretary of War, Pershing described the tactical direction of the American troops in this operation as "excellent."[49] Major General Liggett, Commander of I Corps, and Major General Bullard, Commander of the III Corps, also cited their troops for creditable performance.[50] It is, however, too early in this narrative to make a definite evaluation of the performance of American forces in combat. There is no question that the divisions committed had advanced aggressively; their casualties (fifty thousand) attest to that. But the Aisne-Marne counteroffensive was launched against second-rate troops of the Central Powers. It was planned, directed, and supported by Allied commanders, and its advance was against a force engaged in a deliberate withdrawal. Although it was not recognized at the time, this counteroffensive did signal the turning point in the war. American combat strength (the equivalent of sixteen or seventeen Allied or German divisions) had tipped the balance. On the German side, Graf von Hindenburg (the titular commander of the forces of the Central Powers) was beginning to note signs of lack of discipline and the breakdown of unit integrity in his withdrawing armies. The initiative had passed to the Allies. The German countermarch had begun![51]

5

THE FIRST AMERICAN OFFENSIVE— ST. MIHIEL

In Mid-July General Foch turned exuberant and impatient; he ventured to predict the end of the war in 1919. Meeting with General Haig, General Pétain, and General Pershing at his headquarters in Bombon on 24 July 1918, he proposed a general plan of attack designed to prevent an orderly German withdrawal, a withdrawal that might allow the Central Powers to continue fighting indefinitely. Foch outlined his immediate objectives as the clearing of railway lines, indispensable for later offensive operations: the freeing of the Paris-Amiens railway line by action of the British and French armies, and the freeing of the Paris-Avricourt rail line by eliminating the St. Mihiel salient—the latter operation "to be executed by the American Army, as soon as it has the necessary means."[1] Haig claimed that the British army was "far from being reestablished"; Pétain pled that the French army was "worn out, bled white, anemic." Pershing asserted that the "American Army asks nothing better than to fight; but it has not yet been formed!" Foch demurred; he offered to pace the offensive to the conditions of the armies. The Allies all agreed, then, to Foch's offensive plan. Pétain later advised that he thought an attack on the St. Mihiel salient—in conjunction with clearing the Armentieres Pocket—should be the main offensive for the remainder of summer and autumn.[2]

In consequence of Foch's instructions to attack, and notwithstanding their reservations, the French and British undertook an offensive on 8 August 1918 to reduce the Amiens salient. The attack of British and French infantry with 300 tanks, supported by artillery and 1,700 Allied aircraft, surprised the enemy. The defenders fell back in great confusion; 13,000 prisoners were taken; 300 cannon and much material were abandoned. Up to six miles were gained by the attackers on a twelve-mile front in a single day.

Subsequent days saw equal or greater advances. Ludendorff later called 8 August the "Black Day" for the German army.[3] Jubilant, Foch pressed Haig for a British advance north of the Somme. He also urged the French to extend their offensive east of the Oise. Despite stiffening German resistance on the 13 August, Foch insisted on the resumption of the offensive beginning on the 16 August. Haig, however, refused. He felt that it was necessary for the BEF to reorganize and resupply. The French claimed their forces needed, and they took, the same brief rest.[4]

Finally responsive to Foch's entreaties, the British Third and French Third Armies attacked on the left and right flanks (respectively) of their previous combined movement. Advances were slow and methodical. Aircraft strafed German positions that lay ahead of the advancing infantry, while accompanying tanks knocked out machine gun emplacements. The British Fourth Army extended the attack in the center; then, the British First Army attacked east from Arras. In the face of these attacks, Ludendorff abandoned his salients on 26 August. A strong Canadian attack in the Arras region on 2 September forced a further German withdrawal, to the Siegfried-Hindenburg Line. German losses for this defense and withdrawal were high. The count of prisoners of war captured by the Allies was significant—over one hundred thousand! But the Allies had again outrun their logistics; none of their forces had the remaining capability for an exploitive dash. The front stabilized as all forces reorganized.[5]

At the late July conferences at Foch's headquarters, Pershing had gained approval to activate two American armies: The First Army would take the sector of the French Sixth Army; it would command the two American corps operating against the Marne salient. The Second Army would be formed in the quiet sector of the Woevre Plain, south of Verdun, taking over the sector of the French Third Army.

With the denouement of fighting along the Aisne Vesle Line, Pershing requested, on 9 August, that American forces be concentrated instead in one army in the Woevre, with the St. Mihiel attack their sole responsibility (see Map 2, p. 63). Foch, who had been appointed Marshal of France on 6 August, approved. Accordingly, Pershing activated the American First Army in Lorraine on 10 August 1918. This American force was placed under the "operational control of General Henri Pétain, Commander of the French Armies of the North and Northeast."[6] On that date, there were 1,275,000 Americans in France, including thirty-five divisions.[7] Most didn't have their authorized complement of artillery, the result of the expedited shipment of infantry units. Corps artillery was nonexistent. Initially,

Pershing assigned fourteen divisions to the First Army. He requested a tremendous level of support from the Allies for these forces for the upcoming St. Mihiel offensive:

> 100 batteries of 75 millimeter cannon
>
> 50 batteries of 155 millimeter howitzers
>
> 86 heavy batteries for counterbattery and interdictory fire.

He also brashly requested:

> 300 light tanks
>
> 150 heavy tanks

and a sizable aviation augmentation:

> 7 observation squadrons
>
> 9 pursuit squadrons
>
> 5 day-bombardment squadrons
>
> 10 balloons
>
> plus the support of the British Independent Royal Air Force, for night bombardment.

Nearly all of this requested support (or its equivalent) was provided by the French. Pershing's request to Pétain for one hundred fifty heavy tanks had been passed to the British Marshal Haig, who reported that none were available.[8]

With respect to tanks for the AEF, Pershing had convened an American Tank Board in 19 July 1917. After studying British and French tanks, the Board had recommended the French Renault and a British Mark VI Heavy Tank for the AEF. The British model never reached production. Tank production in the U.S. took so long that the War Department estimated that no tanks could be delivered to France until 1919. (As a matter of fact, the first two American-manufactured Renault tanks arrived at Bourg, France on 20 November 1918.) Even before receiving the report of late arrival of tanks, Pershing had directed purchase of 900 Renault tanks. The Renault Light Tank was the one used by and supporting the AEF in most actions. This tank weighed seven tons, carried a crew of two (a driver and a gunner), and could be equipped with either a 37 millimeter gun or an 8 millimeter machine gun. Mounted on two tracks, the tank could move at seven miles per hour on smooth ground. The turret could turn 360 degrees to allow the gunner to fire at targets at all points of the compass. The AEF was also supported by, but did not crew, French Heavy Schneider and St. Chaumond Tanks. These vehicles, weighing 14 and 23 tons respectively, were lightly armored and underpowered; they carried

75 millimeter cannon, and up to four machine guns, and travelled at a slow five miles per hour. One American Heavy Tank Battalion, manning Mark V British tanks, fought in the British Sector of the Western Front. Many of the purchased Renaults arrived in time for the St. Mihiel Offensive; others were borrowed from the French, and French tank units supported the offensive. A total of 419 tanks participated in the St. Mihiel Offensive, including 168 in the 1st Tank Brigade, under the command of Lieutenant Colonel George S. Patton (144 Renaults in the 326th and 327th Tank Battalions, plus 24 Schneiders in the IV French Groupement), and 251 in the 3d Tank Brigade, under the command of Lieutenant Colonel Daniel D. Pullen (216 Renaults in the 505th Assault Artillery Regiment plus 35 Schneiders and St. Chaumonds in the XI French Groupement.[9]

With respect to aircraft for the AEF, the first American flyers on the Western Front took their training primarily in Nieuport 28 Series Biwing Aircraft. These were powered by a rotary engine of approximately 150 horsepower. The production airplane was armed with two Vickers Caliber .303 light machine guns, mounted center and off center left on the fuselage. This model aircraft had problems with engine malfunction, and fabric separation; also the Vickers guns tended to jam using the AEF ammunition. The Americans preferred the French SPAD (an acronym for the manufacturer) aircraft. The AEF purchased 189 SPAD VIIs, for combat in France and training in the U.S. The SPAD XVI, a two-seat observations and light bombing aircraft, entered combat in 1917; it had two synchronized forward-firing machine guns, and two free-swinging guns for the observer in the rear cockpit. This aircraft was the favorite of many AEF pilots, including the Chief of the AEF Air Service, Colonel Billy Mitchell. The SPAD XIII also flew in 1917; it was similar to the XVI, but was a single-seat aircraft, with a 220 horsepower engine. It was the fastest, most maneuverable, and rated the best Allied pursuit airplane of the war. Most single-engine aircraft had a cruising speed of approximately 120 miles per hour. The U.S. purchased 893 SPAD XIIIs for 15 squadrons. Some of the aircraft for the St. Mihiel Offensive were borrowed from the French. In response to Pershing's request, French observation, day bombardment, and pursuit squadrons were placed under operational control of the AEF, as was a British Royal Air Force night bombardment squadron for the St. Mihiel Campaign. A total of 1,481 aircraft supported this offensive, the largest concentration of aircraft in the war to that date.[10]

The St. Mihiel salient had existed as a threatening bulge into the French lines (fifteen to twenty-six miles south of Verdun) since its seizure by the Germans on 24 September 1914. In 1915, the French had conducted a number of unsuccessful assaults to eliminate this salient. In 1916, the Germans assaulted Verdun from this prominence. After the Verdun bloodletting, both sides had manned the area lightly and used it as a rest and training area.[11] The geography is a giant inverted triangle with the apex at the town of St. Mihiel; the base leg was the front line, running east twenty six miles to Pont-a-Mousson; from St. Mihiel, the vertical leg of the front ran north seventeen miles to Haudiomont. (See Map 2, page 63.) The area is low, rolling terrain, marshy north to south in the center of the salient, lightly wooded, with a line of low hills running north-northeast from the town of St. Mihiel. The towns were small and they were clustered along the few roads. Roads were narrow and unpaved.[12]

German forces in the area were largely "trench" troops, those too old or infirm for offensive combat. They were part of German Composite Army C (General Fuchs in Command); the German Nineteenth Army (General Bothmer) tied in with Army C and held the eastern five miles of the salient. Around the salient from north (Haudiomont) to south (St. Mihiel), the Germans were disposed along wooded high grounds in well-prepared positions, protected by multiple strands of barbed wire. The position was strongly manned in only one sector—the vicinity east of Les Eparges, where one division was arrayed in two-and-a-half miles of multiple defensive works: south of Les Eparges around the salient to Apremont three divisions occupied six miles of front each. For the nineteen miles from Apremont east to the Moselle River, three more divisions were similarly arrayed, generally on low, wooded ground, with lakes and marshy obstacles to their front. One or two divisions were identified in army reserve, with two more within two-day reinforcing capability. Total enemy defensive strength in the St. Mihiel salient and in local reserves was estimated at twenty-three thousand. Across the northern base of the salient were strong defensive emplacements called the "Michel Stellung."[13]

The St. Mihiel region had been selected as the operation for christening the American First Army because it appeared to present a relatively easy task for that large force. It was also likely to provide an early success, more symbolic than important to the Allied cause. It would give the American forces, and their people at home, a long-awaited victory for American arms. From a logistical standpoint, it was the focal point of most of the American lines of supply and communication from their ports in the south and southwest of France.[14]

Strategically, the salient was important, as it posed a constant threat to Verdun and to the flank of any Allied offensive to the

Map 2. Plan of Operation and Advance, American First Army, September 12–18, 1918.

American Battle Monuments Commission. *American Armies and Battlefields in Europe*, Washington: GPO, 1938.

north. Beyond the "Michel Stellung" to the north lay the old, formidable fortress complex of Metz-Thionville. If the Metz defenses were overcome, the Metz-Lille railroad could be disrupted, cutting off supplies to the southern wing of the German armies to the west. Such an offensive would also threaten the Briey iron ore region and the coal mining area of the Saar.

The AEF staff (primarily Lieutenant Colonel George C. Marshall) had been studying the area and planning an offensive there since midsummer.[15] The first concept or "preliminary" study called for a force of four American divisions in the assault, with three in reserve for exploitation or "mopping up." This plan was prepared on 6 August 1918. An important note in this plan was that the offensive should begin no later than 15 September, the onset of the rainy season, because the ground was subject to flooding.[16]

With new guidance, the plan was changed on 9 August to a ten-division drive with French support; by 13 August fourteen divisions were included in the attack. By 16 August, under pressure to use more of the thirty-five American divisions in France, Marshall drew up a plan of attack utilizing seventeen divisions—a grand total of 476,000 men—to attack about 23,000 German troops in an area of approximately three hundred square miles.[17] Were even half of these men to move into the contested area, the troop density would equal approximately eight hundred men per square mile. Such a density makes for uncomfortable urban living; it certainly becomes a crowd difficult to manage on a battlefield![18] The proposed attack would launch nine divisions against the southern face of the salient through Thiaucourt; six divisions would attack the northern face through Fresnes; while two divisions would conduct a supporting attack on the heights east of the Moselle. (The problem of troop density in attack will be taken up later in reviewing the Meuse-Argonne Campaign.) By the end of August, the AEF plan contemplated a drive beyond the salient, to pierce the "Michel Stellung" and open the way for a drive on Metz.[19]

Another problem arose in gaining adequate fire support to assist the infantry attack. According to some planners in the AEF Operations Division, the absence of heavy tanks to crush the barbed wire required the substitution of a long, heavy artillery preparation (fourteen hours) to break gaps in the barbed wire. Others favored an attack without an artillery preparation, to maximize surprise. Pershing seemed attracted to this option; his operations staff finally convinced him to authorize a five-hour preparatory artillery bombardment.[20]

In establishing the forces for the American First Army's attack on the salient, a tremendous reshuffling was necessary to gather

American divisions that had been spread from Flanders to Marseilles. With respect to divisions that were serving with the Allies (in a training status), General Pétain was agreeable to releasing those requested by Pershing; the AEF was taking over a portion of his area of responsibility. As Pershing had feared, Marshal Haig was distressed at having to honor the agreement he had made when the "Six Division Plan" was executed (the agreement to release these divisions on call from Pershing). The British were planning, and hoping for an American army in their zone, based on Dunkerque. Lloyd George was pushing for this plan. The British also appeared to be anxious about the growing association of the Americans with the French. Pershing agreed to British retention of the American II Corps (with the 27th and 30th United States Divisions) for the upcoming fall campaign.[21]

This experience with the British highlighted the continuing pressure being exerted by all the Allies to use American troops to spare their own and to forward their plans. The Italians were pressing for an American front in Italy. Foch also recommended the greater integration of American and French logistical support. The great blow to the independence of the American military effort came on 30 August 1918, the same day General Pershing assumed command of the United States First Army (while retaining command of the AEF). General Foch visited Pershing's headquarters at Ligny-en-Barrois. After the usual pleasantries, Foch presented an entirely new plan for the employment of the American forces. Pointing out the great successes of the ongoing Allied offensives, especially in the north, and the relative disarray of the German forces, Foch then presented his concept for exploiting that continuing success and preventing German reorganization: The British, supported by the left of the French armies, would continue to attack in the general direction of Cambrai-St. Quentin. The center of the French armies would continue their "energetic" actions to throw the enemy behind the Aisne. A combined American-French army on the right of the French center, acting on the Meuse and to the west, would attack in the general direction of Mezieres. Marshal Foch then went on at greater length on his proposal for the employment of American troops: The St. Mihiel operation should begin September 10; the attack should be limited to reaching the Vignuelles-Regneville line (eliminating the salient only). Four to six American divisions should be turned over to the French Second Army for attack between the Meuse and the Argonne Forest. An American army (eight to ten American divisions) should be employed immediately west of the Argonne on both sides of the Aisne River to attack in conjunction with the French Fourth Army. The attacks on either side of the Argonne were to be made between 15 and 20 September. To assist Pershing in planning and in directing the offensive west of the Argonne, two French generals, "with sufficient authority to expedite the solution to all questions," should be assigned to the Commander in Chief of the American Army.[22]

Pershing immediately objected to this late change in plans, and especially to dismembering the American army. He offered to take over the sector from the Meuse west to the Argonne from the French Second Army, rather than split his command. Foch then queried, "Do you wish to take part in the battle?" Pershing replied, "Most assuredly, but as an American army and in no other way." Foch referred to the lack of artillery organic to the American army. Pershing reminded him of his earlier promises to make up for this deficiency, caused by the shipping of American infantry without support that had taken place at Foch's request. Pershing then suggested that the American First Army take over a sector east of the Meuse River; or alternatively, for it to form two armies east and west of the Argonne Forest. Foch rejected both these proposals, according to Pershing. Foch does not record such proposals in his memoirs.[23] (The matter of the location of an American sector is important to the later discussion of the Meuse-Argonne Campaign.) Rising from their conference table, Foch stated, "I must insist upon the arrangements." Pershing replied, "You may insist all you please, but I decline absolutely to agree to your plan. While our army will fight wherever you may decide, it will not fight except as an independent American army!"[24] Foch left, leaving with Pershing a memorandum of his plan. Pershing responded the next day, reiterating his objections, stressing the necessity of eliminating the St. Mihiel salient and the desirability of reserving the decision as to exploiting any success achieved there, even within the limited objectives proposed. He also stated the impossibility of conducting the St. Mihiel operation and of assembling the necessary divisions for the Mezieres operation by the date desired by the marshal. He then proposed to carry out the St. Mihiel operation, then to continue the offensive in the region of Belfort or Luneville, taking over the entire area from St. Mihiel to the Swiss border. His response concluded:

> Finally, however, there is one thing that must not be done and that is to disperse the American forces among the Allied armies. . . . If you decide to utilize American forces in attacking in the direction of Mezieres, I accept that decision even though it complicates my supply system and the care of my sick and wounded. I do insist that the American Army be employed as a whole either east of the Argonne or west of the

Argonne and not four or five divisions here or six or seven there.[25]

Pershing also took the occasion to demand the return of his corps and divisions serving with the British and the French.

Upon receipt of Pershing's response, Marshal Foch called a conference to meet at his headquarters on 2 September 1918 to resolve the matter. At the conference, after considerable discussion and disagreement, it was concluded:

To limit the attack on the St. Mihiel Salient to the objectives of attaining the line Vigneulles-Regneville; the attack to be launched on the 10th of September, with eight to ten divisions. The American Army will attack to the west of the Meuse, covered on its right by the Meuse River, and supported on its left by the attack of the French Fourth Army along the west flank of the Argonne Forest. The American attack will be prepared without delay, to be launched between the 20th and 25th of September. The American Army will attack with all forces which it has available (12 to 14 divisions), and will bring to this attack such of the divisions from the St. Mihiel Region as may become available. Organization of the communications in this sector requires bringing under the same command all the troops operating on the right and left banks of the Meuse. General Pershing will also take under his command for the attack west of the Meuse the front of the II French Army as far as the Argonne. The French divisions holding the passive front to the east of the Meuse will be provisionally retained there and placed under the American command. Operation will be carried out by direction of the Commanding General of the Armies of North and Northeast.[26]

British Marshal Haig was the agent who caused this sudden change in Foch's grand design. British successes in Flanders, and the apparent disarray in the German resistance efforts, convinced Haig that the war might be won in 1918. He inspired Foch to abandon the French and American offensives aimed at freeing the railroad complexes; the weight of the American attack should, he argued, be turned from the axis toward Metz to that of convergence with the British drive. The southern wing of the "pincers" should advance on and seize the Mezieres-Sedan complex. Considering the difficulties Foch had just experienced getting Haig to attack, he was most happy to accept this new offensive projection for early victory proposed by Haig.[27] To what extent Haig's proposal and Foch's subsequent decisions were based upon a desire to reduce the significance of the American role in the climactic campaign can only be surmised. However, the attitude and actions of both the Allies toward the formation of an American army is consistent with such a supposition. Knowledgeable persons, including European authors with whom this author discussed this issue, were nearly unanimous in their disagreement with Allied plans for the piecemeal employment of American forces. As to the political-military motives of the Allies, the following comment by James Stokesbury of Acadia University, author of the text *A Short History of World War I*, is typical of the responses this author received:

> One of the few things Lloyd George and Haig and to a lesser extent, Clemenceau and Foch, agreed upon was that they didn't want too intrusive an American participation in the war . . . if the Americans fought . . . only as fresh blood for the British and French, that was going to give the Americans a lot less clout when it came to making peace terms.[28]

Some authors explain this Allied attitude by noting that the Allies had borne the brunt of a long war and that the Americans were new in this war.[29]

The major changes that had been made in the AEF mission tended to overshadow the upcoming attack on the St. Mihiel salient. Downgraded to a limited offensive by a total of fourteen divisions (only six of which would make the inital assault), the preparations for the attack continued amid a veritable whirlwind of planning and movement for the Meuse-Argonne Offensive to follow.

As railway and motor transport became available, the necessary divisions and their supporting forces were shifted into position. Artillery pieces (numbering a total of 3,000, half of them manned by Americans) had to be moved into positions. Ammunition totalling 40,000 tons was moved into forward dumps. Telephone, telegraph, wireless (radio), and pigeon communications systems were installed. Railheads were established in nineteen locations to break out daily supplies to the combat units. As many as 2,000 French trucks assisted in moving the men and material. 2,000 hospital beds were provided. Engineers stocked material for 300 miles of railway reconstruction. Rock crushed for roadways was over 100,000 tons. Water plants were established at 120 locations able to disperse 1,200,000 gallons per day.[30]

The revised and final order for the St. Mihiel offensive directed an attack by I Corps (82nd, 90th, 5th, 2nd, and 78th Divisions) and IV Corps (89th, 42nd, 1st, and 3rd Divisions) against the south flank of the salient, with the objective of sealing off the salient from Vigneulles to Regneville. The attack was to proceed in four phases during a two-day period. The V Corps (26th, French 15th, and 4th Divisions) was to attack from the west face of the salient to link up with the southern attack along the line of Les Eparges-Vigneulles. The attack was to be conducted in two phases, linking up on the second day. The French II Colonial Corps (with three divisions around the southwest ring of the salient) was to advance after the American attacks had cleared the areas on the flanks. In First Army Reserve for the attack were the 35th and 91st Divisions.[31] (Overlaid on Map 2 is the American attack plan.)

U.S. Colonel Samuel D. Rockenbach, a cavalry officer who had been detailed to the Quartermaster Corps, had been placed in command of the AEF Tank Corps in December 1917. For the St. Mihiel Campaign, he assigned Lieutenant Colonel George S. Patton to command the 1st Tank Brigade, and directed his Chief of Staff, Lieutenant Colonel Daniel D. Pullen, to serve as liaison between Rockenbach's headquarters at Ligny-en-Barrois, and the French Assault Artillery Regiment which was in support of the AEF for the operation. As finally ordered, Pullen's French regiment was directed to support I Corps in their attack from the east, and Patton's 1st Tank Brigade with French attachments supported IV Corps in their attack from the southeast.

George S. Patton Jr., a 1909 graduate of the United States Military Academy, a cavalry officer, was among the first U.S. Army officers assigned with tanks. To get to France, he joined Pershing's staff, and later volunteered for duty with tanks; he organized a light tank training center at Langres, France in 1917. In preparation for the St. Mihiel Offensive, his guidance to his brigade was direct: "No tank is to be surrendered or abandoned . . . if your gun is disabled use your pistols and squash the enemy with your tracks . . . remember, you are the first American tanks . . . American tanks do not surrender." His guidance to his officers was: "Keep up with the infantry; if your tank is knocked out, continue fighting on foot with the infantry."[32]

Aviation support for this offensive was tasked as follows: One observation group, composed of American and French squadrons, was assigned to each corps in the attack. These were under the direct orders of the corps commanders. Observation under direct control of First Army was centered on the 91st Squadron, with two new U.S. squadrons attached, to conduct day reconnaissance over the entire zone. Four French squadrons were assigned to Army Artillery, to direct its fires deep into the zone (including guns which could reach the Metz fortifications). Three hundred and thirty aircraft were tasked with day bombing missions under First Army control. The British night bombing squadrons were tasked to bomb the centers of Longuyon, Conflans, and Metz-Sablon. Pursuit squadrons covered the air over the zone, to engage enemy pursuit aircraft which challenged the bombers and attacked the balloons. Both reconnaissance and pursuit aircraft were to conduct strafing missions in support of ground troops when targets of opportunity were revealed.[33]

Most of these aircraft were assigned to First Army, or under the operational control of Colonel Billy Mitchell, Air Service Officer for First Army. Mitchell was commissioned in the Signal Corps as a volunteer for the Spanish-American War; he accepted a regular commission after that war; in 1916 he was made Chief of the Aviation Section of the Signal Corps. He accompanied Pershing to France, and flew over many of the battlefields on the Western Front. An articulate and iconoclastic spokesman for airpower, he angered many of the conservative officers on the AEF staff. He served as Air Service Officer under Major General Mason M. Patrick, after that officer was appointed by Pershing to command the Air Service. For the St. Mihiel Campaign, Mitchell was appointed Chief of Air Service for First Army.[34]

The long period of preparation for this attack, the frequent moves and countermoves, and the apparent need for most staff officers at all echelons to see the area and coordinate their parts of the offensive, tipped off the Germans well in advance. After considering a number of offensive and defensive alternatives, Ludendorff ordered withdrawal from the salient to the "Michel Stellung" defenses at the northern base of the salient—choosing that option in view of the Allied advances in Flanders and the tremendous American build-up.[35]

Execution of the German withdrawal began on 11 September; the American attack jumped off at 5 A.M. on 12 September. Preceded by an intensive four-hour barrage by 3,000 artillery pieces, the infantry slogged forward in the rain. They struck and quickly overran the German rear guards. The attack came, according to General von Ledebur, Chief of Staff of Composite Army C, at "the most unfavorable moment imaginable." Detailed German plans for a phased withdrawal were scrapped, and their units were told to move quickly through the nearest escape routes.[36] The Combined Aviation Element of fifteen hundred planes (American, French, British, with some Italian and Portuguese flyers also aloft) gained and maintained air superiority and supported the attack. Air and artillery interdicted enemy columns attempting to move north out of the pocket.[37] The American advance was rapid and coordination was good. Most of the tanks fell victim to mechanical failure or ran out of fuel, but the infantry moved rapidly.

Both American and Allied leaders had worried about the U.S. infantry crossing the barbed wire, because artillery had failed to cut gaps, and "bangalore torpedoes" (to blow the wire) and wire cutters were limited. Some of the troops used chicken wire to breach the obstacles. Others stepped on the wire and just walked over it. The French were amazed and claimed it was possible only because the Americans had big feet. Norman Roberts, of the 168th Infantry Regiment, recorded in his diary:

> Day had not broke and you could hardly tell where to go. Bullets, millions of them, flying like raindrops. Rockets and flares in all directions. Shrapnel bursting and sending down its deadly iron. High explosives bursting on the ground and sending bricks, mud and iron. . . . A mad dash of 50 feet, then look for cover. A stop for a minute . . . Then another mad dash![38]

By nightfall of the first day, the converging southern and western divisions were only ten miles from juncture.[39] The American Secretary of War (Baker) visited the front on 13 September. That "pacifist" reported that he was "delighted" with the success of the attack. Pétain and Pershing visited the town of St. Mihiel. Pershing reported that the troops had behaved "splendidly." The action was a good present for him; it was his birthday—Pershing was fifty-eight.[40] During the first night, it was reported that German columns were streaming north through Vigneulles and Thiaucourt. Pershing directed the advance to continue all night. The 26th Division drove east, entering Vigneulles at 2 A.M. on the thirteenth. Soon after dawn, elements of the 1st Division linked up with the 26th from the south.[41] The salient was closed.

Field Order No. 10 from the First Army directed a continuation of the attack. On the morning of 13 September the attacking divisions moved northward, bringing all units on the line of the army objective that day.[42] During the night of 13–14 September, several counterattacks were repulsed; by the sixteenth, strong reconnaissance patrols were probing the German's Michel Stellung—a position that had been reinforced by four divisions. But reports of continuing withdrawals led Pershing to the conclusion that he could have broken through this portion of the Hindenburg Line. Major General Joseph Dickman, Commander of IV Corps during the operation, and Brigadier General Douglas MacArthur of the 42nd Division, argued that the Americans should have been allowed to go for Metz and could have taken it. However, Major General Hunter Liggett, one of the more astute military thinkers in the operation (commanding I Corps), later said, "The possibility of taking Metz . . .

existed only on the supposition that our Army was a well coordinated machine, which it was not, as yet."[43]

The operation ended. Congratulations came from all Allied offices and headquarters, and from the President of the United States.
"We gave 'em a damn good licking, didn't we?" Pershing boasted. In
response to a message of congratulations from Lloyd George who
was on a sickbed, Pershing cabled, "We shall endeavor to supply
you with doses of the same sort of medicine, as needed . . ." Critics,
however, point out that the enemy had presented no challenge.
"The Americans," some said, "merely relieved the Germans."[44] Whatever the case, it is unarguable that two hundred square miles of
territory had been returned to France, and a dangerous salient had
been removed. Prisoners of war were taken, totalling 15,000; also
captured were 450 artillery pieces. American casualties were about
7,000.[45] Major General Robert Bullard, commander of III Corps in
the operation, admits that the gap was not closed quickly enough.
Of the Germans in the salient, perhaps four-fifths escaped capture. Pershing blamed V Corps for not having reacted swiftly enough
to his orders to seal off the escape routes. Bullard adds:

> St. Mihiel was given an importance which posterity will not
> concede it. Germany had begun to withdraw. She had her
> weaker divisions, young men and old and Austro-Hungar-
> ians. The operation fell short of expectations.[46]

There were many examples of individual initiative under fire,
of aggressive leadership, of death-defying, even bizarre deeds. Lieutenant Terry de la Mesa Allen of the 80th Division continued to
drive his men forward though shot through the mouth, with a bleed-
ing gap where his front teeth had been. Sergeant Harry J. Adams of
the 89th Division ran into a dugout full of Germans; out of ammunition he waved his empty pistol and ordered the Germans to surrender; 300 came forward, and Adams led them to the rear, threatening them all the way with instant death if they failed to comply.
"Wild Bill" Donovan (creator of the OSS in World War II) led his men
on a fast drive forward; "What do you think this is, a wake?" he
shouted. Shot off the tank in which he was riding, Patton ran forward to catch up with a tank which was rumbling into Beney alone,
well ahead of the infantry. "I was not the least scared," he later
related; however, he had "run like hell!" In fact, Patton, and a number of his contemporaries were running like hell, too far forward of
the body of their men; they were out of communication with their
support, and with their senior commanders. After the battle, Patton
was severely chastised by Rockenbach ("given Hell," as Patton remembered it) for failing to keep him informed. Rockenbach also

directed that, in the future, all tankers would remain with their tanks when disabled, or face courts-martial; these instructions were taken lightly by the tankers.[47]

Observers, Allies, and even AEF senior officers recognized some essential weaknesses in the AEF, the result of hasty organization, inadequate training, and inexperienced leadership. Enthusiasm, unbounded self-confidence, and a great deal of luck had brought about victory despite weaknesses in command, coordination, and battlefield control. However, the engagement had been a good "shakedown" for part of the American forces. Unfortunately, the units that participated in the St. Mihiel offensive, the most experienced American divisions, would not be available for the start of the greatest effort to come—the attack in the Meuse-Argonne on 26 September 1918.

6

THE AEF ACCEPTS THE CHALLENGE:
THE MEUSE-ARGONNE

The geography of the Meuse-Argonne sector (about eighteen miles east-west) is ideal for defense, deadly for the attacker. The area and the German defenses are depicted on Map 3, page 75. Facing the region (looking north from friendly lines running east to west from Regneville to Binarville), it is apparent that the area is divided by three dominating features: the heights of the Meuse along the east bank of the unfordable Meuse River, the hills of Montfaucon in the center, with approaches from east and west, and the rising terrain of the heavily wooded Argonne Forest, a plateau in the west of the zone. Moving back east from the Argonne Forest, the valley between the Argonne and Montfaucon is drained by the Aire River (fordable in a few places). The valley is narrow, dominated by the buttes of Vauquois and Montfaucon, and dissected farther north into a maze of ridges and valleys connecting with the Barrois Plateau. The valley east of Montfaucon is intersected by east-west parallel ridges and ravines running east to the river. The heights east of the Meuse River, running north-northwest along the east flank of the zone, provide observation over the eastern half of the sector. The wooded hills offer a multitude of concealed locations for machine guns to lay flanking fire on any advance on a south-north axis. The low-lying areas are covered with thick brush varied with open spaces. During the fall rains, the low areas flood and the soil has poor trafficability. Montfaucon (Falcon Mountain) dominates the center of the zone. Three hundred forty-two meters high, it constituted a visible obstacle against which French attacks failed in 1914 and 1915. It was a promontory from which the German crown prince directed the sanguinary assaults on Verdun in 1916. The watershed is the great hogback, the Barrois Plateau, which runs north-northwest from Montfaucon to Romagne, Cunel, and Stonne. This divides the sector in two, allowing crossfire into both valleys.[1]

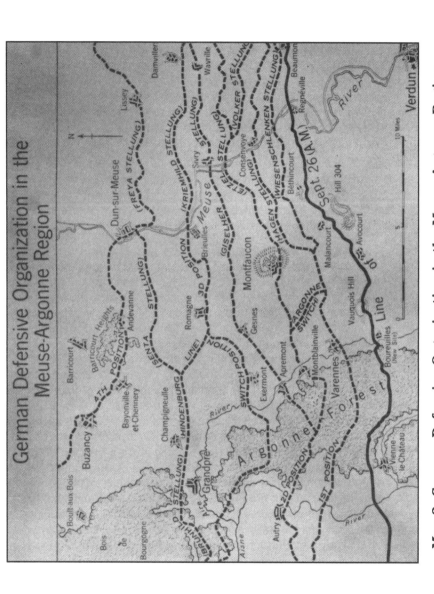

Map 3. German Defensive Organization in the Meuse-Argonne Region.

American Battle Monuments Commission. *American Armies and Battlefields in Europe.* Washington: GPO, 1938.

The Germans had been building an interlocking network of defenses in this area for three years. They had constructed a defensive zone from the line of contact. Three east-west belts of fortifications, named after the witches of Wagnerian lore, crossed the zone: a lightly manned defensive position ran from the line of contact at Regneville on the Meuse west to Bethincourt, to Boureuilles and to Vienne-le-Chateau. Buttressed by pillboxes containing machine guns, it was crossed by cleared lanes, providing successive interlocking bands of fire across the front. Barbed wire entanglements ran along these fire lanes to impede attackers in the killing zones of machine gun crossfire. An intermediate defensive position (Hagen Stellung) ran from Bethincourt to Varennes.

Etzel-Giselher Stellungen. The first major belt of fortifications lay five kilometers behind the first battle positions. This defense line ran from just south of Sivry on the Meuse, west across Montfaucon, to Apremont, to Autry on the Aisne River. The Giselher line was on the high ground north of Montfaucon. Along these lines the defenses were stronger and more continuous. Pillboxes (some made of concrete) were connected by trenches; machine gun fire lanes covered a dense array of multiple barbed-wire fences laid along the "final protective lines" of these guns. Artillery and mortar barrages were registered in defiladed areas, and trench mortar positions were emplaced well forward. The stone houses in the towns contained defensive implacements.

Kriemhilde Stellung. The second belt was the main defensive position, six kilometers north of Montfaucon. The Kriemhilde line was the strongest series of concrete and bunkered emplacements, running from Brieulles on the Meuse west along the east-west rocky ridges of Romagne Heights, through Grandpré, and west through a break in the Argonne Forest. A switch position ran forward from Romagne to Exermont.

Freya Stellung. The last line of German defenses, lightly manned at the time of the offensive, was about eight kilometers north of Kriemhilde; this defensive array extended from just south of Dun-sur-Meuse west through the Barricourt-Buzancy Heights to north of Boult-aux-Bois in the Argonne.

These German defensive lines were continued east and west beyond the American sector. The defensive lines were closer in the Meuse-Argonne than elsewhere, on the front to provide maximum protection for the vital railroad line from Sedan to Metz—the rupture of which was one objective of the right wing of Foch's grand attack plan.[2] The defenses were considered impregnable by the Allies. Pershing allowed that "no Allied troops had the morale or aggressive spirit to overcome the difficulties to be met in that sector."

Pétain thought the Americans would do well to take Mountfaucon before winter halted the fighting. Pershing expected to take Montfaucon the first day.[3]

Before the offensive could begin, a great deal of planning and a gargantuan movement of men and material had to take place—moves and countermoves had to be made over inadequate road and rail nets in a very short period of time. In planning and staffing the wrenching move of First Army from St. Mihiel to the Meuse Argonne, the name of George Marshall stood out among AEF staff. Lieutenant Colonel George C. Marshall had previously distinguished himself as a staff officer for the 1st Division, then for the AEF (as an operations officer), later for the First Army, as G-3, Operations. A 1901 graduate of the Virginia Military Institute, Marshall had served in the usual frontier and staff assignments. He had been noted as a keen mind by senior officers. He was selected for the operations staff of the 1st Division as it sailed for France. In this position, as a captain, he had the courage to rebut Pershing's criticism of the division after a review. Pershing accepted this insubordination, and marked Marshall for later service with him. He became most noted for his effective planning and unflappable disposition.

Marshall described in terse and unemotional terms the terrible task given him during the St. Mihiel Campaign—to move and reorganize the bulk of the First Army for a major offensive campaign in the Meuse-Argonne in a mere two weeks. The campaign was to be conducted in an area sixty miles north of the northern flank of the same army that was just commencing its first independent offensive at St. Mihiel. Marshall was apprised of this task on 8 September 1918 at a meeting called by the Chief of Staff of First Army, Brigadier General Hugh Drum. Drum announced that the army would launch an attack from the Meuse to the Argonne Forest on 25 September; operations section was preparing the attack order. Marshall would be responsible for the move of all units from St. Mihiel to the Meuse-Argonne Front; Marshall's associate, Colonel Walter Grant, would plan and supervise the relief of the French Second Army in the new position, and Colonel Monroe Kerth would arrange for the billeting of the units and coordinate all the actions. Drum then listed the divisions that would be in the first attacking echelon for the Meuse-Argonne offensive, those to be in corps and army reserve, and their supporting artillery. Running over the order quickly and checking locations on a map, Marshall made the hasty judgment that some of these units would have to begin redeploying from the St. Mihiel battle zone on the same day that offensive jumped off. "This appalling proposition rather disturbed my equilibrium," he later wrote. The next few hours he remembered as "the most trying mental ordeal" he experienced in the war.[4]

Marshall's alert order for the movement of organizations from St. Mihiel was considered by him to be the best piece of work he accomplished during the war. Though simple and lacking in detail, it established a good framework for conduct of an extremely complex and delicate redispositioning. Because of its importance to the success of the Meuse-Argonne operation, it is reproduced, in part, below:

Subject: Release and readjustment of units following reduction of St. Mihiel Salient.

1. The following information will serve as a guide to Army Corps commanders during the course of the pending operation. . . .

2. Plan of Readjustment

   As soon as the advance has terminated, and assuming that a threat of a *heavy* hostile counterattack does not exist, Corps Commanders will commence the reduction of the number of divisions in line and regrouping of the divisions so released. . . .

3. Units to be relieved

Organizations	Estimate Date for Relief		Relieving Organizations
		To be	
	To Start	completed	
	(NIGHTS)		
58th F.A. Brig.	D plus 2/3	D plus 3/4 (a)	None
55th F.A. Brig.	D plus 2/3	D plus 3/4 (a)	None
82d Div.	D plus 2/3	D plus 3/4 (b)	French Div.
1st. Corps. Hq. and Troops.	D plus 3/4	D plus 4/5 (b)	IV Corps Hq and Troops

Note: (a) To move by marching.
         (b) To move by bus and marching.[5]

Marshall and his assistants then worked out a similar plan for the nondivisional artillery, mostly French—three artillery brigades and sixty-eight separate artillery regiments—to be relieved of fire-support missions during St. Mihiel, moved, and then given new support tasks and locations. Both these movement schedules would have to be integrated with those of American logistical support and administrative units, and with French and Italian units moving out of the Meuse-Argonne area after relief by the American units. Three corps headquarters, fifteen divisions, and corps support and army troops had to displace forward. The totals involved were approximately 600,000 men moving in; 220,000 moving out. Also moving into the sector were 3,980 artillery guns and 90,000 horses; these moved in a steady stream, forwarding personnel, equipment, or a portion of the required 900,000 tons of ammunition and supplies.[6]

For secrecy, this huge agglomeration of men and materiel had to be moved only at night over three feeder railroads and three roads described as "farm roads." Considering that a division required 900 trucks to move its personnel, and its towed light artillery (seventy-two guns) required fifteen kilometers of road space, some appreciation of the extent of the planning and coordinating effort can be gained. To obviate the problem of the different rates of speed of motor, animal, and foot transportation, Marshall programmed all motor vehicles on the best road, the southernmost, until the convoys turned north at Bar-le-Duc. To carry out the movement in the time allotted required that the road be filled with traffic all night. Marshall's intelligence and decisiveness in planning this move have been praised by many. However, even Marshall knew that writing such an order is infinitely easier than executing it. The implementing movement orders were insufficiently detailed and poorly executed. Their execution immediately revealed their inadequacy. Marshall admits that the night of 15 September was a bedlam of traffic jams, breakdowns, misunderstandings, and changes in movement orders. Since transport had been routed on separate roads according to their rate of movement, unit integrity was destroyed, and control could not be exercised by the normal chain of command. Middle-ranking officers often demanded road priority, while the mixing of French and American columns brought language problems to the routing and sorting process.[7]

Toward the end of the movement, tempers of all transport personnel grew "testy"; animals were worn out, and many of the moving troops were ill with the "flu." Motor breakdowns were numerous and traffic jams continued. With the considerable help of experienced French transport officers, Marshall and his associates were able to program and reprogram the movements so that all units reached their new assembly areas on schedule—according to Marshall's recollection. Marshall's biographer, Forrest Pogue, states that Marshall has left a vivid record of the way in which he had to depend on overworked trucks and drivers, and, in some cases, horse-drawn vehicles.[8]

The assemblage of logistical and administrative elements for the Meuse-Argonne Campaign, mostly units of the Services of Supply (SOS), was itself a complex linking of hundreds of agencies tied together by a fragile network of roads and rails. Ammunition depots were established at twenty-four locations to store and send forward 40,000 tons of ammunition per day (twelve trainloads of over 3,000 tons each). Railheads at nineteen points provided automatic resupply to the army; twelve ordnance depots issued and retrofitted weapons and equipment; nine gas and oil depots provided fuel; nine furnished quartermaster supplies (food and forage); twelve engineer supplies (bridging, road building materials, lumber); eight, water supplies; six, chemical warfare supplies; as well as smaller depots for signal and motor and tank supplies. Thirty-four evacuation hospitals were set up; 164 miles of light railway lines were constructed or rebuilt. Personnel replacement camps were built and freight regulating stations were expanded. Aviation gathered at forward fields. Of the 668,000 personnel assigned to the services of supply, 291,000 were engaged in direct logistical support of the First Army, including personnel of the three divisions used as laborers in the rear.[9]

On 22 September, Marshal Foch fixed the dates and confirmed the objectives of the general offensive for the Allied forces on the Western Front:

—26 September: A France-American attack between the Suippe and Meuse Rivers.

—27 September: An attack by the British First and Third Armies in the direction of Cambrai.

—28 September: An attack by the Flanders group of armies between the sea and the Lys River, under command of the Belgian King.

—29 September: An attack in the center of the Allied line by the British Fourth Army, supported by the French First Army, in the direction of Busigny.

Foch further explained his mission for the Franco-American attack as follows:

(1) The American First Army's attack was to be carried out between the Meuse River and the Argonne Forest in the general direction of Buzancy-Stonne.

(2) The French Fourth Army was to attack between the Aisne and the Suippe Rivers with their axis the Chalons-Mezieres road.

(3) A mixed Franco-American detachment was to maneuver on the right bank of the Aisne to ensure liaison between the French and American operations.

Close reading of Foch's directives indicates that the American attack, which commitment Foch had accepted only reluctantly, was in the nature of a supporting attack to that of the French Fourth Army, which had the mission of seizing Mezieres and clearing the line of the Aisne River. The mission of the American army, which Foch had earlier given as seizing Mezieres, became the lesser strategic task of advancing on Buzancy-Stonne. This change of axis may have been an attempt to keep the American army away from Sedan, a prize desired by the French to expiate their defeat there in the Franco-Prussian War. Pershing recognized this supporting role, for he later stated that the mission was to "draw the best German divisions to our own front and consume them." The Meuse-Argonne offensive would, of course, assist the attack of the French Fourth Army on the Aisne by drawing German reserves east.[10]

The American First Army Headquarters displaced to Souilly on 21 September 1918. At midnight 22 September, Pershing assumed responsibility for the area formerly held by the French Second Army, giving his command the entire sector from the Moselle River west to the juncture with the French Fourth Army on the west of the Argonne Forest. The First Army also assumed operational command of the French II Colonial Corps and XVII Corps, both corps, along with elements of the American III Corps, defending territory from the east bank of the Meuse to the Moselle. In planning the Meuse-Argonne offensive, the AEF staff assumed the ability to concentrate sixteen divisions with ten organic artillery brigades for the initial attack in the Meuse-Argonne area. The additional artillery would be provided by the French from elements relieved in the St. Mihiel area. Pershing approved the plan for a three-corps attack on the front between the Meuse River and including the Argonne Forest, with nine divisions in the initial assault. (The plan for the offensive and the first phase of the attack are depicted on Map 4, page 83.)

The maneuver plan was for the I Corps (Liggett) to drive north along the Aire valley, clearing also the eastern portion of the Argonne Forest; the V Corps (George Cameron) was to advance on Montfaucon and seize that commanding terrain after bypassing it on both flanks. III Corps (Bullard) on the right was to advance in sector. A major mission of the two flank corps was to assist the advance of V Corps by outflanking Montfaucon. Maneuver lines were drawn by the First Army as intermediate objective and control measures. The corps were to come abreast at the corps objective line running east-west north of Montfaucon, then to guide the advance of V Corps (along the high ground) to seize objectives on the army first phase line— from Brieulles (near Ivoiry) west-northwest to and including Cunel and Romagne, then southwest to Apremont and to the boundary with the French Fourth Army near Binarville. Pershing desired the corps to reach the corps objective line in one day; the army first phase line the second day—a projected advance of ten miles. Further advances to link up with the French Fourth Army (at Grandpré) were to be directed as the battle progressed.

Pershing was aware of the restrictive terrain and the extensive defenses which he planned to overcome in such a short time. However, he counted upon surprise to overwhelm the outnumbered defenders before reserve forces could be moved into the Meuse-Argonne to strengthen their positions. Apparently, Pershing also believed the reports of his staff that German morale and fighting capabilities were low. Although the American troops were relatively unskilled and inexperienced, General Pershing counted on their vigor and aggressiveness to compensate for these deficiencies.[11] His assessment was wrong in all respects.

Last minute visual reconnaissance of attack routes and objectives was made by Americans wearing French uniforms to ensure that the American presence would not be tipped to the enemy by this reconnoitering. Units were moved laterally and repositioned during the night of 25–26 September, causing much confusion in their approach to the line of contact. As the assault divisions moved into their attack positions, the remaining detachments of the French Second Army withdrew from the front. The American order of battle for the initial attack, from east to west, was:

III Corps:	33rd, 80th, and 4th Divisions in line; 3rd Division in reserve.
V Corps:	79th, 37th, and 91st Divisions in line; 32nd Division in reserve.
I Corps:	35th, 28th, and 77th Divisions in line; 92nd Division in reserve.
Army Reserve:	1st, 29th, and 82nd Divisions, placed in rear of the III, V, and I Corps respectively; French 5th Cavalry Division vicinity of Souilly.

A total of 2,775 artillery pieces (more than half of them manned by the French) were registered to support the attack. The density of artillery was one gun for eight meters of front.

An AEF deception plan grew out of earlier plans to continue the St. Mihiel Offensive toward Metz. As the Americans moved at night to take up positions in the Meuse-Argonne, a task force from the 1st Tank Brigade was committed to conduct a demonstration,

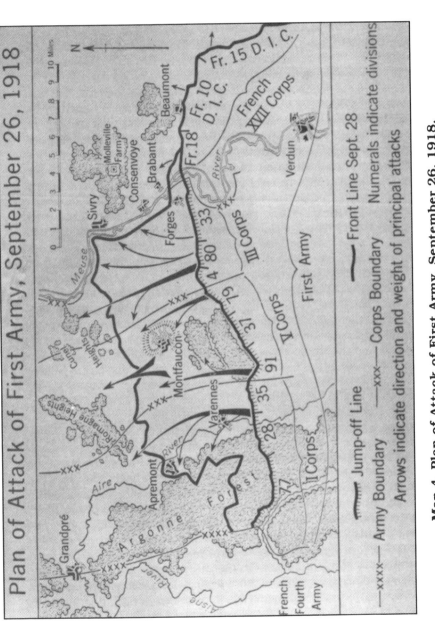

Map 4. Plan of Attack of First Army, September 26, 1918.

American Battle Monuments Commission. *American Armies and Battlefields in Europe.* Washington: GPO. 1938.

feigning a movement to the offensive, near Liverdun, on the night of 19–20 September. This force of 15 tanks, under 1st Lieutenant Ernest A. Higgins, moved through French lines and barbed wire, and maneuvered around "no man's land" in the darkness; this maneuver was repeated in the vicinity of Sivry on the night of 22–23 September, then the tankers returned to their parent battalion.[12] For the coming Meuse-Argonne Offensive, Rockenbach allocated Patton's 1st Brigade to I Corps, to operate along the western fringes of the Argonne Forest in the Aire Valley. Pullen's 3d Brigade was to support V Corps in its drive around Montfaucon, and to assist the advance of III Corps advance on the right of the zone, "wherever practicable." Patton's reconnaissance revealed only a narrow zone in the Aire Valley in which his tanks could support the I Corps advance. He planned to commit his battalions in column, with the 334th Tank Battalion in the van until first objectives were taken; then he intended to leap-frog the 345th Battalion to pass through the 334th and continue the advance. Rockenbach, concerned that earlier operations had been hampered by the tanks running out of fuel, placed large depots in support of both brigades. Patton established additional dumps of gasoline and oil forward of those; he also directed that each tank carry two cans of gas on the rear deck, despite the vulnerability of these to enemy fire. As a result of his experience with breakdowns during the St. Mihiel operation, Patton also organized a maintenance detachment to repair on the battlefield those tanks which broke down, or to tow them to the rear for salvage.[13]

Air support for the initiation of the Meuse-Argonne Offensive suffered from the rapid shift of the First Army while the St. Mihiel operation continued, and also the withdrawal of the British night-bombing squadron and a number of French squadrons as well. A total of 840 aircraft, most of them American, was committed to support the offensive on 26 September. Still, Mitchell's air armada outnumbered the Germans' by three to one. AEF air support was also augmented during the campaign by addition of three newly-organized U.S. squadrons, including the 166th Bombing Squadron equipped with U.S.-manufactured DH-4 aircraft. The combat missions for the air service were generally the same as for the earlier St. Mihiel Offensive. Thirteen balloons were deployed across the Army front, to adjust artillery fire and provide intelligence of enemy activity. "Cavalry Reconnaissance Patrols" were added to conduct aerial scouting forward of advancing infantrymen, and drop messages to lead elements of attacking troops concerning enemy positions ahead. An entire pursuit group was also tasked to combat low-flying enemy planes.[14]

The Americans had little or no experience in active combat; only four of the divisions had had any front line duty. Over half of the troops were recent draftees; some had only received individual training; a few said they had never had the chance to fire their rifles.[15] As "H Hour" (the hour for the assault) approached, all of the one hundred thousand men in the first wave felt tension, as they crouched in the night, waiting for the order to move out. George Marshall recorded that the troops were tired from the exertions of the move forward; sickness (the flu) had spread through the ranks. Marshall expressed his empathy with Pershing, "as yet untried in the role of commander of a great combat army, accepting battle under most unfavorable circumstances—his reputation was decidedly in jeopardy.[16]

Arrayed in attack and support positions facing the Meuse-Argonne defenses was the greatest military force which America had ever sent into battle. The Americans had overwhelming superiority in fighting strength—on the order of eight to one, depending upon who and what is counted. They were far stronger in artillery, in aircraft, and in tanks—the Germans had no tanks in this campaign. The enemy, however, were in strong fortifications; the Argonne Forest was a maze of camouflaged, mutually supporting strong points. The front from Verdun to the Argonne Forest was the responsibility of German Army Group "von Gallwitz." Along this front were eighteen divisions, with twelve more in reserve, most of the reserve clustered around Metz. Five divisions were in defense between the Meuse and the Argonne under command of the German Fifth Army. It was estimated by AEF G-2 (Intelligence) that the Germans could reinforce the front with four divisions the first day, two the second, and nine the third day.

The enemy troops were of poor quality; a large number were Saxons and Austro-Hungarians, who were of doubtful dedication to the German cause. The enemy divisions were at one-third authorized strength. However, the command structure was effective, and the German high command had stressed the need for stubborn defense in Lorraine. The entire German army was at risk, the high command stated, if their southern flank were turned. The intelligence estimate of von Gallwitz' headquarters on 16 September 1918 concluded that a large-scale French and American attack was due in the direction of Conflans (on the Woevre Plain). Other estimates cited Metz as the purported ultimate objective.[17] Donald Smythe, author of two texts on the life of General Pershing, has found evidence that despite the secrecy of the movement of the AEF at night into attack positions facing the Meuse-Argonne, the Germans divined U.S. intentions, pulled some of their outposts back, and started reinforcements toward the Meuse-Argonne area before the Americans launched their attack. The British historian, Hubert Essame, in his text *The Battle for Europe, 1918*, noted that the Germans were prewarned, adding that the Germans learned of the planned American attack in the Meuse-Argonne from French deserters. The German Commander, von Gallwitz, also told of the capture of a soldier from the U.S. 4th Division west of the Meuse, which gave him some indication that the American attack was to be in that area.[18]

Pershing had, again, opted for a short (three-hour) artillery preparation—to achieve surprise. Bullard (III Corps) described this preparation, observed from the infantry attack positions:

> At 2:30 A.M. September 26, silent blackness gave way to what one vivid imagination described as the sound of the collision of a million express trains. Besides the noise there was the feel of concussion, quivering ground, livid skies—and that inevitable wait, while officers scanned luminous watch faces, and engineers and sergeants gazed at compasses with which, by dead-reckoning, they were to lead through a No Man's Land where past shell fire and present fog obliterated landmarks.

On the other side of the line, von Gallwitz recorded that his windows rattled at Montmedy, 25 miles away. Captain Eddie Rickenbacker, later the first American "Ace" among aviators, remembered that the entire horizon was lighted up as if someone had thrown an electric switch, and the area was illuminated "by a mass of jagged flashes."[19]

At 5:30 A.M. the assault troops moved forward behind a rolling barrage one hundred meters to their front. In a heavy fog, mixed with cordite smoke, accompanied by the incessant roar of artillery, the "Doughboys" climbed in and out of great shell holes, "bunching up" at the barbed wire. Someone cut some of the wire, some worked their way over and through it; whistles sounded in the mist, and shouting. Then the enemy machine guns opened up, and their artillery and trench mortars joined in firing heavy defensive barrages. Crouched in their positions in the Argonne from La Harazee east to Vauquois was the 1st Prussian Guards Division. Behind them on the Kriemhilde Stellung were the 5th Prussian Guards, both good units, but low in strength. The 117th and 7th Reserve Divisions east of Montfaucon were reinforced by the 5th Bavarian Reserve, all rated as "poor" units. But they were fighting tenaciously. Among the Americans, cries went up for aidmen and litters. Some men in the assaulting units became lost; others drifted into the low ground, where they gathered in groups. But their spirit was up, and the pressure of those advancing from behind pushed the line of contact forward. The initial German defenses were quickly over-run—the enemy had manned these lightly and would make his stand on the Etzel-Giselher Stellungen. Control of the supporting artillery was poor because it was difficult to ascertain the exact locations of the attackers. The artillery continued firing blindly their prearranged barrages. Some of the infantry insisted their own artillery was firing into them.[20]

At 9:30 A.M., the sun broke through the mist—at the same time, some of the American "mystique" evaporated too! Whenever the doughboys burst into a patch of open terrain, they were hit by frontal and flanking fire from hidden machine guns. The "green" troops moved fast until they hit the first effective enemy fire; then, according to friendly and enemy observers, they tended to "mill about," remaining in the killing zone, taking no action to silence the fire.[21] This was, clearly, a failure in small unit leadership, and in training. Another early observation: The Americans were not using their grenades! Many had none; either they had failed to draw any or they had dropped the ones they were issued. In the close-in fighting, they could not see targets for direct rifle fire. They did not think either to lob grenades at hidden machine gun nests or to call for supporting fire from their trench mortars. Many had also neglected to don gas masks when gas shells struck. Obviously, the lack of training, appropriate training, was paying off the wrong way—in casualties.[22]

The tanks supporting the American attack came forward slowly, many breaking down a few hundred meters into the attack. Many tanks "hung up" in ditches, and many were hit by German artillery while attempting to negotiate the rough ground in the sector of the 28th Division, and to maneuver around the boggy terrain along the Aire in the sector of the 35th Division. German minefields were encountered, but the Germans had so carefully marked these that the "Tankers" had no trouble avoiding them. German machine gun fire was intense, and artillery fire blanketed the area, knocking out tanks and scattering units across the fire-swept areas. On the ground, Patton gathered some tankers and infantry around him, with the entire group under fire. Dispatching his Renaults and Schneiders toward Cheppy, he shouted, "Let's go get them; who's coming with me?" About 100 men jumped up, but upon receiving withering machine gun fire at the crest of a hill, most scattered and ran for cover. Patton asked for volunteers to go with him to knock out the machine guns. Only seven volunteered. As these brave men advanced, the machine guns picked them all off. Patton was wounded in the upper leg; his men dragged him to cover of a shallow shell hole. The tanks, however, joined the 138th Infantry (35th Division) in flanking the town; Cheppy fell at 1:30 P.M. on the first day of the attack. Patton was evacuated to a hospital; his brigade had lost 43 tanks during the first day's operation.[23]

Most of the infantry had advanced little beyond their first contact with the German defensive fires. Confused by the smoke and fire, the attacking units lost organization and internal communications. When the infantry was held up, some individual tanks continued alone, often encountering German sappers who used infantry guns, explosives, and grenades to knock them out. The attacking infantry failed to destroy bypassed German pillboxes; they then found themselves virtually isolated in small groups in the valleys, with Germans on their flanks and in their rear, firing into their hiding areas. In the words of George Marshall, who later studied this campaign, the attackers "became disorganized or confused to a remarkable degree."[24]

The initial situation reports from the attacking corps, received at 9:00 A.M. by First Army Headquarters, stated that all units were advancing with light contact. Later reports—vague and uncertain as to locations of forward elements—showed III Corps moving well on the right of the advance; V Corps was held up in front of Montfaucon; I Corps, on the left, was tangled in the heavy brush of the Argonne interlaced with concrete bunkers and machine gun fire lanes.[25] By 12:30, First Army reported four hundred prisoners had been taken. Allied planes had established air superiority throughout the zone; they were strafing enemy positions and directing artillery on deep targets. Tallies of twenty enemy planes and three balloons were reported "shot down." The 2:30 P.M. AEF press reports confirmed the air action, adding that enemy planes had been swept from the skies.[26] On the ground, from east to west, the 33rd Division (George Bell, Jr.), on the right of the III Corps, had swept through the Bois de Forges against heavy enemy machine gun fire, and had turned half right to occupy a flanking position along the Meuse by 4:00 P.M.[27] The right flank brigade of the 80th Division (Adelbird Cronkhite) fought its way through strong machine gun defenses in the Bois Jure, clearing that woods by noon; the left of the division succeeded in capturing Hill 262 after an all-day fight.[28] The 4th Division (John Hines) took Septsarges early; its left advanced one mile beyond Montfaucon, on the low ground to the east, but, because of its exposed position, it was withdrawn to the forward limits of the rest of the division between Nantillois and Septsarges. III Corps advanced about five miles the first day. The 4th Division repulsed three counterattacks during the afternoon.[29]

Bois de Cuisy   Bois de Montfaucon

German defenders' view of the sector of the U.S. 80th Division, looking west-southwest from the heights of the Meuse vicinity of Harremont.

American Battle Monuments Commission, *Terrain Studies, Meuse-Argonne.* Washington: Battle Monuments Commission, n.d. Reproduced with permission of U.S. Army Military History Institute, Carlisle Barracks, Pennsylvania.

V Corps in the center was meeting the most resistance. The 79th Division (Joseph Kuhn) on the corps' right took Melancourt, but encountered heavy machine gun and artillery fire in the open ground before Montfaucon. The division assaulted the "mountain" during the late afternoon and evening, but they were driven back by a hail of machine gun and artillery fire.[30] The 37th Division (Charles Farnsworth), in the center of the corps, drove through strong defenses in the Bois de Montfaucon, moving abreast of the mountain on the low ground to the west. The division established positions just south of Ivoiry.[31] The 91st Division (William Johnson) advanced rapidly against strong initial resistance and took Epinonville in the late morning; it was driven out by immediate counterattack and fire, turned left, and occupied Very.[32]

I Corps (on the left of the army) made good progress, except on their left. The 35th Division (Peter Traub) captured Vauquois and Cheppy against strong resistance. Some elements got to the corps objective line (east of Charpentry) but were withdrawn to divisional positions west of Very. The left brigade of the 35th Division was held up between Varennes and Cheppy. A further attack carried it to the high ground south of Charpentry.[33] The 28th Division (Charles Muir) took the western half of Varennes and moved a mile north. The left brigade of the division was unable to overcome intense machine gun fire down the eastern spurs of the Argonne from the vicinity of Champ Mahaut.[34]

The 77th Division (Robert Alexander), on the left of the corps and army, made small progress (about one mile) against strong, well-sited positions in the Argonne Forest during the first day.[35] The 77th was a spottily trained aggregation of city-dwelling draftees from New York City and environs, given one of the more difficult and man-killing tasks along the entire Meuse-Argonne front: digging out an enemy well-fortified and camouflaged within a wooded area, with many of the approaches to the German bunkers cleared from ground to knee-high, to give defenders visibility, and leaving the higher brush to limit the visibility of the attackers. Like many of the National Army divisions activated late, the 77th had been subject to a number of personnel levies and changes in commanders. They had shipped from the Port of Baltimore on the 11th of March, 1918, and arrived at Brest, France on the twenty-eighth, the first National Army division to reach the theater. Called the "Metropolitan Division," the 77th was a training status for a period of four months, during which time they were being subjected to personnel changes and levies, to fill not only combat forces but also the structure of the burgeoning AEF logistical and administrative complex. The 77th occupied the Baccarat Sector of the fighting line in Lorraine, and the Vesle Sector in Champagne, then participated in the Oise-Aisne Operation in August and September 1918.

Training of the 77th had been interrupted so frequently that they had been unable to complete unit training at a level higher than rifle company; they were forced to reinstitute small unit training three times during their training in France. On 16 September, the division was moved from the Aisne to the Argonne Forest. The "Metropolitan Division" was given the difficult task of conducting a direct offensive through the Argonne Forest, to maintain pressure on an enemy in fortified positions, while divisions on their right attempted to outflank the forest. It was also required to maintain liaison with the French Fourth Army, their boundary an indefinable line on a map which bisected the Argonne Forest north to south. Evaluated by AEF Headquarters to be in "fair shape" for the Meuse-Argonne Offensive, the 77th Division was committed into horrendous conditions of combat and physical exertion on a murky, damp, hilly battlefield. Disoriented in the forest gloom, out of communication with each other, units became separated, lost; senior commanders, including the Commanding General, Robert Alexander, walked the woods straightening out the order of battle. In the days that followed the jump-off, the division was required, in fact ordered repeatedly, to continue a rate of advance which would keep it abreast of other divisions moving through more open ground on their right.[36]

A detailed review of the battle for Montfaucon is instructive.[37] This was the most critical attack along the entire line for the First Army. It involved the highest, most defended peak, which provided observation over most of the First Army's zone. Nevertheless, it was assumed by First Army planners that Montfaucon would fall more easily than would the associated woods on its flanks. First Army assigned the mission for this critical assault to the V Corps. The First Army order directed: V Corps will attack on the front, Melancourt including Vauquois. This included Montfaucon, but not by direct statement. III Corps, on the right of the army line, was to drive through its sector outflanking Montfaucon from the east by its advance. To the left of the 79th Division was the 37th Infantry Division, which was to make small advances on the west of Montfaucon. Both the 79th and the 37th were totally "green" divisions, never having been in significant combat before.

The 79th Division was an unfortunate choice for this critical mission. Composed of draftees from Maryland and the District of Columbia, it was one of the National Army divisions that had been depleted in the U.S. by two personnel levies to fill other divisions going overseas. Fifty percent of its personnel had been assigned since 25 May 1918, the date when the unit was alerted for overseas shipment. A War Department inspector had visited the division at Camp Meade and had recommended that its personnel receive more training before going overseas. Before the publication of the inspector's report, the unit was on its way overseas. Arriving in France in July 1918, the division had moved into a training site that had insufficient water. The 79th was moved to another area, began training, then nearly all their senior officers were transferred; new officers were assigned late in the division's training. The 79th was placed in a quiet defensive sector behind the front in Lorraine. There they conducted some individual and small-unit training. AEF headquarters judged them to be well-trained.

While the fighting was going on at St. Mihiel, the 79th was among the divisions that were moved quickly into position on the Meuse-Argonne front. The division's artillery remained in their training area in Lorraine; the 79th was given the artillery of another division, which joined them in the attack position. The division's attack frontage was changed twice, as the combat elements were poised for the Meuse-Argonne attack; it was not until nearly midnight on the twenty-fifth—five hours before the attack—that the troops were

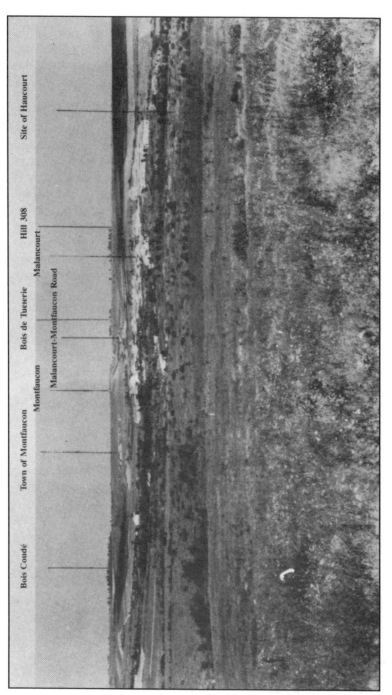

Attackers' view of Montfaucon and vicinity, looking north-northwest from the center of the area of the U.S. 79th Division.

American Battle Monuments Commission. *Terrain Studies. Meuse-Argonne.* Washington: Battle Monuments Commission, n.d. Reproduced with permission of U.S. Army Military History Institute, Carlisle Barracks, Pennsylvania.

finally able to halt, dig in, and reorganize in the mud. Some of the soldiers claimed they had not yet fired their individual weapons. Former Private Robert Hoffman, who served in Company E, 315th Infantry Regiment (79th Division) during this campaign, said his training before being sent into combat was poor; it involved primitive tactics and poor equipment.[38] Most of the soldiers did not know their commanders, above the immediate leaders in their squads or platoons. This "green" and ill-organized unit had been given the major mission of the offensive—capturing the notorious Butte des Montfaucon, with its twin strong points heavily fortified and protected. Also, the town of Montfaucon on the immediate left of the highest peak, from which the German Crown Prince had directed the attack on Verdun two years before, and the Bois de Tuilerie on the right of the second peak, high against the skyline, were both fortified and defended. There were open fields in front of all these promontories, "zeroed in" by machine gun, artillery, and mortar fire.

Major General Joseph Kuhn, Commander of the 79th, was a Regular Army officer, well respected in the AEF. His plan was to attack with his 157th Brigade leading the assault, followed by the 158th moving in support and acting as reserve. The 157th moved out on the attack at 5:30 A.M. on 26 September, with the 313th Infantry Regiment on the left and the 314th Infantry Regiment on the right.

At seven in the morning, the telephone line between the 79th Division Headquarters and the 157th Brigade went out; all communication with the brigade was lost until about noon. At the same time, the 157th Brigade lost contact with its 314th Infantry Regiment, and was only able to maintain contact with the 313th by moving the brigade's command post forward behind that unit. Twelve thousand men of the 79th Division were moving in an area approximately one-and-a-half miles wide in heavy fog and smoke, through barbed wire and shell holes, over ground pockmarked and shattered by former years of fighting. On the left, the 313th moved initially without significant resistance. Colonel Claude Sweezey, the Regimental Commander, reported to Brigadier General William Nicholson (157th Brigade Commander) at 8:30 A.M. that everything was progressing well, with no fire from the enemy. However, the smoke that was being fired in support of the movement caused some of the troopers to shout "gas," and there was some delay while gas masks were adjusted; then the "all clear" order was given. The line moved forward again. The 313th overran the first enemy position with comparative ease, and entered the Bois de Melancourt within their sector without serious fighting. By eight o'clock in the morning this regiment had come out in the open in the Golfe de Montfaucon, with the menacing slopes of Hill 282 looking down upon the attackers.

From these heights, the Germans opened up with heavy machine gun fire. The artillery loaned to the 79th had been scheduled to provide a rolling barrage ahead of the infantry; now, it moved fast and fired far ahead of the attackers. Communications could not be established with the artillery to slow its rolling barrage. Without artillery support, struggling through mud, barbed wire, shell holes, deep trenches, around fallen trees, and pools of water, the "Boys from Baltimore" climbed the slopes of Hill 282 and seized the position; but it took five hours, and their losses were heavy.[39]

Enemy artillery had by now become very accurate; machine gun fire from the heights and the Bois de Cuisy was taking its toll. The 158th Brigade, following the assault, was pressing forward into the ranks of the 314th Infantry Regiment, resulting in a mix of troops, commanders, equipment, wounded, and supply parties. The supporting divisional artillery was ordered to displace forward, but it became mired in the mud along the north-south road and was unable to move to support the advance. Unsupported, the 313th, leading the entire divisional attack, fought its way into the Bois de Cuisy and was able to drive the enemy almost entirely from the position. Counterattacked, they were forced to dig in and reorganize, as they attempted to "mop up" the enemy in the woods. Higher headquarters informed the 79th that a German counterattack from Ivoiry was driving back the 37th Division on the left of the 313th, and that they should be prepared for heavy counterattacks. Colonel Sweezey determined to hold the Bois de Cuisy at all costs.

On the right of the divisions sector, the 314th Infantry Regiment, out of touch with higher headquarters, had continued to move forward almost without opposition, taking Haucourt and Melancourt by ten o'clock in the morning. As they moved up the slopes toward the high ground of Montfaucon north of Melancourt, they came under heavy automatic weapons fire and were pinned down in a hollow between two noses of land approximately one half mile north of Melancourt. The regiment dug in and called for artillery support. None came. Receiving neither support nor direction from the rear, the 314th dug in. Colonel William Oury, the Regimental Commander, decided to hold in position on the high ground north of Melancourt.[40]

The "chain of command" from the 79th Division to V Corps headquarters to First Army headquarters was also not operating. Very little information was sent back from the fighting positions, and little direction or support came from "on high." As is so often the case in the absence of communications, the higher echelons tended to believe that all was going well. At 10:40 A.M., V Corps reported to First Army headquarters that the line of contact was "at the north edge of the Bois de Montfaucon, running from there in a northeasterly direction."[41] Such a line as drawn put the 79th Division far ahead of where it really was; in fact, it showed that the division had already taken Montfaucon. This location plot was easily believed, however, because the 4th Division on the right of the 79th had already moved beyond Cuisy and was moving on Septsarges, generally east of the Montfaucon heights. V Corps headquarters, in a surge of optimism, called the Chief of Staff of the 79th Division, advising him to be sure to report when the division reached the corps objective, which was many kilometers beyond Montfaucon.

At 4:30 P.M., the First Army's Liaison Officer at V Corps headquarters notified the corps, "Aviator reports our patrols entering Montfaucon." At 7:30 P.M., the V Corps Operations Report sent to First Army headquarters the information that the 79th Division was a kilometer north of Montfaucon; a later report from the corps stated, "The report of the capture of Montfaucon has been verified by aviation reports, balloon reports, and by statements of prisoners captured within a hundred yards of Montfaucon."[42] The daily communique from AEF Headquarters announced to the world that Montfaucon had been seized on 26 September 1918. But it wasn't so![43]

The only report that the 79th could have given on 26 September 1918 was that the division's men were dying on the slopes leading to the heights of Montfaucon. Colonel Sweezey of the 313th Infantry Regiment had been calling for artillery and tank support all afternoon. Colonel Oury of the 314th Infantry had been calling for artillery support all day. Both regiments were stalled by heavy enemy fire. The 314th finally overcame machine gun nests on the hill south of Cuisy by maneuvering the infantry without artillery support, without even the fires of the division's machine gun battalion or the one-pounder guns both designated for direct support of the 314th. By afternoon of the first day, the 4th Division on the right of the 79th had moved past Septsarges and was approaching the Bois de Septsarges, receiving only intermittent fire from the woods. On the left, of the 79th the 37th Division had moved swiftly through the woods of Melancourt and Montfaucon (the First Army attack plan had assumed a slow advance through those woods). The 37th, under fire, was approaching the town of Cierges by nightfall. Directly south of Montfaucon, the enemy fire was thickest. With the help of some remnants of the 314th Infantry Regiment, the 313th, late in the day, had taken the right portion of the Bois de Cuisy.[44]

At about the same time, the word went out from First Army through V Corps to the 79th Division: You must take Montfaucon tonight. The 79th Division is holding up the whole army! Guidance such as this is of little help to hard-pressed commanders. Runners from division headquarters stumbled through shellfire and over obstacles to find the command post of the 157th Infantry Brigade and that of the 313th Infantry Regiment in front of Montfaucon. Under pressure of the army's orders, Colonel Sweezey of the 313th Infantry, in spite of previous failures, made preparations to advance out of the woods of the Bois de Cuisy against the slopes of Montfaucon after dark. He was advised that V Corps would support the advance with artillery fire upon the heights of Montfaucon. He was also informed that tanks were also moving up the valley to assist in the attack. It was nearly 8:00 P.M. before the tanks arrived. Artillery support could not be obtained, because communications were again interrupted. Nevertheless, despite all the confusion and lack of support, the 313th broke out of the Bois de Cuisy at 9:00 P.M., heading across the fire-swept draw toward the ruins of the town of Montfaucon two kilometers to the north. Although they were concealed by the darkness, the leading troops were immediately engaged by heavy machine gun fire from the southern slopes of Montfaucon. These fires were joined by flanking fires on the advancing elements and by artillery raining down on them, adjusted by observers on the mountain. Under heavy fire, the tanks deserted the infantry and moved to the rear. Every "field grade" officer except the colonel himself was wounded. Casualties mounted quickly, as the fire appeared to come from all directions. The regiment, what was left of it, fell back and dug in again in the Bois de Cuisy. Montfaucon had not been taken. It had been a fight against pillboxes and machine gun nests; fighting had been at close range with grenades, rifles, and bayonets.[45]

On the right and left, the divisions flanking the 79th had moved considerably forward, at least abreast of the heights of Montfaucon. The 4th Division had gained a position east of Nantillois, well north of Montfaucon. This division, three kilometers ahead of the 79th, was stopped and driven back. One of their elements had become lost and had actually moved up a ridge of Montfaucon, temporarily occupying a position in the Bois de Tuilerie. Later commentators have stated that this action, if it had been reinforced, could have caused the fall of the heights the first day. Perhaps so, but the amount of fire received by the forward elements of the 4th Division ultimately forced it back to Septsarges.[46]

During the night of 26 September 1918, III Corps, on the right of the 79th, ordered the 8th Brigade of the 4th Division to move by night march through the position of its 7th Brigade (which was south of Nantillois) to attack north against the Cunel Heights, seizing a position on the army first phase line. This was a bold move, which, if it had been properly executed, certainly would have turned the defenders out of their defenses on Montfaucon. The 79th Division, attempting to reorganize under fire from the defenses on Montfaucon, received word that the 4th Division was going to send a brigade across its front that night to seize the high ground behind Montfaucon. This action would require delicate coordination to ensure that the supporting fires of the 79th Division did not engage the attacking troops of the 4th Division moving across their front. However, no such problem was actually to occur, for the 8th Brigade of the 4th Division got only as far as Cuisy, still far in the rear of the fighting organizations of the 79th and of the 4th Division's own 7th Brigade—and, for some inexplicable reason, halted there until daylight, 27 September. Whether the anticipation of the movement by the 8th Brigade caused the 79th to remain in position for the remainder of the night can only be a matter of conjecture. Survivors, veterans of the 79th, say that anticipation of the movement of the 8th Brigade was the reason they did not take Montfaucon the first night. Postwar studies show that the enemy on Montfaucon, part of the 11th Grenadier Regiment, were actually planning to withdraw, but the absence of continued pressure during the first night of the American attack caused them to dig in and reinforce.[47]

Just before midnight on 26 September, V Corps sent word to the commander of the 79th Division: "Commander in Chief expects the 79th to advance to positions abreast the 4th Division in the vicinity of Nantillois." This would mean that the remnants of the 313th Infantry Regiment would have to gather their forces and take Montfaucon as soon as possible. The 314th, in intermittent communication with their brigade headquarters, was to be moved left to join the attack of the 313th. The division commander had only uncertain contact with the 158th Brigade in the rear of the moving units and was, for the most part, out of contact with the 157th Brigade in the lead. The commander of the 157th, Brigadier General William Nicholson, was maintaining his command post with the lead battalion of the 313th, and had no knowledge where his other regiment, the 314th, actually was. Runners were scattering across the dark, battlescarred landscape, attempting to establish contact and to relay orders. Nevertheless, a calm prevailed back at First Army headquarters that was exemplified by the following situation report:

The enemy has been driven back on the whole front of attack. American First Army will continue its advance to the Army Objective; the V Corps will continue its advance at 5:30 o'clock this morning. Divisions will advance independent of each other to the Army First Phase Line; troops will be organized to resist counterattack and will be sent forward in exploitation.[48]

At approximately midnight on the 26 September, the commander of the 79th Division, Major General Kuhn, got in touch with the commander of the 158th Brigade, Brigadier General Evan Johnson. The 158th was ordered to move forward at once, to advance through and to the right of the 157th Brigade, and to establish contact with the 4th Division in the vicinity of Nantillois. The 158th Brigade commander had the same problem as the others; his units were scattered throughout the dark battle area. The 316th Infantry of his brigade had swept to the west into the low ground between the hills west of Melancourt and had wound up in the rear of the 313th Infantry of the 157th Brigade. The 79th Division commander seemed to realize the disorganization of his troops, for he amended his orders to the 158th Brigade; this brigade was now to move forward on the right of the division sector with the 315th Infantry Regiment (the only regiment which the brigade commander could contact), take command of the 314th Regiment of the 157th Brigade as the brigade advanced, then attack and take a position on the left flank of the 4th Division in the vicinity of Nantillois. Brigadier General Johnson made a valiant attempt to organize and move his forces, but by 6:00 A.M. of 27 September, they had not moved. He was relieved of his command![49]

The division commander then reorganized his two brigades; the two regiments on the left of his sector became part of the 157th Brigade, those on the right became part of the 158th Brigade. The division attack was executed that morning with two brigades abreast. The 313th on the left went up through the ridges and captured the town of Montfaucon and the ridge on the left of the mountain by 11:45 A.M., under heavy fire and with severe losses. They used their one-pound Infantry Gun to knock out enemy machine guns; they overcame nests of hard-fighting enemy troops with grenades and with bayonets. On their right, the 314th, somewhat in the rear of them, pushed along a ridge in the face of heavy fire and finally broke through the Bois de Tuilerie, coming abreast of the 313th about noon. German resistance weakened. Montfaucon was declared in the hands of the 79th by noon on 27 September 1918.[50]

Studies made of this attack by the Inspector General of the AEF, and by the AEF operations staff, indicated that the 79th Division had achieved all that could have been expected of it under the unique pressures of enemy resistance, terrain, and weather. The division's attached light artillery had been too far to the rear to continue in support of the advancing forces during their surprisingly easy advance from their assembly positions. Once that artillery started to shift forward, it became stuck on the roads and trails and was, in effect, lost to the division for several days. The heavy artillery had been scheduled to fire a rolling barrage in support of the advancing infantry; but this schedule of fire-shifting was much too optimistic, and the artillery outran its infantry, who were moving slowly forward against heavy opposition. Communications between the infantry and artillery were, as we have seen, sporadic to nonexistent. The roads in the rear of the 79th Division, indeed, in the rear of the entire First Army, were so badly blocked by vehicles and by the collapse of the roadbed that it took twenty-four hours for a truck to move approximately ten kilometers. Pioneer engineer troops and other units in the vicinity of the roads were directed to assist in hauling rocks from the fields to attempt to establish a roadbed. The entire division special staff, including the two judge advocates (lawyers), the maintenance officer, and the division's ammunition officer, were pressed into service directing traffic; they did a miraculous job untangling the terrible traffic jams. The AEF inspector general's report concludes:

Considering the fact that this was the first time under fire for some divisions, and that none had received prior training considered necessary, these operations were very creditable to all concerned.[51]

The fact remains that a green division was given the main offensive mission on the entire army front; it was given inadequate support by an artillery organization that was unfamiliar with its operations; it was out of contact with headquarters and relatively unsupported during its operation; it was given little aid by V Corps and the First Army; and it was literally driven forward by "guts" and determination. The employment of the 79th may be a grand story for military history, but it does no credit to the commander of First Army in the Meuse-Argonne Campaign.

Along the First Army front the first night of the attack, divisions and corps reported a total of approximately 950 prisoners of war (POWs) taken. However, the army report for the same period lists five thousand POWs and fifty guns captured. Heavy casualties were reported by the 35th, 79th, 4th, and 80th Divisions. Others reported light casualties or gave no casualty reports. Situation reports from the divisions were poor in content throughout. All corps reported increasing resistance as the Kriemhilde Stellung was approached. All reported supply and evacuation problems and increasing traffic congestion in their rear. Unit locations were reported and corrected frequently during the night of 26 September.[52]

In his book, *My Experiences in the World War*, Pershing stated that the initial advance had been relatively rapid. The First Army had outgained the French Fourth Army on their left. The forward defenses had been lightly manned; the Germans were obviously not fully prepared for an attack in the Meuse-Argonne sector. The German commanders agreed with Pershing's judgment. They were strong on the Aisne, expecting the attack there because of the long French artillery preparation.[53] Enemy fire from the Argonne Forest had delayed the American advance in the west of the army sector, and from Montfaucon in the center. German artillery fire directed from the heights of the Meuse (on the east of the river) was effective, but it had not developed the volume and accuracy it later attained. General Bullard, Commander of III Corps (speaking also for Liggett of I Corps), later stated that the flanks corps should not have been required to wait on the Corps Objective Line for the V Corps to come abreast. Pershing and his corps commanders have also been criticized for not having committed a reserve division to take Montfaucon from a flank when the center corps was held up.[54] Both criticisms have some validity. But allowing the flank corps to get too far forward of a strong defensive position such as Montfaucon might subject the forward elements to the risk of isolation and defeat, especially as German reserves were reinforcing defenses along the ridges running toward Montfaucon.

As to the propriety of committing a reserve, Pershing already had approximately 140,000 men struggling in an area of about seventy square miles. The few roads and trails into "no man's land" were jammed with human, animal, and vehicular traffic. Communications with moving units was almost nil. Situation reports were few and highly inaccurate.

In the quiet of this author's library, almost sixty-eight years after the battle, with faded maps spread all over the room, he, acting as Pershing at Souilly, would remove the limits on advance, and would direct the corps commanders to reinforce their forward elements to outflank resistance. But, reading Liggett's description of his lack of information and control: "100,000 men were trying to kill each other within clear vision of a normal eye, and yet, as came often to be the case in this war, we couldn't see a single living person." And Bullard's: "At headquarters, all dumb, blind, deaf. Even I, a corps commander, was told nothing." Noting the information available to the higher commanders at this stage of the fighting, Essame said, "The fog of war had come down like a blanket."[55] If this author were in command on that confused battlefield that September day, he probably would have taken no action—waiting until the situation cleared.

It rained the night of 26 September 1918, and it was raining hard when the troops moved forward again the next morning. The Doughboys ran into immediate fire from the German main defenses along the Kriemhilde Stellung. The Germans were reinforcing their lines, although heavy U.S. and Allied artillery fire was interdicting the forward movement of some of their reserves. When the attack commenced, General von Owen, commanding Group Meuse West, ordered the 5th Bavarian Division, apportioned behind the 117th Division near Melancourt, and the bulk of the 7th Reserve Division to the Nantillois area. On 26 September, von Gallwitz ordered the 115th Division to move west, while the German Supreme Command directed the 236th Division toward Dun and ordered their 28th Division to march northwestward from the Moselle Region. These units were supposed to close into the Meuse-Argonne area before nightfall on the twenty-sixth; they arrived, however, on 27 September. On the same day, elements of the 37th German Division moved west across the Meuse and counterattacked at Ivoiry.[56]

After the American 79th Division, as hard-pressed by the chain of command as by the enemy, captured Montfaucon on the twenty-seventh, the 4th Division captured Nantillois, but was driven out by counterattacks. That town was retaken by the 4th Division on 28 September with the assistance of the 79th Division. The 4th moved on to seize the Bois de Brieulles; it fought in and lost the Bois des Ogons.[57] The American 37th Division advanced west of Montfaucon on 27 September but was driven back by heavy artillery fire. On 28 September, it crossed the Cierges-Nantillois road and attacked Cierges, but was again driven back.[58] The 91st Division fought through Epinonville to Eclisfontaine, but it could not hold those towns. On 28 September Epinonville fell and the Bois de Cierges was taken in hard fighting. Two American attacks from the Bois de Cierges on the 28 and 29 September were forced back, but on 30 September, the 91st Division took Gesnes, with heavy losses. The U.S. 37th Division was unable to advance and form on the right of the 91st, and the 91st had to withdraw to the forward positions of the rest of V Corps.[59]

In the I Corps zone, the 35th Division on the corps' right, took Charpentry on 27 September, suffering heavy casualties. The next day, it took Montrebeau Woods and reached Exermont on 29 September; but a strong counterattack drove the division south of Montrebeau Woods.[60] The 28th Division made headway in the east of the Argonne Forest, capturing Montbainville on 27 September and Apremont on 28 September, against strong defenses and counterattacks.[61] The 77th Division in the Argonne crawled forward another mile by 29 September, against strong, hidden defenses. Casualties were high, especially in the 35th and 79th Divisions. The Germans later reported that they had trapped both of these divisions in the open. Firing artillery directly into the ranks of Americans and raking them with machine gun crossfire, the Germans reported that their "enemy" streamed to the rear out of control. The 35th Division Commander, Major General Peter Traub, went without sleep for four days, going from unit to unorganized group, attempting to spur them on. He lost contact with his command post, got gassed, and almost wandered into German lines. By his own admission, he "had a helluva time." His men had a worse time; by the twenty-ninth, according to Smythe, thousands of them were missing, and the division was combat-ineffective.[62]

The 35th, the "Sante Fe" Division, was organized from federalized National Guard units from Missouri and Kansas on 18 July 1917. It arrived in France during May 1918 and trained for one month with the British and one month with the French. It occupied the Wesserling Sector on 20 June, then the Gerardmer Sector, both in Alsace; it then moved to the Meuse-Argonne, on the right of I Corps sector. The division was rated satisfactory for participation in the offensive, and had its own supporting artillery. After the initial advance up the Aire Valley, it was scattered, and driven back to Very. The division was relieved by the 1st Division on 30 September. The poor performance of the Sante Fe Division in this offensive was as much a result of the intense concentration of enemy fire as for any other reason.[63]

By this time the Germans had moved six additional divisions into First Army's area and had placed five more in local reserve. The defenses stiffened all along the line and counterattacks were strong. Front line and rear areas of First Army were saturated with gas. The Germans were ordered to hold their Argonne positions at all costs. Casualties were high in all U.S. divisions; the American offensive had run out of steam.[64] Reluctantly, on 29 September, Pershing accepted the need to go over to the defensive temporarily—to reorganize and to bring his experienced divisions from St. Mihiel into the line.[65] The location of the First Army's line on 30 September was approximately along the corps objective line, shown as front line 28 September on Map 4, page 83.

Rain continued to fall, and the roads and trails through no man's land turned into quagmires. Craters and shellholes from earlier fighting had limited the capacity of these routes at the beginning of the offensive; by this time they were virtually impassable. Long lines of traffic were stalled for days. Wounded could not be evacuated; food and ammunition could not get forward. Smythe stated that by 29 September, First Army "was dead in its tracks." He cited Sir Frederick Maurice's conclusion that the Americans had created the worst traffic jam of the war.[66]

Overworked engineers struggled to shore up the roadbeds with any solid material they could find. Reserve units, headquarters personnel, and even malingerers drifting to the rear were pressed into service to move the traffic and shore up the roadway. By the evening of 28 September, all artillery had been shifted forward. Divisions, however, continued to report communication and supply problems through the end of the month. Many units were without food for days. Tank strength had been reduced to one third by breakdowns and by accurate enemy artillery fire. Front-line units conducted local attacks, repulsed counterattacks on 29 and 30 September, and improved their defensive positions. Relief of the most depleted divisions by "veteran divisions" began on 30 September. The 1st Division (Charles Summerall) relieved the 35th Division in I Corps. The 32nd Division (William Haan) relieved the 37th Division; the 3rd Division (Beaumont Buck) relieved the 79th Division on 1 October 1918, and the 91st Division was withdrawn to corps reserve—a complete change of front-line units in V Corps.[67] Despite the continuing bad weather, and resulting from herculean efforts by engineers and logistic units, supplies were stockpiled forward, and personnel replacements were moved to understrength divisions. Positions were improved, units reorganized, patrols sent forward—and the men gained some badly needed rest. The AEF had undergone its "baptism of fire." It had met the challenge of the Meuse-Argonne and advanced. Badly mauled and mired in the mud in front of the main German defenses, the Kriemhilde Stellung, it was hardly a victorious army.[68]

7

THE TEST OF BATTLE: FIGHTING THROUGH TO VICTORY

When the offensive was halted, units began refitting and reorganizing. General Pershing and his staff analyzed the deficiencies of First Army, as these had been revealed in the offensive thus far, and they set about correcting them. It was apparent that the infantry unit leaders were inadequately trained and not sufficiently motivated to continue to press an attack against strong defenses. Fred Ross, who served as a sergeant in Company I, 317th Infantry Regiment, 80th Division, stated that his company's officers were former sergeants who knew nothing but drill; German fire cut the unit to pieces, while the officers did nothing. Sergeant Stephen Murphy, Company B, 307th Infantry Regiment, 77th Division, noted that his company officers were learning the hard way, by making mistakes and getting men killed.[1] "The gaining of objectives, for the present, does not seem possible without undue casualties," stated an AEF report on 29 September 1918. The AEF Headquarters was, it seemed, beginning to appreciate the effectiveness of well-directed defensive fire. "Every goddam German who didn't have a machine gun had a cannon," remembered one veteran.[2] The author Hubert Essame called the Kriemhilde Line the most difficult sector on the whole front, excepting Ypres.[3]

Communications between major organizations and with the French had been poor, as had fire-support coordination at all levels. Divisional artillery had given poor support. It continued firing preregistered barrages, and lifting fires according to a planned schedule of advance, despite information that the advance was slowed or stopped. The Germans merely took cover until the barrages passed, then resumed withering fire on the attackers. Most of the divisional artillery was too far in the rear at the beginning of the attack, and most failed to move forward as the battle line advanced. Artillery was often out of communication with the advancing infantry, and made little attempt to restore communications; thus, artillery support was not flexible nor responsive to changes in requirements.[4] Enemy artillery fire, on the other hand, was devastatingly effective. Observed fire from the Heights of the Meuse on the right of the zone, and from the foothills of the Argonne Forest on the left was wiping out entire small units, while enfilading machine gun fire was killing those who continued to advance.[5]

Pershing visited corps and division command posts. "[We] must push on, night and day, regardless of men or guns," was his message. However, he was beginning to recognize that his determination, and the pressure he generated down the chain of command, were not enough to make an untrained army advance against well-organized defenses. To his diary, Pershing confided, "I . . . certainly have done all in my power to instill an aggressive spirit." The German Third Army War Diary for 29 September recorded, "The entire American front between the Aire and left wing to the [German Third] army is moving back. Concentrated artillery fire struck the masses streaming to the rear with an annihilating effect."[6]

Units were not digging in immediately after taking their objectives, leaving them vulnerable to counterattacks. The Americans had taken heavy casualties from enemy gas, but they had not used gas intensively. The deteriorating health of the troops was of growing concern; the number of influenza cases grew each week (sixteen thousand new cases during the week ending 5 October 1918).[7]

The personnel replacement picture was bad. The War Department had included in its breakout of the "80-Division Program" divisions to be used as replacement and depot units, while the AEF was working on an eighty-division combat force—therefore, the personnel requirement schedules of the two headquarters were different. The War Department also used a lower figure than the AEF for the number of support personnel required in relation to combat personnel. In any case, the War Department was unable to fill its own personnel shipping quotas, even though these were lower than those requested by the AEF. Also, losses through combat and disease were higher than projected. The AEF had to break up two newly arrived divisions in September 1918 to supply replacements. The authorized strength of the rifle company was reduced from 250 to 175 men; some divisions needing rest and refitting were retained in the line.[8]

Meanwhile, Pershing and his staff conducted a furious schedule of visits and inspections and published correctional directives.[9] Pershing continued to relieve commanders who were not able to tolerate the physical and emotional strains of combat. Allied criticisms of the conduct of the American offensive thus far hit Pershing at the same time as the German fire slackened. The mood of the senior Allied commanders reflected an "I told you so" attitude. Premier Clemenceau visited Pershing on 29 September and insisted on visiting Montfaucon. Moving forward despite Pershing's admonitions, he became enmeshed in a gigantic traffic jam on the road to Montfaucon (the 1st Division was relieving the 35th). Returning to Paris without completing his visit, Clemenceau told Foch that the American attack had stalled and the AEF was in "complete chaos." He demanded that Foch relieve Pershing. Foch stated, "The Americans have got to learn sometime. They are learning now, rapidly."[10] Despite repeated demands from Clemenceau over the next few weeks, Foch did not relieve Pershing; however, he did take action to goad Pershing forward. On 30 September, he sent Major General Weygand (his Chief of Staff) to Pershing to announce his intention to "allocate" the American I Corps to the French Second Army, which would be injected between the American First Army and the French Fourth Army, to operate through the Argonne. Pershing would command the remainder of the American army to the west and east of the Meuse. Pershing reacted with hostility to this change, and he convinced Weygand to withdraw the proposal. Foch got his point across, however, in a letter to Pershing on 2 October 1918, in which he stated:

> Amending what I wrote you September 30, I agree to maintaining the present organization of command, as you propose, under the condition that your attacks start without delay and that, once begun, they be continued without any interruptions such as those which have just arisen.[11]

Foch's reasoning behind this proposition may have been more devious than it appears to be on the surface. Marshal Haig, whose troops had broken through the Hindenburg Line in the north, criticized the slowness of the American advance and that of the French on the Aisne. The British and the French had long been suspicious, each that the other was trying to hold down its own casualties, at the other's expense. In attempting to assign I Corps to the French Second Army, Foch was likely trying again to infuse American strength into the French drive to increase their advance by adding American reinforcements. During this period, Lloyd George had also importuned Secretary of War Baker to let him retain the American troops that had been sent to the BEF for training. The historian Cyril Falls, in his text, *The Great War, 1914–1918*, added to his review of problems of the AEF at the end of September the offsetting note that Anglo-Belgian forces in Flanders had halted at the same time for the same reasons.[12]

Criticism of the AEF's rear-area services was also coming from the fighting divisions. Sergeant Major Harold Craig of the G-2 office of the 79th Division admitted he had better living conditions than the men in the attacking echelons. Still, he complained of the food: "Beans and slum [stew] for the 119th time." He also stated that the traffic jams on the roads were unimaginable; it took five hours to move five miles along the roads, he estimated.[13]

Criticism of the logistical tangles in the Services of Supply and all the way forward along the line of communications had reached Washington. Pershing blamed the War Department for having failed to provide horses and trucks in the amounts programmed. The War Department criticized Pershing's management and began, again, to propose the reorganization of the Services of Supply. The French were demanding the return of their truck trains, on which the AEF depended for survival. To ensure that Secretary of War Baker understood the AEF's perspective on the problem, Pershing sent Major General Harbord (Commander of the SOS) to talk to Baker, who was then in Paris. Baker promised to expedite the shipment of transport. Meanwhile, roads and trails had been made "passable" for the twenty-five thousand tons of supplies which had to be moved daily across "no man's land" in the Meuse-Argonne.[14]

German strength facing the Americans from the Moselle to the Argonne (as estimated by AEF G-2 on 4 October 1918) increased to twenty-three divisions in line and in local reserve. In the next week, this strength increased to twenty-seven divisions, with eleven between the Meuse and the Argonne. Many of these divisions were very low in strength. Orders from their supreme command were to defend "until the last man."[15]

The Order of Battle for the Resumption of First Army's attack was, from east to west:

—III Corps (Bullard) on the right: 33rd Division (Bell), 4th Division (Hines), and 80th Division (Cronkhite) in assault, with no reserve designated.

—V Corps (Cameron) in the center: 3rd Division (Buck) and the 32nd (Haan) in assault; the 42nd (Menoher) and the 91st (Johnson) Divisions in reserve.

—I Corps (Liggett) on the left: 1st Division (Summerall), the 28th Division (Muir), and the 77th Division (Alexander) in assault; the 82nd (George Duncan) and the French 5th Cavalry Divisions in reserve.

—Army Reserve: 29th Division (Charles Morton), 35th Division (Traub), and the 92nd Division (Charles Ballou).[16]

The relative strengths of the units in contact between the Meuse and the Argonne totaled about nine Americans to one German, according to some accounts. The Germans, however, were less vulnerable in hidden, strong defenses; they were making maximum use of preregistered machine gun and artillery fire, including heavy use of poison gas. The Americans, with about two hundred thousand men pressing forward in an area of restricted terrain a mere twelve miles wide, were counting on manpower to overcome the German defenses. The author David Kennedy, who wrote *Over Here,* a text on the attitudes of U.S. and Allied personages, says:

> The AEF had an immense numerical superiority over the Germans in the Meuse-Argonne, and made most of its advances simply by smothering the enemy with flesh. One American commander estimated that ten of his men perished for every dead German.[17]

Such a trade-off—bodies for bullets—was certainly not intended, but the restrictiveness of the terrain, the quality of the defenses, and the poor training of the massed attacking forces brought about that result.

On 4 October, the First Army resumed its offensive with rested troops, and wiser, somewhat more experienced leaders. These attacks were being made against the main German defenses of the Kriemhilde Stellung. Key positions in this defensive complex were the Heights of Cunel in III Corps' zone, Romagne (including the Cote Dame Marie) in V Corps' sector, and Hill 272, St. Juvin, and the Argonne Ridges in I Corps' zone. (See Map 5, page 109.) These defenses were supported by interlocking direct fires and observed artillery fire from flanking promontories and from the heights east of the Meuse. Pershing instructed his corps commanders to keep smoke on the high "observation points," and to maneuver so as to avoid flanking fire. III Corps and V Corps, acting in concert, were to seize both the Cunel Heights and those on the east of Romagne. Pershing specified that their main effort should be concentrated on the western approaches to Cunel to avoid the galling fire from the heights of the Meuse. Elements of V Corps and I Corps were to take the Romagne Heights. I Corps was also directed to neutralize the artillery fire coming from the eastern flanks of the Argonne Forest by means of smoke and heavy counterbattery fire. Strong supporting fires were planned throughout the First Army's zone, using high explosives and gas shells.[18]

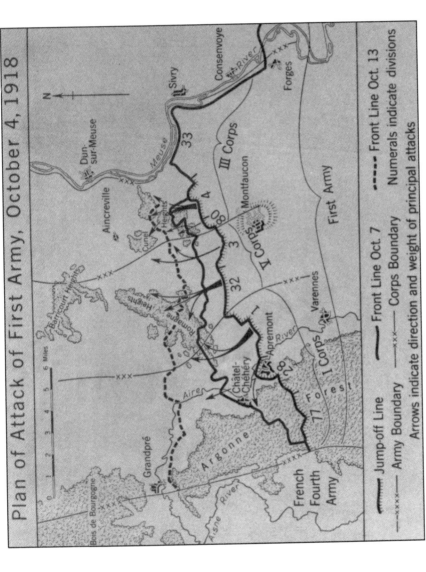

Map 5. Plan of Attack of First Army, October 4, 1918.
American Battle Monuments Commission. *American Armies and Battlefields in Europe.* Washington: GPO. 1938.

The Heights of the Meuse, looking over the river northeast from positions of U.S. 33d Division north of Consenvoye.

American Battle Monuments Commission. *Terrain Studies. Meuse-Argonne.* Washington: Battle Monuments Commission. n.d. Reproduced with permission of U.S. Army Military History Institute, Carlisle Barracks, Pennsylvania.

Bois de Chaume

Route Natl. 64

Meuse River

Bois de Consenvoye

Consenvoye

The infantry attack moved out at 5:30 A.M., 4 October 1918, and immediately made heavy contact with the enemy all along the front. In the center of the III Corps area, the 4th Division fought its way into the Bois du Fays southeast of Cunel, but only after three days of bitter fighting. Heavy and accurate German artillery fire was delivered from the Heights of the Meuse; American counterbattery fire was neither masking nor suppressing that enemy fire. The 4th Division's attempts to seize the Bois de Peut de Faux were unsuccessful; sharp counterattacks drove the division back to positions in the Bois du Fays, about one mile from their original line of departure.[19] The 80th Division on the left of the 4th gained and held a foothold in the Bois des Ogons south of Cunel against unusually heavy machine gun fire.[20] Both divisions reported that the enemy was entrenched in strong positions along the Cunel heights and that they could make no further headway.[21] In the V Corps' attack, the 3rd Division (Preston Brown), on the corps' right, made repeated sallies into the Bois de Cunel but was driven back, with little gain and heavy casualties.[22] The 32nd Division, on the left of the 3rd, advanced against Gesnes (south of center of Romagne Heights), with tanks clearing enemy from the low ground south of the town. Although they encountered strong resistance in the town and fire from Hill 265 and from the Romagne Heights, the 32nd seized Gesnes on 5 October and held it.[23]

I Corps, attacking down the Aire Valley behind a rolling artillery barrage, made the greatest gains. Led by tanks, the 1st Division (on the corps' right) attacked Hill 240 (on the west of Romagne Heights) moving against frontal and flanking machine gun fire from the Argonne, from the hill, and from farms in the valley. The division's attack was slowed by the enemy's accurate adjustment of artillery, including gas shells, on their moving elements. In two days, the 1st Division gained three miles and seized Hill 240 and Arietal Farm. The 28th Division, on the left of the 1st, captured Chatel Chehery. Their western brigade, however, could make no progress in the Argonne Forest.[24]

The 77th Division, on the corps' left, continued its grinding assault, day after day, in the gloomy Argonne Forest—the fighting characterized by small-unit attacks against well-dug-in machine gun emplacements.[25] The Yiddish, Polish, Italian, Latin, city-bred soldiers of the 77th were learning woodsmanship and soldiering the hard way. One man, caught malingering, complained, "I can't make the bullets go into this thing." Only 10 percent of the men knew how to use hand grenades. The morale of the division continued to be low, casualties high.[26] On 2 October, several units of the 77th reached Charlevaux Creek (approximately on the 7 October line in the forest, Map 5), then fell back. Elements of the 1st Battalion, 308th Infantry Regiment, remained forward of the others, and was surrounded by the Germans. This became the "Lost Battalion" of later legend. For several days, attempts by the 77th Division to link up with this battalion were thwarted, while the battalion fought off repeated enemy attacks. German guns "zeroed-in" on the battalion's perimeter, and American casualties quickly reduced the fighting strength of the unit to half of the 550 men assigned to the unit. Runners sent to request support were captured. Ammunition and food ran out, and the water point remained under fire.[27] Still, the commander, Major Charles Whittlesey, refused the repeated demands of the Germans to surrender. Walking among his men, the major saw a soldier eating a chunk of black bread. "Where did you get that?" he asked. "Off one of the dead Boches; want some?" the soldier rejoined. "No," said Whittlesey, "you deserve it all." By messenger, he sent a plea: Men are suffering from hunger and exposure and the wounded are in very bad condition. Cannot support be sent at once? There was no reply. With his last pigeon, the major informed his headquarters: "Our artillery is dropping a barrage directly on us. For heaven's sake, stop it!" Finally, the artillery ceased. After six days of fighting off the German attacks, the 77th broke through to the beleaguered battalion, their advance assisted by a flank attack by the 82d and 28th Divisions. Only 194 men of the "Lost Battalion" were able to walk to the rear, but they walked with pride.[28]

On 5 October, the Germans threw fresh troops into counterattacks all along the front. Front-line divisions reported close-in fighting, with many hand-to-hand engagements. Enemy planes were active over the front during the early hours every morning. Casualties were reported as "heavy" in all corps. The roads, however, had improved, as had the supply situation. Even the weather had improved; but in the valleys, the mud, which is the soldier's constant companion, clung to everything. New enemy units were identified, especially opposing the I Corps' advance. There were reports of German tanks with the counterattacking forces in the Aire Valley. As stated earlier, there were no German tanks in the Meuse-Argonne. Reports of German tanks firing on the Americans may be related to other reports that a few Germans took over disabled Allied tanks in the Aire Valley and fired the tank weapons. The tank was one new weapon whose effectiveness the Germans were late to recognize.[29]

Remembering the fighting in the Meuse-Argonne, Brigadier General Edwin Randle said, "Junior officers, mostly, were courageous, and motivated by patriotism, but their training was poor for that kind of war. Some of the senior officers were poor. . . . Attack plans were mostly forward movements. Platoon and company commanders had little chance to maneuver their units.[30] By the evening of 7 October 1918, the United States First Army held a line shown on Map 6 (page 126) from Bois de la Cote Lemont west through Bois du Fays, Gesnes, Hill 240, Fleville, southwest to Chatel Chehery, and through the Argonne.

It was time, past time, for Pershing, the large AEF staff, and the small First Army staff to examine, in detail, how they were meeting the German challenge. Despite Pershing's emphasis on "Open Warfare," the attack plan had, thus far, been nothing more than a frontal assault on a fortified position. Was this operation an American Battle of the Somme? It's true that the casualties (approximately 75,000 up to 6 October) were not as great as they had been on the Somme, but the uninspired tactics were the same as had prevailed during that earlier Allied debacle.[31] Fortunately, below army level, some lessons had been learned and some innovations developed. The "trooper" had learned not to pass a German machine gun nest whose personnel "appeared" to be dead. Too many of these dead men had "opened up" on our troops after they had passed. Private Wiley Goudy of Battery F, 314th Field Artillery Regiment, 8th Division, remembers running into booby traps placed in houses and on dead bodies.[32] The Americans were also becoming accustomed to throwing grenades into apertures of machine gun nests. More fire-and-movement was being used in the ravines and defiles to knock out barricaded emplacements. It became apparent also that much of the German direct and indirect fire was "unobserved." Machine guns and artillery were firing their "final protective fires" on order, as the Americans approached, without exposing their gunners and observers—the Americans were advancing into "blind fire." It was also concluded that many machine gun emplacements forward of the main positions were manned by well-trained, fatalistic veterans. Engaging these by fire and bypassing them was the best technique.[33] Corporal William Sibley, Company B, 109th Infantry Regiment, 28th Division, reported that his unit was told some of the German "sacrifice" gunners were chained to their machine guns.[34] The Americans were also learning that most of the enemy's defensive positions were mutually supported by the fires of other positions throughout the depth of the defenses. American wounded being evacuated were passing on battle tips, and replacements were being oriented on the state of the enemy defenses.

Ludendorff was reinforcing in the Meuse-Argonne, even at the expense of his defenses in Flanders, where the Allied offensive had gained much more ground. It was apparent to the German high command that they must hold the line from Verdun to the Aisne in

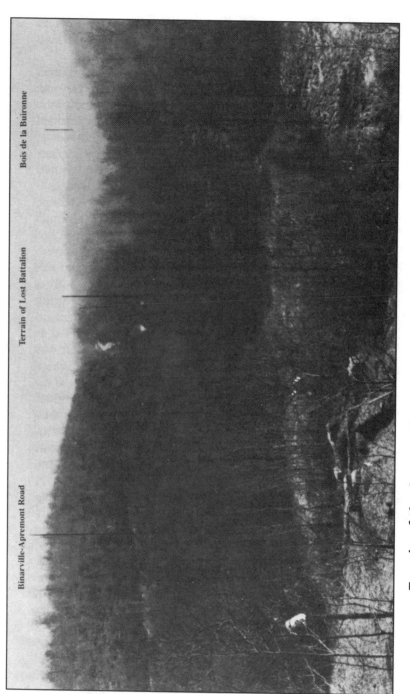

Terrain of the Argonne Forest, looking north-northeast at the area where the "lost battalion" was surrounded.

American Battle Monuments Commission. *Terrain Studies. Meuse-Argonne.* Washington: Battle Monuments Commission. n.d. Reproduced with permission of U.S. Army Military History Institute, Carlisle Barracks, Pennsylvania.

order to withdraw the bulk of their armies from positions to the north and the west. It was also apparent to Ludendorff that the end was fast approaching. American troops were landing in France at the rate of three hundred thousand per month, and he had no reserves of manpower to oppose these reinforcements. By the end of September, Ludendorff and Hindenburg both urged Germany's political leaders to request an armistice. On 6 October 1918, Prince Max von Baden, the new German chancellor, cabled President Wilson requesting an armistice based on Wilson's "Fourteen Points."[35]

On the battlefield, artillery support was improving; but the artillery had failed in one major mission: to silence the galling fire from the ridges of the Argonne Forest and from the Meuse Heights flanking the line of advance on both sides.[36] There are four ways to attenuate hostile fire directed from a promontory: mask it (with smoke); knock it out by counterbattery fire; bypass the area beyond the range of effective observation and fire; or attack the promontory itself. In the First Army's attack thus far, the first alternative to silence the enemy artillery had failed—as any private lying in the "beaten zone" of the German artillery fire, working, methodically, up and down the Aire Valley, could have told Pershing. To bypass the German observation points meant, for all practical purposes, to attack outside the Meuse-Argonne, for it would have been necessary to advance beyond the limits of visual observation from the two hill masses. Observation from the eastern Heights of the Argonne only covered the Aire Valley; from the Heights of the Meuse only the approaches to the Cunel heights were visible. The only bypass alternative for the AEF was sufficiently east of the Heights of the Meuse to prevent both effective enemy observation and fire. Unfortunately, this alternative had not yet been considered. Pershing, in *My Experiences,* later said that there was a contingency to attack the Heights of the Meuse as part of the initial attack plan. Apparently, this was not approved for execution; First Army attack orders through 4 October 1918 only required the divisions on the right of the army to protect the army's flank along the Meuse.[37] By 6 October 1918 it was apparent that in order to seize the Cunel-Romagne Heights (the key positions of the Kriemhilde Stellung west of the Meuse), the defenses on the Heights east of the Meuse would have to be neutralized.

Pershing's directive for continuing the attack tasked the French XVII Corps along the Meuse River to assault and seize the Heights of the Meuse, while the American corps of First Army drove forward from their line of contact in the Meuse-Argonne.[38] The XVII Corps, reinforced by the American 29th and 33rd Divisions (which attacked across the Meuse) stormed the heights on 8 October. They took

Consenvoye and fought up the slopes of Richene Hill, but they were stopped just short of the high ground.[39] This attack was fiercely resisted, because the area was the hinge of the German defenses of their entire westward extension into France (the so-called Loan Bulge). This author concludes that this should have been Pershing's main attack—on the Meuse Heights, or farther to the east to flank the heights. It is possible that Pershing, in *My Experiences*, was reacting to postwar criticism of his concentration of force between the Meuse and the Argonne, for he went into some detail to explain the narrowness of the ridges and the difficulty of access to the Heights of the Meuse. True, the heights were nearly ideal for observation and defense, but so was the Cote Dame Marie against which III and V Corps were committed. Although the attack of XVII Corps against the Heights of the Meuse was stalled, it did so press the defenders of the heights that flanking fire upon III and V Corps was considerably attenuated.[40]

I Corps, whose left was entangled in the Argonne Forest, was ordered to take the eastern ridges of the forest without delay. This time, the corps delivered a fifteen-hour preparatory artillery bombardment on the ridges; on 7 October the infantry moved against the wooded hills, supported by a well-controlled rolling barrage. The Corps Commander, Major General Hunter Liggett, then demonstrated an innovativeness unique among AEF commanders: pulling the 82nd Division up from Corps Reserve, he flung this division, together with elements of the 28th Division, in a westward drive across the Argonne Hills, cut off the forest, and sent the Germans tumbling back into Grandpré.[41] This oblique attack enabled the 77th to move forward rapidly, relieving the "Lost Battalion." This attack also cleared the way for the French Fourth Army to advance on the west of the Argonne.

V Corps, relieved of the observed fire from its right, launched an all out assault on the Bois de Romagne on 9 October. By nightfall, the leading elements had seized Fleville and were fighting up the slopes of Hill 255. III Corps advanced on the right on 10 October, and the whole army line moved forward against stubborn resistance. The Bois de Romagne fell on 10 October, but strong enemy fire stopped the right of V Corps and the left of III Corps short of Romagne and Cunel. By the night of 10 October, the advance had slowed. First Army went into a temporary defense on 11 October.[42] The halt was necessary in order again to reorganize and resupply. The brutal fighting had rendered some of the divisions ineffective for further attack. The 91st Division, bled of its strength from repeated assaults against Hill 255 (which it had seized) and against the Cote Dame Marie (from which it had been driven back),

The Heights of the Meuse flanking the route of the attack of the U.S. 5th Division, looking over the Meuse east-northeast from Clery le Petit.

American Battle Monuments Commission, *Terrain Studies, Meuse-Argonne.* Washington: Battle Monuments Commission, n.d. Reproduced with permission of U.S. Army Military History Institute, Carlisle Barracks, Pennsylvania.

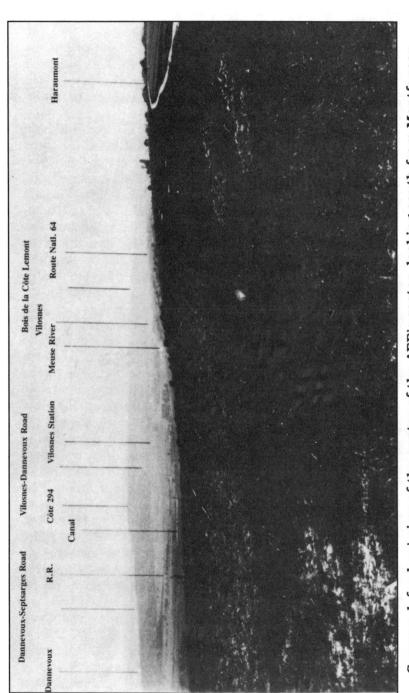

German defenders' view of the center of the AEF's sector, looking south from Montfaucon.

American Battle Monuments Commission. *Terrain Studies, Meuse-Argonne.* Washington: Battle Monuments Commission, n.d. Reproduced with permission of U.S. Army Military History Institute, Carlisle Barracks, Pennsylvania.

Dannevoux-Septsarges Road   Vilosnes-Dannevoux Road   Bois de la Côte Lemont

Dannevoux   R.R.   Côte 294   Vilosnes Station   Meuse River   Vilosnes   Route Natl. 64   Haraumont

Canal

was relieved on 11 October. The 1st Division, which had wrested Hill 272 from the enemy, was pulled out the same night; it had lost 9,387 officers and men, the highest casualty figure of the campaign. The 1st's position was taken over by the 42nd Division. The 80th Division came out of the line also, replaced by the 5th Division (John McMahon). On 13 October, the front line (shown on Map 6 by a marked line) ran from south of Brieulles on the Meuse directly west through the lower Cunel Heights south of the Cote Dame Marie, through the Bois de Romagne to the break in the Argonne Forest south of Grandpré.[43]

Casualties had risen to over one hundred thousand, according to later estimates. Adding to the army's other woes, the weather had turned cold; rain slashed the troops dug-in along the line of contact. Sickness was increasing in the war theater.[44] Bugler Herbert Summers of Company I, 314th Infantry Regiment, 79th Division, remembers the cold, the rain, and the mud. Everyone had diarrhea; eating cheese from the ration helped.[45] The replacement situation was bad—not more than forty-five thousand replacements were available for all the combat divisions; the divisions were short a total of eighty thousand personnel. The "flu" was so bad at home that President Wilson had considered stopping the replacement flow altogether. Pershing's request for the return of the American divisions with the British and French resulted in requests from these Allies for more American units.[46]

It finally became obvious to Pershing that he would have to expand his zone of attack to the east—a conclusion his staff and he should have reached much earlier. Pershing created the Second Army, effective on 12 October 1918, to take responsibility for operations on the east of the Meuse River, from Fresnes-en-Woevre to the Moselle River. Major General Robert Bullard of III Corps took over this command. Pershing turned over the First Army to Major General Liggett, formerly commanding I Corps, effective on 16 October. Pershing replaced the two vacant corps commands, with Major General Joseph Dickman taking I Corps and Major General John Hines to command III Corps. Major General Charles Muir replaced Dickman as commander of IV Corps. At his own request, Major General George Cameron stepped down from command of V Corps to retake his old command, the 4th Division; Major General Charles Summerall replaced Cameron as commander of V Corps.[47]

It was well Pershing made these changes, including removing himself from field command. He had driven his corps and division commanders unmercifully. Goaded on by Allied criticisms and by his own driving ambition to succeed in breaking the strong German defenses, fighting the War Department for men and supplies,

Argonne Forest   Pleinchamp Fme.   Croix de Bayle   Cornay   R.R.   Aire River
                                    Côte 180

The sector through which the U.S. 82d Division operated in its flank attack, looking west along the route of the 82d on the north of the forest.

American Battle Monuments Commission, *Terrain Studies, Meuse-Argonne.* Washington: Battle Monuments Commission, n.d. Reproduced with permission of U.S. Army Military History Institute, Carlisle Barracks, Pennsylvania.

U.S. Cemetery   Bois des Rappes   Bois de la Pultière   Cunel   Romagne-Clerges Road   Bois de Cunel   Romagne-Charpentry Road

Hills around Cunel and Romagne in the center of the sector of the U.S. 32d Division, looking northeast from Gesnes.

American Battle Monuments Commission. *Terrain Studies. Meuse-Argonne.* Washington: Battle Monuments Commission. n.d. Reproduced with permission of U.S. Army Military History Institute, Carlisle Barracks, Pennsylvania.

beset by wet and cold weather, tired and ill himself from the flu that was affecting his army, Pershing appeared to be losing his sense of judgment and perspective.[48] Our French ally may have chosen this moment to again attempt to reduce the American force, and with it U.S. influence on the war and on the coming peace settlement. According to Frank Vandiver, a Pershing biographer, Marshal Foch sent General Weygand to Pershing on 12 October with a curt message relieving him of command of the U.S. First Army (to be replaced by the French General Hirschauer), and assigning him to command a southern region from Pont-à-Mousson, on the Moselle, south to the Selle. Pershing rejected the order. "It would forever obliterate the part America has taken in the war," he (allegedly) said to his French aide.[49] If effected, this action would have been in line with Foch's earlier attempt to shift Pershing eastward and to employ American forces on both sides of the Meuse. Now, however, Pershing would be relegated to a sector well to the east of the Meuse only. Vandiver, citing a memorandum concerning this incident, believed Foch was, in fact, attempting to relieve Pershing. Neither Pershing nor Foch mentioned this attempt in their memoirs. The historian Donald Smythe, whose second volume of his biography of Pershing (Pershing: General of the Armies) covers this period, was skeptical that Foch would have attempted a direct relief, as is this author. However, all major headquarters had heard gossip that the French were trying to have Pershing relieved. Hearing this talk, Secretary of War Baker said, "It will be a long time before any American commander would be removed by any European premier." This statement reflected the prevailing opinion that Clemenceau was behind the attempt to remove Pershing.[50]

The records show that, on 13 October, Pershing had a conference with Foch at Bombon. Foch, disarmingly, queried Pershing about Wilson's position on an armistice, hoping, ever tactfully, that "Wilson would not presume to speak for the Allies!" Pershing's icy manner forced Foch to the main issue: The Americans were not advancing as rapidly as the other Allies, he stated. "I judge only by the results. . . . If an attack is well planned and executed, it succeeds with small losses. If not, the losses are heavy and there is no advance," said the small marshal—apparently forgetting the stalemates and Allied defeats of the past three years. He then brought up the fact that Pershing had "selected" the area for the American army and was therefore responsible for the results. To break the impasse, Weygand mentioned Pershing's plan for creating two American armies. Commenting again on "results," Foch approved the plan. He insisted, however, that Pershing operate near the front.[51] The new First Army Commander, Major General Hunter Liggett, was thus saddled with Pershing's presence until nearly the end of the war. According to Charles Dawes, Pershing's Chief of Procurement, Paris was buzzing with rumors that the French were going to relieve Pershing—to reduce American influence in the coming peace settlements.[52] The weary American army was tasked again with producing immediate results against an enemy reinforcing his strongest, most strategically important defenses. The result was more bloodshed and only minor gains. But the reasoning behind the American drive, and the Allied criticisms, was obviously political— the AEF had to fight to gain for the United States a position of influence at the peace conferences soon to come. Bliss warned the War Department that France and Britain would "attempt to minimize the American effort as much as possible. They think they have got the Germans on the run and they do not need as much help as they were crying for a little while ago."[53]

As is often the case, a political problem had to be solved on the battlefield. Pershing had "selected" the area; now he had to get an offensive going there. The new American Second Army east of the Meuse was, relatively, ignored by Pershing. Given fewer forces than the First Army, it was tasked to lean forward from its defenses, while Pershing kept his attention on the heights of Romagne.

There was no relaxation of the pressures applied by Pershing on his commanders; nor was there slackening in the German defensive efforts. The First Army was fighting its way directly through a series of defiles to break the "crown" of the German defenses. It was a hard, costly, uphill battle, not rendered easier by rotten weather and increasing sickness among the troops. Criticism of the sterile tactics of the AEF came now even from the troops themselves.[54] Pershing ranged over the battle area, lectured commanders, and even sent his aviators into the trenches so that they could learn how better to support the infantry. The organization of captured terrain for immediate defense, maximizing fire support of moving elements, coordination, command presence at the point of contest—these lessons were stressed by Pershing in his visits to commanders.[55]

Supplies, equipment, weapons, and transport to support and sustain the AEF were inadequate and declining. Railway and truck transport from the SOS forward was approaching a breakdown, and needed supplies were piling up on ports and railroad sidings. Horse transportation was severely short, by 43 percent; the AEF needed over 100,000 horses to fill basic transport needs. Every day, the French were less compliant in the way of furnishing transport, suggesting strongly that these and other shortages could be accommodated by breaking up the American armies and distributing corps and divisions among the Allied armies. The War Department was also unable to make up the supply and transport shortages, claiming that ship bottoms could not be secured to provide a surge of replacement materiel.[56] However, a brighter result was achieved in the air, where the AEF Air Service controlled the skies over the battlefield, and continued to drive German planes north of the Meuse River, despite unfavorable flying weather over the zone. On 9 October, an AEF air armada of about 200 bombing planes, 100 pursuit planes, and 53 tri-place aircraft struck between Wavrille and Damvilliers, dropping 32 tons of bombs. This bombing raid brought up the Germans; 12 German planes were shot down, while only one AEF aircraft was lost.[57] The tanks of the AEF had fought along with the infantry; however, the battlefield was littered with their carcasses. By the middle of October, more than half of the remaining tanks were inoperable; lack of spare parts had led to cannibalization, and maintenance crews roamed the Aire Valley pulling parts from wrecked and disabled machines. Patton returned from the hospital on 28 October; he was very angry at the condition of the men and tanks of his command. He was particularly distressed at the lack of military courtesy and issued a spate of directives demanding improvements in saluting and wearing of the uniform. Patton also set about refitting his tanks and his command during the two-week standdown which General Liggett had directed for the First Army.[58]

(The First Army plan for continuing the attack is on Map 6, page 126.) The offensive was resumed on 14 October 1918. After advancing around Romagne, the 5th Division of III Corps became disorganized, under a hail of enemy fire in the Bois de Rappes, and withdrew in confusion. The division commander, Major General John E. McMahon (a West Point classmate of Pershing) excused the performance to Pershing by saying that the men were "tired." Pershing thought that the commander was tired—McMahon was relieved, replaced by Major General Hanson E. Ely, who had won fame at Cantigny. Earlier the same day, Pershing had relieved Major General Beaumont B. Buck from command of the 3rd Division; Pershing was distressed to note that the 3rd, a "regular army" division, was low in morale. He replaced Buck with the hard-driving Brigadier General Preston Brown. Buck was notified that his reassignment was in accordance with a policy of rotating commanders home to provide experienced officers for stateside units.

The most controversial relief was that of Major General Clarence R. Edwards from command of the 26th Division, the National Guard division from New England. Major General Edwards was respected and well liked by his men, who affectionately called him "Daddy." A graduate of the U.S. Military Academy (1883), he had served on the frontier, in the Spanish-American War, and in the Philippine Insurrection. He later served in Hawaii, and in Panama, returning home to organize the 26th Division for the call to the colors. Pershing considered him a "politician," probably because of Edwards' command of a National Guard division; Pershing also disliked Edwards' unmilitary manner and lack of deference to him. The 26th "Yankee Division" was criticized by AEF staff for poor organization and discipline; it was said that their officers did not know where their men were, they failed to meet commitments on time, and failed to keep AEF informed. In relief of the 1st Division in the Toul Sector, Edwards had criticized the officers of the "Big Red One" for leaving their defenses in poor condition; Pershing took the side of the 1st Division. Later, the 26th Division was criticized for fraternization with some Germans. It was well known that Pershing had been dissatisfied with Edwards and with the 26th. Its commander, Edwards, seemed to be unable to organize and direct the division; the division had done poorly in training, movement, and battle. Edwards and his subordinates were convinced that Pershing was "down on them" because they were National Guard—and this may have been true: Pershing and his "regular" elite considered the National Guard to be commanded by poorly qualified "political generals. The relief caused a political storm at home, despite Pershing's note to Edwards that, like Buck, he was merely being rotated to gain experienced leadership in the stateside training base.[59]

While III Corps was driving against the fortified defenses of Cunel, the French XVII Corps, with the American 29th and 33rd Divisions in the lead, attacked and were stalled on the ridges leading to the Heights of the Meuse, the 29th taking the wooded heights north of Molleville Farm (see Map 4, page 83, for location of Molleville Farm). V Corps, under its hard-driving commander Major General Charles P. Summerall, had the major task: to drive the enemy from the Barricourt Heights, the crown of the Kriemhilde defenses. The main attack mission was assigned to the 42d Division, one of the stalwart organizations of the AEF. The 42d Division was called the "Rainbow Division" because it was formed on 1 August 1917 by combining National Guard units from 26 states and the District of Columbia. It was moved overseas beginning in October 1917, and entered the line of French defenses on 21 February 1918. From its first combats, the division was noted for high discipline, esprit, and aggressiveness. The division engaged in 12 major battles and advanced well under fire, taking very high casualties largely because of its direct attack against enemy machine guns. It attacked aggressively in the French Aisne-Marne Counteroffensive and in

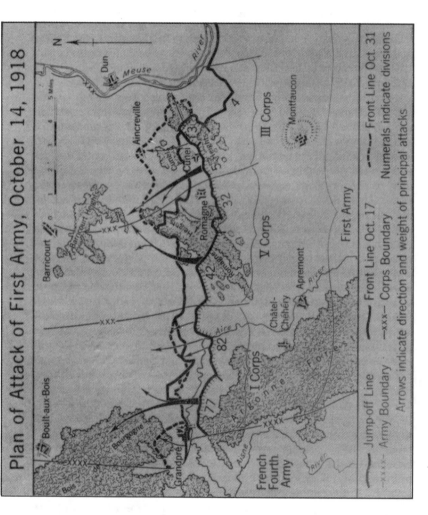

Map 6. Plan of Attack of First Army, October 14, 1918.

American Battle Monuments Commission. *American Armies and Battlefields in Europe.* Washington: GPO, 1938.

the St. Mihiel Offensive. Observers attributed the effectiveness of this National Guard division, which equalled that of the regular divisions, to competitiveness between units of the division from the different states; the division was also blessed by having outstanding commanders. Major General Charles T. Menoher commanded the division during most of its combats.[60]

The key to the Barricourt Heights was the Cote de Chatillon, which was the objective for the division's 84th Brigade, under Brigadier General Douglas MacArthur. Graduate of the U.S. Military Academy Class of 1903, MacArthur's exceptional military abilities, personal drive and ambition, and his flair for dramatic actions, made him one of the most effective commanders in the AEF. As Chief of Staff, MacArthur had brought the 42d Division to France. Wounded twice, he was decorated for bravery by award of two distinguished service crosses and seven silver stars prior to the Cotillon assault. MacArthur roamed the trenches and battlefields wearing a blazer and scarf without rank or accoutrements, causing him once to be detained as a German. Promoted by the War Department to Brigadier General in July 1918, over the objection of Pershing who did not recommend him, MacArthur led the 84th Infantry Brigade of the 42d in the St. Mihiel Offensive in September, driving north to St. Benoit. The brigade advanced rapidly and captured 10,000 prisoners, according to MacArthur's later recollection. MacArthur also recalled that he and his adjutant sneaked through the lines to the outskirts of Metz, discovering it to be lightly defended. He then proposed that the 84th be allowed to lead a drive on Metz; this proposal was turned down, as the First Army was redisposing for the Meuse-Argonne Offensive. MacArthur stated that this refusal was one of the worst mistakes of the war, as the Germans in France could have been cut off at the hinge of their line of communications.[61]

As MacArthur disposed his brigade for the attack on the Cote de Chatillon, Major General Summerall told him, "Give me Chatillon, or a list of 5,000 casualties!" MacArthur responded quickly, "All right, General; we'll take it or my name will head the list."[62] Assaulting aggressively, with the 32d Division on its flank, the 84th took the heights on 16 October; the 32d had taken the Cote Dame Marie on 14 October. The entire corps then moved forward to the Bois de Bantheville.[63]

The advance of I Corps was less rapid. The 77th crossed the Aire River under heavy fire and attacked Grandpré. This was the western anchor of the German defenses in the area, and the town was strongly defended. Former Private Lawrence Meyers, Battery A, 303rd Field Artillery of the 77th Division, related that he manned a single artillery piece called forward to fire directly at machine gun nests. Artillery so used were called "Pirate Guns," he said. This was a very effective way to knock out machine guns that were in strong emplacements.[64] After two days of close combat in Grandpré, some of it being hand-to-hand and some with bayonets, the 77th was relieved by the 78th Division. Meanwhile, the 3rd Division and the 5th Division of III Corps penetrated the woods and heights from Cunel to Romagne.

The Kriemhilde defenses finally had been penetrated, and the Americans now occupied part of the dominant heights. The Metz-Sedan-Mezieres railroad lay within heavy artillery range. But the attack had been another costly frontal assault, and the First Army had to go into a defensive posture, again. Later, local attacks by I Corps cleared the woods north and east, and finally captured Grandpré on 27 October after heavy fighting. The Bois de Bantheville was cleared by V Corps, while III Corps fought through the Bois de Rappes and held it against counterattacks.[65]

The 5th Division (III Corps) took Aincreville on 30 October. Thus the last strongholds of the Kriemhilde Stellung were taken, and the First Army was on good terrain for the renewal of the offensive. (The line of contact for the First Army at the end of October and the plan for continuing the attack are shown on Map 7, page 129.) Pershing turned his attention to proposals for an armistice, and Liggett refitted and trained his army.[66] Ludendorff admitted that the defense of the "Kriemhilde Stellung" had been costly: "Our best men lay on the bloody battlefield." A general withdrawal plan was adopted, and Ludendorff pinned his hopes on the tenuous defenses of the "Freya Stellung." No major reserves remained available to the defenders.[67]

Although Pershing remained too close to First Army headquarters and repeatedly urged Liggett to continue the offensive, the new army commander showed a surprising firmness with his boss: he refused to attack before the army was "tightened up." And much tightening was needed. Divisions, such as the 4th and 33rd, had been in the line since the beginning of the offensive. The 33rd had taken over 2,000 gas casualties. The 32nd Division was probably lowest in strength, with less than 2,000 combat-effective soldiers. These divisions needed to go into reserve, to reorganize and refit. The combatants of all divisions needed to rest, to be better trained in fire and maneuver and in the techniques for attacking fortified positions; unit commanders needed to learn to maximize the use of supporting fires. The artillery had again bogged down; the chief problem was the acute shortage of draft horses. Men of the 6th

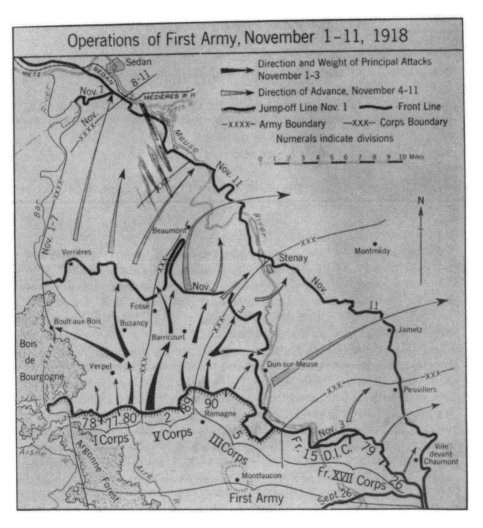

Map 7. Operations of First Army, November 1–11, 1918.

American Battle Monuments Commission. *American Armies and Battlefields in Europe.* Washington: GPO, 1938.

Division, which division never saw active combat, labored along the roads, manually hauling artillery and supplies forward. Ammunition had to be stocked forward to support a new offensive. Most of the commanders were still deficient in the use of smoke to screen their locations and movements. And, despite the terrible effects of the poison gases, with which the Germans literally drenched the Americans, corps and lower commanders were still reluctant to employ this weapon to disable enemy units.

A further major problem, truly a disgrace to the AEF, was the large number of stragglers and malingerers, lounging around kitchens and aid stations, hiding in dugouts, stealing and drifting about in the rear. Liggett thought there were as many as 100,000 "stragglers," who needed to be rounded up. In the 3rd and 5th Divisions, badly mauled and disorganized, only about one-fourth of the combat infantry were present for duty. While many were casualties and many more were evacuated because of influenza, a great many— too many—had fled to the rear. Military police set up straggler lines and routed out hidden groups. Still, Pershing had to break up two more newly arrived divisions to provide replacements to units in the field. The authorized strength of divisions was reduced by 4,000 men each. Pershing again requested that the Allies return the American divisions with their forces, in order to build the strength of his Second Army.[68] The high rate of "straggling" is a clear indication of poor morale in First Army at this time.

By agreement with the French Fourth Army (on the west), the continuation of the attack of the First and Second American Armies was set for 1 November 1918. Foch had attempted (on 28 October) to turn the American First Army west against the Bois du Bourgogne, but Pershing considered these instructions to be beyond Foch's charter, and he directed a general attack to the north, with his main objective being the seizure of the Barricourt Heights in the center of the First Army's zone. He did order the Bois du Bourgogne to be cleared after the Barricourt operation. The Second American Army, well to the south and east of Meuse, was directed to conduct only local attacks and to improve their positions. For this attack, Pershing set no limits on the advance; he prescribed only an all-out and continuing attack to uncover the line of the Meuse and the defenses of Sedan.[69]

Liggett's First Army was rested; it had been retrained, really "remodeled," for attack against fortified positions. Artillery supporting plans had been developed to isolate the hills under attack by interdictory fires on rear slopes and rear approaches, while heavy counterbattery fires were planned on likely German artillery and infantry reserve positions. Heavy use of gas, including mustard gas, was planned. Special training had been given to infantry squads grouped into heavily armed "assault teams." These teams were trained to eliminate machine gun bunkers by fire and movement, crawling up to lob grenades or explosives into the bunkers. While these teams engaged the men in the bunkers, the rest of the infantry were trained to bypass these strong points. The other Allied ground armies were also attacking: the British and Belgians were driving on Brussels; the British right and the French center were flattening the "Laon Bulge" slowly, while the French right and the American First Army were closing the gap from the south.[70]

The First Army was deployed to attack, from east to west, as shown below:

—III Corps (Hines), with the 5th (Ely) and 90th (Henry Allen) Divisions in line east to west and the 3rd Division (Brown) in reserve.

—V Corps (Summerall), with the 89th (Wright) and 2nd (John Lejeune) Divisions in line and the 1st (Frank Parker) and 42nd (Menoher) Divisions in reserve.

—I Corps (Dickman), with the 80th (Cronkhite), 77th (Alexander), and 78th (McRae) Divisions in attack, and the 82nd (Duncan) in reserve.

—The 32nd (Haan) was in Army reserve.

This time, Liggett was not going to have First Army attack all along the front. V Corps was to conduct the main attack, seizing the ridges from Barricourt west to Fosse. The 1st and 42nd Divisions were located in the rear of V Corps to exploit the V Corps' attack. The other corps were to support the V Corps, with III Corps seizing the high ground east of Barricourt and I Corps striking northwest to seize Boult-aux-bois. All divisions in the attack were veteran. All were ready.[71]

The army's artillery was well prepared to support the attack. Heavy artillery had been moved well forward, including railcar-mounted fourteen-inch naval guns, which guns began hurling 1,400-pound shells deep into the enemy's rear late in October. Two days prior to the infantry attack, the army's artillery began to place heavy fires, including all types of gas, on known and suspected enemy artillery and reserve-troop locations. For the first time, the AEF artillery was saturating the defensive area. All of the artillery was supporting this attack, including those guns that would normally support divisions now in reserve. "Cannon enough to conquer hell," said the writer Fairfax Downey.[72]

At 3:30 A.M. on 1 November, the black of night burst bright as day as the last great barrage of the war struck the enemy positions "like a million hammers."[73] Gun barrels glowed as the artillery rained fire on enemy battery locations, reserve positions, crossroads, headquarters, bridges, and areas suspected of being occupied by reserve units.[74]

The infantry assault jumped off at 5:30 A.M., the Doughboys following the customary rolling barrage. This time, however, smoke and gas were adjusted along the flanks of the advancing forces. The artillery preparation had devastated the enemy's defenses. The attackers closed quickly on their objectives; active strong points were invested by direct-fire weapons, while the bulk of the troops swung around these and surged forward. The German defenses broke, the defenders fleeing northward, followed by the fast-moving Yanks. III Corps quickly took Andevaune (west of Dun-sur-Meuse), protecting V Corps' flank. V Corps stormed and seized the Heights of Barricourt. After supporting V Corps' movement by fire, I Corps drove the Germans out of Buzancy on 2 November, and the entire army line moved north. By the end of 3 November, V Corps had seized the town of Barricourt and had advanced to the southern edge of Beauclair. In a daring night advance, the 2nd Division moved through the Bois de la Folie, their columns slipping between enemy defenses, and took the high ground east and north of Fosse on the morning of 3 November. That same night, they again moved through a gap in the Germans' positions and captured some headquarters men in their billets. By midnight, they had taken La Tuilerie farm just south of Beaumont.

The Second Division was Regular Army division. Organized in September 1917 in France, it was formed from units in France or en route, including one brigade of marines. The initial complement of personnel and units contained a high percentage of Regular Army and regular marine NCOs and officers. Called the "Indianhead Division" because of an Indianhead shoulder patch, the division forged a bloody record of aggressiveness in stopping the 1918 German drive in the Chateau Thierry area. After leading the Allied offensive at Soissons, and attacking vigorously in the U.S. First Army's St. Mihiel Campaign, the division had been committed to join the French Champagne offensive. Capturing Blanc-Mont Ridge, the Second Division again demonstrated high esprit and aggressiveness in battle, under Major General James G. Harbord. The outstanding record of this division was attributed to its cadre of regulars, as well as to rivalry between army and marine components. Under the command of Marine Major General John Lejeune, the division was committed into the Argonne in V Corps on 21 October 1918. The 1 November drive up the Aire Valley to the Meuse River was its crowning achievement.[75]

These advances compelled the withdrawal of the German forces facing I Corps and the French Fourth Army.[76] The 77th now advanced beyond Champigneulles to Harricourt. The 78th attacked again on 3 November 1918 and captured Germont and Verrieres.[77] III Corps, on 1 November, captured Clery-le-Grand, turned northeast, and drew up along the Meuse south of Stenay. By 4 November, the First Army had advanced twenty kilometers. At First Army headquarters, staff officers could hardly keep up posting locations on the maps.[78]

On the night of 4 November 1918, German forces on the Western Front began a phased, general withdrawal, designated the *Kriegsmarsch;* it was designed to break contact with the Allied advance, then to reestablish the German defenses along the northeast bank of the Meuse River. The American First Army, having reached open ground, was preparing for pursuit.[79] German bodies littered the roads and fields. Von Gallwitz knew that the situation was hopeless. On 2 November, he had reported:

> All of the front line commanders report that the Americans as [*sic*] attacking in mass formations in the general direction of Stenay, that the German troops are fighting courageously but just cannot do anything. Therefore, it has become imperative that the Army be withdrawn in the rear of the Meuse and that said withdrawal be effected immediately.[80]

On 5 November, Pershing ordered the continuation of the pursuit: The First Army was to cross the Meuse and advance in sector to clear the region between the Chiers and Bar Rivers. The Second Army finally was ordered to advance between the Moselle and Etang Rivers toward Gorze and Chambley and to prepare plans for a broad offensive in the direction of Briey. All forces were to advance in zones, without regard to terrain objectives or the advance of forces on their flanks.[81]

On 8 November 1918, the soldiers' newspaper, *The Stars and Stripes,* reported:

> The thick walls of German resistance in the Argonne, against which the First American Army has been hammering since the last week in September, gave way with a crash on November 1. . . . The very earth and sky seemed in alliance with the doughboys. For a week, the weather has been kindlier. . . .[82]

The First Army was already on the move. By 5 November, 5th Division of III Corps had crossed the Meuse under fire and established bridgeheads south of Dun-sur-Meuse. The division then captured Milly and extended its line south to the Bois de Chatillon. The 79th Division fought against strong defenses on the Heights of the Meuse, turning south against the Borne de Cornouiller. The

The area through which the U.S. 2d Division conducted its night attack, looking north-northeast along their route of march from Bois de la Folie.

American Battle Monuments Commission. *Terrain Studies, Meuse-Argonne.* Washington: Battle Monuments Commission, n.d. Reproduced with permission of U.S. Army Military History Institute, Carlisle Barracks, Pennsylvania.

enemy forces were fighting to keep their pivot anchored there until forces to the north could withdraw. The Borne de Cornouiller fell on 7 November. The following day, the 79th, part of the French II Colonial Corps, took Wavrille on the east flank of the Heights of the Meuse. (These locations are north of Ville-devant-Chaumont on Map 7.) On 8 November the 79th Division drove southeast and seized Ville-devant-Chaumont. The 81st, on the night of 7 November, captured Mantieulles and Moranville, southeast of Ville-devant-Chaumont.[83]

In V Corps' zone, the 89th captured Beaufort on the fourth and reached the Meuse north of Stenay. The 2nd Division took heavy casualties in its attack along the Barricourt Heights, but it reached the Meuse south of Villemontry (where the Meuse turns again north seven miles north of Stenay, Map 7).[84] In I Corps, the 80th Division fought through a German unit committed to a "last-man battle" and captured Vaux-en-Dieulet and Sommauthe. The enemy then withdrew, and the 80th pursued them to a line north and west of Beaumont by the night of 5 November. The 80th was relieved the next morning.[85] The 77th was still meeting stubborn resistance. On 5 November, however, it pushed its forward elements north of Stonne and La Besace. By the evening of 6 November, it had driven to the Meuse, sending patrols northward into Villers and Remilly (five miles southeast of Sedan). The 78th Division captured Les Petites Armoises (northwest of Verrieres) on 4 November. The 42nd Division took over from the 78th, and by 6 November had established its line north of Bulson (six miles south of Sedan).[86] The 1st Division entered the offensive on the left of V Corps on 6 November (taking over from the 80th Division) and immediately attacked and secured Villemontry on the Meuse.[87] Von Gallwitz remembers that it was about this time (6 November) that he was out of reserves and could only hold on as long as possible, while the German armies fought back to a line along the trace Meuse-Antwerp.[88]

Meanwhile, Pershing had been playing politics during early November, pronouncing himself to be for the continuation of the war until the "unconditional" surrender of the Germans, in contravention, even in defiance, of the known stand of President Wilson, who favored an armistice. For a brief period, it again seemed that Pershing might be relieved, this time by his own national authorities. The President's advisor, Colonel Edward House, talked the matter over with Pershing and advised President Wilson that nothing further should be done.[89] On 6 November 1918, Pershing caused another furor by announcing that it was his desire that American forces take Sedan. At Pershing's request, First Army directed I Corps,

Bois de Remoiville

Brandeville-Breheville Road

Looking over the plain of the Woevre, north-northeast from the 5th Division's forward positions.

American Battle Monuments Commission. *Terrain Studies, Meuse-Argonne.* Washington: Battle Monuments Commission, n.d. Reproduced with permission of U.S. Army Military History Institute, Carlisle Barracks, Pennsylvania.

assisted by V Corps, to bend all its energies to capturing Sedan. Although Pershing says he had the approval of the commander of the combined French Fourth and American First Armies (General Maistre), he reckoned without the sense of pride of the French. Sedan was the site of the great French defeat in the Franco-Prussian War! Understandably, the French were determined to have the honor of liberating Sedan—but the Doughboys were on the way, while the French fumed. Pershing finally halted his more aggressive commanders just before the 42nd Division and the 1st Division became hopelessly entangled, partly in the zone of the French Fourth Army, on the heights overlooking Sedan. The American Second Army moved east in the Woevre Plain on 9 November, reaching a line, Marcheville-Lachausee. Both armies of the AEF continued their attacks on the 11th of November and took casualties. The armies were planning further pursuits north and east when the Armistice instructions were received. At the eleventh hour on the eleventh day of the eleventh month of 1918, all fighting ceased![90]

Units fought until the last minute, and some Allied artillery, it was later charged, "shot" past the deadline. For most of the soldiers, the Armistice came as a gradual realization—of silence! Then the question: Is it really over? asked of buddies for reassurance, half in disbelief. It is over! I'm alive, I made it. Some of the bolder soldiers on both sides of the front advanced, haltingly, toward each other. Almost shyly, they waved, came closer, then shook hands. Corporal William Sibley, Company B, 109th Infantry Regiment, 28th Division, recalls the happy sensation: "One of our platoons was over a hill.... A few Germans came to them to shake hands; they gave our men coins, and even pulled buttons off their clothes to give them.[91] The wounded George Patton wrote in his diary, "Got rid of my bandage. Wrote a poem on peace."[92] And peace it was for the tired, victorious soldiers from America. The AEF had fought through the Argonne, uncovered the Meuse. The Americans passed the terrible test of battle in the Meuse-Argonne. They had punched through strong defenses by frontal assault—with heavy casualties. Their leadership had revealed that it was insufficiently trained and experienced to meet this trial by fire.

Looking north at Sedan from positions at which U.S. 1st Division was halted on the heights south of the city.

8

DENOUEMENT AND DEPARTURE

During the last few hours before the Armistice, Pershing paced in front of a large wall map at his headquarters at Chaumont. He was obviously glad that the war was over; however, he could not lay aside the dream of invading Germany. "I suppose our campaigns are ended," he remarked, "but what an enormous difference a few days more would have made." Pershing had opposed the Armistice, to the point of provoking the anger of President Wilson; he still opposed it. Shortly after the Armistice, he had made the point strongly: "If they had given us another ten days, we would have rounded up the entire German army, captured it, humiliated it...What I dread is that Germany doesn't know that she was licked. Had they given us another week, we'd have taught them."[1]

Pershing sent a congratulatory message to his AEF, laden with admonitions and directives:

The enemy has capitulated. It is fitting that I address myself in thanks directly to the officers and soldiers of the American Expeditionary Forces who by their heroic efforts have made possible this glorious result . . . I congratulate you upon the splendid fruits of victory which your heroism and the blood of our gallant dead are now presenting to our nation. These things you have done. There remains now a harder task, which will test your soldierly qualities to the utmost . . . Every natural tendency may urge towards relaxation in discipline, in conduct, in appearance, in everything that marks the soldier. Yet you will remember that each officer and each soldier is the representative in Europe of his people and that his brilliant deeds of yesterday permit no action of to-day to pass unnoticed by friend or foe . . . Whether you stand on hostile territory or on the friendly soil of France, you will so bear yourself in discipline, appearance and respect for all civil rights that you will confirm for all time the pride and love which every American feels for your uniform and for you.[2]

Celebrations of the victory varied from some front-line troops taking a long sleep to wild parties by aviators, in keeping with their newly established social traditions. Eddie Rickenbacker remembers that "pandemonium broke loose. Shouting like mad, falling over one another, the airmen grabbed anything that could shoot...and dashed outside to light up the night in one delirious, semihysterical orgy of noise, laughter, and light." Paris had literally gone mad with joy. Crowds jammed the streets, shouting and singing the Marseilles. Pershing's car took two hours across the Place de la Concorde; not given to displays of emotion, he was nevertheless profoundly moved by the occasion. Encountering Clemenceau a few days later, Pershing admitted, "We fell into each other's arms, choked up, and had to wipe our eyes. We had no differences to discuss that day." Pershing visited the headquarters of the Allied commands, presenting the Distinguished Service Medal to Marshals Foch, Pétain, Joffre, and Haig. Regarding the rapprochement of the Allies and Americans, Harbord commented, "The Armistice thus ended two wars for us—the one with our friends, the other with our enemies."[3]

The celebratory mood of the AEF turned quickly sour, as the soldiers came to appreciate that the mission for which they had been called to the colors and shipped overseas was complete. The AEF staff and administrative commands had the difficult task of stopping the surge of men and materiel forward, and quickly reversing the flow. Camps became crowded, conditions were bad, food was poor, and free time, which is deleterious to morale, led to rising complaints. Pershing directed a full program of training, coupled with emphasis on discipline and the "school of the soldier." He and his staff initiated a round of inspections and talks to the men. These visits led to improvements in conditions; however, on a number of occasions, Pershing was greeted with boos, and chanting: We want to go home! Congressmen, politicians, and other prominent Americans visited the soldiers, and commented upon the inadequacies of living conditions, and of plans for redeploying the troops home. Pressed by high-level complaints and investigations, Pershing reduced the rigor of the training and initiated a sports and entertainment program; these activities improved morale somewhat.

On 13 December, President Wilson arrived in France. Pershing had hoped that the President would visit the AEF in a battle position, site of a great victory. However, President Wilson begged off a visit to the front; after persuasion, Wilson agreed to visit the troops in Langres at Christmas. The President's visit and talk to the troops were conducted on a cold, wet Christmas afternoon. Wilson's talk was uninspiring, and the troops were unresponsive. The President excused himself early, avoiding Christmas dinner with the AEF; Pershing appeared happy to see him leave.[4]

The AEF staff was busier than during much of the war. In addition to planning and directing the redeployment of troops, weapons, and equipment to the United States, and organizing the occupation of the American Sector of Germany, a veritable flood of studies and after-action reports was generated by Pershing, the senior commanders, and even the staff itself. On 19 November 1919, General Pershing submitted a "Preliminary Report of the Commander in Chief, American Expeditionary Forces to the Secretary of War." This report was a summary of organization and operations of the AEF in France, including totals of personnel, weapons and equipment, casualties, and enemy prisoners of war and equipment captured. The Final Report of General John J. Pershing to the Secretary of War, dated 1 September 1919, was a detailed review of the experiences of the AEF from organization until the dissolution of the AEF. The final report included a chronological summary of AEF organization, operations, and sustenance. Policies with respect to relations with Allies, missions and combat operations, relations with the offices of the Secretary of War and the Chief of Staff of the U.S. Army, establishment of the theater, including the SOS, augmentations and replacements of men and materiel, and ancillary matters were reviewed, as well as summaries of staff organization and operations. There were no significant differences in this extended final report from earlier reports and operational summaries. In this final report, reasoning and justification for decisions made by Pershing and his major commanders were also given.

As with military "after action reports" through history, this report revealed Pershing's judgments to have been timely, necessary, and correct. The wording of the report was particularly facile in justifying conditions and decisions about which U.S. and Allied authorities had been critical. The points of contention which were rationalized included Pershing's "Open Warfare" training guidance, commitment of U.S. forces under Allied command, establishment of a separate American army, selection of the Meuse-Argonne operational area, First Army's attack plan, Allied combat support, attrition tactics, failure of AEF combat and logistical support, Allied criticism of AEF operations and leadership, and post-Armistice tasking and relationships with Allies and the enemy. Pershing's report ended with commendations to officers and men of the AEF, American civilians in Europe, social and religious societies, the U.S. federal government, and a commendation to the nation itself. Pershing's main report makes no recommendations, although the reports of staff sections and agencies do cite failings and recommend improvements for the future.[5]

After the Armistice, the AEF established boards of officers to consider and evaluate Tactics and Organization, Staff Organization, Field Artillery, Heavy Artillery, Cavalry, Infantry, Signal Corps, Engineer Corps, Medical Corps. These boards were diligent in their inquiries; they made many recommendations for modernization in weapons, equipment, operations, logistics, and military procedures. These recommendations were later incorporated into the omnibus report of the AEF Superior Board. One of the boards whose recommendations gained prominence was the "Hero Board," so called because it was headed by Brigadier General Andrew Hero, Jr.; it was formed on 9 December 1918 to make a study of the experience gained by the artillery of the AEF, and to submit recommendations for future artillery organization and functions based upon that study. The Board conducted a great many interviews and searched records; their recommendations were submitted to the Chief of Artillery of the AEF on 27 March 1919. Of the Board's many recommendations, most dealt with the need for increases in caliber of guns and improvements in materiel to bring greater fire upon targets more quickly and more effectively. Motorization of all batteries was recommended so that artillery would be able to move and displace quickly. The Board also recommended increases in staffing and liaison and strongly recommended artillery training for officers of all combat branches. The Board recommended improvements in observation and ranging, including having artillery officers assigned as aerial observers (to adjust artillery), and requiring these officers to live with the units for which they were adjusting fire. The report did not emphasize forward observer positions or training; this omission is difficult to understand, considering the lack of effective forward observer operations in most AEF campaigns.[6]

On 19 April 1919, the AEF created a board of officers to "consider the lessons to be learned from the present war in so far as they affect tactics and organization." This Board, headed by Major General Joseph T. Dickman and consisting initially of three major generals, two brigadier generals, and two colonels, was given the title, "Superior Board on Organization and Tactics," and has been called "The Superior Board" ever since. The Board adjourned and submitted its report to the Commander in Chief of the AEF on 1 July 1919. The report addressed the organization of an army operating with its own supply system. However, recognizing that future wars may call for several armies, the Board also considered a theater command (called a Directing Head), and a separate Service of Supply.[7]

The Superior Board's recommendations were unsurprising and mostly affirmed the organization and operations of the AEF as the model for the future field army. The Board stressed the principle of war, Unity of Command, leading off its report with the statement that all activities "must be controlled by the single mind of the commander." Without a doubt, this statement was an affirmation of Pershing's earlier dictum on the War Department's plan to separate the SOS from his command. The Board then sketched a theater organization containing Combat Arms (Infantry, Artillery, Cavalry, and Aeronautics), and Services (consisting of Administrative, Technical, and Supply functions). At theater headquarters, called G.H.Q., the Board called for a chief for each of the combat arms, to act as the focus for the technical development of each of the combat arms.[8]

The Superior Board's report then presented "tactical lessons of this war" for each of the arms and services. For Infantry, the Board postulated that this arm will be dominant in future war as it was in the war just concluded. Future tactics would, according to the Board, be similar to those employed by the AEF; however, the Board noted that the theater of the next war might not be bound by oceans, thus allowing for envelopment of the enemy's defenses. The Board deplored the tactic of "artillery attack," which it stated was the primary method of "limited objective" attack on the Western Front during 1915, 1916, and 1917. The Board also condemned the lack of aggressiveness and initiative which prevailed on the front at that time as well. For the Infantry to be aggressive, and not dependent upon the other arms, soldiers must be well-trained in time of peace—a standard which the board admitted was unlikely to be achieved. Ignoring criticisms of the great size of the U.S. combat division in the last war, the Board recommended that this organization remain about the same. It did recommend more automatic weapons in forward units, especially machine guns organized for offensive combat, and improvement in infantry cannon. The Board also strongly recommended that the tank be recognized as "an infantry weapon," incapable of decisive independent action. "There is no such thing as an independent tank attack!" said the Board. A separate tank branch was rejected by the Board; however, tanks should be assigned to G.H.Q., available for attachment to armies, corps, and divisions as each situation indicates.[9]

Calling for the assignment of an Air Squadron of 10 planes for each Infantry Division, the Board came down strongly in favor of assigning aerial weapons to the field army and its subordinate organizations. "Nothing so far brought out in the war shows that Aerial activities can be carried on, independently of ground troops, to such an extent as to materially affect the conduct of the war as a whole," concluded the Board. The Board assigned reconnaissance aircraft to division and corps, and tactical combat aircraft and bombing aircraft to corps and army.[10]

With respect to artillery, the Superior Board confirmed the judgments of the Hero Board. Recommending that measures be taken for better cooperation with the other combat arms by habitual commitment of the same units to work with each other, the Board agreed that provisions must be made for single guns to accompany infantry in certain cases, possibly by tractor transport. The report also called for artillery liaison officers to "move with the infantry commanders to keep the guns informed of the infantry needs"; however, like the Hero Report, it did not specifically address forward observers to adjust fire from the forward positions. The report does refer to "forward observation stations," but these are a far cry from a system for adjusting artillery by artillery officers from the infantry positions. Calling for more motorization for all but the heaviest artillery in the future, the report generally recommended acquisition of artillery with longer ranges. The report also called for development of anti-aircraft artillery, based on the ad hoc systems of the AEF. To better coordinate ammunition supply, the report recommended that the artillery assume this function entirely from the Ordnance Corps.[11]

Like most senior officers in the AEF, the members of the Superior Board could not bring themselves to recommend elimination of the horse cavalry. Admitting that the cavalry charge was little used on the Western Front, the Board went into some detail to show when and how it was used elsewhere. "When the detailed history of [campaigns] is written," predicted the Board, ". . . more use was made of cavalry than at present is generally supposed...also, many opportunities for important achievements [by cavalry] were missed...The Board sees no reason for change in the American conception of the tactical employment of cavalry." The Board then described an organization of future cavalry up to division.[12]

The Board made many good recommendations for organization of administrative and logistical services for the theater and field army in future war. These reflect primarily the experiences of the SOS in the war. There were some offhand complaints of rear-area services as to their being misused or given less than the respect they deserved. For example, the Engineers complained that engineer units should not be routinely considered as reserve infantry.[13] The Board attached recommendations of other combat arms and services to the report; these attachments were similar in summaries and recommendations to those in Pershing's final report.[14]

As memories of the combined struggle faded, relations between the AEF and the French soured in association. Pershing rejected Foch's order for American units to assist in the rehabilitation of France, by filling in trenches, rolling up barbed wire, and reconstructing roads. "It would be unjust, and even criminal . . . to use our soldiers as laborers," he said. This disagreement began a period of testiness between French and American commanders, ill feeling which ultimately extended down the ranks. "The French," Pershing said to Haig, "have never once said a word of thanks or complimented the American troops for what they had done . . . The Americans would never forget the bad treatment which they had received from the French, and it was difficult to exaggerate the feeling of dislike for the French which existed in the American army."[15]

The terms of the Armistice required Germany to evacuate all territory in Belgium, Luxemburg, and France, including Alsace-Lorraine. The Germans were also required to withdraw their military forces east of the Rhine River. The agreement provided that the Allies be permitted to occupy three bridgeheads across the Rhine, the French at Mayence (Mainz), the Americans at Coblenz, and the British at Cologne, each bridgehead to be 18 miles in radius. A neutral zone six miles in depth was to be established along the east bank of the Rhine and around the perimeters of each of the bridgeheads, in which neither the Allies nor the Germans would station troops (see Map 8, page 147). On 7 November 1918, General Pershing activated the Third Army, with Major General Joseph T. Dickman (former Commander of I Corps) as commander. On 14 November, this army was designated as the Army of Occupation. Initially, this army consisted of III Corps with the 2d, 32d, and 42d Divisions, and the IV Corps with the 1st, 3d, and 4th Divisions. On 22 November, the army was increased with the assignment of the VII Corps containing 5th, 89th, and 90th Divisions.[16]

The withdrawal of the German armies and the advance of the Allies to their bridgeheads were delayed a week by German disputations of terms of the Armistice. Under pressure of an imminent Allied offensive, the Germans withdrew in good order, and the Allied advance to the Rhine was begun on 17 November 1918 (see Map 9, page 148). Considering the organizational and logistical difficulties in moving and sustaining the Third Army and associated elements, with a total strength of 287,975, the advance was accomplished smoothly. The American advance passed through Luxemburg City on 21 November, arriving at the German border on 23 November. The troops were in good spirits, buoyed by the wild demonstrations of the liberated French and Luxemburgians. The Allies paused on the German frontier to allow the Germans forces to clear the area west of the Rhine, then began their advance into Germany on 1 December. The German populace was curious but generally undemonstrative as the Americans passed through the towns. The leading elements of the Third Army arrived at the Rhine on 9 December. The Allies crossed the Rhine on the thirteenth, with III Corps of Third Army crossing at and below Coblenz to occupy the American Zone; the corps completed its occupation of the zone on 14 December. IV Corps and VII Corps took up positions in Germany west of the Rhine in a 50-mile-wide zone held by Third Army from the German border to the Rhine. The U.S. Second Army assumed responsibility, primarily for security of transport and logistics facilities, in a zone of similar size in Luxemburg from the western frontier of Germany to France.[17]

Uppermost in the minds of nearly all of the 2,000,000 men in the AEF immediately after the Armistice was the desire to return home. Despite Foch's desire to retain 15 U.S. divisions in France during the first months of 1919, when the Germans were refusing to sign the peace treaty, Pershing continued to report to him the departure of divisions of the AEF as quickly as shipping became available. For the approximately one million soldiers who had months to wait for transport, a vigorous program of athletics, entertainment, travel, and education was offered. AEF sports teams competed against teams from 18 Allied and friendly nations in the Inter-Allied Games sponsored by the AEF. Two hundred and thirty thousand soldiers enrolled in education programs ranging from primary education, through trade school, to university classes. Over 8,000 officers and men attended European universities through AEF sponsorship. Men took leave to visit Great Britain, Belgium and Italy, and that part of Germany occupied by the Allies.[18]

With respect to the soldiers shipping home, Pershing demanded sharp appearance and high military discipline. He was vehement on the subject of the health of soldiers returning home. Although about one soldier in 20 had venereal disease upon entering service, Pershing desired that none be so infected upon discharge. He preached a high moral standard to troops awaiting shipment home, and he demanded frequent medical inspections of soldiers due to depart. Depart they did; the monthly rate of return in 1919 exceeding the highest rate of arrival during the previous year. By May of 1919, all combat divisions of the AEF in France had departed or were processing to do so. In August 1919, the 1st Division, the first to arrive in France, departed for home. Five divisions remained in occupation duty in Germany in 1919, but with the dissolution of

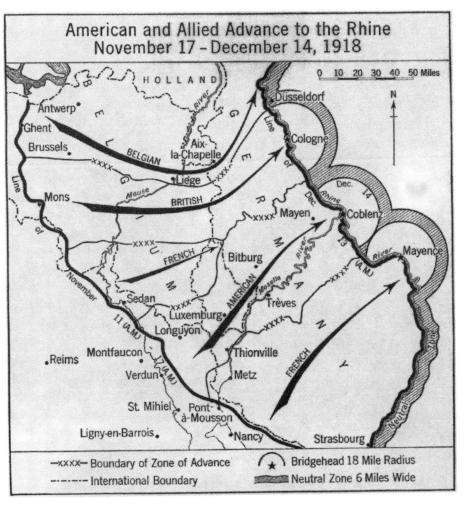

Map 8. Allied Advance to the Rhine.

U.S. Army in the World War, Washington: GPO, 1948.

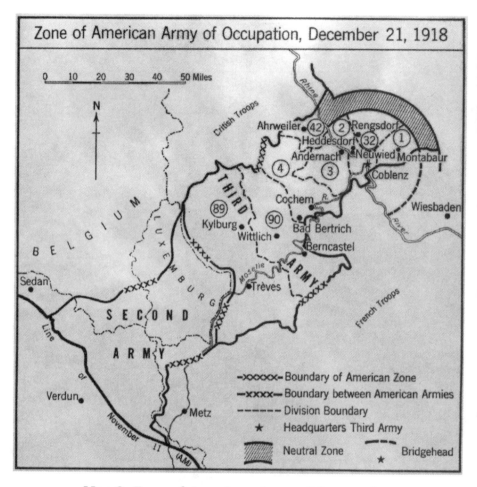

Map 9. Zone of American Army of Occupation.

U.S. Army in the World War. Washington: GPO, 1948.

Third Army on 2 July 1919, most of these began moving to the French ports. Replacing Third Army, American Forces in Germany, at a strength of 6,800, was formed. These forces remained in occupation on the Rhine until January 1923, when the last American flag on the Rhine was lowered, and the area turned over to the French. As far as America was concerned, The Great War, The War for Humanity, The War to Save the World for Democracy, the War to End all Wars had ended.[19]

9

IN RETROSPECT

Although the government and people of the United States had turned away from supporting the noble endeavor which had brought the AEF to France, there was every reason for the American people to be proud of the effective military force which their fighting, work, and sacrifice had deployed upon the Western Front in a short time: Of the 2,084,000 American soldiers who had reached France before the Armistice, 1,390,000 saw active service at the front. Of the forty-two United States divisions that had reached France, twenty-nine took part in active combat service. Seven of these were Regular Army divisions, eleven were from the National Guard, and eleven were organized as part of the National Army. Draftees made up the bulk of the soldiers in all of these divisions.

The American army had a total of two hundred days in battle and engaged in thirteen major operations. From the middle of August until the end of the war, the American divisions actually held a bigger part of the front than that held by the British during the same period. During October and November, American divisions occupied 134 kilometers of the southern portion of the Allied line (21 percent of the Western Front). On 1 April 1918, the Central Powers possessed a superiority on the Western Front of 324,000 riflemen. As a result of the arrival of American reinforcements, Allied strength exceeded that of the Germans in June and was more than 600,000 over the enemy strength by the time of the Armistice.

American battle losses in this war were 50,280 killed and 205,690 wounded. These were heavy losses, considering the short period of intensive fighting for the Americans; they are small, however, when compared with the 7,485,000 lost by the Allies during the four years at which they were at war. The European belligerents had killed nearly a whole generation of their young men.[1]

The Meuse-Argonne Campaign lasted forty-seven days. A total of 1,200,000 Americans were engaged in the campaign, of which 850,000 were combat troops. Twenty-two American divisions were engaged in the battle; 2,417 artillery pieces supported this fighting, firing a total of more than four million shells (a greater tonnage of ammunition than was used by Union forces during the entire five years of the American Civil War). The American ground battle was supported by 840 airplanes, most of these manufactured by the Allies. In addition, 324 tanks also supported the American campaign in the Meuse-Argonne; all of these tanks were of Allied manufacture, and many were manned by Allied troops. The AEF claimed to have drawn to the Meuse-Argonne a total of 44 enemy divisions; this figure was disputed by the Allies and could hardly be proven. The First Army reported the capture of 26,000 prisoners of war in this campaign, though other statisticians cite only 16,000. They also listed the capture of 874 artillery pieces and over 3,000 machine guns.[2] The First Army claimed to have inflicted 100,000 enemy casualties, at a cost of 117,000 American casualties.[3]

With regard to costs of the war, the total expenditure of the United States came to thirty-three billion dollars, of which ten billion were lent to the Allied nations. The United States spent about two million dollars per hour during its period of war. This cost was about equal to that of Great Britain and Germany, and one third greater than the cost to France in dollar equivalents. However, the cost to the United States was only 14 percent of its estimated prewar wealth, while the cost to Great Britain, for example, was 44 percent of its prewar wealth.[4]

Following the celebrations and parades came Allied criticisms and deprecations of the importance of the American effort on the Western Front and of performance of the AEF in battle. The Allies definitely wanted to "play down" the significance of the American military contribution to the victory of the alliance. The writer David Kennedy makes the point that Wilson himself recognized "Pershing's modest military successes against Germany had given him little diplomatic leverage on the Allies."[5] To demonstrate by statistics the importance of the effort by the United States, AEF Headquarters, in its postwar report, concluded that the presence of "fresh" American divisions on the Western Front was the main factor leading the Germans to accept a settlement.[6]

In Appendix 3 a tabular representation of the report of the status of divisions on the Western Front on 11 November can be found. The summary makes the point that of the thirty fully equipped American divisions in France, seven were considered to be in good condition, their strength equalling fourteen divisions of the other contestants. The other Allies had fifty-seven divisions considered to be "fresh," while the Germans were estimated to have a total of only forty-nine divisions considered to be in good condition. The table also shows that the Allies, on 11 November, had 127 divisions in reserve, while the Germans/Austrians on the same date had a total of only 41.[7]

In considering the relative manpower strength of the Allies, augmented by the tremendous American presence, compared to the Germans, one must take into account the fact that the Germans had succeeded in withdrawing their forces, in good order, along their line of communications to a front that was 150 kilometers shorter than that which existed during the height of the 1918 German advance. If they had had to continue the war, they would have been able to stand on the defensive anchored on the difficult terrain of the Ardennes; they should have been able to put up a creditable defense against Allied attacks from there.[8]

How effective were the Americans in combat, as compared to the Allies and to their enemies? The Allies were critical of the Americans' performance, partly for reasons that would serve their own military and political ends. However, in their secret official reports to their headquarters, Allied observers were equally critical of the Americans from a professional standpoint. A French military report in October of 1918 stated that American troops under Allied command "have done splendidly," but, "owing to inexperience, particularly in the higher ranks, American divisions ... under their own command, suffer wastage out of all proportion to results achieved." The blame for this state of affairs was laid to Pershing's "insistence on the premature formation of large American armies."[9] A British official report of 21 October 1918 declared that:

> the American Army is disorganized, ill-equipped and ill-trained with very few non-commissioned officers and officers of experience. It has suffered severely through ignorance of modern war and it must take at least a year before it becomes a serious fighting force.[10]

Marshal Haig made a similar judgment, but withdrew the statement when challenged by Pershing.[11] It is difficult to refute such professional condemnations of American leadership—unless one rejects all criticism of the AEF as biased, which this author does not. In responding to questions concerning the American battlefield performance, about half of this author's correspondents tended to give the Americans credit for greater combat effectiveness than did the Allied leaders at the time of the appearance of the AEF in battle. Inexperience was the deficiency most often cited.

The British author of military histories, Correlli Barnett, made the point that the Americans were probably equally as good in 1918 as were the Allied troops in 1915.[12] Barnett's comment was echoed by Peter Simkins, Historian of the Imperial War Museum, with the proviso that such a comparison can be faulted by dozens of exceptions. The similarities between the Kitchener Divisions on the Western Front in 1915 (about which Simkins has made a four-year study) and the AEF in 1918 is worth noting. Both had been given poor and inappropriate training and most performed poorly in early combat, he stated. However, a few of the Kitchener Divisions did very well on The Somme, in 1916. What many of the Kitchener Divisions possessed was a "social cohesion"—units such as the "Pals Battalions," which came from small neighborhoods or specific industries. Simkins posited that such social commonality gave esprit, competitiveness, and moral support to these men, enabling these units to hold up in combat better than others, despite their poor training. The Dominion divisions had similar spirit and seemed eager to prove their worth and their superiority over the English organizations. It may be postulated that the Dominion units were better in combat than English units because of their pride in their uniqueness. Simkins made the point, however, that a study of social cohesion and its contribution to morale and combat effectiveness remains to be made.[13]

Some who observed the AEF in early combat gave similar evaluations to U.S. National Guard Divisions, for similar reasons. Some guard divisions, notably the 28th and the 42nd, did indeed do as well as any division called "regular"; others were rated poor in leadership and discipline. Captain Frank W. Showman, who commanded Company H, 110th Infantry of the 28th Division during the campaign, stated, "The National Guard proved that they could fight as well as the Regular Army. We are proud of the 28th."[14] Any rating in this regard is subject to the questioning of the rater's prejudice; such prejudice is, unfortunately, easier to document than to discount in any rating.

Returning to the rating of the AEF, the military author and analyst Trevor Dupuy maintained that the Americans were the best soldiers on the Western Front in 1918, all the others being spent.[15] George Marshall reflected his and Pershing's opinions in a postwar article in *Infantry Journal:* "The Americans who fought only at St. Mihiel and the Meuse-Argonne will probably never realize the vast difference between the enemy then and the German of April or May."[16] Marshall's point can be translated to a general postulate: excessive personnel losses in combat units can more than offset capabilities gained by the combat experience. This statement can be applied to Allied armies as well as to those of the Germans. In commenting on problems of the AEF, the historian Allan Millett noted that all armies had and still have problems displacing artillery and moving supplies;

however, veteran organizations perform better than "green" units.[17] This author agrees substantially with the above comments, as a result of his research and combat experience. Fighting capability may decline as the number and quality of replacements diminish, but administrative and logistical infrastructure generally improves with experience.

Combat performance results from the interaction of a great many factors; among these are leadership, training, experience, physical condition, and unit spirit (or esprit). Using statistics supplied by the AEF, it is interesting to attempt an evaluation of the "veteran" divisions as against the relatively inexperienced ones.[18] Statistics on the number of days spent by each division of the AEF in quiet sectors of the line and in active military operations are shown in Appendix 4. This chart confirms the very natural assumption that those American divisions that had arrived in France the earliest had the most time in combat, the 1st Division, the first to arrive in Europe, having had the most combat time. However, some divisions, notably the 3rd, 27th, and 30th, had all of their front line time in active combat, extending over periods of about two months; the 36th and 80th Divisions were in active combat for their entire experience, which totaled one month each.

The distance advanced against enemy forces by each division is graphically indicated in Appendix 5. A relatively good match can be made between the lengths of the bar graphs for each division in Appendixes 4 and 5, which generally indicates that those divisions with the longest period in active combat advanced the farthest. The distance advanced, however, has a great deal to do with the nature of the ground being traversed, the strength and effectiveness of the opposing enemy forces, and the mission (offensive or defensive) given to each division. The graph shows that the 77th National Army Division, whose ranks were filled largely by draftees from New York City and vicinity, made the longest advance; it also did some of the toughest fighting. Dividing miles advanced by the number of days in active combat shows the 42nd Division slightly higher than the 77th in miles advanced per active day (.87 to .67 miles per day). In this comparison, both the 42nd and 77th rank well ahead of the 1st and 2nd Divisions. Again, the point is made here that these indicators are inadequate, in themselves, as a means to rate the combat capabilities of an organization.[19]

One reasonable criterion of combat success is the number of awards for valor in action given to combat units. Individuals are generally so rated. The chart at Appendix 6 shows this breakout for the Congressional Medal of Honor (the highest decoration given by the United States government for military action) and for the Distinguished Service Cross (the second highest award given for combat action). While it may be argued that the award of decorations is very much a consequence of location, timing, and luck, as well as command policy, it is this author's opinion that awards are, in general, fairly representative of combat effectiveness, and by their number reflect a degree of unit performance as well. In this criterion the 2nd Division is highest, followed by the 1st and 3rd. Appendix 7 lists casualties by division. Again, it may be argued that the number of casualties is as indicative of enemy proficiency as it is of friendly, and that it may even indicate poor unit performance, leading to excessive casualties. However, this author's research and experience lead him to sense a positive relationship between casualties and unit combat effectiveness. Those units that perform well are given, unfortunately, the harder tasks, and they are given these more frequently than other units. This was true for the Meuse-Argonne Campaign. Thus, over time, the higher standards of these units led to higher casualties. The chart at Appendix 8 shows the number of prisoners of war (POWs) captured by each division in the AEF. With the aforementioned reservations, it is affirmed here that a relatively direct relationship exists between numbers of POWs captured and combat proficiency.

For the purposes of determining the degree of relationship among these factors, the figures for each division in each category, except time in combat, have been juxtaposed upon a graph in Appendix 9. Although there are many exceptions in specific categories, the chart shows a positive relationship of each of these categories to the total. The eighteen highest scoring divisions are shown on the chart. The totals, unfactored, yield a ranking of: 2nd Division, 1st, 3rd, 26th, 42nd, 32nd—in that order. Factoring by days in active combat yields this ranking: 2, 42nd, 26th, 28th, 1st and 77th. It is readily admitted that these gross figures give far greater numerical import to casualties and prisoners of war than to other categories. However, factoring and weighting each category does not change the ranking order significantly. These ratings appear to be in line with the subjective judgments of those observers of the AEF in combat and those historians who have made qualitative comment, including this author. Pershing and his associates would likely reject the high rating of the 26th National Guard Division from New England, and that of the 77th National Army Division from New York, and so does this author. These divisions rank high primarily because of unique circumstances under which they suffered.[20]

One may conclude from these few rankings that the Regular Army divisions and those of the National Guard performed generally better than those of the National Army. Since all divisions were filled with draftees at the lower levels of rank, the discriminator in combat performance may be in leadership. Experienced leaders at all levels were assigned to the units deploying early; the numbers of experienced leaders available for assignment thinned out considerably as the pace of deployment accelerated in the spring of 1918. Thus, one may also make the unsurprising conclusion that units performed well, in part, according to the degree of military experience possessed by their leaders. Not a great deal of difference can be found in the performance indicators for National Guard organizations and those of the Regular Army using this gross method. An extension of this examination might provide an argument for the American "Militia System" versus a large regular military establishment. Such examination may have some relevance to the ongoing debates about downsizing the U.S. Army since the end of the Cold War.

Considering, again, these criteria, the British Expeditionary Forces (BEF) far outstripped the AEF in time in combat and ground gained for the same period. They and the French gave fewer awards, however; thus they would show up less well in that category. In terms of casualties, one can judge that for the personnel involved in the war during this period, the American figures were the highest. Also, as Smythe noted, the British captured twice as many guns and nearly four times the number of POWs as the Americans. The AEF staff did not make a national statistical comparison—and it is just as well they didn't.[21]

Attempts at finite measurements of relative combat proficiency suffer from a plethora of unquantifiables, as noted by General Theodore Conway and the historians Edward Coffman and Theodore Ropp, in responding to some of this author's questions. John Keegan, in his book, *Six Armies in Normandy,* found a distinct cultural bias in national armies that predisposes the way they fight; in his comments to this author, Keegan reflected on the complex nature of any qualitative judgments. Pershing himself rejected the AEF comparisons as invalid.[22]

The efficiency of the AEF Headquarters may be more readily evaluated, as it was the subject of debate ever since the headquarters began operations. Marshall took pride in the output of the overworked staff of which he was a key director. However, even he commented upon the inflexibility and the inexperience of the hundreds of staff officers placed in responsible positions.[23] Allied observers were vociferous in criticizing the AEF staff for poor management of human and material resources, particularly citing the logistical tangles that occurred early in the Meuse-Argonne Campaign. This criticism was also reflected in reports of visitors from the War Department.[24] Pershing blamed the War Department Headquarters for having failed to coordinate with and to respond to his requests and guidance.[25] The War Department blamed Pershing for trying to manage too large and complex an organization.[26] Each was justified in criticizing the other! John Toland, author of *No Man's Land*, sympathizes with the overworked AEF staff, citing the adverse weather conditions and restrictive terrain that affected planning; but he did judge the AEF staff's planning and staff actions as "second rate."[27] The British author Correlli Barnett blamed the clumsiness of AEF staff work on their inexperience, "a condition facing all hastily expanded forces."[28] James Rainey agreed with Barnett's judgment.[29] Gordon Brook-Shepherd, author of *November 1918: The Last Act of the Great War*, commenting on AEF staffwork, concluded that the great problem of the AEF was certainly logistical.[30] Donald Smythe declared that there were at least two occasions when the AEF and its First Army were in a state of virtual paralysis (the last days of September and mid-October 1918).[31] AEF staff were at least partly to blame for that condition. Commenting specifically upon First Army staff, Edward Coffman noted that "First Army planners were gambling that the sheer weight of numbers they committed in the Meuse-Argonne would achieve the breakthrough."[32] The fact that the army's headquarters was a new organization when it directed the Meuse-Argonne Campaign could explain their failings; however, most officers assigned to First Army's staff had had staff experience in the theater. Allan Millett made a key observation: "If the First Army staff can be faulted, it is for underestimating the limitations of its troops."[33] Timothy Nenninger, whose text, *The Leavenworth Schools and the Old Army*, dealt with command and staff training and experience, added another key point:

> The remoteness of general staff officers from the combat troops . . . led to operations orders based on incomplete information, especially on the conditions and capability of the troops to carry out the assigned missions. Consequently, operational demands were made that could not be fulfilled.[34]

These are key points. While noting these problems, Russell Weigley stated, "American staff work was remarkably good considering our newness to large-scale war."[35] In general, the historians Theodore Ropp and Irving Holley, Jr. echoed Weigley's judgment.[36]

This author concludes that the comments made about the AEF staff are generally correct. The staffs produced adequate orders, directives, instructions, and other guidance—perhaps too much paper guidance to be of value to commanders in intensive combat. They did not give enough thought to problems that might occur in executing these plans and orders. Probably, there was not enough time for "wargaming" each major plan, but the staff should have done a better job in anticipating operational constraints, communications failures, logistical chokepoints, and enemy reactions. They should have asked themselves and each other, "What if . . . ?"

The AEF staffs did not master the techniques of forward positioning of support and supplies, automatic resupply and evacuation, alternate transport, task organization and reorganization, and the full employment of the massive combat power available to them. They operated in an *ad hoc* experimental fashion throughout the campaign. Chronically short of transportation, forced to buy or borrow aircraft, tanks, supporting weapons, and equipment, saddled with management problems that would have strained even the most experienced of Allied headquarters, the staffs met and overcame most of their challenges by hard work, sheer willpower, and improvisation upon encountering obstacles. They improved daily; however, General Harbord said after the war that had the Armistice not occurred when it did, the AEF would have had to cease fighting until its logistical problems could be solved.[37]

The initial strategic plan for employment of the AEF from the St. Mihiel area, driving east in the direction of Metz, was a good strategic concept. Probably, the fortified zone around Metz was too tough a bastion for the fledgling First Army to have seized, as Liggett judged; an early assault that far east in isolation from the Allied main thrust may have provoked a disastrous defeat, as Rainey theorized.[38]

However, the AEF could have broken out of the St. Mihiel area to the northeast, on the axis Etain-Longuyon, created a Second Army at that time to tie in with the First Army, while the Second echeloned east of the Meuse, and advanced on a broad, new front, against the very vitals of the Laon Bulge held by the Germans. Ludendorff stated after the war that had the Americans launched such an attack, he would have been compelled to make a general withdrawal of all forces in the bulge.[39] Pershing stated after the war that this was just what he wanted to do.[40] Positioned well, as they were at St. Mihiel, the AEF could have launched, expanded, and supported a broad offensive on this axis. If this American offensive had been even partially successful, it would have cut off the prospect of retreat for the southern armies of the Central Powers; in any case, it would have required the Germans to reinforce quickly and to make a major defensive effort on their southern flank, thus easing the situation for Allied advances elsewhere on the front.

Assuming, however, that Haig and Foch were correct in August 1918, in changing direction of the American offensive in order to make it converge with those of the British and French in the Mezieres area, why did Pershing not opt to launch his main attack east of the Meuse in the more negotiable terrain of the Woevre Valley? It is likely that when Foch first discussed with Pershing abandoning the St. Mihiel Campaign, he was mainly interested in securing American divisions for the French operation along the Aisne. The right pincer of Foch's grand envelopment was drawn along the west of the Meuse, as Foch said, to give that pincer a relatively secure flank. Foch also dismissed Pershing's offer to operate the American army entirely east of the Meuse, saying there were "no communications." This author has conducted a detailed reconnaissance of the area east of the Meuse, flanking the area in which First Army attacked. True, the hills are higher, but the valleys are wider and the trafficability is fair. At the time of the American offensive, the roadways on the east of the Meuse were more extensive and in better condition than on the west. Foch may have been concerned that the Meuse was, at that time, unfordable; Pershing may have also considered the unfordable river an obstacle to operations on both sides of the river. But there were many bridges, the river is fordable in many places, and the AEF was strong enough to support operations east and west of the river, in any case. Reviewing the Allied demands and Pershing's counterproposals of late August-early September 1918, this author gains the impression that Pershing, under terrible pressure to accept one of a number of undesirable alternatives, opted to take the Meuse-Argonne area because it appeared to be the only choice open to him for employment of an American army, from the tenor of Foch's discussion.[41] Having accepted that area, Pershing was, possibly, reluctant to suggest modification or expansion of the zone, since such a proposal might result in a reopening of the earlier issue of splitting American forces. The mission accepted, Pershing focused his attention straight ahead. Once surprise was lost, attrition of the defenders was the only means of advancing. As noted earlier, Pershing even described the First Army's mission: "to draw enemy forces to our sector and consume them."[42] However, a commander cannot consume more enemy forces than his own by direct assault on strong defenses; the German General Erich von Falkenhayn discovered this fallacy at Verdun in 1916.

An offensive strategy based on the attrition of an enemy in strong defenses is really no strategy at all. In the First World War, technology had given a primacy to the forces in defense. It is understandable that there was a nadir in strategic innovation, confronted, as the belligerents were, with a deadlock in France with no land flanks to turn. One could criticize the Allies, who controlled the sea, for not using it to envelop the northern flank of the German front with an invasion behind their lines.[43] But ship transport was slow, communications limited, and the Germans could have reinforced within their perimeter faster than the Allies could from without. It is fair to criticize the American military leadership for not bringing their power to bear over a broader front in France.

This critique now turns to AEF tactics in the Meuse-Argonne Campaign. In the main, there weren't any tactics employed. Committing hundreds of thousands of infantrymen in a narrow zone directly against heavily fortified and defended positions guaranteed high casualties and small gains. The zone should have been adjusted and expanded, allowing for more flexibility in advance and maneuver. The left boundary of First Army was mainly within the tortuous fortified maze of the Argonne Forest. The French Fourth Army was supposed to operate along the left and provide a "liaison detachment" to maintain contact with the Americans. This was a bad arrangement, and it did not work: First Army's left flank was often open, and contact between the First Army and the French Fourth Army was made only sporadically. It is generally bad attack tactics to divide a major defensive position between two forces that are not under the same battlefield commander. Pershing should have arranged to include the Argonne and its western approaches within his sector, or to have shifted his sector east, giving the entire forest to the French Fourth Army, as Foch desired him to do after the battle had commenced.

In a similar vein, it has already been argued that the AEF should have launched a major offensive east of the Meuse. This author walked the commanding terrain in the region, asking himself, why did Pershing, or his subordinate commanders not move to the flanks, particularly the right flank of the First Army's zone, to break out of the killing cauldron of enemy fires? During these walks, a hypothesis formed on this vexing question, and it is offered as just that: Pershing, and his subordinates, in the heat of battle, were afflicted with a myopia which could be called "Battlefield Fixation." There are many examples in history of commanders who focus on the killing zone because the enemy is also focused therein. General Robert E. Lee at Gettysburg is one example which comes to mind. Pressed by General James Longstreet to break off the battle and envelop the Union forces around the strategic flank connecting them to Washington, Lee said, "The enemy is there, General Longstreet (indicating Cemetery Ridge), and there I am going to strike him."[44]

A summary critique of the conduct of the Meuse-Argonne Offensive itself is appropriate at this juncture, before the smoke of battle clears from this book. The criteria for the performance of a modern armed force in the field is that it be able to shoot, move, and communicate. Inherent in that simplification is the ability to deliver fire effectively, to maneuver to destroy the enemy, to seize terrain, and to communicate in order to orchestrate both fire and movement. Judged by even these simple criteria, the performance of the First Army in the Meuse-Argonne must be given a fairly low rating. With respect to shooting, over four million artillery shells were expended in the contested area. However, the artillery was poorly employed. For a variety of reasons, human and natural, the artillery did not displace forward swiftly enough to continue giving support to the attacking infantry. While it was in position, it tended to move its rolling barrages forward too swiftly for the rate of infantry movement in difficult terrain, and it continued to fire upon prearranged targets, rather than shifting to engage "targets of opportunity" discovered during the attack. The artillery used too few foot-mobile forward observers accompanying the advancing infantry commanders; the artillery fired too often solely by map coordinates. This method of adjustment of fires limited the support of attacking infantry. This failing was at least partly due to poor communications. Effective adjustment of artillery fire in support of attacking infantry requires mobile communications; radios were, as noted, heavy and fragile, and were generally left in the rear. Fires were adjusted by using telephone lines, which nearly as often as radio went out. Signals for shifting fire were given by a complex code of colored flares; in the smoke and other obscurations of battle these were often not seen or misinterpreted. One of the main problems in artillery support was the adherence of artillery commanders, and their fire-direction centers, to standardized procedures and mathematical formulae. While these procedures enabled relatively precise computation of indirect parabola for insuring that fires were delivered on desired targets, the system inhibited the flexible shifting of fires to strike enemies who appeared where they were not expected to be.

Infantry and artillery commanders can also be faulted for their infrequent use of smoke to screen movements, and their reluctance to use poison gas to disable enemy artillery and reserves. Pershing was very desirous of using more gas, in order to break the enemy's defenses and allow for the open warfare he desired.[45] In his study "Gas Warfare in World War I," Rexmond Cochrane concluded that, until the 1 November offensive, American corps and lower commanders did not use much gas to support their attacks. He believed that the commanders feared retaliation by gas fired by the enemy, and they particularly declined to use persistent gases because they feared these gases would injure their troops as they advanced.[46] But the Germans were already using gas against the Americans—the most effective use of gas during the entire war, according to Liddell Hart.[47] Cochrane also showed that the AEF did not employ smoke efficiently. Smoke was not delivered in sufficient volume nor for periods long enough to provide effective screening. Commanders had no experience with either gas or smoke and used them poorly, according to Cochrane.[48] These criticisms were echoed by Charles Heller in his study "Chemical Warfare in World War I." Heller believed that American revulsion at the use of poison gas resulted in our being unprepared to engage in chemical warfare when we joined the war. Heller told of the poor training provided the personnel of the Ist U.S. Gas Regiment, and the departure of the unit for France "without gas masks"![49]

A major problem affecting all others was the failure to maintain communications, front-to-rear and especially rear-to-front. In military organizations, then and now, the responsibility for maintaining communications is upon the higher headquarters to establish and maintain contact with its lower unit headquarters. In the Meuse-Argonne, commanders were often out of contact with their subordinates. Thus they did not maintain control of the battle nor give good, continuing support to their units in attack. The higher headquarters were much too far in the rear to appreciate the conditions encountered by the fighting troops and commanders. Reliance on long telephone lines, laid across the ground as units advanced, pinned higher commanders to their headquarters, while the movement of troops, animals, and vehicles across the wires and the bursting of artillery often knocked out the wire connections. As mentioned, the radios, called "wireless," were heavy, unreliable, and of limited range in the rugged terrain and wet weather.

Major headquarters used motor messengers, air delivery of messages, and carrier pigeons. Units moving in battle used flares to signal for support. But, in general, units sent messengers back and forth, mostly on foot in the forward areas. These messengers often as not got lost or were turned back by encounters with enemy personnel or fire. As with other bearers of bad news, the messengers also appeared to change the messages to allow the messengers' units to avoid dangerous missions. The result was that there was not much command influence during a fight; combat communications were a problem for all the armies at the time. Still, the Germans and the Allies controlled and supported their combat forces better than did the AEF, using the same state-of-the-art means. The difference appears to be related to experience in planning for interruptions, and planning for alternate means of communications.[50]

Insufficient attention was given to solving the problem of moving supplies over no man's land, despite the recurrence of this problem throughout the campaign. Combat units frequently had to send guides to the rear to find and lead food and ammunition supply parties to their units. Scanning some 5,000 responses of veterans of World War I to the MHI Questionnaire mentioned earlier, this author noticed that nearly half mentioned being hungry during the fighting because their food supplies did not come forward. (A summary of these comments is in Appendix 10; comments will be made on these later in this critique.)[51]

A great many of the veterans commented about the lack of resupply of water. Although it rained frequently, water sources were often under fire; some sources had been poisoned or polluted, and, again, water supplies did not get forward regularly. Many of the veterans complained of being sick or wounded and of not being promptly evacuated from the fighting. Those who could walk usually made their way to aid stations in the rear. Many had to wait until the attack moved forward and medical aides could get to them. Many died waiting.

These problems could have been partly resolved by prior planning for automatic resupply and by evacuation of wounded by returning supply parties. Knowing that the soldiers were going to be in intensive combat, resupply of ammunition, food, and other expendables should have been started forward as soon as the attackers jumped off. Supplies should have been stocked well forward, even if some were destroyed by fire. Some of these procedures were taken by the AEF late in the war, but not enough attention was given to these problems.

It has been mentioned that influenza was a great killer, and the cause of most of the attrition of front-line strength in the AEF in France. A great many of the veteran respondees complained of dysentery, and most complained of being cold, wet, lice-infested and otherwise ill. While being cold and wet is a natural condition for a soldier in battle, treatment for illness, even by the medical standards of those days, was rather primitive in the AEF. Dr. Claude Moore, former surgeon at the AEF General Hospital in Langres, France, remembers that the normal treatment of a wounded man was to clean the wound, sew up the opening, and hope for the best. The treatment for influenza and other respiratory diseases was to pump out the lungs where there was fluid accumulation, then give the patients rest. Medical troops dealing with influenza cases wore gauze masks. However, according to Dr. Moore, it was the cold and somewhat drier weather of December that helped to end the influenza epidemic shortly after the Armistice.[52]

Commanders at all levels of the AEF are also criticized herein for failure to employ reserves properly during the Meuse-Argonne Campaign. Commanders appeared to utilize their reserves more to redeem failures, plugging the reserves behind units that were pinned down by fire, than to exploit successes by extending a successful advance. This option (reinforcing success) was limited by the restricted terrain and the narrow zone, but much more could have been done in the employment of reserves to outflank and turn enemy positions.

Until very late in the offensive, commanders did not properly employ close-support weapons, such as machine guns, trench mortars, and direct-fire artillery, in conjunction with the maneuver of attacking infantry. These weapons were positioned by commanders to support the beginning of an attack; then they were not ordered forward to continue support. It is only human that the personnel manning these support weapons continued their support from the relatively safe positions in the rear unless ordered and even driven forward.

Failure to use natural cover and concealment in approach to enemy defenses, infrequent movement and attack under cover of night—these failings also are charged to AEF commanders. General Mark Clark, commenting about the tactics of the AEF in which he served, said, "Each division was given a narrow sector, and it was just massed infantry stuff." General Theodore Conway remembered that General Omar Bradley and other veterans of the World War, in postwar discussions, often expressed criticism of the tactics employed by the AEF.[53]

The combat training of the AEF has already been reviewed herein. In summary, it is believed that such training was misdirected. It was not based upon effective tactics, and the training that was provided did not emphasize those combat techniques that would prepare a soldier to kill and to remain alive on a modern battlefield. The failure of the AEF to enunciate a sound, relevant tactical doctrine led to faulty, incomplete training for soldiers and their leaders. Allan Millett stated, "This uncertain emphasis denied small unit commanders the training necessary to provide fire support to attacking units, and to develop fire and maneuver."[54] Donald Smythe stated, "The key weapon in World War I was not the rifle, but the machine gun which killed many, and artillery which killed more. Against them, the American infantryman pitted raw courage, enthusiasm, inexperience, guts, some support from his auxiliary arms, and his own blood."[55] Pershing and his AEF trainers were correct in their criticism of the Allied leaders and soldiers for their failure to emphasize rifle marksmanship; they were incorrect in declaring the rifle to be the most effective weapon for the war they were preparing to fight. This failing must be placed clearly on the shoulders of John J. Pershing, not only because he was the Commander in Chief of the AEF, but also because he promulgated an erroneous doctrine and demanded adherence to it. Pershing took satisfaction in noting (in *My Experiences*) that the French finally admitted that he was right in emphasizing open warfare and the importance of the rifle.[56] However, Donald Smythe stated that Pershing's research assistant for *My Experiences* searched for over a month but could not find any statement to that effect by a French leader; neither could Smythe.[57] Of Pershing's doctrine, Liddell Hart said, "He thought he was spreading a new gospel of faith when actually it was an old faith exploded. That was the one flaw in the great structure he had built. It may even be said that he omitted but one factor from his calculations—German machine guns—and was right in all his calculations but one—their effect."[58]

Some understanding, even sympathy, can be gained for Pershing and his commanders in their attempts to develop doctrine for infantry attack through lethal defenses. From the period after the American Civil War, innovative military thinkers struggled with little success to devise tactics which could maximize, or neutralize, the effects of the mass-casualty-producing weaponry on the modern battlefield. Regarding that tactical dilemma, a book by Perry Jamieson, *Crossing the Deadly Ground: United States Army Tactics, 1865–1899*, catalogues the general belief in the U.S. Army in the late 19th century that the devastating firepower of improved direct-fire weapons and artillery made defense dominant on the battlefields of the future. Many military writers of the period immediately before World War I assayed the cost of "crossing the deadly ground" as prohibitive of success in any measure. Committees and boards examined this problem for the U.S. Army; these committees modified small-unit tactics, as these were described in the Field Service Regulations and in infantry manuals, to employ less-vulnerable dispersed formations.

A problem in spreading attack formations, which problem persists today, is the amount of dispersion between individual riflemen which can be achieved without sacrificing control of the attacking unit. The greater the spread of the attackers, the more difficult it becomes for the commander to exercise control. This was especially a difficult task for small-unit commanders in The Great War, as they had to communicate by voice and gestures in the roaring inferno of the enemy's final protective fires. Jamieson makes the point that this problem was partly solved with the development of the field radio. However, this author's pertinent experience leads to the conclusion that the problem of assault against final protective fires is even greater than one of control. It becomes very difficult to mass assault fires while attacking in spread formation; further, and more important, the spreading of individuals involved in a very dangerous action, assault against deadly fire, increases individual fear, and leads to faltering of movement forward, as the effect of group esprit it lost. Jamieson concludes that assaulting against modern defensive fires was a harrowing experience through World War I.[59] This author's later experience leads to the conclusion that the problem is as great today, and as unsolved by military tacticians, as it was at the turn of the century.[60]

Whatever the pressures upon the U.S. authorities and upon their general in the field, there was insufficient reason to send a man into battle untrained in his basic weapon. Of the 514 veterans of the Meuse-Argonne who commented upon training in response to the MHI questionnaire, nearly half spoke of poor training, and many specifically stated that they had not been trained in using the weapon they were given in France. Smythe cited a pithy summary on this matter by the American military author Harvey DeWeerd: "The AEF learned to fight through bitter experience, not through any legerdemain with the rifle."[61] That's the sum of it! This author wishes he'd said that.

Returning to the review of the campaign, this author offers comment upon the desire of senior AEF commanders to gain the assignment of cavalry to their forces. Richard Goldhurst, in his biography of Pershing, *Pipe Clay and Drill,* recorded that Pershing attempted, until the end of the war, to find ways to employ cavalry in an attack—this effort despite the terrible casualties that Allied cavalry had taken on the few occasions when they were committed, mounted, against machine guns in defense. Pershing's request for two cavalry divisions for the AEF was quietly pigeonholed by General March; that request did not come to light until many years after the war.[62]

Pershing and his "old army" associates were deprecatory about the value of the tank in warfare. It is true that tanks at that time were blind monsters, underpowered and frequently disabled. Pershing thought that their value was maximized by moving with and assisting the advance of infantry by clearing barbed wire obstacles. Pershing did establish a tank corps in the AEF; he also complained that he had too few tanks to support the infantry. But he did believe that the tank had a limited role. Pershing was an accomplished horseman, as were most of his associates. After the war, he solemnly dedicated a plaque in the War Department building to the memory of the horses and mules which died in the war.[63]

This attitude—love of the horse and disdain for its replacement, the tank—continued in the army until well into World War II. General Dwight Eisenhower recorded the fact that in 1920 he was forced to recant statements he had made in an article that he had co-authored with then-Colonel George Patton on the importance of the tank in future warfare. Eisenhower was told by the Chief of Infantry that he would refrain from any statement contrary to existing doctrine, which limited tanks to support of infantry, or face court-martial.[64] The purpose of citing these tactical precepts regarding cavalry and its successor arm, the tank, is to show that there was a mind-set on the part of General Pershing and his senior officers that changed very little, despite a great deal of bloody experience on the Western Front.

The prejudice against the tank was expressed by the old army officers equally against the airplane. Perhaps this was because the early advocates of air power were brash young men who tended to view themselves as, literally, "above" the ground officers whom they supported. Pershing formed an air service and directed that it be employed in combat; he gave little attention, however, to the employment of this arm, certainly less than did the Germans opposing him. General Mark Clark made the comment: "German bombardments by air-dropped bombs played havoc with columns in approach and with the organization of the rear area of the AEF."[65] Pershing's lack of attention to the employment of air power may have been the result of his experiences in Mexico, where most of the aircraft employed in chasing Villa crashed or were otherwise disabled. Because the staffs of the divisions and corps gave little attention to air support, it tended to operate as an independent element, engaging in bombardments of the enemy's rear, in pursuit, and in observation. Thus, the close association of air with the advance of the ground troops was not established in the AEF.[66] It was very well established across the line in the German armies. In Pershing's defense, it must be admitted that the airplane, like the tank, was not a very reliable weapons system in that war. Its effectiveness and its role were growing rapidly in the last years of the war, and its potential should have been more appreciated by the command of the AEF. It is often stated that generals train their troops to fight the previous war. Pershing appears to be at least partially guilty of that failing.

A few summary comments are necessary on the subject of American leadership. This is a difficult task, for this author believes that "leadership," like "love," is easier to recognize and appreciate than it is to analyze. Most of the authors who commented on this subject agreed that American leadership was somewhat better than the Allies credited it with being. Edward Coffman made the point that the Allied analysis of new American officers coming into the theater was likely very self-serving, but that it was probably to some extent correct. "They were the experienced leaders and we were not," he stated.[67] Irving B. Holley, Jr. agreed that the Americans were probably far less capable than were the Allied officers at the time the AEF arrived in theater. "The whole generation of professional American Army officers, Holley stated, "came out of an animal-powered era. Thus, their appreciation for the application of the industrial revolution to the battlefront took some time to develop."[68] General Theodore Conway stated that it was undoubtedly true that the Allies downgraded American leadership even before it had had a chance to demonstrate its capability. "From the European point of view," he stated, "we in the United States have always been thought of as amateurs in military affairs. This is the result of the fact that our nation has not chosen, until after World War II, to retain a large standing army; thus, our officer corps has not had direct experience with leading major military organizations."[69]

At this point in the critique, some balance to the generally critical comments on American officership should be made. In response to this author's queries on leadership in the AEF, Irving Holley, who has had considerable military experience, stated that the Regular Army officers did rather well, all things considered.

> They built an AEF staff from scratch into a sophisticated staff organization by the end of 1918. . . . This could be done only by men who were well-grounded professionals with a good deal of ability to begin with. What they lacked was specific experience with the kinds and scale of problems they encountered in France. This they acquired on the run.[70]

Holley's comment was expanded upon by Timothy Nenninger, in his text *The Leavenworth Schools and the Old Army*. Nenninger concluded that training provided by the military school system paid off later in France.[71] Without withdrawing any earlier criticisms, this author can agree with Holley and Nenninger. The creation of a modern theater of war—training, fighting, and sustaining a force (which grew quickly to two million men, requiring a million tons of supplies and materiel per month) was a nearly impossible task.[72] That it was accomplished at all, however fragile the structure of the AEF, was little short of a miracle. Credit must go to the small cadre of Regular Army officers and noncommissioned officers who directed much of this effort, and particular credit must be given to the "old army" schools. Their graduates did learn relatively modern army command and staff techniques. However, an old army limerick keeps coming to mind as this author writes and rewrites this section:

> Here's to the brave Captain White,
> The pride of this institution,
> Who went out like a light,
> In his very first fight,
> Following the school solution![73]

Recognizing that established doctrine did not always conform to reality, Nenninger noted that Leavenworth graduates in the AEF "exhibited too much self confidence, too great a belief in the rationality of warfare, and too high expectations of what the combat troops could accomplish . . . [this] compounded the problems that arose from the dichotomy between reality and doctrine.[74] Nenninger quoted Frederick Palmer. the war correspondent:

> Regular as well as reserve officers who had never been in action were to prove again that no amount of study of the theory of war, invaluable as it was, may teach an officer . . . how to keep his head in handling a thousand or three thousand men under fire. West Point cadet drill, Philippine jungle and "paddy" dikes, Leavenworth Staff School, army post routine, and border service had no precedent of experience for the problems of maneuver which they [the AEF] now had to solve.

Nenninger also stated his conclusion: "Clearly, the AEF learned to fight by fighting, not because of Pershing's insistence on open warfare or because the prewar Leavenworth had expounded the proper tactical doctrine."[75]

Certainly there were leaders of vision and high intelligence in the AEF. George Marshall, Douglas MacArthur, Charles Summerall, John Hines, Hunter Liggett, and Hugh Drum come to mind. They saw the doctrinal and operational errors; they just did not have the time to make significant changes during the fighting. Billy Mitchell was something of a visionary, but he was right about the role of airpower in future war. Though he was a bit of a nuisance to the senior officers, he came up with a number of plans to restore maneuver to the modern battlefield. Harvey DeWeerd stated that Mitchell had even gained Pershing's approval, in concept, to air drop the soldiers of the 1st Division from a fleet of multipassenger airplanes (each soldier with a single parachute) behind enemy lines, in conjunction with a motorized ground attack.[76]

A judgment of the leaders in the AEF who were not regulars is more difficult to make. Many of the senior officers of the National Guard and National Army divisions were regulars. Some of the National Guard officers were too old, physically unfit, and/or not competent to lead at the level of the rank they held. This was also the condition of some of the senior regular officers whom Pershing rejected or dismissed. Those officers newly minted by the preparedness camps, the Reserve Officers' Training Corps, Student Army Training Corps, and Officer Training Camps and Schools suffered from insufficient training and lack of pertinent experience. Those technical and administrative experts and doctors appointed to military rank to coordinate, primarily, the logistical support of the AEF, brought an expertise that was sorely needed and generally did a great job. If forced, this author would rate the regular officers and noncommissioned officers as the best two groups of leaders in the AEF; those of the prewar National Guard next best, and those leaders who held National Army rank only as the last. The regulars were criticized as being too stiff, not only in manner but in problem solving; the others were criticized as being, in varying degrees, unqualified and unmilitary.[77] This author could think of perhaps sixty individual exceptions to the group ratings just made, and perhaps there were thousands. If fired upon on this matter, this author will retreat!

It is to the credit of the American people and their way of life that, when challenged, the nation brought forth a great number of citizens who were innovative, able to improvise, self-confident, and success-oriented—the raw material for effective military leadership. To the observation of this author, many amateurs in military leadership, after some training and experience, have done as well as professionals on the battlefield. What they lack in military knowledge and experience they make up for by a greater degree of innovation and experimentation than many of the professional military leaders. The key problem is the time required for the knowledge and experience to be gained; if military experience must be gained during battle, the cost of such on-the-job-training can be expressed in high casualties among those being led.[78]

Peter Simkins, in discussing the BEF, stated that the National Army officers joining the AEF were probably similar in socioeconomic background to the young officers of Kitchener's Army; they were graduates of the British public (read private) school system, who marched into battle with enthusiasm, intelligence, and not much leavening experience.[79] It is likely that the American officers in the AEF came from a broader spectrum of our society than those in the BEF; yet there was a resemblance, as noted by Simkins.

The Regular Army officers in the AEF did look with disdain upon the officers from other components. This was only natural: they were the professionals; the others were less so. There was a marked dislike between the Regular and National Guard officers. For the Regulars, the ranks held by officers of the Guard, possibly higher than those of Regulars of the same age, was a source of irritation. For the Guard officers, with long unit and regional association, their second-class status was insulting. Liggett gave a fairly balanced analysis of the officers in the AEF from all sources. He found a mix of abilities among Regulars and the others. An officer deemed unfit to lead in the AEF was sent before a fitness board in the town of Blois, France. The board would reassign him or send him home as unfit. The town was called "Blooey," in the AEF, Liggett said; being sent there meant one's status had "gone Blooey," according to the slang of the AEF.[80]

From their common trial-by-fire in the Meuse-Argonne, officers of the AEF from all sources developed friendships and mutual respect, which offset, to some extent, the ill feelings between them because of their different sources of commission. By the end of the war, Pershing himself had come to appreciate the contributions of the Guard and National Army divisions and leaders. By the time he became Chief of Staff of the army, Pershing favored a relatively small Regular Army, one of whose major tasks would be to train a larger, civilian reserve force.[81]

Having been very critical of the leadership of the AEF, this author should admit to be also critical of his own leadership in past wars. In the later wars, this author lost a lot of men in battle; some of the losses were due to poor judgment on his part. These losses are a painful memory.

As in all wars, the soldiers of the AEF criticized their officers as a group and blamed them for failings in leadership. Interesting to note is the fact that many of the AEF veterans who commented upon leadership in responses to the MHI Questionnaire, most of them privates, had a high regard for the officers and noncommissioned officers under whom they served directly. Of 523 veterans of the Meuse-Argonne who commented on leadership (not all did), only 22 made derogatory remarks; most of these said their leaders lacked experience. The remaining 501 responses were positive; most told of a respect and affection for their unit leaders and admiration for their abilities.[82] Again, one could discount the comments of these aged veterans as having been mellowed by time. Nevertheless, the number of favorable responses speaks well for the human relations aspect of the leadership of the AEF.

When this author undertook this study, he wanted to avoid commenting upon General Pershing's leadership, mainly out of a concern that such comments, if laudatory, are usually dismissed as patronizing; if critical, they call into question the judgment of the rater and any animus against the rated or his group that maybe attributed to the rater. Frank Vandiver saw Pershing in heroic stature; a strong, dedicated leader, venerated by his soldiers, his nation, and our Allies.[83] And so he was. Donald Smythe was more critical of Pershing, faulting him for his stubbornness and inflexibility. Smythe concluded, however, that, given the tremendous challenges he faced, Pershing performed as well as could any other American military leader.[84] The historian T. Harry Williams found Pershing to have been to obstate and self-centered.[85] B. H. Liddell Hart credited Pershing with great strength of will, but faulted him for an aloofness, a coldness of manner, "lacking in personal magnetism which can make men lay down their lives gladly."[86] This author concurs with these criticisms: Pershing was venerated; he was not loved by his men! James Stokesbury rated Pershing as the equal of Foch or Haig, when the limits under which he operated are considered.[87] The British author John Terraine acknowledged such limits on Pershing; yet he questioned Pershing's capacity as a leader in a coalition.[88] John Toland saw Pershing as a stubborn, solid leader with a reasonable leadership capability. Toland, as well as Theodore Ropp, questioned the ability of any analyst or historian to rate leaders on a qualitative scale.[89] Russell Weigley faulted Pershing's tactical concepts and his judgment.[90] Trevor Dupuy rated Pershing the equal of Haig, but judged both to be of lesser attainments than either Foch or Ludendorff.[91] Allan Millett saw Pershing as equal in leadership to any of his Allied contemporaries.[92] Edward Coffman credited Pershing with great organizational ability and with the ability to select capable subordinates; but he (Coffman) found Pershing to be no great strategist or tactician.[93]

This analysis of the Meuse-Argonne Campaign cannot be rounded out without commenting on Pershing's leadership. This will be done directly: Mindful of the short period of this campaign, and of the unfairness of evaluation by hindsight, this author evaluates Pershing with empathy. Pershing was a strong leader. His strength and forcefulness were certainly needed during this period; otherwise, the American effort might have been diffused. He certainly was a bold commander, forceful and relentless in attack despite high casualties and little progress. His manner was cold and taciturn, although those close to him said he could be warm and personable. Donald Smythe believed that had the German offensives of 1918 gone all the way to the Loire River, with Pershing still refusing to amalgamate his forces with those of the Allies, he would likely have been relieved. But the offensive did not reach the Loire. As Smythe said, "Pershing was right in believing that the Allies could hold without the widespread amalgamation of American units; they did!"[94]

So agreeing, this author rates Pershing's leadership as too narrow, too self-centered, too authoritarian, somewhat vain, lacking in flexibility and innovativeness, and bound by tradition and experience to the extent that he was unable to master the requirements of the modern battlefield. Pershing's insistence on controlling the AEF Headquarters, the First Army, and the Services of Supply overloaded his span of effective control, strained him physically, and prevented him from evaluating the failures of the offensive, and determining new tactics and new procedures for winning the campaign, and for support and sustenance of the AEF. Had the fighting continued into 1919, a thorough reorganization of the AEF would have been necessary, in this author's opinion. The historian David Trask concurred with this judgment, and added that the management of the AEF was so bad that Pershing may well have been relieved had the war continued.[95] In his review of Pershing's *My Experiences*, Liddell Hart accused Pershing of so writing history as to show that all of his decisions were correct and appropriate.[96] On balance, however, Liddell Hart saw in Pershing "a man who has rare moral courage, driving force, bold vision, constructive power, and an ability to rise above professional prejudices in selecting his instruments."[97] This author agrees with Liddell Hart's analysis except on the question of Pershing's "ability to rise above professional prejudices." After giving this matter some thought and doing some rereading about Pershing, he (Pershing) appears to have been rather provincial and biased. A man of strong opinions, he did not tolerate dissenting views well. In fairness to Pershing, it must be stated that the tenor of military leadership in his era was very authoritarian. Pershing's machinations against the Chief of Staff of the army, General Peyton C. March, also revealed a pettiness in his nature.

DeWeerd judged Pershing's final report as Commander in Chief to have been of little value as a guide for the future. "To insist that 'the rifle is the master of the battlefield' in a day when the pace of technical advancement foreshadowed the possibility of fleets of monster tanks and swarms of dive bombers was to invite military stagnation," said DeWeerd.[98] However, DeWeerd agreed with and quoted Liddell Hart on Pershing: There was, perhaps, no other man who would or could have built the structure of the American Army on the scale he planned. And without that army the war could hardly have been saved and could not have been won.[99]

No question: Pershing put his stamp on the AEF. Those closest to him felt ennobled by that association. He was certainly a role model for a Commander in Chief, as was noted by Smythe.[100] He was respected, even by those who did not like him. He was America's hero. There were many admirable traits in his personality; his failings—no worse than those of other great men. But, a poorly trained draftee in the 79th Division at the foot of Montfaucon, ordered to attack directly into machine gun fire, might think less of Pershing than those who have been referenced herein.

While our Allies questioned and deprecated American leadership, they were unanimous in praise of the American soldiers, both amateur and professional. Certainly the Allies saw these men as fresh reinforcements for their depleted forces; but they found in the "Yank" more than they had expected. British Marshal Haig was particularly generous in his compliments concerning the abilities of the Americans with the BEF—their morale, their stamina, and their competitiveness. Other Allied commanders and observers spoke similarly.[101] The AEF veterans who responded to the MHI questionnaire spoke well of the Allied soldiers with whom and beside whom they served. They were critical of the food provided by the Allies, particularly of sour French wine and British "hardtack." Some, particularly those who stayed overseas after the Armistice, made complaints and uncomplimentary remarks about the French people. But they had very few complaints regarding their associations with the "Tommy" and "Poilu." The comment by former Second Lieutenant Waldo Moore of the 109th Field Artillery is typical: "I had a high opinion of all the troops from those countries with which I had contact, particularly the British, French and Belgian."[102] The "Yanks" gave even more praise to the soldiers from the British Dominions; they felt a greater kinship with the Australians and Canadians than they did with the Europeans.[103]

Mindful of the intense hatred of the "Hun" during the war, it is surprising that the American veterans who responded gave to the enemy soldiers, particularly the Germans, high compliments. Former private Ira Lacey of Battery B, 107th Field Artillery, said, "The Germans must have been pretty good fighters . . . the cost in lives that it took to defeat them." Of the 378 veterans who commented about the enemy, only twenty-nine had negative comments; twenty-two said the enemy were fairly good soldiers, while the other 227 described the Germans as good soldiers, good fighters.[104] It is probable that less commendatory statements would have been made about the enemy had the U.S. veterans endured four years of war on the Western Front, as did the Allied soldiers.

Some lessons may be deduced from this war regarding the problems of coalition warfare. For three years of war prior to America's entry into the conflict, the Allies suffered from the inability to gain unity of command over the forces on the Western Front. From the Battle of the Frontiers in August 1914 until the Battle of Caporetto in the fall of 1917, the Allies had seen their common aims frustrated by the unique aims and purposes that each member of the alliance considered separately paramount.[105] During the fighting on the Marne in 1914, the French suspected that the British might fall back on the Channel—and the Germans focused their drives on the juncture of the British Expeditionary Force and the French armies to lead to that result. Later, the French openly stated that the British were withholding a substantial portion of their combat power from the Western Front to retain and expand their colonial empire, and this was apparently true. The British, on the other hand, suspected that the French were not committing all of their manpower to the defense of their own country, while they were encouraging the British to commit the last of their manpower to the defense of France.[106] Earlier mentioned were British reservations about accepting orders from the Allied high command. Defending the British attitude, Peter Simkins stated that it was not appreciated by the

French and others that Great Britain was keeping the sea lanes open, bottling up the German fleet, and fighting, nearly alone, in the Middle East and Africa against the Central Powers.[107]

It was this combination of suspicious Allies that the United States joined in April 1917. Almost immediately, the Allies contested with each other for American manpower, and each whispered suspicions to American political and military leaders regarding the other. The French stressed the point that the Americans were in France and could learn the most from their associations with the French on the battlefield in which they would both fight. They also stressed long-term political associations, going back to the French commitments during the American Revolution. The British made the point that our troops would find a common language with the British and share a commonality of culture. The British desired the establishment of an American army in association with the BEF, while the French suspected that they were doing exactly that. The French complained regarding the number of American replacements being trained with the British as a result of their having been transported to France in British ships, and the British complained when Pershing attempted to withdraw those troops placed with them for training; the British had assumed the U.S. troops would remain indefinitely. Thomas Lonergan (former Lieutenant Colonel, general staff, AEF) in his text *It Might Have Been Lost,* cited documents from British and French archives that proved, as he saw it, that both sides were making desperate attempts to procure American manpower for their armies, at the same time that each attempted to prevent the other from gaining American reinforcements. Lonergan's sources can hardly be contested; his conclusions seem to be correct.[108] On the other hand, the Allies can hardly be faulted. During the German offensives of 1918, the AEF had a million men in France, at least another million in the United States who could be sent—and the Allies were fighting "with their backs to the wall."

The problems that the United States experienced in this, our first modern wartime coalition, were repeated with varying intensities of problem and pattern in World War II with the same Allies in Europe. The designation in World War II of a combined Allied command for the invasion of Europe, and General Dwight Eisenhower's success in directing multinational forces and leaders, give hope for successful coalition operations in current and future peacekeeping or warmaking operations. However, it is in the nature of partners in coalitions of "sovereign" powers to distrust each other and to give less than full assistance when it is not in their clear selfinterest to do so. It is also a characteristic of a coalition of sovereign nations to be slow in decision making, and to fail to obey decisions of the combined command that seem to some of the members to be unwise. These experiences are relevant to our international military associations today and for the foreseeable future.

From the Armistice until today, the importance of the AEF contribution to Allied victory on the Western Front is debated. Colonel John Elting (military historian and author) credited the Americans with having played a major role in stopping the 1918 German drives, and thought that their reinforcement of the Allies' forces was the decisive element in the final Allied offensive.[109] Edward Coffman reflected the opinion of many historians on both sides of the ocean that it was the appreciation of U.S. reinforcements, current and projected, which caused Ludendorff to give up the fight.[110] As to the significance of the Meuse-Argonne Campaign itself, the AEF commanders and staff, of course, believed it was the most decisive action on the Western Front.[111] One could as well argue, as did Correlli Barnett, that the British and French actions in stopping the German offensives of 1918, and the Allies' later advances were more significant.[112] However, the leader of the forces which fought the Americans and their Allies, General Ludendorff, said, "The American infantry in the Argonne won the war."[113]

The matter of the American contribution to the victory became a subject of contention in the press upon the publication of Pershing's *Experiences* in 1931. The *New York Times* selected the British military commentator, B. H. Liddell Hart, to review the text; it was mentioned earlier that Liddell Hart was rather critical of the work. In his review, he stated that the American battlefield contribution was an important one, but hardly the most decisive.[114] Hart's views prompted rebuttals in letters to the editor of the *New York Times.* Thomas M. Johnson of New York City cited Prince Max of Baden, General Ludendorff, and General Groener on the enemy's side, who stated that the Meuse-Argonne was the most critical point along the front.[115] Wendell Westover, former infantry captain in the AEF, took on Liddell Hart for criticizing Pershing's insistence on forming an American army. Slashing at Hart for "rank deception," Westover stated that the German reserves were known to have concentrated against the American drive, while the British forces, filled with "war torn veterans and last resort infants" were hardly doing "great offensive deeds."[116] This last comment provoked a response from Liddell Hart. Citing figures to prove the sacrifices and achievements of the BEF and of the British people, Liddell Hart defended his position on the relative merits of the campaigns of the BEF and the AEF, and huffily restated his experience in battle (a matter alluded to derogatorily by Westover).[117] From this vantage point in time, Liddell Hart seems to have got the better of the argument. His judgment—that the American reinforcement, in toto, was vital to victory, but that the

American military commitment in the Meuse-Argonne was not the most decisive action—seems to be reasonable.

As recently as 1983, this matter came up again in the press. John Giles, founder and president emeritus of The Western Front Association (an active group, centered in England, which studies and memorializes the events of the First World War), wrote to this author about a contretemps concerning credit for hastening the departure of the Germans from the Western Front. In his letter, he enclosed a clipping from *The London Daily Telegraph* of 3 August 1983, in which a British reader, who had been in World Wars I and II, stated that he was fed up with the carping against the Americans. He wanted to record his opinion that the Americans had won the First World War for the Allies. Giles answered in *The Telegraph* to the effect that had the war gone into 1919, the Americans would have had to bear the brunt of the fighting and could then have been considered to have won the war for the Allies—but it just did not turn out that way."[118] This author agrees with Giles.

It is concluded that the Meuse-Argonne Campaign was "a decisive action." It contributed to the Allied victory, but it was not the only nor the most decisive offensive of the war. For the Americans, it was a hard-won victory, won only in the last stages and at a great cost in lives. It was a victory produced mostly by improperly trained leaders and soldiers, and it was won by determination, esprit, and the exhaustion of the enemy. The victory was a tribute to the vitality and strength of the United States when sorely tried. The losses should have served as a lesson of the price of military unpreparedness. That lesson was not learned. After the Great War, U.S. military and civil leaders attempted to establish a permanent military structure that would keep the nation strong in time of peace. Secretary Baker and General March argued for a large, modern standing army. Pershing, commenting that "our traditions are opposed to the maintenance of a large standing army," proposed a smaller Regular Army, with a major commitment to train large, well-equipped civilian reserve organizations. Both Baker's and Pershing's proposals called for "universal military training for all males at age nineteen."[119] But the American people and their Congress would have none of it.

By the National Defense Act of 1920, a Regular Army of 288,000 was authorized; appropriations allowed for only 200,000. In response to the public's mood, Congress reduced funds in successive years. By the end of Pershing's tour as army chief of staff in 1924, the active army was down to 110,000. The American people were disillusioned with their European Allies and with the political results from the war in which they had sacrificed their young men and spent their money. Isolationism was running strong; equally strong was antimilitarism.[120]

What lessons were learned from the war? From their wartime experiences, the French were to adopt the "Maginot-line strategy," in which near total reliance was placed upon a strong defensive line on their eastern border. The British, horrified by their disastrous experiment in land warfare on the continent of Europe, relied again on their navy and looked to an indirect approach to any future threat from the continent. The postwar politics of England were increasingly dominated by a clique which held that military threats could be defused by diplomatic negotiations. The United States slammed the door on European affairs, at least for a time. The U.S. solution to modern war was international disarmament, and nearly domestic disarmament as well. We had no warfighting strategy worthy of the title. The German military, alone among the major powers, forged an offensive strategy from the very edge of developing technology: swift, deep penetration of an enemy's defenses by the combined "Blitzkrieg" of massed tanks supported by fighter aircraft.

The American people had every reason for concluding that their noble effort to save the Allies had been in vain. American participation in the Great War did not "make the world safe for democracy." The elites in the Allied nations had no intention of surrendering elective power to the lower classes; the democracies that were formed in Europe by the peace treaties were short lived—most giving way to dictatorships. The American public, too, shrank away from Woodrow Wilson's grand design for international order and peace. Finally, it became apparent that the war had not really been won; the "war to end all wars" had only postponed some international struggles that were building again in the 1930s.[121]

But, it can be argued that America's entry into World War I was both necessary and inevitable—necessary to defeat worldwide aggression, at least on the seas, which if successful would have posed great problems for the United States. Our step into the Great War was inevitable, the assumption of a contributory role in international leadership, made necessary by the growing economic power of the U.S. in an increasingly interdependent and dangerous world. However much we may have wished to isolate ourselves, there was no turning back. The world of the twentieth century would not allow America to be secure in isolation. The historian C. Vann Woodward characterized this change in U.S. affairs as "the passing of the Age of Free Security."[122] The author Daniel Smith said in *The Great Departure: The United States and World I*: "World War I marked a great departure for the United States, from the less demanding world of the past into the more dangerous but challenging world of the twentieth century."[123] It would take another generation and another world war for America to understand and accept the thankless role of world leadership, and to arm herself adequately to exercise that role.

In a hollow framed by the hills of Romagne, France, facing the heights on which the Kriemhilde defenses were anchored, an American cemetery was established in 1919. This is the resting place for fourteen thousand Americans who died during the Meuse-Argonne offensive. It is a well-landscaped, carefully tended shrine, a memorial for those who made the supreme sacrifice. French schoolchildren still visit the graves, and many plots are decorated with fresh flowers. A visitor may muse on the luck, or the lack of it, that brought these men here instead of home in victory. Luck does discriminate in any war. But some—no, many of these men lie here because they were committed to battle with insufficient training, poor tactics, and inadequate leadership. Of all that the United States gave to the Allied cause in the Great War, these young men were our most precious resource. Their unfulfilled lives, their hopes and dreams can only be imagined—and the loss remembered for all time. General Pershing dedicated this cemetery in 1919. This narrative and analysis of the test of battle in the Meuse-Argonne Campaign ends with the final words he spoke:

"And now, dear comrades, farewell. Here, under the clear skies, on the green hillsides and amid the flowering fields of France, in the quiet hush of peace, we leave you forever in God's keeping."[124]

The United States Military Cemetery at Romagne, France.

Author's Collection

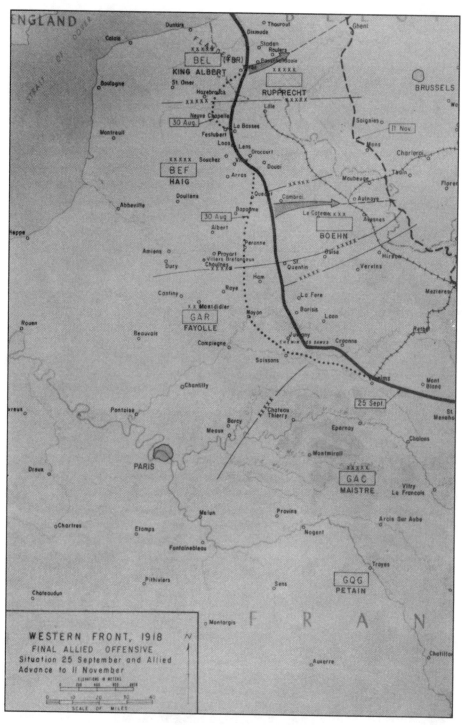

Map 10. The Western Front, 1918.

Department of History, United States Military Academy, map to accompany interim text, *The Great War*. West Point U.S.M.A , 1979.

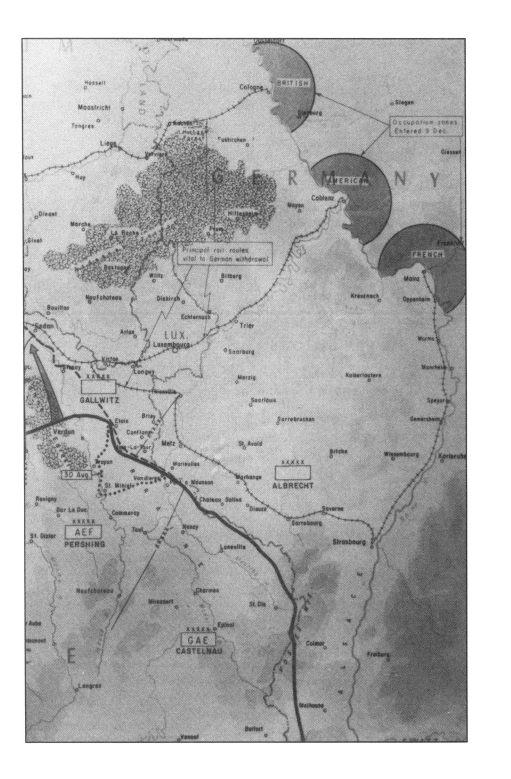

APPENDIX 1

DEFINITIONS OF MILITARY TERMS, ABBREVIATIONS, AND SYMBOLS

AEF = American Expeditionary Forces. The land forces, Army and Marines, which the United States sent to France in World War I.

BEF = British Expeditionary Force. The land force of British and Colonial troops which Great Britain sent to France.

= The United States First Army, commanded by General Pershing. The four X's over the rectangle indicate an Army, consisting of a number of corps. The U.S. is used when foreign armies are also shown.

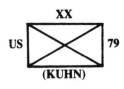

= The United States First Corps (corps are designated by Roman numerals), commanded by General Liggett. A corps consists of a number (variable according to mission) of divisions. Three X's over the rectangle indicate a corps.

= The United States 79th Infantry Division, commanded by General Kuhn. An infantry division consisted of 28,000 personnel; its infantry combat units were two infantry brigades (8500 men each). The name of the commander is also shown after the title where the name is significant.

= The 57th Infantry Brigade (General Nicholson in command).

= 113th Infantry Regiment (about 3500 men).

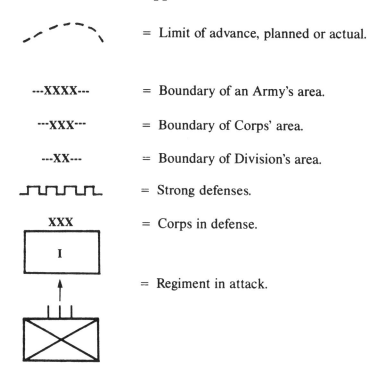

	= Limit of advance, planned or actual.
---XXXX---	= Boundary of an Army's area.
---XXX---	= Boundary of Corps' area.
---XX---	= Boundary of Division's area.
	= Strong defenses.
XXX	= Corps in defense.
	= Regiment in attack.

Objective = A geographical area to be attacked and seized.

Objective Line, Phase Line, Maneuver Line = Lines drawn on a map to control the movement of attacking units by order (e.g., "move to" "hold at").

TO&E = The Table of Organization and Equipment which shows the personnel, weapons, and other equipment allocated to a unit, broken out by subunits and sections.

LOC = Line of Communications. The route along which an organization communicates with its supporting elements in its rear and with higher headquarters and support, and by which it receives support and supply.

Strategy = the plan for the employment of military forces in major groupings to place them in a favorable position for battle.

Tactics = The disposition and maneuver of units on a battlefield. Higher Tactics refers to the maneuver of major forces beyond a single battle area.

Turning or Outflanking = The act of moving an attacking unit around the sides or flanks of a defender to the extent that he is forced to withdraw or fight at a disadvantage.

Fire and Movement/Maneuver = Directing the fires of weapons upon a defensive position to prevent return fire, while moving a unit to attack the position or to move around it.

Final Protective Fires/Line = Fires of weapons from defensive positions which fires are preset along a single line, to be fired together when the defended position is under attack.

Company Grade Officers = Lieutenants and Captains; Field Grade Officers—Majors, Lieutenant Colonels, and Colonels; General Officers—all Generals.

Beaten/Killing Zone = That area, usually prearranged, where the fires of defensive weapons are concentrated.

Barrage = The coordinated firing of a number of artillery weapons or mortars so that the projectiles land at the same time in a selected area.

Interdictory Fire = The employment of the fire of weapons to deny an area to enemy usage.

APPENDIX 2

TIME SPENT IN TRAINING AND COMBAT

```
Divi-        1917                        1918
sion  Jul Aug Sep Oct Nov Dec Jan Feb Mar Apr May Jun Jul Aug Sep Oct N

1st   ooooooooooooooo/////////////////////////XXXXXXXXXXXXXXXXXXXXXXXXXXX
2d     odooooooooooooo0000000000000000000///////////XXXXXXXXXXXXXXXXXXXXX
26th           oooooooooo000000000000/////////////////XXXXXXXXXXXXXXXXXX
42d        ooooooooooo0000000000000//////////////////XXXXXXXXXXXXXXXX
41st           oooooooooooo000000000000000000000000000000000000000000000
32d       ooooooooooooooooooooooo000000000000///////XXXXXXXXXXXXXXX
3d             ooooooooooooooooooooo//////XXXXXXXXXXXXXXXXXXXXXX
77th         ooooooooooooooooooooooo000000000//////XXXXXXXXXX
5th              ooooooooooooooooooooo0000//////////XXXXXXXXX
27th          ooooooooooooooooooooooooooooo00000000XXXXXXXXXXXXXXXXX
35th          ooooooooooooooooooooooooooooo0000000000//////////XXXXXXXXX
82d       oooooooooooooooooooooooooooo00000///////XXXXXXXXX
4th                oooooooooooooooooooooo0000000XXXXXXXXXXXXXXXX
28th      oooooooooooooooooooooooooooooooooo00000000XXXXXXXXXXXXXXXX
30th        boooooooooooooooooooooooooooooooooo000000XXXXXXXXXXXXXXXX
33d      oooooooooooooooooooooooooooooooooo000000000000//XXXXXXX
80th      oooooooooooooooooooooooooooooooooo0000000000//XXXXXXX
78th      ooooooooooooooooooooooooooooooooooo00000000000XXXXXXXXX
83d       ooooooooooooooooooooooooooooooooo000000000000000
92d            oooooooooooooooooooooooooooooooo0000000/////////
89th        ooooooooooooooooooooooooooooooooooo00000///XXXXXX
90th        oooooooooooooooooooooooooooooooooo00000///XXXXXX
37th        ooooooooooooooooooooooooooooooooooo000//////XXXXX
29th     ooooooooooooooooooooooooooooooooooooooo00//////XXXX
91st       oooooooooooooooooooooooooooooooooooo000000//XXXXX
76th    oooooooooooooooooooooooooooooooooooooooo0000000000000
79th      ooooooooooooooooooooooooooooooooooooo000000//XXXXX
6th           ooooooooooooooooooooooooooooooooo00000/////////
36th     oooooooooooooooooooooooooooooooooooooo000000XXXXXXX
85th        ooooooooooooooooooooooooooooooooo00000000000
7th              ooooooooooooooooooooooooooooooo000000////
81st     ooooooooooooooooooooooooooooooooooooooo00000/////
88th      ooooooooooooooooooooooooooooooooooooo0000//////
40th        ooooooooooooooooooooooooooooooooooo000000000
39th      oooooooooooooooooooooooooooooooooooo0000000000
87th      oooooooooooooooooooooooooooooooooooo000000000
86th      ooooooooooooooooooooooooooooooooooooo00000000
84th        ooooooooooooooooooooooooooooooooo00000000
34th    ooooooooooooooooooooooooooooooooooooooo0000000
38th     ooooooooooooooooooooooooooooooooooooooo00000
31st      oooooooooooooooooooooooooooooooooooooooo0000
8th             oooooooooooooooooooooooooooooooooooooooo0
```

ooooo Organization or entry on active duty until arrival in France.
00000 Arrival in France until entering the line.
///// In the line; quiet sector.
XXXXX Active combat.

From: *Final Report of Assistant Chief of Staff G-1 to Commander-in-Chief, American Expeditionary Forces*, 22 April 1919 (NA, RG 120, Folder 29), 32.

APPENDIX 3

STATUS OF DIVISIONS ON THE WESTERN FRONT, 11 NOVEMBER 1918

Armies	Divisions on Line			Divisions in Reserve			Total
	Fresh	Tired	Total	Fresh	Tired	Total	Avail.
United States	4	12	16	3	11	14	30
France	19	17	36	19	53	72	108
Great Britain	5	24	29	6	29	35	64
Belgium	3	1	4	2	1	3	7
Italy	1	0	1	0	1	1	2
Portugal	0	0	0	2	0	2	2
TOTAL ALLIES	32	54	86	32	95	127	213
Germany/ Austria	47	97	144	2	39	41	185

NOTE: American divisions are approximately twice the size of those of other nations.

From: *Final Report of A C of S, G-3 to CINC AEF*, 2 July 1919 (NA, RG 120, Series 274), 88.

APPENDIX 4

DIVISION DAYS ON THE LINE IN FRANCE

Division	Quiet Sector	Active Sector	QUIET / ACTIVE	TOTAL DAYS
1st	127	93	//////////////XXXXXXXXX	220
26th	148	45	//////////////////XXXXx	193
42d	125	39	/////////////XXXX	164
2d	71	66	//////XXXXXXx	137
77th	47	66	////XXXXXXx	113
5th	71	32	//////XXX	103
82d	70	27	//////XXX	97
35th	92	5	////////x	97
32d	60	35	/////XXXx	95
3d	0	86	/////////	86
89th	55	28	/////XXX	83
29th	59	23	/////XXx	82
28th	31	49	///XXXXX	80
90th	42	26	///XXx	68
37th	50	11	////X	61
33d	32	27	//XXx	59
27th	0	57	XXXXXx	57
30th	0	56	XXXXXx	56
92d	51	2	/////x	53
79th	28	17	///Xx	45
4th	7	35	/XXXx	42
6th	40	0	////	40
78th	17	21	//XX	38
7th	31	2	///x	33
81st	31	0	///	31
91st	15	14	/Xx	29
88th	28	0	///	28
36th	0	23	XXx	23
80th	1	17	Xx	18

///// Quiet Sector
XXXXX Active Combat

From: *Final Report of Assistant Chief of Staff G-3 to Commander-in-Chief, American Expeditionary Forces,* 2 July 1919. (NA, RG 120, Series 274), 9.

APPENDIX 5

DISTANCE ADVANCED AGAINST FIRE

Division	Distance	Miles
77th	XXXXXXXXXXXXXXXXXXXXXXXXXXXXXXXXXXXXXXXXXXXXXXXx	44.5
2d	XXXXXXXXXXXXXXXXXXXXXXXXXXXXXXXXXXXXXXXXx	37.5
42d	XXXXXXXXXXXXXXXXXXXXXXXXXXXXXXXXXXXX	34
1st	XXXXXXXXXXXXXXXXXXXXXXXXXXXXXXXXXX	32
89th	XXXXXXXXXXXXXXXXXXXXXXXXXXXXXXXX	30
3d	XXXXXXXXXXXXXXXXXXXXXXXXXXXx	25.5
80th	XXXXXXXXXXXXXXXXXXXXXXXXXXx	23.5
26th	XXXXXXXXXXXXXXXXXXXXXXXX	23
32d	XXXXXXXXXXXXXXXXXXXXXXXx	22.5
33d	XXXXXXXXXXXXXXXXXXXXXXXx	22.5
91st	XXXXXXXXXXXXXXXXXXXXXX	21
37th	XXXXXXXXXXXXXXXXXXXX	19
30th	XXXXXXXXXXXXXXXXXXXx	18.5
5th	XXXXXXXXXXXXXXXXXX	18
90th	XXXXXXXXXXXXXXXXX	17
4th	XXXXXXXXXXXXXXX	15
78th	XXXXXXXXXXXXX	13
36th	XXXXXXXXXXXXX	13
79th	XXXXXXXXXXXX	12
82d	XXXXXXXXXXx	10.5
35th	XXXXXXXX	8
27th	XXXXXXX	7
28th	XXXXXX	6
92d	XXXXX	5
29th	XXXX	4
91st	XXXx	3.5
7th	x	.5
6th		0
88th		0

From: *Final Report of Assistant Chief of Staff G-3 to Commander-in-Chief, American Expeditionary Forces*, 2 July 1919. (NA, RG 120, Series 274), 7.

APPENDIX 6

AWARDS FOR VALOR, AGGREGATED BY DIVISION

Division	Medal of Honor	Distinguished Service Cross	Oak Leaf Cluster	Total
2d	7	673	13	693
1st	2	415	3	420
3rd	2	328	2	332
30th	12	307	-	319
26th	2	269	5	276
32d	-	250	-	250
42d	2	239	4	245
77th	6	202	3	211
33d	9	202	-	211
5th	2	197	-	199
27th	6	161	2	169
29th	3	159	-	162
4th	-	159	-	159
91st	4	143	1	148
89th	9	137	-	146
28th	1	138	4	143
78th	1	116	-	117
82d	2	94	-	96
90th	-	88	-	88
79th	-	88	-	88
35th	2	85	1	88
93d	1	69	-	70
37th	-	52	-	52
80th	-	50	-	50
36th	2	39	-	41
7th	-	37	-	37
81st	-	23	-	23
92d	-	22	-	22
6th	-	15	-	15
88th	-	1	-	1

NOTE: Oak Leaf Cluster means a second award of the same decoration.
From: *A C of S, GI, Final Report to CINC AEF*,
22 April 1919 (NA, RG 120, Folder 29), 11.

APPENDIX 7

CASUALTIES, AGGREGATED BY DIVISION

Division	Casualties	Total
2d	CCCCCCCCCCCCCCCCCCCCCCCCCCCCCCCCCCCCCCCCCCCCCCCCCCC	25,232
1st	CCCCCCCCCCCCCCCCCCCCCCCCCCCCCCCCCCCCCCCCCCCCCCCCC	23,496
3d	CCCCCCCCCCCCCCCCCCCCCCCCCCCCCCCCCCCCCC	18,468
28th	CCCCCCCCCCCCCCCCCCCCCCCCCCCCCCCCCCC	17,003
42d	CCCCCCCCCCCCCCCCCCCCCCCCCCCCCCCCC	16,107
26th	CCCCCCCCCCCCCCCCCCCCCCCCCCCCCCCC	15,619
4th	CCCCCCCCCCCCCCCCCCCCCCCCCCCCC	14,255
32d	CCCCCCCCCCCCCCCCCCCCCCCCCCCCC	14,040
77th	CCCCCCCCCCCCCCCCCCCCCCCC	12,361
27th	CCCCCCCCCCCCCCCCCCCCCc	11,446
30th	CCCCCCCCCCCCCCCCCCCC	11,158
5th	CCCCCCCCCCCCCCCCCC	9,981
33d	CCCCCCCCCCCCCCCCC	9,379
89th	CCCCCCCCCCCCCCC	8,838
82d	CCCCCCCCCCCCCCC	8,467
78th	CCCCCCCCCCCCCCc	8,282
90th	CCCCCCCCCCCCCC	8,090
35th	CCCCCCCCCCCCCC	8,025
79th	CCCCCCCCCCCCC	7,670
80th	CCCCCCCCCCCC	6,864
91st	CCCCCCCCCCCC	6,524
29th	CCCCCCCCCCCc	6,226
37th	CCCCCCCCCCC	5,946
36th	CCCCC	2,735
7th	CCCC	1,838
92d	CCCC	1,697
81st	CCC	1,102
6th	C	679
88th		99

NOTE: Total casualties included killed in action, wounded, and evacuated for illness.

From: *Final Report of Assistant Chief of Staff G-3 to Commander-in-Chief, American Expeditionary Forces,* 2 July 1919. (NA, RG 120, Series 274), 33.

APPENDIX 8

PRISONERS OF WAR, AGGREGATED BY DIVISION

Division	Prisoners of War	Total
2d	PPPPPPPPPPPPPPPPPPPPPPPPPPPPPPPPPPPPPPPPPPPPPPPPPP	12,026
1st	PPPPPPPPPPPPPPPPPPPPPPPPPPP 6,469	
89th	PPPPPPPPPPPPPPPPPPPPPPP 5,061	
33d	PPPPPPPPPPPPPPPPP 3,987	
30th	PPPPPPPPPPPPPPPP 3,848	
26th	PPPPPPPPPPPPP 3,148	
4th	PPPPPPPPPPPP 2,756	
91st	PPPPPPPPP 2,412	
27th	PPPPPPPPP 2,357	
5th	PPPPPPPPP 2,356	
3d	PPPPPPPP 2,240	
29th	PPPPPPPP 2,187	
32d	PPPPPPPP 2,153	
90th	PPPPPPP 1,876	
80th	PPPPPP 1,813	
37th	PPPPP 1,495	
42dh	PPPPP 1,317	
79th	PPPP 1,077	
28th	PPP 921	
82dh	PPP 845	
35th	PPP 781	
77th	PPP 750	
36th	PP 549	
78th	PP 432	
81st	P 101	
7th	69	
92d	38	
6th	12	
88th	3	

From: *Final Report of Assistant Chief of Staff, G-3 to Commander-in-Chief, American Expeditionary Forces*, 2 July 1919. (NA, RG 120, Series 274), 8.

APPENDIX 9

CONSOLIDATION OF PERFORMANCE FACTORS

Division	Total of Indicators
2d	IIIIIIIIIIIIIIIIIIIIIIIIIIIIIIIIIIIIIIIIIIII
1st	IIIIIIIIIIIIIIIIIIIIIIIIIIIIIIIIIIIIIII
3d	IIIIIIIIIIIIIIIIIIIIIIII
26th	IIIIIIIIIIIIIIIIIIIII
42d	IIIIIIIIIIIIIIIIIIII
32d	IIIIIIIIIIIIIIIIII
77th	IIIIIIIIIIIIII
5th	IIIIIIIIIIIII
30th	IIIIIIIIIIIII
89th	IIIIIIIIIIII
4th	IIIIIIIIIII
33d	IIIIIIIIIII
91st	IIIIIIIIII
90th	IIIIIIIIII
28th	IIIIIIIII
27th	IIIIIIII
78th	IIIIIII
29th	IIIIIII

APPENDIX 10

RESPONSES OF 728 VETERANS OF THE MEUSE-ARGONNE CAMPAIGN TO ARMY SERVICE EXPERIENCES QUESTIONNAIRES

Criterion	# Responses	Yes/Good	OK/Fair	No/Poor	Comment
Training	514	12	16	486	Lack of time.
Leadership	503	467	14	22	Leaders cared.
Discipline	429	358	34	27	Hard but fair.
Weapons	371	40	2	329	German's better.
Equipment	316	39	25	252	Allied issue.
Food	431	21	54	346	Bad, insuff.
Supplies	319	10	28	281	Transp. Problems.
Health	380	16	44	320	Wet, flu, cooties.
Morale	467	375	53	39	High, except no supplies.
Allies	251	210	30	11	OK except food
Enemy	378	327	22	29	Good soldier.
Fellow soldiers	481	415	44	22	Great friends.
Value of service	427	413	10	4	Proud to serve; no pension.

NOTE: It is likely that far more of the 6,700 respondees to the MHI questionnaire actually participated in the Meuse-Argonne Campaign. Of the 5,000 responses scanned by this author, only 728 could be identified as having participated in the fighting.

(Figures were collected by author from the Responses of Veterans of World War 1 to Army Service Experiences Questionnaires and request for memorabilia made by U.S. Army's Military History Institute; with permission of the director and staff of that Institute.)

NOTES

CHAPTER 1. EUROPE CHOOSES WAR

1. Barbara W. Tuchman, *The Guns of August* (New York: Macmillan, 1962) conveys well the emotional stimuli to war that swept Europe at that time.

2. A Polish banker turned military analyst, Ivan Bloch, published in 1898 a six-volume study, *The Future of War in Its Technical, Economic, and Political Relations*, trans. R. C. Long (Boston: Doubleday and McClure, 1899). This treatise accurately forecast huge casualties from modern weapons and mass armies equipped by industrialized societies. The text so shocked the Czar of Russia that it prompted him to call the first Hague Peace Conference in 1899. Bloch himself lectured the delegates on the slaughter that could be effected by automatic weapons and explosive artillery shells. Neither his efforts nor those of the conferees appear to have prevailed against the appeals of war. See Theodore Ropp, *War in the Modern World* (New York: Collier, 1962), 218–220.

3. For greater explication of these martial developments, see Bernard and Fawn Brodie's *From Crossbow to H-Bomb* (New York: Dell Books, 1962), 137–153.

4. Naval developments, such as the screw propeller and turret gunnery, are not covered in this summary of land fighting. The military applications of the internal combustion engine will be taken up later.

5. Trevor N. Dupuy, *The Evolution of Weapons and Warfare* (New York: Bobbs-Merrill, 1980), 288, 289.

6. Ropp, *War in the Modern World*, 215–221.

7. Bloch, *The Future of War*, xvi, xli.

8. Ropp, *War in the Modern World*, 221–227.

9. The elan of the intelligentsia for war is exemplified by quotations from poets of that time in *The Great War*, James B. Agnew et al. (West Point: United States Military Academy, 1979), 443ff.

10. Robert Leckie, *The Wars of America*, vol. 2 (New York: Harper and Row, 1968), 76.

11. Like the armies of the Entente powers, the Germans had regarded the machine gun as a general support weapon, assigning two to each front line battalion. The wars of the early twentieth century, however, convinced the Germans of the effectiveness of the machine gun as a forward support weapon. They formed Jäger (Hunter) companies, with six machine guns each, to operate with rifle units. The armies of the Entente did not increase their machine gun strength until after the frontier battles of 1914. See John Ellis, *The Social History of the Machine Gun* (New York: Pantheon Books, 1975), 113–116.

12. Vincent Esposito, ed., *The West Point Atlas of American Wars*, vol. 2 (New York: Praeger, 1959) gives a succinct and graphic summary of these war plans and their execution, maps and text 2–6.

13. One of the many excellent accounts of the German offensive and the First Battle of the Marne is John Keegan, *Opening Moves: August 1914* (New York: Viking Press, 1971); also Cyril Falls, *The Great War, 1914–1918 (First World War)* (London: Longman's 1960), 79ff.

14. In the nineteenth century, the Prussian military philosopher Karl von Clausewitz announced the superiority of the defensive form of war (although he did prescribe a counteroffensive as a requisite to victory). Karl von Clausewitz, *Vom Kriege* (Berlin, 1832; trans. J. J. Graham, 1908; pub. by Pelican Books, Hammondsworth, England as *Carl von Clausewitz: On War*, 1968.

15. *West Point Atlas*, maps and text 16–21.

16. Excellent accounts of the British-led campaign in the Dardanelles are Robert R. James' *Gallipoli* (London: Longman's, 1965) and Alan Morehead's *Gallipoli* (London: Hamilton, 1956); a personal attempt at exculpation is General Sir Ian Hamilton, *Gallipoli Diary* (London: Arnold, 1920).

17. Luigi Villari, *The War on the Italian Front* (London: Unwin, 1932).

18. The strategic deadlock is well summarized by Hanson Baldwin in his pithy text, *World War I: An Outline History* (London: Hutchinson, 1963).

19. Ibid., 73.

20. Col. G. L. McEntee, *Military History of the World War* (New York: Scribner's Sons, 1937), quoted by Baldwin, *World War I*, 79.

21. The British official history of the Great War is entitled *History of the Great War*. The history of the BEF is entitled *Military Operations France and Belgium*, James E. Edmonds, ed., 1917, 3 Vols; 1918, 5 vols. (London: Macmillan, 1935–48). The French official history is État-Major de l'Armée, Service Historique, *Les Armées Françaises dans la Grande Guerre*. Volumes 5–7 are germane to this period (Paris: Imprimerie Nationale, 1923–38). The German official history is *Der Weltkrieg, 1914 bis 1918*. Volumes 1, 5–7 are germane to this period (Berlin: Reicharchiv, 1925).

22. A military account of the "face off" of the two great fleets is given in Commander Halloway H. Frost, *The Battle of Jutland* (Annapolis: U.S. Naval Institute, 1936). A good account of the controversies surrounding the conduct of the battle from a British viewpoint is given by Admiral Sir Reginald Bacon in *The Jutland Scandal* (London: Hutchinson, 1925).

23. An American account of the blockade and submarine warfare, critical of the British, is Thomas G. Frothingham, *The Naval History of the World War*, vol. 1, 3 vols. (Cambridge: Harvard University Press, 1925). A more reasoned account is Louis Guichard's *The Naval Blockade, 1914–1918* (Paris: n.p., 1930).

24. The U.S.M.A. text, *The Great War*, gives a good summary of these operations and their effects in chapter 4, "Deadlock and Attrition on the Western Front, 1914–1916."

25. Criticism during the years of attrition was strongest and most public in the capitals of the Entente powers; however, dissatisfaction at the highest levels did result in the relief of the heads of the British, French, Russian, and German armies in 1915, and again, for the French and Germans, after the disasters of 1916. After the war, a torrent of criticism came from the home front and the trenches, their authors newly released from the restrictions of censorship. See bibliography.

26. Baldwin, *World War I*, 49ff., Dupuy, T. N., *Weapons and Warfare*, 217–229.

27. C. S. Forester, *The General* (Boston: Houghton Mifflin, 1936).

28. Wilhelm Balck, *Development of Tactics--World War,* trans. Harry Bell (Fort Leavenworth: General Staff School Press, 1922).

29. Ibid., 71ff.

30. Captain G. C. Wynne, *If Germany Attacks: The Battle in Depth in the West* (London: Faber and Faber, 1940), 83ff.

31. Ibid. 85–104.

32. Maurice is quoted by H. A. DeWeerd (no small critic himself) in the foreword to DeWeerd's text, *Great Soldiers of Two World Wars* (New York: W. W. Norton, 1962), 14.

CHAPTER 2. 1917—THE YEAR OF HOPE AND DESPAIR

1. German strategy and its changes are presented in some detail in Fritz Fischer, *Germany's Aims in the First World War* (New York: W. W. Norton, 1961); another view is that of Hans Gatzke, *Germany's Drive to the West* (Baltimore: The Johns Hopkins University Press, 1950).

2. U.S.M.A., *The Great War,* 210–221; also Baldwin, *World War I,* 95–104.

3. D. F Fleming, *The Origins and Legacies of World War I* (Greenwich: Fawcett, 1968), 270–277.

4. The taking of Vimy ridge by the Canadians cost 100,000 lives and set a record for slaughter in a war where high casualties had become routine (Fleming, *Origins and Legacies,* 277). For an intriguing account of the political-military discussions preceding this offensive, see Gen. Sir E. L. Spears, *Prelude to Victory* (London: Cape, 1930).

5. The "first" battle of the Aisne was a prelude to the Allied "race to the sea," which occurred in September 1914.

6. U.S.M.A. Text, *The Great War,* 207–222. For an account of the causes and effects of the French mutinies, see Richard M. Watt, *Dare Call It Treason* (New York: Simon and Schuster, 1963).

7. U.S.M.A., *The Great War,* 222–227; also Baldwin, *World War I,* 102–104. For an indictment of the futility of this offensive, see Leon Wolff, *In Flanders Fields: The 1917 Campaign* (London: Longman's, 1958).

8. U.S.M.A., *The Great War,* 225, 226, 230–233.

9. The best account of the confusing political-military maneuvers of this theater is Winston Churchill, *The Unknown War* (New York: Scribner's Sons, 1932), 353ff. The insertion of Lenin into the Russian political arena was a masterstroke on the part of the Germans; Lenin's presence had much to do with Russia's surrender and much more to do with postwar troubles for the Allies and for Germany.

10. *West Point Atlas,* map and text, 43.

11. A good account of the new German offensive tactics (the so-called "Hutier Tactics") was given by Erwin Rommel in *Infantry Attacks,* trans. G. E. Kidde (Washington: GPO, 1944), 168–207.

12. *West Point Atlas,* map and text, 41.

13. Villari, *War Italian Front,* 126ff. For a detailed study of the disaster at Caporetto, see Cyril Falls, *Caporetto 1917* (London: Weidenfield, 1965).

14. *West Point Atlas,* maps and text, 52–56.

15. Allied shipping losses (largely British) were 868,000 tons in 1915; 1,236,000 tons in 1916; and two million tons during the first four months of 1917 (Fleming, *Origins and Legacies,* 276). A good account of the controversy over the convoy system is Arthur Marder, *From Dreadnaught to Scapa Flow,* vol. 2 of 5 vols. (New York: Oxford University Press, 1961–1970), 134–159.

16. Most authorities agree concerning the tremendous material and capital (loan) reinforcement provided by the U.S. before and after it became a belligerent.

CHAPTER 3. AMERICA SENDS AN ARMY TO FRANCE

1. Wilson's statement was paraphrased by Robert Leckie in *The Wars of America*. 2:75–76.

2. Ibid., 2:76.

3. Oliver L. Spaulding (Col., U.S. Army), *The United States Army in War and Peace* (New York: G. P. Putnam & Sons, 1937), pp. 406–408.

4. Leckie, *The Wars of America*, 2:78–104.

5. Tuchman writes interestingly of this crisis in her book, *The Zimmerman Telegram* (New York: Dell, 1958).

6. Leckie, *The Wars of America*, 104–106.

7. Daniel R. Beaver, *A Progressive at War: Newton D. Baker and the American War Effort, 1917–1919* (Ph.D. diss., Northwestern University, 1962), Preface.

8. Ibid., preface. also Maurice Matloff, ed., *American Military History* (Washington: GPO, 1973), 372, 373.

9. Department of the Army, *The Army Lineage Book, Vol. II, Infantry* (Washington: GPO, 1953), 34–39, 60, 61.

10. Spaulding, *The U.S. Army*, 410.

11. Paul S. Bond (Col., U.S. Army) and Col. Clarence O. Sherrill, *America in the World War: A Summary of the Achievements of the Great Republic in the Conflict with Germany* (Menasha, Wis.: Collegiate Press, 1921), 47–53.

12. Ibid., 47–49.

13. Ibid., 52–55.

14. Richard Goldhurst, *Pipe Clay and Drill* (New York: Thomas Y. Crowell, 1977), 254–259. The attitude of the Allies regarding the capabilities of America's military leadership are well summarized in an unpublished thesis by Major James W. Rainey, *The Training of the American Expeditionary Forces in World War I* (Philadelphia: Temple University, 1981), 15, 16.

15. Edward M. Coffman, *The War to End All Wars* (New York: Oxford University Press, 1968), 47.

16. Josiah B. Miller, "Development of Departmental Direction of Training. . . ." (Washington: Dept. of Army, n.d.), 1, 2.

17. Ray Stannard Baker, *Woodrow Wilson: Life and Letters; Facing War, 1915–1917*. (New York: Doubleday, 1937), 490–506; also Arthur S. Link, *Woodrow Wilson and the Progressive Era, 1910–1917* (New York: Harper, 1935), 277–282.

18. House was quoted by Rainey, *The Training of American Forces*, 11.

19. Ibid., 12.

20. Baker, *Woodrow Wilson*, 507.

21. In his *Reminiscences*, General Douglas MacArthur (New York: McGraw-Hill, 1964), 46, 47, said Funston had been selected to lead the AEF. There is no reliable evidence to support MacArthur's recollection.

22. Peyton C. March, *The Nation at War* (Garden City: Doubleday, 1932), 247–248.

23. Ibid., 249.

24. Frank E. Vandiver, *Black Jack: The Life and Times of John J. Pershing*, vol. 2 (College Station: Texas A&M Press, 1977), 695.

25. At the risk of killing yet another pleasant myth, it must be reported that Pershing did not utter the words, "Lafayette, we are here!" He was present at a review of the 16th Infantry Regiment on the 4 July 1917 at Lafayette's tomb when those

words were uttered by a quartermaster colonel. See Matloff, ed., *American Military History*, 273.

26. "Final Report of Assistant Chief of Staff for Operations (G-3) to Commander in Chief, AEF," 2 July 1919. National Archives, Records Group 120, Series 274, 7. Hereafter, these archival groups records will be referred to by the notations "NA" and "RG."

27. Ibid., 8.

28. The identities of those in the picture are:

Left to right, standing: (1) Col. Benjamin Alvord, A.G. of AEF; (2) Maj. Robert Bacon, A.G. Dept.; (3) Lt. Col. George S. Simonds, War Dept. Inf; (4) Col. Charles P. Summerall, W.D. Artillery; (5) Maj. Alvin B. Barber, Gen. Staff, AEF (g-l); (6) Lt. Col. John Barker, Gen. Staff, AEF; (7) Lt. Col. Dwight E. Aultman, W.D. Artillery; (8) Lt. Col. Fox Conner, Gen. Staff, AEF (G-3); (9) Col. William S. Graves, W.D.G.S.; (10) Maj. Gen. John J. Pershing, C-in-C, AFF; (11) Maj. Arthur L. Conger, Gen. Staff, AEF (G-2); (12) Col. Chauncey B. Baker, Q.M.C.; (13) Lt. Col. Hanson E. Ely, W.D.; (14) Lt. Col. James G. Harbord, Chief of Staff, AEF; (15) Col. Mark L. Hersey, W.D.; (16) Lt. Col. Sherwood A. Cheney, Engineers, W.D.; (17) Lt. Col. Edward D. Anderson, Gen. Staff, W.D.; (18) Maj. Marlborough Churchill, AEF, Field Artillery. *Left to right, sitting:* (1) Maj. Morris E. Locke, W.D., Artillery; (2) Maj. Nelson F. Margetts, A.C.C., AEF; (3) Lt. Col. Kirby Walker, Cav. W.D.; (4) Lt. Col. John McA. Palmer, G.S., AEF (G-3), (5) Lt. Col. Dennis E. Nolan, G.S. AEF (G-2); (6) Capt. Martin C. Shallenberger, ADC, AEF; (7) Capt. William O. Reed, Cav. AEF (G-2); (8) Maj. Hugh A. Drum, G.S., AEF; (9) Capt. Jas. L. Collins, ADC, AEF; (10) Maj. Robert H. Dunlap, Marine Corps, Washington; (11) Maj. Frank Parker, Cav. AEF. Source of Photo: Copy from U.S. Army Signal Corps Photo #94307, held in the Archives of the Military History Institute, Carlisle Barracks, Pennsylvania.

29. *AC of S G-3, Final Report,* 8, 9.

30. Dupuy, R. E., T. N. Dupuy, and Paul Braim, *Military Heritage of America* (2 Vols). Dubuque, Iowa: Kendall/Hunt Pub., 1992, 258, 259, 598.

31. Ibid.

32. Ibid.

33. Matloff, ed., *American Military History,* 374–375.

34. Rainey, *Training of AEF;* also *Final Report of AEF G-3,* 12.

35. Report of the Chief of Staff, U.S. Army to the Secretary of War, 1919 (Annual Reports, War Department, Washington: GPO, 1920), 18–19.

36. War Department General Order No. 53, 27 May 1918 (NA RG 94).

37. Edward M. Coffman, *The Hilt of the Sword: The Career of Peyton C. March* (Madison: University of Wisconsin Press, 1966), chap. 5.

38. Historical Division, U.S. Army, *The United States Army in the World War, 1917–1919,* 17 vols. (Washington. GPO, 1948) 3:38, 39.

39. Coffman, *Hilt of Sword,* 48–51.

40. Ibid., 60, 61.

41. Ibid., 58, 59; also Donald Smythe, *Pershing: General of the Armies* (Bloomington: University of Indiana Press, 1986), 56, 167, 168.

42. John J. Pershing, General of the Armies, *My Experiences in The World War,* 2 vols. (New York: Stokes, 1931), 1:103; *Final Report of G-3,* 45, 46; Matloff, *American Military History,* 382, 383.

43. Pershing, *My Experiences,* 1:100–110, 128, 129.

44. A detailed presentation of the organization, growth, and problems of the AEF logistics system is in Johnson Hagood, *The Services of Supply* (New York: Houghton Mifflin, 1927).
45. Pershing, *My Experiences,* 1:28, 29, 150–154.
46. Rainey, *Training of AEF,* 1–16.
47. Ibid.; also Pershing, *My Experiences,* 1:150–154.
48. Letter to the author from Maj. Gen. Irving B. Holley Jr., professor of history, Duke University, author of the text *General John M. Palmer: Citizen Soldiers and the Army of a Democracy* (Westport, Conn.: Greenwood Press, 1982).
49. George S. Pappas (Col., U.S. Army), *Prudens Futuri: The U.S. Army War College, 1901–1967* (Carlisle: USAWC, 1967), 89. Pappas argued that 30 percent of general officers serving at the time of the Armistice were War College graduates. He also quoted Maj. Gen. Hugh Scott (chief of staff in 1917) as to the tremendous demand for War College graduates for high-level command and staff positions.
50. Rainey, *Training of AEF,* 16.
51. Cable 228-S, 19 October 1917, Pershing to Adjutant General, War Department, quoted in *The United States Army in the World War, 1917–1919,* 14:316.
52. Pershing, *My Experiences,* 1:151–152.
53. See the program for training for the 1st Infantry Division, issued by headquarters, American Expeditionary Forces, in October 1917, reproduced in vol. 14, *The United States Army in the World War,* 304; also, Pershing, *My Experiences,* 1:152–154.
54. War Department Document No. 394, *Infantry Drill Regulations, United States Army 1911* (Washington: GPO, 1911); the revisions to the *Infantry Drill Regulations* are reviewed in a text published by the United States Infantry Association, *Infantry Drill Regulations, United States Army 1911, With Changes One to Eighteen* (Philadelphia, J. B. Lippincott, 1917).
55. Russell F. Weigley, *History of the United States Army* (New York: Macmillan, 1967), 391. In a letter to the author dated 11 March 1983, Weigley referred again to the obtuse thinking of Pershing (and his associates) and their lack of clarity in strategy training and doctrine.
56. Rainey, *Training of AEF,* 28–30, quoted Kennedy and gave his own summary.
57. War Department Document No. 583, *Instructions on the Offensive Conduct of Small Units* (Washington: GPO, 1917); this document is a translation of a French document printed and distributed by the War Department in May 1917 and by AEF Headquarters in August 1917; it contained the standard French pessimism: "Infantry of itself has no offensive power against obstacles defended by fire . . . reinforcement of riflemen . . . will simply increase the losses." A War Department "translation notice" reinforced this pessimism by stating that "recent developments confirmed the power of the machine gun and the inability of infantry forces to capture or break through modern entrenchments unless heavily supported by massive artillery fire" (Ibid., 5–9).
58. This memorandum to the AEF chief of staff was provided the author by Colonel William R. Griffiths, a longtime student of the AEF in World War I in a letter dated 2 March 1983. The authenticity of the memo from the American chief of training was verified by reference to the National Archives, RG 120, Folder 695-B. Griffiths is the author of "Coalition for Total War: Field-Marshal Sir Douglas Haig and Entente Military Cooperation, 1916–1918" (M.A. Thesis, Rice University, 1920).

59. Memorandum, Lt. Col. H. A. Drum to the Assistant Chief of Staff G-3, 18 May 1918. This memorandum, including summary comments from American division commanders in France, is reprinted in *The United States Army in the World War,* 2:406–412.

60. Ibid., 412.

61. U.S. *Army in the World War,* 3:131.

62. Weigley made this point in a letter to the author dated 11 March 1983. Weigley averred that there was "a good deal of confusion in Pershing's mind" as to just what was meant by "open warfare" tactics. Allan Millett voiced the same opinion in a letter dated 18 February 1983.

63. GHQ, AEF, "Combat Instructions," dated 5 September 1918. NA, RG 120, Series 248.

64. Russell F. Weigley, *The American Way of War: A History of U.S. Military Strategy and Policy* (New York: MacMillan, 1973), 202.

65. Rainey details this personnel turbulence and its effects on training in his work, *Training of AEF,* 139.

66. E. S. Wallace, ed., *The Twenty-Eighth Division: Pennsylvania's Guard in the World War,* 5 vols. (Pittsburgh: Twenty-Eighth Division Publishing Co., n.d.), 5:52, 54, 55.

67. Weigley, *History of the United States Army,* 371–375.

68. Pershing, *My Experiences,* 1:266.

69. Ibid.

70. Rainey, *Training of AEF,* 69.

71. Vandiver, *Black Jack,* 2:772; Pershing, *My Experiences,* 1:151–152.

72. Rainey, *Training of AEF,* 73–76.

73. Pershing, *My Experiences,* 1:264–265.

74. Memo, Assistant Chief of Staff G-5 to the Chief of Staff, AEF dated 27 August 1917. Subject: School Project for American Expeditionary Forces. NA, RG 120, Series 230, Folder 211.

75. Ibid. This plan was approved by Gen. Pershing for immediate execution, the order signed by Col. J. C. Harbord, Chief of Staff, on 31 August 1917.

76. Rainey cites one directive that required that nine of the division's twelve infantry battalion commanders attend staff school at Langres (See *Training of AEF,* 208–213, 240.)

77. Weigley, *History of the Army,* 392.

78. Rainey, *The Training of AEF,* 226.

79. Ibid., 215–225.

80. Ibid., 227–229.

81. Final Report of Assistant Chief of Staff G-5 (Training) to Commander in Chief AEF 2 July 1919, NA, RG 120, Series 274, 2. Numerical totals summarized by this author.

82. AEF Document No. 251, "Program of Training for the 1st Division," dated 6 October 1917, NA, RG 120, Series 331.

83. Rainey, *Training of AEF,* 246, 247.

84. Ibid., 253–259.

85. Ibid., 253–259.

86. Ibid., 251–266.

87. Ibid., 266–270.

88. Weigley stated his agreement with Rainey's thesis (he was thesis advisor to Rainey) in a letter to this author dated 11 March 1983.

89. Dr. Jay Luvaas, author of many military texts (e.g., *The Military Legacy of the Civil War* (Chicago: University of Chicago Press, 1959), offered this opinion in a letter to this author dated 13 April 1983. Ropp states that all U.S. leaders were inexperienced and desperately overworked. Letter to author, 15 February 1983.

90. Gen. Theodore J. Conway (U.S. Army, Ret.) is deceased. He expressed these opinions in a letter to this author dated 6 March 1983.

91. Letters from Gordon Brook-Shepherd (9 March 1983); Correlli Barnett (12 March 1983); Michael Howard (23 February 1983); Brian Bond (22 February 1983); and John Terraine (25 February 1983).

92. Letter from Dr. James L. Stokesbury (Acadia University), 12 March 1983. Stokesbury is author of the text *A Short History of World War I* (New York: Merrow, 1981); also Dr. A. J. M. Hyatt (Univ. of Western Ontario), who has written on Canadian participation in World War I; letter to author dated 21 April 1983. Both expressed the opinion that American aggressiveness and adaptability made up quickly for their lack of training and experience.

93. MHI WWI Questionnaire; MHI archives.

CHAPTER 4. THE AMERICANS MOVE INTO THE LINE

1. Barrie Pitt, *1918: The Last Act* (New York: Ballantine Books, 1962), Prologue.

2. Two excellent texts on American participation in the Supreme War Council are David F. Trask, *The United States in the Supreme War Council: American War Aims and Inter-Allied Strategy, 1917–1918* (Middletown: Wesleyan University Press, 1961) and Frederick Palmer's text, *Bliss, Peacemaker: The Life and Letters of General Tasker Howard Bliss* (New York: Dodd Mead, 1934).

3. A colorful account of the last year of war is John Toland's *No Man's Land: 1918—the Last Year of the Great War* (New York: Doubleday, 1980).

4. Pershing, *My Experience*, 1:202-217.

5. *AC of S G-3, Final Report to CINC, AEF*, 17.

6. Ibid.

7. Pershing, *My Experiences*, 1:78, 256.

8. Frederick Palmer, *Bliss, Peacemaker*, 227–239.

9. *AC of S G-3, Final Report*, 18–22. See also Pershing, *My Experiences* 1:254–257.

10. For a complete and emotional tale of British attempts to "latch on" to U.S. manpower to save their own, see T. C. Lonergan's *It Might Have Been Lost: A Chronicle from Alien Sources of the Struggle to Preserve the National Identity of the AEF* (New York: Putnam's Sons, 1929).

11. *AC of S G-3, Final Report*, 2:22.

12. Pershing, *My Experiences*, 1:311–316.

13. Matloff, *American Military History*, 385–386.

14. *AC of S G-3, Final Report*, 23.

15. Matloff, *American Military History*, 385–387.

16. The "Paris Gun" was a specially cast, long-range German artillery piece which could fire a shell 75 miles.

17. Matloff, *American Military History*, 385–387.

18. Ibid., 388–389.

19. Toland, *No Man's Land*, 95.

20. Ibid.

21. Pershing, *My Experiences*, 1:360–363.
22. Pershing, *My Experiences*, 1:365; Foch, in his memoirs, remembers the commitment as more absolute than does Pershing. See *The Memoirs of Marshal Foch*, Col. T. Bentley Mott, trans. (New York: Doubleday, 1931), 270.
23. Pershing, *My Experiences*, 1:360–367.
24. Ibid.
25. Pershing, *My Experiences*, 2:7–13; Foch, *Memoirs*, 307–309.
26. Coffman, *The Hilt of the Sword*, 70–75.
27. Pershing, *My Experiences*, 2:20, 21.
28. Pershing, *My Experiences*, 2:28, 29; Coffman, *The Hilt of the Sword*, 71–72; Vandiver, *Black Jack*, 2:367.
29. Pershing, *My Experiences*, 2:31.
30. Ibid., 32–34.
31. Matloff, *American Military History*, 389–391; Baldwin, *World War I*, 143, 144.
32. Matloff, *American Military History*, 390–392.
33. Letter, John Toland to author, 18 February 1983.
34. Letter, Don Lawson to author, 4 March 1983.
35. Letter, William Griffiths to author, 2 March 1983.
36. Coffman, *Hilt of the Sword*, 71–74.
37. Ibid., 80–83.
38. Ibid., 84.
39. Pershing, *My Experiences*, 2:79, 80; Coffman, *The Hilt of the Sword*, 75.
40. *AC of S G-3, Final Report*, 48.
41. Ibid.
42. Coffman, *Hilt of the Sword*, 86, 87.
43. Ibid.
44. Coffman, *Hilt of the Sword*, 75, 111–115.
45. Baldwin, *World War I*, 144–146; *AC of S G-3, Final Report*, 45-47.
46. Matloff, ed., *American Military History*, 392–393
47. *Order of Battle of U.S. Land Forces in World War I* (Washington: GPO, 1988), vol. 2, 1–17; also Garey, E. B. et al., *American Guide Book to France and its Battlefields* (New York: Macmillan, 1920), 207–209.
48. *West Point Atlas*, vol. 2, Map 66; Matloff, ed., *American Military History*, 392-394.
49. John J. Pershing, *Report of General John J. Pershing, Commander-in-Chief American Expeditionary Forces*, HQ, AEF, 20 November 1918. HQ AEF, 1922.
50. Liggett, Hunter, Maj. Gen., USA, *Ten Years Ago in France* (New York: Dodd, 1928), 89ff., and Lt. Gen. Robert L. Bullard, USA, *American Soldiers Also Fought* (New York: Longman's, 1936), 64ff.
51. Toland, *No Man's Land*, 314–331.

CHAPTER 5. THE FIRST AMERICAN OFFENSIVE—ST. MIHIEL

1. Foch, *Memoirs*, 369–371.
2. Ibid., 372–374.
3. Erich von Ludendorff, *Erich von Ludendorff's Own Story August 1914–November 1919* (New York: Doubleday, 1929), 2:326.
4. *West Point Atlas*, Maps 66, 67.
5. Matloff ed., *American Military History*, 396; *West Point Atlas*, Map 67. With respect to exploitation, the British had earlier taken heavy casualties in attempting to

exploit with horse cavalry. The tanks were too blind and subject to breakdown to operate in an independent, fast-moving role.

6. Pershing, *My Experiences*, 2:175; see also *United States Army in the World War, 1917–1919*, 8:1–9.

7. Figures taken from *AC of S G-3, Final Report*, 58; also Bond and Sherrill, *America in War*, 110.

8. *U.S. Army in the World War, 8:10–15.*

9. Wilson, Dale E., *Treat 'Em Rough: The Birth of American Armor, 1917–20*. (Novato, Calif.: Presidio Press, 1989), 100–107.

10. *U.S. Army in the World War*, vol 15, 230–232.

11. R. E. Dupuy and T. N. Dupuy, Cols., U.S. Army, Ret., *The Encyclopedia of Military History* (New York: Harper and Row, 1970), 940, 947, 959, 982.

12. American Battle Monuments Commission, *A Guide to the Battle Fields in Europe* (Washington: GPO, 1927), 68–69.

13. AEF Assistant Chief of Staff G-2 Study 191-30.8, "Analysis of German Defensive System in St. Mihiel Salient," dated 18 August 1918. NA, RG 120, Series 191.

14. U.S.M.A., *The Great War*, 289–290.

15. Central to this planning, and to that for the Meuse-Argonne Campaign, was Lt. Col. George C. Marshall, of later military and diplomatic fame. Marshall wrote memoirs of this period through 1919. In later years, distressed by the arguments in print of his World War I mentors, he declined to publish any memoirs and directed that those from World War I be destroyed. After his death in 1959, his widow found a copy and authorized the Army to publish it. It was published in 1976 as *Memoirs of my Services in the World War* (Boston: Houghton Mifflin, 1976).

16. Marshall, *Memoirs*, 131–133; AEF G-3 Report, 59ff.

17. Larry I. Bland, ed., *The Papers of George Catlett Marshall: Vol. I, The Soldierly Spirit, December 1880–June 1939* (Baltimore: The Johns Hopkins University Press, 1981), 152–155.

18. These troop density figures were developed by this author from personnel data earlier cited and a study of the area, including that area east of the Meuse. While the specific figures may be subject to refutation, the tendency of the AEF planners to press too many troops into an attack is clear.

19. U.S.M.A., *The Great War*, 289–290.

20. *AC of S G-3, Final Report*, 15, 21; Bland, *Papers of Marshall*, 157–160.

21. Pershing, *My Experiences*, 2:215–219.

22. Pershing, *My Experiences*, 2:243–255, recounts the contretemps with Foch as a bitter disagreement. Foch, *Memoirs*, 395–401, smooths the whole matter over with a few sentences regarding a friendly give-and-take discussion on the new strategy. However, the record of this discussion supports Pershing. *U.S. Army in the World War*, 8:38–40.

23. Pershing, *My Experiences*, 2:246, 247.

24. Ibid., 2:247.

25. *AC of S G-3, Final Report*, 47–49.

26. *U.S. Army in the World War, 8:47.*

27. For Haig's reasoning see Robert Blake, ed., *The Private Papers of Douglas Haig, 1914–1919* (London: Wiedenfeld, 1952), 325. Foch records his judgments in *Memoirs*, 389–401.

28. James Stokesbury, *A Short History of World War I* (New York: William Morrow, 1981). Stokesbury is a professor of history at Acadia University, Canada. He

expressed the opinion quoted in a letter dated 12 March 1983 in response to questions from this author on World War I.

29. Among those who commented to this effect were John Keegan, Forrest Pogue, Russell Weigley, Gordon Brook-Shepherd, Correlli Barnett, and T. N. Dupuy. See Bibliography: Interviews and Correspondence.

30. Pershing, *My Experiences,* 2:260, 261.

31. *U.S. Army in the World War,* 8:177–180.

32. Wilson, 100–107.

33. *U.S. Army in the World War,* vol. 15, 230–232.

34. Ibid., 290.

35. *U.S. Army in the World War,* 8:291–300.

36. von Ledebur is quoted in Barry Gregory's *Argonne* (New York: Ballantine Books, 1972), 78.

37. Matloff, ed., *American Military History,* 390–398; *West Point Atlas,* Map 68.

38. William Matthews, and Dixon Wecter, *Our Soldiers Speak* (Boston: Little Brown and Co., 1943), 303.

39. GHQ AEF Assistant Chief of Staff for Operations, G-3, "Situation Report 12 Hours, 13 September 1918" NA, RG 120, Series 137. Hereafter, Situation Reports will be identified as "Sit. Rep.," showing the headquarters and the date. The story on big feet is in Pershing, *My Experiences,* 2:268.

40. Pershing, *My Experiences,* 2:266, 267.

41. GHQ AEF Sit. Rep., 14 September 1918.

42. *U.S. Army in the World War,* 8:258.

43. Pershing, *My Experiences,* 2:269–271; the information on the Metz controversy is taken from the U.S.M.A., *The Great War,* 290.

44. Quotation taken from Matloff, ed., *American Military History,* 398.

45. Pershing, *My Experiences,* 2:270.

46. Bullard, *American Soldiers,* 91.

47. Smythe, 184, 185; Wilson, 115–119.

CHAPTER 6. THE AEF ACCEPTS THE CHALLENGE: THE MEUSE-ARGONNE

1. Douglas W. Johnson, *Battlefields of the World War—Western and Southern Fronts: A Study in Military Geography* (New York: Oxford University Press, 1921) 339–406. Johnson's description in his text on Military Geography was verified and expanded by this author's reconnaissance of the area.

2. The description of these defenses was taken from Frank Vandiver's *Black Jack,* 2:955–956; J. F C. Fuller's *Decisive Battles of the U.S.A* (London: Harper, 1942), 383–384; The American Battle Monument Commission's *Guide,* 116–117; and Pershing's own account, *My Experiences,* 2:281–283.

3. Vandiver, *Black Jack,* 2:956.

4. Marshall, *Memoirs,* 137–138; Bland, *Papers of Marshall.* 1:160.

5. Marshall, *Memoirs,* 141–149; Pershing, *My Experiences,* 2:284–285.

6. Ibid., 149–156.

7. Ibid.

8. Letter, Forrest Pogue to author, 5 April 1983. Pogue is the author of the text *George C. Marshall: Education of a General* (New York: Viking Press, 1963) among his many writings.

9. Pershing, *My Experiences*, 2:285, 286; Johnson Haygood, *The Services of Supply* (New York: Houghton Mifflin, 1927) 320, 335–337.

10. Pershing was quoted by Lieutenant General (then Major General) Robert L. Bullard in his text *American Soldiers also Fought*, 89.

11. Secret Order, Headquarters French Second Army, 21 September 1981;NA, RG 120, Series 268. First Army Field Order No. 20, 20 September 1918; *U.S. Army in the World War*, 9:4, 47, 82–87. Pershing's views were expressed in *My Experiences*, 2:292–294.

12. Ibid.; also Toland, *No Man's Land*, 408; Fairfax Downey, *Sound of the Guns* (New York: David McKay, 1955), 231; Wilson, 127–131.

13. Wilson, 127–131.

14. *U.S. Army in the World War*, vol.15, 232–235; Smythe, 195.

15. *AC of S G-3, Final Report*, 75–81. Comments on training status are in Bullard, *American Soldiers*, 91, 92 and Rainey, *Training of AEF*, 262–378.

16. Marshall, *Memoirs*, 143.

17. Matloff, *American Military History*, 399; "Estimate of the Situation No. 235," Group of Armies von Gallwitz, 16 September 1918, *AC of S G-3, Final Report*, 80.

18. Donald Smythe advised about German foreknowledge of the coming American attack in the Meuse-Argonne in his text *Pershing, General of the Armies* (Bloomington: University of Indiana Press, 1986), 194, 195. Hubert Essame also stated that the Germans learned of the attack from French deserters; see his *Battle for Europe, 1918* (New York: Charles Scribner's Sons, 1972), 168.

19. Von Gallwitz's statement is in George Viereck, ed., *As They Saw Us* (New York: Doubleday, 1929), 239, 240. Bullard, *American Soldiers*, 93, 94; Smythe, 195.

20. This description is a collage taken from the American Battle Monuments Commission (BMC) texts *Summary of Operations in the World War* (Washington: GPO, 1944) prepared for each of the divisions in the AEF. Hereafter, these texts will be referred to as *BMC summary, ——Division*. See also Dale van Every, *The AEF in Battle* (New York: Appleton, 1928); Barry Gregory, *Argonne* (New York: Ballantine Books, 1972); Liggett, *AEF: Ten Years* Ago in *France;* Bullard, *American Soldiers Also Fought;* Robert Maddox, "The Meuse-Argonne Offensive" *American History Illustrated* April 1975; Laurence Stallings, *The Doughboys: The AEF in World War I* (New York: Harpers and Row, 1963); Frederick Palmer, *America in France* (Westport, Conn.: Greenwood Press, 1981); and John Toland, *No Man's Land.*

21. "Estimate of Strength, Capabilities, and Combat Value of American Forces by the German Supreme Command, 1917–1918," unpublished staff study, 1935, United States National War College Library, Fort McNair, Washington, D.C. Also Viereck, *As They Saw* Us, 286–287, 294–295, 297–298.

22. Viereck, *As They Saw Us*, 50–51, 296–297; Liggett, *AEF: Ten Years Ago*, 250–251.

23. Wilson, 142–145.

24. Smythe, 196.

25. First Army Sit. Rep., 9 A.M. 26 September 1918. NA, RG 120, Series 137.

26. First Army Sit. Rep., 12:30 P.M. NA, RG 120, Series 770.

27. BMC Summary, 33rd Div., 28, 29.

28. BMC Summary, 80th Div., 20-23. 195A.

29. BMC Summary, 4th Division, 52, 53.

30. BMC Summary, 79th Division, 13–15.

31. BMC Summary, 37th Division, 12, 13.

32. BMC Summary, 91st Division, 14–16.

33. BMC Summary, 35th Division, 14–16.

34. BMC Summary, 28th Division, 35, 36.

35. Pershing, *My Experiences,* 2:295–297; First Army Sit. Rep., 4 P.M., 26 September 1918. NA, RG 120, Series 137; BMC Summary, 77th Division, 16–19.

36. U.S. Army Center of Military History. *Order of Battle of the United States Land Forces in the World War, American Expeditionary Forces: Divisions* (Washington: GPO, 1931), 296-307; Smythe, 197.

37. This description is taken, in part, from an article by Major Elbridge Colby, "The Taking of Montfaucon," *Infantry Journal* (March–April, 1940) 1–14, and one by Colonel Conrad H. Lanza, "The Battle of Montfaucon," *Field Artillery Journal* (issues of May–June, July–August, November–December 1933, and July–August 1934).

38. Hoffman's statement is in his response to a questionnaire sent to him by the U.S. Army's Military History Institute (MHI) at Carlisle Barracks, Pennsylvania, 315th Infantry Regiment folder, 79th Division, MHI archives.

39. Colby, "Taking Montfaucon," 7.

40. Ibid.

41. V Corps Sit. Rep., 10:40 A.M., NA, RG 120, Series 137.

42. V. Corps Operations Report, 26 September 1918; NA, RG 120, Series 137. Hereafter, operations reports will be called *Op. Rep.*

43. AEF Headquarters Daily Communique, 26 September 1918; NA, RG 120, Series 137.

44. Colby, "Taking Montfaucon," 8, 9.

45. Ibid., 9.

46. Ibid., 9; *BMC Summary, 4th Division,* 12–14.

47. Colby, "Taking Montfaucon," 10, 11.

48. First Army Sit. Rep., 7:30 P.M., 26 September 1918; NA, RG 120, Series 137.

49. Colby, "Taking Montfaucon," 11.

50. Ibid., 12.

51. Ibid., 13.

52. First Army Sit. Rep., 4:30 A.M., 27 September 1918. I Corps Op. Rep., 26 September 1918; III Corps Op. Rep. 26 September; V Corps Op. Rep., 26 September; division Op. Reps., same period. NA, RG 120, Series 137, 271.

53. Pershing, *My Experiences,* 2:296, 297; Viereck, *As They Saw Us,* 32, 33, 238, 239.

54. Bullard, *American Soldiers,* 94; Maddox, "Meuse-Argonne," 26.

55. Liggett, *AEF, Ten Years Ago,* 180; Bullard, *American Soldiers,* 92. Essame, *Battle,* 169.

56. Viereck, *As They Saw* Us, 239–243.

57. *BMC Summary, 4th Division,* 54, 55.

58. *BMC Summary, 37th Division,* 14, 15.

59. *BMC Summary, 91st Division,* 121.

60. *BMC Summary, 35th Division,* 14–20.

61. BMC Summary, *28th* Division, 46, 47.

62. Daniel R. Beaver, *Newton D Baker and the American War Effort, 1917–1919* (Lincoln: University of Nebraska Press, 1967), 195; Smythe, *Pershing,* 197–199.

63. *Order of Battle...* Vol. 2, 210, 211; Smythe, 196, 197.

64. Beaver, using several sources, estimates combat casualties at between 45,000 and 50,000 for the four days of September. Beaver, *Newton D. Baker,* 195.

65. First Army Op. Reps., 28–29 September 1918; NA, RG 120, Series 271; AEF G-3 memo, "Study of the Situation Considering the Defensive Plan," 29 September 1918; NA, RG 120, Series 271.

66. Smythe, *Pershing*, 200, 201.

67. I Corps and V Corps Op. Reps., 1 October 1918; NA, RG 120, Series 271; *BMC Summary, 1st Division*, 64; *3d Division*, 59; *32d Division*, 37; *91st Division*, 23.

68. Beaver, *Newton D. Baker*, 196; Smythe, 200; Essame, *Battle*, 173–195.

CHAPTER 7. THE TEST OF BATTLE: FIGHTING THROUGH TO VICTORY

1. MHI WWI Questionnaire; MHI archives.

2. Smythe, 196, 197; AEF G-3 Memo, "Defensive Plan," 29 September; AEF G-3 Memo, "Study of the Changes in Zone of Action of Corps," 29 September 1918; NA, RG 120, Series 270.

3. Essame, 171.

4. Smythe, 197.

5. Ibid., 188, 189.

6. *U.S. Army in the World War.* vol. 9, 522; Smythe, 198, 199.

7. Pershing, *My Experiences*, 2:327; Charles E. Heller, "Chemical Warfare in World War I," Leavenworth Papers No. 10, Fort Leavenworth, Kansas: U.S. Army Command and General Staff College, September 1984.

8. Pershing, *My Experiences*, 2:311ff.

9. Ibid., 303.

10. Smythe, *Pershing*, 200, 201; Essame, *Battle*, 173, 174; Toland, *No Man's Land*, 415.

11. Letter, Marshall Foch to General Pershing, 2 October 1918, *U.S. Army in the World War*, 2:619.

12. Pershing, *My Experiences*, 2:chaps 46, 47. Vandiver, *Black Jack*, 2: 967–968; Beaver, *Newton D. Baker*, 197, 198; Falls, *Great War*, 357.

13. MHI WWI Questionnaire; MHI archives.

14. Pershing, *My Experiences*, 2:327ff.

15. AEF *AC of S G-3, Final Report*, 81; First Army Op. Rep., 4 October, reported POWs' statements on defense orders of German Supreme Command; NA, RG 120, Series 271.

16. *AEF G-3, Final Report*, 82, 83.

17. David M. Kennedy, *Over Here: The First World War and American Society* (New York: Oxford University Press, 1980), 204.

18. Pershing, *My Experiences*, 2:321–322.

19. BMC Summary, 4th Division, 63, 64.

20. BMC Summary, 80th Division, 20, 30.

21. III Corps Op. Reps., 4, 5, 6 October 1918; NA, RG 120, Series 271; *AEF G-3, Final Report*, 81.

22. BMC Summary, 3rd Division, 62, 63.

23. V Corps Op. Reps., 4, 5 October 1918; NA, RG 120, Series 271; BMC Summary, 32nd Division, 38–43.

24. BMC Summary, Ist Division, 9, 10; 28th Division, 67, 68.

25. I Corps Op. Reps., 2, 3, 4, 5 October 1918; NA, RG 120, Series 271.

26. Matthews, *Our Soldiers Speak*, 305.

27. James M. Merrill, *Uncommon Valor* (New York: Rand McNally, 1964), 326-330. Also Matthews, *Our Soldiers Speak*, 306.

28. Merrill, *Uncommon Valor*, 330–335.

29. Discussion with veterans of World War I who were members of Region 3, Veterans of World War I Assn. of the USA, under direction of Dana J. Pyle, on 12 April 1983, at Wilmington, Del.. Martin Apostolico claims to have seen Germans firing from U.S. tanks; others said they had heard about that.

30. Letter, Edwin Randall to author, 3 August 1983.

31. Pershing admits this total of casualties in *My Experiences*, 2:328.

32. MHI WWI Questionnaire; MHI Archives.

33. Vandiver, *Black Jack*, 2:968–969.

34. MHI WWI Questionnaire; MHI Archives.

35. Pershing, *My Experiences*, 2:299–304; Ludendorff, *Ludendorff*, 2:404.

36. First Army Field Order No. 33, 1 October 1918, *U.S. Army in the World War*, 9:191–192.

37. First Army Field Order No. 20, Pershing, *My Experiences*, 2:289–293.

38. First Army Field Order No. 39, 5 October 1918, *U.S. Army in the World War*, 9:215.

39. BMC Summary, 28th Division, 13, 14; 33rd Division, 35–38.

40. Vandiver, *Black Jack*, 2:969-970; 33rd Division Op. Reps., 8, 9, 10 October 1918; NA, RG 120, Series 271. Pershing, *My Experiences*, 2:331–333.

41. BMC Summary, 28th Division, 63–69; 82nd Division, 25–27.

42. Pershing, *My Experiences*, 2:327-334; I, III, V Corps Op. Reps., 8, 9, 10, 11 October 1918, NA, RG 120, Series 271; *AC of S G-3, Final Report*, 81-82; 1st Division Op. Reps., 8, 9, 10, 11 October 1918, NA, RG 120, Series 271.

43. BMC Summary, 1st Division, 77, 78; 5th Division, 27, 28; 80th Division, 35, 36.

44. *AC of S G-3, Final Report*, 82; Bullard, *American Soldiers*, 107.

45. MHI WWI Questionnaire; MHI archives.

46. *AC of S G-3, Final Report*, 82; Pershing, *My Experiences*, 2:327, 328; Smythe, *Pershing*, 206, 207.

47. Pershing, *My Experiences*, 2:335.

48. Smythe, *Pershing*, 208, 209. Smythe also expressed his opinion of Pershing's condition at this time in an interview with this author on 1 March 1985.

49. Vandiver, *Black Jack*, 2:972. Vandiver cites a memo of conversation between General Preston Brown and French Colonel de Chambrun at the Army War College, 2:30 P.M., 18 January 1920. Vandiver footnotes that a copy is in the Pershing Papers, Box 35. This author holds a copy of the memo, but he believes the recollections of de Chambrun or possibly of Brown are in error.

50. Secretary Baker's statement is recorded by Richard O'Connor, *Black Jack Pershing* (New York: Doubleday, 1961), 316. Hereafter, to avoid confusion with Vandiver's text, O'Connor's text will be referred to by the short title *Black*. I gained Smythe's opinion in an interview on 1 March 1985. Pershing, *My Experiences*, 2:335, reports only a meeting with Foch at the time at which he (Pershing) discussed the reorganization of his armies. Foch, *Memoirs*, 432–442, states his defense of Pershing against demands by Clemenceau for his relief. Vandiver, however, believes that both Foch and Pershing failed to record the attempted relief of Pershing out of courtesy. Vandiver, *Black Jack*, 2:956, Note 86.

51. Vandiver, *Black Jack*, 2:973–975; Pershing, *My Experiences*, 2:335.

52. Charles C. Dawes, *A Journal of the Great War,* 2 vols. (Boston: Houghton Mifflin, 1921), 2:189.

53. Bliss is quoted in O'Connor, *Black,* 313.

54. *Army Times* Editors, *The Yanks are Coming: The Story of John J. Pershing* (New York: Putnam's Sons, 1960), 128.

55. Pershing, *My Experiences,* 335–339.

56. Smythe, 208.

57. *Army in World War..,* vol. 15, 235.

58. Wilson, 176–178.

59. Smythe, *Pershing,* 214–216; *Order of Battle...,* vol.2, 113–129.

60. *Order of Battle...,* vol.2, 272–286; Garey, E. B. et al., *American Guide Book to France and its Battlefields* (New York: Metropolitan, 1920), 255–258.

61. BMC Summary, 29th Division, 21; 33d Division, 41,42; MacArthur, Douglas, *Reminiscences.* (New York: McGraw-Hill, 1964), 42–66.

62. MacArthur, 66.

63. BMC Summary, 42d Division, 61–65.

64. MHI WWI Questionnaire; MHI archives.

65. BMC Summary, 78th Division, 21;3d Division, 83, 84; 5th Division, 31, 34; Pershing, *My Experiences,* 2:340, 341, 351, 352.

66. Pershing, *My Experiences,* 2:351, 352.

67. Beaver, *Newton Baker,* 202, 203.

68. Vandiver, *Black Jack,* 2:978, 970; Smythe, *Pershing,* 217–219; Heller, "Chemical Warfare," 83–90.

69. Letter, AEF Chief of Staff to Commanders, First and Second Armies, 22 October 1918; *U.S. Army in the World War,* 2:364; Letter of Instructions to Commanding General, First Army, 21 October 1918; First Army Field Order No. 88, 27 October 1918, *U.S. Army in the World War,* 9:332, 333.

70. Vandiver, *Black Jack,* 2:978, 979; Pershing, *My Experiences,* 2:372–374.

71. *AC of S G-3, Final Report,* 83.

72. Raymond C. Cochrane, "The Use of Gas in the Meuse-Argonne Campaign, September–November, 1918," Study Number 10, U.S. Army Chemical Corps Historical Office, Army Chemical Center, 87; Fairfax Downey, *Sound of the Guns: The Story of American Artillery* (New York: David McKay, 1955), 233.

73. Downey, *Sound of the Guns,* 233.

74. Ibid.

75. BMC Summary, 2d Division, 70, 71.

76. Ibid.

77. BMC Summary, 78th Division, 42, 43.

78. Smythe, *Pershing,* 226.

79. *AC of S G-3, Final Report,* 84, 85; Beaver, *Newton Baker,* 208, 209; First Army Field Order No. 99, 3 November 1918; First Army Op. Rep., 4 November 1918, U.S. *Army in the World War,* 9:377–380.

80. Beaver, *Newton Baker,* 209.

81. Pershing, *My Experiences,* 2:378.

82. *Stars and Stripes,* 8 November 1918, 1.

83. First Army Op. Reps., 4, 5 November 1918, *U.S. Army in the World War,* 9:382–386; Pershing, *My Experiences,* 2:378–381; BMC Summary, 5th Division, 47; 79th Division, 24–32; 81st Division, 14–20.

84. BMC Summary, 2nd Division, 84-87; 89th Division, 31.

85. BMC Summary, 80th Division, 38–55.

86. BMC Summary, 78th Division, 20, 44, 45; 42nd Division, 77, 78.

87. First Army Op. Reps., 6, 7, 8 November 1918; *U.S. Army in the World War,* 9:388–394; BMC Summary, lst Division, 83, 84.

88. Viereck, *As They Saw Us,* 280–281.

89. Vandiver, *Black Jack,* 2:982, 983.

90. Pershing, *My Experiences,* 2:383–387; First Army Field Order No. 104, 7 November 1918; Memo, Chief of Staff, First Army, to deputy (1st Division out of Sector), 7 November 1918; *U.S. Army in the World War,* 9:481–482; BMC Summary, lst Division, 85; 42nd Division, 88–91. Smythe, *Pershing,* 227, 228.

91. MHI WWI Questionnaire; MHI Archives.

92. Patton is quoted by Toland, *No Man's Land,* 557.

CHAPTER 8. DENOUEMENT AND DEPARTURE

1. Smythe, 232.

2. Pershing, II, 390.

3. Pershing, II, 394–396; Smythe, 232, 233.

4. Smythe, 245–247.

5. *U.S. Army in the World War,* vol. 12, 2-70; staff reports are in Volumes 13–15.

6. Ibid., vol. 15, 177–219.

7. *Report of Superior Board on Organization and Tactics,* 19 April 1919, 1–3.

8. Ibid., 5–11.

9. Ibid., 18–31.

10. Ibid., 80–83.

11. Ibid., 31–42.

12. Ibid., 60–78.

13. Ibid., 89.

14. Conclusions and recommendations about other combat arms and services follow in the report.

15. Smythe, 245–247.

16. *American Armies and Battlefields...,* 487, 488.

17. *U.S. Army in the World War...,* vol. 10, Part 1, 93–154; *American Armies and Battlefields...,* 488, 489.

18. *American Armies and Battlefields...,* 492, 493; Smythe, 248, 249.

19. *U.S. Army in the World War...,* vol. 10, Part 2, 1132, 1133; Smythe, 250,251.

CHAPTER 9. IN RETROSPECT

1. Bond Paul S. and Clarence O. Sherrill, *America in the World War.* Menasha, Wis.: Banta Pub, 1921, 140–146.

2. Bond and Sherrill, *America in the War,* 144–146; also Pershing, *My Experiences,* 389. Bond and Sherrill show a total of 63,000 prisoners of war captured by Americans on all fronts (page 145), while Pershing in his *Report to the Secretary of War,* 20 November 1918 (Washington: G.P.O., 1922), 23, cites a total prisoner of war count of 44,000.

3. Bond and Sherrill, *America in the War,* 146.

4. Ibid.

5. Kennedy, *Over Here,* 348–359.

6. *AC of S G-3, Final Report,* 87.

7. Ibid., 87.

8. Ibid.

9. Kennedy, *Over Here*, quotes French "Notes on American Offensive Operations," 200.

10. Kennedy, *Over Here*, quotes from the notes of a British War Cabinet meeting, 200.

11. Kennedy, *Over Here*, 200; also Smythe, *Pershing*, 112.

12. Letter to author from Correlli Barnett, 12 March 1983.

13. Interview with Peter Simkins, historian of the Imperial War Museum, London, England, on 13 May 1983.

14. MHI WWI Questionnaire; MHI Archives.

15. Letter to author from Trevor N. Dupuy, 15 February 1983.

16. Marshall's statement is quoted by O'Connor, *Black*, 354.

17. Letter to author from Allan R. Millett, 18 February 1983.

18. Charts are composed from data supplied in AC *of S G-3, Final Report*, as amplified by data from Bond and Sherrill, *America in the War*. See charts for specific sources.

19. The 77th had leadership problems from the division commander down the chain of command. Pershing cited the 1st in general orders for excellence; he did not select any other division for such a unique rating. Smythe believes the 1st was Pershing's favorite, *Pershing*, 230. Many cite the 2d Division as first in performance. This author would find it difficult to rank the 1st, 2d and 42d, all having performed well in combat, but he wouldn't rate the 77th as high as those three.

20. One recent attempt to quantify combat capabilities is in Trevor N. Dupuy's text, *The Evolution of Weapons and Warfare* (New York: Bobbs-Merrill, 1980). Dupuy has come closer in establishing combat value criteria than any other work seen by this author. However, his work is criticized by many.

21. Smythe, *Pershing*, 237.

22. Letters to the author from Theodore Conway, 6 March 1983; from Edward Coffman, 4 February 1983; from Theodore Ropp, 15 February 1983; and from John Keegan, 30 March 1983. Keegan, *Six Armies in Normandy* (London: Sharp, 1982). Pershing's rejection of AEF comparisons is cited by John Palmer, *America in Arms* (New Haven: Yale University Press, 1941), 352.

23. Marshall, *My Service*, 13ff.

24. Smythe, *Pershing*, 82, 83, 161-166.

25. O'Connor, *Black*, 195; Pershing, *My Experiences*, 1:182–186, 321, 322, 388, 389; 2:180, 181.

26. Richard Goldhurst, *Pipe Clay and Drill—John J. Pershing: The Classic American Soldier* (New York: Thomas Crowell, 1977), 285, 286; Coffman, *The Hilt*, 81, 82, 104–117.

27. Letter, John Toland to author, 18 February 1983. Toland, *No Man's Land* (Garden City, N.Y.: Doubleday, 1980).

28. Letter, Correlli Barnett to author, 12 March 1983.

29. Letter, James Rainey to author, 4 April 1983.

30. Letter, Gordon Brook-Shepherd to author, 9 March 1983. Brook-Shepherd, *November 1918: The Last Act of the Great War* (London: Collins, 1981).

31. Smythe, *Pershing*, 200, 217.

32. Letter, Edward M. Coffman to author, 4 February 1983.

33. Letter, Allan Millett to author, 18 February 1983.
34. Timothy Nenninger, *The Leavenworth Schools and the Old Army* (Westport, Conn.: Greenwood Press, 1978).
35. Letter, Weigley to author, 11 March 1983.
36. Letters, Ropp to author, 15 February 1983; I. B. Holley to author, 15 March 1983.
37. Harbord's statement is reported by Smythe, *Pershing*, 230.
38. Liggett's statement taken from U.S.M.A., *Great War*, 290; Rainey's opinion given in a letter to this author, 14 April 1983.
39. Viereck, *As They Saw Us*, 31–33.
40. Pershing, *My Experiences*, 2:270.
41. Pershing, *My Experiences*, 2:243–250; Foch, *Memoirs*, 400, 401.
42. Bullard, *American Soldiers*, 79.
43. David Lloyd George and Winston Churchill were among British leaders who wanted a seaborne strategy.
44. Among the many references to this dispute between Lee and Longstreet, the conversation is cited in the text *For the Common Defense*, by Allan R. Millett and Peter Maslowski (New York: Free Press, 1984), 206.
45. Pershing, *My Experiences*, 1:205, 207.
46. Rexmond C. Cochrane, "Gas Warfare in World War I," Study Number 10, U.S. Army Chemical Corps Historical Studies, Army Chemical Center, Maryland, 75, 76.
47. Liddell Hart is quoted in Cochrane, "Gas Warfare," 76.
48. Cochrane, "Gas Warfare," 83–87.
49. Heller, "Chemical Warfare," 44, 87–90.
50. Smythe illustrates communications problems in *Pershing*, 197.
51. The appendix is my summary of comments from veterans whom this author could definitely associate with the Meuse-Argonne Campaign. Certainly there are hundreds of others whose service merits more detailed research on these records.
52. Interview with Dr. Claude Moore, 16 June 1983.
53. Letter from General Mark Clark to author, 16 June 1983; letter from General Theodore Conway to author, 6 March 1983.
54. Allan Millett, *The General: Robert L. Bullard and Officership in the U.S. Army, 1881–1925* (Westport, Conn.: Greenwood, 1975), 247.
55. Smythe, *Pershing*, 235, 236.
56. Pershing, *My Experiences*, 1:153.
57. Smythe, *Pershing*, 235.
58. Basil Liddell Hart, *Reputations Ten Years After* (Boston: Little, Brown, 1928), 314, 315.
59. Jamieson, Perry D., *Crossing the Deadly Ground: United States Army Tactics, 1865–1899* (Tuscaloosa, Ala: Univ. of Alabama Press, 1994), 113–154.
60. *U.S. Army Field Service Regulations* of 1911, 1914, and 1917, all contain instructions for assault in line formation. As late as 1977, the Infantry School at Fort Benning, Georgia was teaching "Marching Fire," essentially assault in erect posture by troops in line formation; recent issues of infantry field manuals modify this guidance by allowing for fire and movement onto the objective.
61. Smythe, *Pershing*, 235.
62. Goldhurst, *Pipe Clay*, 233, 234, 301.

63. Downey, *Sound*, 207.

64. Dwight D. Eisenhower, *At Ease: Stories I Tell to Friends* (New York: Doubleday 1967), 173.

65. Letter from Clark to author, 16 June 1983.

66. Smythe, *Pershing*, 143, 144, 285.

67. Letter from Coffman to author, 14 February 1983.

68. Letter from Holley to author, 15 March 1983.

69. Letter from Conway to author, 6 March 1983.

70. Letter, Holley to author, 15 March 1983.

71. Nenninger, *Leavenworth Schools*, 149.

72. Figures are from Thomas G. Frothingham, *The American Reinforcement in the World War* (Freeport, N.Y.: Books for Libraries Press, 1971), 332–340.

73. This limerick was often recited to deride officers who came from military schools to their first combat experience.

74. Nenninger, *Leavenworth Schools*, 151.

75. Ibid.

76. Harvey A. DeWeerd, *Great Soldiers of Two World Wars* (New York: W. W. Norton, 1941), 365; see also Smythe, *Pershing*, 143, 144, 284, 285, for Mitchell's relations with other AEF officers.

77. Matloff, *American Military History*, 377; Liggett, *Ten Years Ago*, 255, 256.

78. The historian T. Harry Williams, *Americans at War: The Development of the American Military System* (New York: Collier Books, 1960), 135, found unique qualities in the American similar to my listing.

79. Interview with Peter Simkins, 13 May 1983.

80. Liggett, *Ten Years Ago*, 252–257.

81. Smythe, *Pershing*, 262, 263.

82. MHI WWI Questionnaire; MHI archives.

83. This author has summarized Frank Vandiver's opinions on Pershing, expressed in Vandiver's two-volume biography of Pershing, *Black Jack*.

84. Smythe, *Pershing*, 238–244; also interview with Smythe, 1 March 1985.

85. T. Harry Williams, *The History of American Wars* (New York: Knopf, 1981), 402, 403.

86. Liddell Hart, *Reputations*, 314, 315.

87. Letter, James Stokesbury to author, 12 March 1983.

88. Letter, John Terraine to author, 21 February 1983.

89. Letter, John Toland to author, 18 February 1983; Theodore Ropp to author, 15 February 1983.

90. Letter, Russell Weigley to author, 11 March 1983.

91. Letter, Trevor Dupuy to author, 15 February 1983.

92. Letter, Allan Millett to author, 18 February 1983.

93. Letter, Edward M. Coffman to author, 14 February 1983.

94. Interview with Donald Smythe, 1 March 1985.

95. Interview with David Trask, 14 March 1983. Trask is the author of the text *The United States and the Supreme War Council* (Middletown: Wesleyan University Press, 1961).

96. *The New York Times Book Review*, 26 April 1931, 1.

97. Liddell Hart is quoted by DeWeerd, *Great Soldiers*, 185.

98. Ibid., 184.

99. Little Hart, *Reputations*, 316; DeWeerd, *Great Soldiers*, 186.
100. Smythe, *Pershing*, 244.
101. Pershing, *My Experiences*, 2:354; Kennedy, *Over Here*, 200.
102. MHI WWI Questionnaires; MHI archives. For totals, see Appendix 10. "Tommy" and "Poilu" were nicknames for the British and French soldiers, respectively.
103. Ibid.
104. Ibid.
105. Trask, *Supreme War Council*, chap. 4.
106. Interview with Peter Simkins, 13 May 1983.
107. Ibid.
108. Thomas Lonergan, *It Might Have Been Lost* (New York: C. P. Putnams, 1929).
109. Letter, John Elting to author, 14 May 1983.
110. Letter Edward Coffman to author, 14 February 1983.
111. *AEF G-3, Final Report*, 87.
112. Letter, Correlli Barnett to author, 12 March 1983.
113. Ludendorff is quoted by Smythe, *Pershing*, 237.
114. *The New York Times Book Review*. 26 April 1931, 1.
115. *The New York Times Book Review*, 24 May 1931, Letters to the Editor.
116. *The New York Times Book Review*, 10 May 1931, Letters to the Editor.
117. *The New York Times Book Review*, 2 August 1931, Letters to the Editor.
118. Letters, John Giles to author, 28 July 1983, 12 August 1983.
119. Smythe, *Pershing*, 261, 262.
120. Walter Millis, *Arms and Men: A Study of American Military History* (New York: Mentor Books, 1958), 214ff.; Smythe, *Pershing*, 278, 279.
121. Millis, *Arms and Men*, 216, 217.
122. Woodward is quoted in the Preface of Daniel M. Smith, *The Great Departure: The United States and World War I, 1914–1920* (New York: J. Wiley and Sons, 1965).
123. Smith, *The Great Departure*, 201.
124. Smythe, *Pershing*, 259.

BIBLIOGRAPHY

ARCHIVAL MATERIAL

National Archives. There is a veritable gold mine of records of the American military effort in World War I in the old Army and Navy Division of the National Archives. For this author's research, the most valuable sources were:

Record Group (RG) 120. Records of the American Expeditionary Forces (AEF), 1917–1923. Approximately 18,000 linear feet, comprising orders, records, reports, memoranda, and studies collected from divisions, corps, armies, headquarters, and staff sections of the AEF and the supporting services of supply (SOS). A mimeographed inventory (NM-91) is available to researchers; it is a valuable guide to this extensive collection. Cartographic material (maps and photographs) are mostly in separate storage under the care of the cartographic and audio-visual branches of the archives. A guide to this material is in Franklin W. Burch's *Cartographic Records of the American Expeditionary Forces, 1917–1918*, Preliminary Inventory 165, National Archives.

Microfilm listings (Microcopy T-900) of the "Index to Correspondence of the Adjutant General, AEF Headquarters, 1917–1920." This extensive index is an excellent guide to specific orders and directives.

Microfilm bibliography (Microcopy T-619) "History of the U.S. Army Air Service, 1917–1919," compiled by Colonel Edgar S. Garrell, gives a complete listing of documents related to the development and employment of our air services.

RG 165. Records of the War Plans Division, War Department General Staff. These files also contain a collection of Austro-Hungarian and German military records of World War I as well as some records on Allied forces, British, French, and Italian.

215

RG 94. Records of the War Department, general and special staffs and the adjutant general for the period of World War I and earlier.

RG 177. Records of the chief of air service of the War Department for 1917–1922. These files also contain records for the chief of arms for the War Department for World War I and other periods.

RG 107. Records of the Office of the Secretary of War for World War I and some other eras.

RG 156. Records of the Ordnance Department, machine guns and artillery.

RG 166. Records of the War College Division (Historical Branch) General Staff of the War Department. Contains monographs and studies on the war and related matters.

The Congressional Library contains a large collection of published material for World War I, listed under the title "European War, 1914–1921." It also holds the personal papers of many of the luminaries of the period including some of the Pershing papers.

The Library of the National War College, Fort McNair, Washington, D.C., contains a wealth of studies and monographs on military operations in World War I and related matters.

The Library of the Center of Military History of the Department of Army, Washington, D.C., contains a random collection of un-published studies on World War I and related subjects.

The U.S. Army's Military History Institute at the U.S. Army War College, Carlisle Barracks, Pennsylvania, contains much unpublished material on World War I. An ongoing collection of over sixty-seven hundred responses of World War I veterans to Army Services Experience Questionnaires (World War I Research Project) is a rich source of personal observations awaiting further scholarly exploitation. In this research effort, the collection (segregated by military organization) was reviewed to gain verification/refutation of official records and to add the color of personal narration of events. The responses of those 728 veterans who were found to have participated in the Meuse-Argonne were collated for determining group opinion on matters related to the campaign.

The Army War College holds a quantity of student monographs on World War I and related subjects. The U.S. Army's Command and General Staff College at Fort Leavenworth, Kansas, also holds a number of student monographs on U.S. participation in World War I.

The American Battle Monuments Commission produced a series of 69 volumes of photographs of the terrain of the Meuse-Argonne, taken from vantage points to show the ground as viewed by the personnel of the AEF and their enemies. Each of the 1,396 photographs is accompanied by a 1:20,000 scale map, marked to show the location of the camera and the direction of the photograph. The series is entitled *Terrain Photographs, American World War.* A copy of this collection is in the archives of the Military History Institute, Carlisle Barracks, Pennsylvania.

INTERVIEWS AND CORRESPONDENCE

Apostolico, Martin. Former corporal, U.S. Marine Corps, assigned to 2d Infantry Division during the Meuse-Argonne Campaign. Interviewed on 12 April 1983.

Barnett, Correlli. British military historian; author of *The Swordbearers: Supreme Command in the First World War.* New York: William Morrow, 1964. Letter to author 12 March 1983.

Blumenson, Martin. American military historian; author of *The Patton Papers, 1885–1940.* 2 vols. Boston: Houghton Mifflin, 1972, and "The Outstanding Soldier of the AEF" *American History Illustrated* 1 (February 1967): 4–13, 50–54. Letter to author 12 March 1983.

Bond, Brian. *British Military Policy between the Two World Wars.* Oxford: Clarendon Press, 1980. Letter to author 22 February 1983.

Brook-Shepherd, Gordon. British journalist; author of *November 1918: The Last Act of the Great War.* London: Collins, 1981. Letter to author 9 March 1983.

Clark, Mark W. General, U.S. Army (retired). Served in the AEF in World War I. Letter to author 16 June 1983.

Coffman, Edward M. American military historian; author of *The Hilt of the Sword: The Career of Peyton C. March.* Madison: University of Wisconsin, 1966; and *The War to End All Wars.* New York: Oxford University Press, 1968. Letter to author 14 February 1983.

Conway, Theodore J. General, U.S. Army (deceased), Ph.D. candidate; dissertation topic: "The U.S. Army Prepares for World War II." Letter to author 6 March 1983.

Dupuy, Trevor N. Colonel, U.S. Army (retired). Military historian and analyst; author of *The Evolution of Weapons and Warfare.* New York: Bobbs Merrill, 1980, and with his father, Colonel R. Ernest Dupuy, *Brave Men and Great Captains.* New York: Harper & Brothers, 1955. Letter to author 15 February 1983.

Elting, John R. Colonel, U.S. Army (retired). Military historian and analyst; author of *American Army Life.* New York: Scribner's Sons, 1982. Letter to author 14 February 1983.

Giles, John. Military historian and chairman emeritus of *The Western Front Association;* author of many studies on World War I. Letters to author 28 July, 12 August 1983.

Griffiths, William R. Colonel, U.S. Army. Military historian; coauthor of *The Great War.* West Point, N.Y.: United States Military Academy, 1979. Letter to author 2 March 1983.

Holley, Irving B. Major General, U.S. Air Force (retired). Military historian; author of *General John M. Palmer: Citizen Soldiers and the Army of a Democracy.* Westport: Greenwood Press, 1982. Letter to author 15 March 1983.

House, Jonathan. Major, U.S. Army. Military historian; author of "John McAuley Palmer and the Reserve Components," *Parameters,* 12 (September 1982): 11–18.

Jewett, Richard L. Brigadier General, U.S. Army (retired); has written on military logistics in World War I. Letter to author 31 August 1983.

Keegan, John. British military historian; author of *Opening Moves: August 1914.* New York: Viking Press, 1971, and *The Face of Battle.* New York: Viking Press, 1976. Letter to author 30 March 1983.

Lawson, Don. American writer; author of *The United States in World War I.* New York: Scholastic Book Services, 1963. Letter to author 4 March 1983.

Luvaas, Jay. American historian; author of *The Military Legacy Of the Civil War: The European Inheritance.* Chicago: University of Chicago Press, 1959. Letter to author 13 April 1983.

Maddox, Robert J. American historian; author of "The Meuse-Argonne Offensive." *American History Illustrated* (April 1975): 22–31. Letter to author 29 March 1983.

Matloff, Maurice. American military historian; editor of *American Military History.* Washington: GPO, 1973. Note to author 4 April 1983.

Millett, Allan R. American historian; author of *The General: Robert L. Bullard and Officership in the United States Army, 1881–1925.* Westport: Greenwood Press, 1975, and *Semper Fidelis: The History of the United States Marine Corps.* New York: Macmillan, 1980. Letter to author 18 February 1983.

Moore, Claude. Former chief surgeon, Langres Base Hospital, AEF. Interviewed 22 March 1983.

Pogue, Forrest C. American historian; biographer of General of the Army George C. Marshall. Letter to author 5 April 1983.

Pyle, Dana J. Commander, Region 3, Veterans of World War I. Interviewed 12 April 1983.

Rainey, James W. Lieutenant Colonel, U.S. Army; author of "The Training of the American Expeditionary Forces in World War I" M.A. thesis, Temple University, 1981. Letter to author 4 April 1983.

Randle, Edwin H. Brigadier General, U.S. Army (retired); rifle company commander in AEF in Meuse-Argonne. Letter to author 3 August 1983.

Ropp, Theodore. American historian; author of *War in the Modern World.* Durham, N.C.: Duke University Press, 1959. Letter to author 15 February 1983.

Simkins, Peter. Historian, British Imperial War Museum; writing a text on Kitchener's Army. Interviewed 13 May 1983.

Smythe, Donald. American historian; author of a two-volume biography of General of the Armies John J. Pershing. Interviewed 1 March 1985.

Stokesbury, James L. Canadian historian; author of *A Short History of World War I.* New York: William Morrow, 1981. Letter to author 12 March 1983.

Terraine, John. British military historian; author of *To Win a War.* London: Sidgwick, 1978. *The Smoke and Fire.* London: Sidgwick, 1980. Letter to author 25 February 1983.

Toland, John. American writer; author of *No Man's Land.* New York: Doubleday, 1980.

Trask, David F. Chief Historian, U.S. Army Center of Military History; author of *The United States in the Supreme War Council.* Middletown: Wesleyan University Press, 1961. Interviewed 14 March 1983.

Weigley, Russell F. American historian; author of *The American Way of War: A History of United States Military Strategy and Policy.* Bloomington: Indiana University Press, 1973, and *Towards an American Army: Military Thought from Washington to Marshall.* New York: Columbia University Press, 1962. Letter to author 11 March 1983.

SECONDARY SOURCES

Abrahamson, James L. *American Arms for a New Century.* New York: Free Press, 1982.

American Battle Monuments Commission (ABMC). *American Armies and Battlefields in Europe: A History, Guide and Reference Book.* Washington: GPO, 1938, 1992.

————. *Summary of Operations in the World War.* 44 vols. Washington: GPO, 1944.

Aron, Raymond. *The Century of Total War.* Garden City, N.Y.: Doubleday, Doran, 1954.

Army Times Editors, *The Daring Regiments.* New York: Dodd, Mead, 1954.

Asprey, Robert B. *At Belleau Wood.* New York: Putnam's Sons, 1965.

Ayres, Leonard P. *The War with Germany: A Statistical Summary.* Washington: GPO, 1919.

Bacon, Eugene H., and C. Joseph Bernardo. *American Military Policy: Its Development Since 1776.* Harrisburg, Penna.: Stackpole, 1955.

Baker, Newton D. "America's Duty." *National Geographic* 31 (May 1917): 453–457.

————. "America's War Effort." *Current History Magazine of the New York Times* (August 1918): 229–232.

————. "Return of the Soldier." *Review of Reviews* 59 (February 1919): 143–144.

Baker, Ray Stannard. *Woodrow Wilson: Life and Letters.* Vol. 6, *Facing War: 1915–1917*; Vol. 7, *War Leader: April 6, 1917–February 28, 1918*; and Vol. 8, *Armistice: March 1–November 11, 1918.* Garden City, N.Y.: Harper & Brothers, 1937–1939.

Baker, Ray Stannard, and William E. Dodd, eds. *The Public Papers of Woodrow Wilson.* 6 vols. New York: Harper & Brothers, 1925–1927.

Balck, Wilhelm von. *Development of Tactics—World War.* Translated by Harry Bell. Leavenworth, Kans.: General Service Schools Press, 1922.

Baldwin, Hanson. *World War I: An Outline History.* London: Hutchinson, 1963.

Barnes, Harry E. *Genesis of the World War.* New York: Alfred Knopf, 1962.

Barnett, Corelli. *The Swordbearers: Supreme Command in the First World War.* New York: William Morrow, 1964.

Baruch, Bernard M. *American Industry in the War.* New York: Prentice-Hall, 1941. First printed in 1921 by Government Printing Office, Washington, D.C.

Beard, Charles A. *The Devil Theory of War.* New York: Vanguard Press, 1936.

Beaver, Daniel R. *Newton D. Baker and the American War Effort.* Lincoln: University of Nebraska Press, 1966.

Bernstorff, Johann H. von. *My Three Years in America.* New York: Scribners, 1920.

Blake, Robert, ed. *The Private Papers of Douglas Haig, 1914–1919.* London: Spottswood, 1952.

Bland, Larry I., ed. *The Papers of George Catlett Marshall.* Vol. 1, *The Soldierly Spirit, December 1880–June 1939.* Baltimore: Johns Hopkins University Press, 1981.

Bliss, Tasker H. "The Evolution of Unified Command." *Foreign Affairs* 1 (December 1922): 1–30.

———. "The Strategy of the Allies." *Current History* 29 (November 1928): 197–211.

Bloch, Ivan. *The Future of War in its Technical, Economic and Political Relations.* 6 vols. Translated by R. C. Long. Boston: Doubleday and McClure, 1899.

Blumenson, Martin. *The Patton Papers, 1885–1940.* 2 vols. Boston: Houghton Mifflin, 1972.

———. "The Outstanding Soldier of the AEF" *American History Illustrated* 1 (February 1967): 4–13, 50–54.

Bond, Brian. *British Military Policy between the Two World Wars.* Oxford: Clarendon Press, 1980.

Bond, Paul S., and Clarence O. Sherrill. *America in the World War.* Menasha, Wis.: Banta Pub. Co., 1921.

Brodie, Bernard, and Fawn Brodie. *From Crossbow to H-Bomb.* New York: Dell, 1962.

Brook-Shepherd, Gordon. *November 1918: The Last Act of The Great War.* London: Collins, 1981.

Broun, Heywood. *The AEF: With General Pershing and the American Forces.* New York: Harcourt, 1918.

Brown, L. Ames. "The General Staff." *North American Review.* (August 1917): 229–240.

Buchan, John. *A History of the Great War.* Boston: Houghton Mifflin, 1922.

Bullard, Robert Lee. *Personalities and Reminiscences of the War.* Garden City, N.Y.: Doubleday, Page, 1925.

———. *American Soldiers Also Fought.* New York: Longmans, Green, 1936.

Callwell, Sir Charles Edward. *Field Marshal Sir Henry Wilson, His Life and His Diaries.* 2 vols. New York: Scribners, 1927.

Carver, Sir Michael. *The War Lords.* Boston: Little, Brown, 1976.

Carnegie Endowment for International Peace. Preliminary History of the Armistice, Official Documents Published by the German National Chancellery by Order of the Ministry of State. New York: Oxford University Press, 1924.

Cate, James Lea. "The Air Service in World War I." *The Army Air Forces in World War II*. Edited by Cate and Wesley Frank Craven. Vol. 1, Chicago: University of Chicago Press, 1948.

Chambers, Frank P. *The War Behind the War, 1914–1918*. New York: Harcourt, Brace, 1939.

Chandler, David, ed. *A Guide to the Battlefields of Europe*. Philadelphia: Chilton, 1965.

Chase, Joseph C. *Soldiers All: Portraits and Sketches of the Men of the AEF*. New York: Scribners, 1920.

Churchill, Allen L., Francis T. Miller, and Francis J. Roynolds. *The Story of the Great War: History of the European War from Official Sources*. 8 vols. New York: P. E. Collier and Son, 1916–1920.

Churchill, Winston S. *The Unknown War*. New York: Scribners, 1932.

———. *The World Crisis*. 4 vols. New York: Scribners, 1923–1929.

Clemenceau, Georges. *Grandeur and Misery of Victory*. New York: Harcourt, Brace, 1930.

Cochrane, Raymond C. "Gas Warfare in World War I" Study Number 10. *U.S. Army Chemical Corps Historical Studies*. Army Chemical Center, Maryland, 1958.

Coffman, Edward M. *The Hilt of the Sword: The Career of Peyton C. March*. Madison: University of Wisconsin, 1966.

———. "Conflicts in American Planning: An Aspect of World War I Strategy." *Military Review* (June 1963): 78–90.

———. *The War to End All Wars*. New York: Oxford University Press, 1968.

Colby, Eldridge. "The Taking of Montfaucon." *Infantry Journal* (March–April 1940): 1–13.

Cramer, Clarence C. *Newton D. Baker*. Cleveland, Ohio: World Press, 1961.

Creek, George. *How We Advertised America*. New York: Harper & Brothers, 1929.

Crowder, Enoch H. *The Spirit of Selective Service*. New York: Century, 1920.

Crowell, Benedict, and Robert Forrest Wilson. *How America Went to War, An Account from Official Sources of the Nation's War Activities, 1917–1920*. 6 vols. New Haven: Yale University Press, 1921.

Crowell, J. Franklin. *Government War Contracts.* New York: Oxford University Press, 1920.

Crozier, William. *Ordnance and the World War.* New York: Scribners, 1920.

Cruttwell, Charles R. M. F. *A History of the Great War.* Oxford: The Clarendon Press, 1934.

Culver, Wallace W. "A Look Back at a Long Time Ago—World War I." *Officer Review* (March 1984): 9–11.

Curti, Merle. *The American Peace Crusade.* Durham, N.C.: Duke University Press, 1929.

Daniels, Jonathan. *The End of Innocence.* Philadelphia: J. B. Lippincott, 1954.

Daniels, Josephus. *The Wilson Era: Years of War and After, 1917–1923.* Chapel Hill, N.C.: University of North Carolina Press, 1946.

Dawes, Charles G. *A Journal of the Great War.* 2 vols. Boston: Houghton Mifflin, 1921.

DeWeerd, Harvey A. *Great Soldiers of Two World Wars.* New York: W. W. Norton, 1941.

Dickinson, John. *The Building of an Army, A Detailed Account of Legislation, Administration and Opinion in the United States, 1915–1920.* New York: Century, 1922.

Dickman, Joseph T. *The Great Crusade: A Narrative of the World War.* Boston: Appleton, 1927.

Dreiziger, N. F., ed. *Mobilization for Total War: The Canadian, British and American Experience, 1914–1918, 1939–1945.* Waterloo, Canada: WLV Press, 1984.

Dupuy, Trevor N. *The Evolution of Weapons and Warfare.* New York: Bobbs-Merrill, 1980.

———. *Brave Men and Great Captains.* New York: Harper and Row, 1955.

Earle, Edward M., ed. *Makers of Modern Strategy, Military Thought from Machiavelli to Hitler.* Princeton: Princeton University Press, 1943.

Ebelshauser, G. A. *The Passage: A Tragedy of First World War.* Huntington, Va.: Griffin Books, 1984.

Edmonds, James E., ed. *Military Operations, France and Belgium.* 1917, 3 vols.; 1918, 5 vols. London: Macmillan, 1935–1948.

———. *A Short History of World War I.* London: Oxford University Press, 1951.

Eisenhower, Dwight D. *At Ease: Stories I Tell to Friends.* Garden City, N.Y.: Doubleday, 1967.

Ellis, John. *The Social History of the Machine Gun.* New York: Random House, 1975.

Elting, John R. *American Army Life.* New York: Scribner's Sons, 1982.

Ely, Hanson. "The Attack on Cantigny." *National Service* 7 (April 1920): 201–208.

Esposito, Vincent J. *The West Point Atlas of American Wars.* New York: Praeger, 1959.

Essame, Hubert. *The Battle for Europe.* New York: Scribners, 1972.

———. "Night Counterattack." *Military Review* (January 1962): 7.

Every, Dale van. *The AEF in Battle.* New York: Appleton, 1928.

Falkenhayn, Erich von. *The German General Staff and its Decisions, 1914–1916.* New York: Dodd, Mead, 1920.

Falls, Cyril. *The Great War.* New York: Putnam's Sons, 1959.

———. *War Books: A Critical Guide.* London: Davies, 1930.

———. *Caporetto, 1917.* London: Weidenfeld, 1965.

Ferro, Marc. *The Great War: 1914–1918.* Translated by Nicole Stone. London: Routledge, 1972.

Fleming, D. F. *The Origins and Legacies of World War I.* Greenwich, Conn.: Fawcett, 1968.

Foch, Ferdinand. *The Memoirs of Marshal Foch.* Translated by T. Bentley Mott. Garden City: Doubleday, Doran, 1931.

Foley, William. "Restraints in Gas Warfare." *Military Review* (October 1963): 23.

Foulois, Benjamin D. "Why Write a Book?" *The Air Power Historian* (April 1955): 17–35.

Fortescue, Sir John. *History of the British Army.* 13 vols. London: Macmillan, 1910–1935.

France. Etat-Major de l'Armee. Service Historique. *Les Armees Francaises dans la Grande Guerre.* Vols. 5–7 with annexes. Paris: Imprimerie Nationale, 1922.

Frothingham, Thomas G. *The American Reinforcement in the World War.* Garden City, N.Y.: Doubleday, Page, 1927.

———. *The Naval History of the World War.* Cambridge: Harvard University Press, 1925.

Fuller, J. F. C. *The Military History of the Western World.* 3 Vols. New York: Funk and Wagnalls, 1954.

———. *Decisive Battles of the U.S.A.* London: Harper and Row, 1942.

Fussell, Paul. *Siegfried Sassoon's Long Journey.* New York: Oxford University Press, 1984.

Ganoe, William A. *History of the United States Army.* Washington: GPO, 1924.

———. "General Pershing in France." *Current History* 6 (July 1917): 6–11.

———. "General Pershing's Homecoming." *Current History* 11 (October 1919): 1–9.

———. "General of the Armies Wins Another Victory. " *Life* (2 May 1938): 9–12.

Gershater, E. M. "Chemical Agents and Battlefield Mobility." *Military Review* (June 1963): 37.

Gibbs, Philip. *Now It Can Be Told.* New York: Harper & Brothers, 1920.

Giehrl, Hermann von. "Battle of the Meuse-Argonne." *Infantry Journal* 19 (August–September, October–November 1921): 131–138.

Goldhurst, Richard. *Pipe Clay and Drill—John J. Pershing: The Classic American Soldier.* New York: Thomas Y. Crowell, 1977.

Grattan, C. Hartley. *Why We Fought.* New York: Vanguard Press, 1929.

Graves, Robert. *Goodbye to All That.* Garden City, N.Y.: Doubleday Anchor Books, 1929.

Great Britain Public Records Office, List 53. *Alphabetical Guide to War Office and Other Military Records Preserved in the Public Records.* London: PRO, 1931.

Gregory, Barry. *Argonne.* New York: Ballantine Books, 1982.

Griffiths, William R. (with editing by Thomas Griess). *The Great War.* West Point: United States Military Academy, 1979.

———. "Coalition for Total War: Field-Marshal Sir Douglas Haig and Entente Military Cooperation, 1916–1918." Unpub. MA Thesis, Rice University, 1970.

Gudmundsson, Bruce I. *Stormtroop Tactics: Innovation in the German Army, 1914–1918.* New York: Praeger, 1989.

Gurney, Gene. *A Pictorial History of the United States Army.* New York: Bonanza Books, 1966.

Hagedorn, Herman. *The Bugle That Woke America.* New York: John Day, 1940.

———. *Leonard Wood, A Biography.* 2 vols. New York: Harper & Brothers, 1931.

Hagood, Johnson. *The Services of Supply.* Boston: Houghton Mifflin, 1927.

Hankey, Maurice. *The Supreme Command, 1914–1918.* 2 vols. London: Longman's, 1951.

Harbord, James G. *The American Army in France.* Boston: Little, Brown, 1936.

———. *Leaves from a War Diary.* New York: Dodd, Mead, 1925.

———. *America in the World War.* Boston: Houghton Mifflin, 1931.

Haythornthwaite, Philip J. *A Photohistory of World War I.* London: Arms and Armour Press, 1994.

Heller, Charles E. "Chemical Warfare in World War I: The American Experience, 1917–1918." *Leavenworth Papers No. 10.* Fort Leavenworth, Kansas: U.S. Army Combat Studies Institute, September 1984.

Hedges, Arthur. *Lord Kirchener.* London: Thornton Butterworth, 1936.

Henig, Ruth. *The Origins of the First World War.* 2d Ed. Lancaster Pamphlets. London: Routledge, 1993.

Higham, Robin. *Official Histories.* Manhattan, Kans.: Kansas State University Library, 1970.

———. *A Guide to the Sources of British Military History.* Berkeley: University of California Press, 1971.

Hill, Jim Dan. *The Minute Man in Peace and War.* Harrisburg, Pa.: Stackpole, 1964.

Hindenberg, Paul von. *Out Of My Life.* New York: Cassell, 1920.

Hoffman, Max. *The War of Lost Opportunities.* New York: International Publishing, 1925.

Holley, Irving B. *Ideas and Weapons.* New Haven: Yale University Press, 1953.

———. *General John M. Palmer: Citizen Soldiers and the Army of a Democracy.* Westport, Conn.: Greenwood Press, 1982.

Hoover, Herbert. *The Memoirs of Herbert Hoover: Years of Adventure, 1874–1920.* New York: Macmillan, 1951.

House, Jonathan. "John McAuley Palmer and the Reserve Components." *Parameters* 12 (September 1982): 11–18.

Howard, Michael. *Studies in War and Peace.* New York: Viking Press, 1970.

———. *War in European History.* London: Oxford University Press, 1976.

Huntington, Samuel P. *The Soldier and the State.* Cambridge: Belnap Press of Harvard University, 1957.

Hurley, Edward M. *The Bridge to France.* New York: J. B. Lippincott, 1927.

Huston, James A. *The Sinews of War: Army Logistics, 1775–1953.* US. Army Historical Series. Washington: GPO, 1966.

Infantry Journal. "Infantry in Battle." Washington: Infantry Journal, 1939.

Ironside, Sir Edmund. *Tannenberg.* Edinburg: Blackwood and Sons, 1933.

Jackson, Robert. *Fighter Pilots of World War I.* New York: St. Martin's Press, 1977.

James, D. Clayton. *The Years of MacArthur.* 2 vols. Boston: Houghton Mifflin, 1970,1985.

Jamieson, Perry D. *Crossing the Deadly Ground: United States Army Tactics, 1865–1899.* Tuscaloosa, Ala.: Univ. of Alabama Press, 1994.

Joffre, Joseph. *Personal Memoirs.* 2 vols. Translated by T. Bentley Mott. New York: Harpers, 1932.

Johnson, Douglas. *Battlefields of the World War—Western and Southern Fronts: A Study in Military Geography.* New York: Oxford University Press, 1921.

Johnson, Ellis L. *The Military Experiences of General Hugh A. Drum from 1898–1918.* Wisconsin: University of Wisconsin Press, 1975.

Johnson, Hubert C. *Breakthrough: Tactics, Technology, and the Search for Victory on the Western Front in World War I.* Novato, Calif.: Presidio Press, 1994.

Johnson, Thomas M. *Without Censor: New Light on our Greatest World War I Battles.* Indianapolis, Ind.: Bobbs-Merrill, 1928.

Jusserand, Jean J. *What Me Befell.* Boston: Houghton Mifflin, 1933.

Keegan, John. *Opening Moves: August 1914.* New York: Viking Press, 1971.

———. *The Face of Battle.* New York: Viking Press, 1976.

Kennedy, David M. *Over Here: The First World War and American Society.* New York: Oxford University Press, 1980.

Keyes, Sir Roger. *The Naval Memoirs of Admiral of the Fleet Sir Roger Keyes.* Vol. 2, 1916–1918. London: Butterworth, 1935.

Kreidberg, Marvin A., and Merton G. Henry. *History of Military Mobilization in the United States Army, 1775–1945.* Washington: GPO, 1955.

Lasswell, Harold B. *Propaganda Techniques in the World War.* New York: Alfred Knopf, 1927.

Lawson, Don. *The United States in World War I.* New York: Scholastic Book Services, 1964.

Leckie, Robert. *The Wars of America.* 2 vols. New York: Harper and Row, 1968.

Leland, W. G., and W. D. Mereness. *Introduction to the American Official Sources for the Economic and Social History of the World War.* New Haven: Yale University Press, 1925.

Liddell Hart, Sir Basil H. *History of the World War, 1914–1918.* Boston: Little, Brown, 1935.

————. *Reputations Ten Years Later.* Boston: Little, Brown, 1928.

————. *Through the Fog of War.* New York: Random House, 1938.

————. "Pershing and His Critics." *Current History* (November 1932): 135–140.

Liggett, Hunter. *Ten Years Ago in France.* New York: Dodd, Mead, 1928.

Link, Arthur. *Woodrow Wilson and the Progressive Era, 1910–1917.* New York: Harper & Brothers, 1954.

Lloyd George, David. *War Memoirs of David Lloyd George.* 6 vols. Boston: Little, Brown, 1934.

Lockmiller, David A. *Enoch A. Crowder: Soldier, Lawyer and Statesman.* Columbia, Miss.: University of Missouri Press, 1945.

Lonergan, Thomas C. *It Might Have Been Lost.* New York: G. P. Putnam's Sons, 1929.

Lossberg, Fritz von. *Meine Tätigkeit im Weltkrieg 1914–1918.* Berlin: Mittler, 1939.

Lowry, Edward G. "The Emerging Mr. Baker: A Pacifist Who is in this War Business to 'See it Through.'" *Colliers Weekly,* 6 October 1917, 6, 7, 35, 36.

Lucas, Pascal. *The Evolution of Tactical Ideas in France and Germany during the War.* Translated by P. V. Kieffer. Fort Leavenworth, Kans.: Army Service Schools Press, 1925.

Ludendorff, Eric von. *Ludendorff's Own Story: August 1914–November 1918.* 2 vols. New York: Harper & Brothers, 1920.

Lupfer, Timothy T. "The Dynamics of Doctrine: The Changes in German Tactical Doctrine during the First World War." Leavenworth Papers No. 4. Fort Leavenworth, Kans.: U.S. Army Command and General Staff College (July 1981).

Lutz, Ralph H. *The Causes of the German Collapse in 1918.* Stanford, Calif.: Stanford University Press, 1934.

Luvaas, Jay. *The Military Legacy of the Civil War: The European Inheritance.* Chicago: Chicago University Press, 1959.

Lyddon, William G. *British War Missions to the United States, 1914–1918.* London: Oxford University Press, 1938.

MacArthur, Douglas. *Reminiscences.* New York: McGraw-Hill, 1964.

MacDonald, Charles B. "The Neglected Ardennes." *Military Review* (April 1963): 74.

MacDonald, Lyn. *Somme.* New York: Michael Joseph, 1984.

McEntee, Gerald L. *Military History of the World War.* New York: Scribners, 1937.

McLean, Ross H. "Troop Movements on the American Railroads during the Great War." *The American Historical Review* (April 1921): 464–488.

McMaster, John B. *The United States in the World War.* 2 vols. New York: Appleton, 1918, 1920.

Maddox, Robert. "The Meuse-Argonne Offensive." *American History Illustrated* (April 1975): 22–31.

Magnus, Philip. *Kitchener: Portrait of an Imperialist.* London: Arrow Books, 1958.

March, Francis A. *History of the World War.* Philadelphia: John Winston Co., 1921.

March, Peyton C. *The Nation at War.* Garden City, N.Y.: Doubleday, Doran, 1932.

Marder, Arthur J. *From Dreadnaught to Scapa Flow: The Navy in the Fisher Era, 1904–1919.* London: Oxford University Press, 1961.

Markey, John D. "That Was Pershing." *American Legion Magazine* (January 1949): 28.

Marshall, George C. *Memoirs of My Services in the World War, 1917, 1918.* Boston: Houghton Mifflin, 1976.

———. "Some Lessons in History." *Maryland Historical Magazine* (September 1945): 175–184.

Marshall, S. L. A. *The American Heritage History of World War I.* New York: American Heritage Pub., 1964.

Matloff, Maurice, ed. *American Military History.* Washington: GPO, 1973.

Matthews, William, and Dixon Wecter. *Our Soldiers Speak.* Boston: Little, Brown, 1943.

May, Ernest R., ed. *The Ultimate Decision: The President as Commander in Chief.* New York: Braziller, 1960.

Merrill, James M. *Uncommon Valor.* Chicago: Rand McMally, 1964.

———. "Submarine Scare, 1918." *Military Affairs* (Winter 1953): 181–190.

Messenger, Charles. *Trench Fighting 1914–1918.* New York: Ballantine, 1972.

Meyer, Herman. *A Check List of the Literature and Other Materials in the Library of Congress on the European War.* Washington: GPO, 1918.

Miller, Josiah B. "Development of the Departmental Direction of Training and Training Policy in the United States Army, 1789–1854: Background for Twentieth Century Training 1899–1917." Draft manuscript in offices of the Chief of Military History, Department of the Army, Washington, D.C., n.d.

Millett, Allan R. *The General: Robert L. Bullard and Officership in the United States Army, 1881–1925.* Westport, Conn.: Greenwood Press, 1975.

———. *Semper Fidelis: The History of the United States Marine Corps.* New York: Macmillan, 1980.

Millett, Allan R., and Peter Maslowski. *For the Common Defense: A Military History of the United States of America.* New York: Macmillan, 1984, Free Press, 1994.

Millis, Walter. *Arms and Men: A Study of American Military History.* New York: G. P. Putnam's Sons, 1958.

———. *The Road to War: America, 1914–1917.* Boston: Houghton Mifflin, 1925.

Mitchell, William. *Memoirs of World War I, From Start to Finish of Our Greatest War.* New York: Random House, 1960.

———. *Our Air Force.* New York: E. P. Dutton, 1921.

———. "The Air Service at the Argonne-Meuse." *World's Week* 38 (September 1919): 552–560.

Moll, Kenneth L. "Writing on Water with a Fork. " *Military Review* (August 1964): 29.

Morison, Elting E., ed. *The Letters of Theodore Roosevelt.* 8 vols. Cambridge: Harvard University Press, 1951–1954.

———. *Admiral Sims and the Modern American Navy.* Boston: Houghton Mifflin, 1942.

———. *Turmoil and Tradition: A Study of the Life and Times of Henry L. Stimson.* Boston: Houghton Mifflin, 1960.

Mott, L. Bentley. *Twenty Years as a Military Attache,* Garden City, N.Y.: Doubleday, Doran, 1937.

Nagel, Fritz. *Fritz: The WWI Memoirs of a German Lieutenant.* Huntington, W.Va.: Griffin Books, 1984.

Nelson, Otto L. *National Security and the General Staff.* Washington: Infantry Journal Press, 1946.

Nenninger, Timothy K. *The Leavenworth Schools and the Old Army: Education, Professionalism, and the Officer Corps of the United States Army, 1881–1918.* Westport, Conn.: Greenwood Press, 1978.

Newman, George P. *The German Air Force in the Great War.* London: Hodder and Stoughton, 1920.

O'Connor, Richard. *Black Jack Pershing.* New York: Doubleday, 1961.

Ormsby, Hilda. *France, A Regional and Economic Geography.* New York: E. P. Dutton, 1931.

Otto, Ernst. "The Battles for the Possession of Belleau Woods, June 1918." *U.S. Naval Institute Proceedings* (November 1928): 940–962.

Page, Arthur W. *Our 110 Days Fightings.* Garden City, N.Y: Doubleday, Page, 1920.

Palmer, Frederick. *Bliss, Peacemaker: The Life and Letters of General Tasker Howard Bliss.* New York: Dodd, Mead, 1934.

————. *John J. Pershing: A Biography.* Westport, Conn.: Greenwood Press, 1948.

————. *Newton D. Baker: America at War.* 2 vols. New York: Dodd, Mead, 1931.

————. *Our Greatest Battle.* New York: Dodd, Mead, 1919.

————. "Looking Back on the World War." *World's Week* 53 (April 1927): 587–593.

Palmer, John M. *America in Arms: The Experience of the United States with Military Organization.* New Haven: Yale University Press, 1921.

————. "Reorganization of the War Department." *Army and Navy Journal* (27 August 1921): 1365.

Pappas, George. *Prudens Futuri: The War College, 1901–1967.* Carlisle, Pa.: U.S. Army War College, 1967.

Paxson, Frederic L. *American Democracy and the World War.* 3 vols. Boston: Houghton Mifflin, 1937, 1984.

————. "The Great Demobilization." *American Historical Review* 44 (January 1939): 237–251.

————. "The American War Government, 1917–1918." *American Historical Review* 26 (October 1920): 54–76.

Perkins, Dexter. *America and Two World Wars.* Boston: Little, Brown, 1944.

Pershing, John J. *My Experiences in the World War.* 2 vols. New York: Frederick Stokes Co., 1931.

———. "The Meuse-Argonne." *Foreign Service* 15 (August 1927): 6, 7.

———. "Our National Military Policy." *Scientific American* 127 (August 1927): 83, 142.

———. *Final Report of General John J. Pershing, Commander-in-Chief, American Expeditionary Forces.* Washington: GPO, 1920.

Pershing, John J., and Hunter Liggett. *Report of the First Army, American Expeditionary Forces: Organization and Operations.* Fort Leavenworth, Kans.: General Service Schools Press, 1923.

Pétain, Henri P. *Verdun.* New York: Dial Press, 1930.

Peterson, Horace C. *Propaganda for War.* Norman, Okla.: University of Oklahoma Press, 1939.

Peterson, Horace C., and Gilbert C. Fite. *Opponents of War, 1917–1918.* Madison, Wis.: University of Wisconsin Press, 1957.

Pierce, C. Fredericks. *The Great Adventure: America in the First World War.* New York: E. P. Dutton, 1960.

Pitt, Barrie. *1918: The Last Act.* New York: Ballantine Books, 1963.

Pogue, Forrest C. *George C. Marshall: Education of a General, 1880–1939.* New York: Viking Press, 1963.

———. *George C. Marshall: Ordeal and Hope, 1939–1942.* New York: Viking Press, 1966.

———. *George C. Marshall: Organizer of Victory, 1943–1945.* New York: Viking Press, 1973.

Preston, R. A., S. F. Wise, and H. O. Werner. *Men in Arms: A History of Warfare.* New York: Praeger, 1962.

Rainey, James W. "Training of the American Expeditionary Forces in World War I." MA Thesis, Temple University, 1981.

———. "Ambivalent Warfare: The Tactical Doctrine of the AEF in World War I." *Parameters* (September 1983): 34–46.

Read, James M. *Atrocity Propaganda, 1914–1918.* New Haven: Yale University Press, 1941.

Reilly, Henry J. *Americans All, The Rainbow at War: The Official History of the 42d Rainbow Division in the World War.* Columbus, Ohio: F. J. Heer, 1936.

Remak, Joachim. *The Origins of World War I, 1871–1914.* Hinsdale: Dryden Press, 1967.

Renn, Ludwig [Arnold von Golssenau]. *War.* London: Martin Secker, 1929.

Repington, Charles. *The First World War, 1914–1918.* 2 vols. Boston: Houghton Mifflin, 1920.

Reynolds, E. A. B. *The Lee-Enfield Rifle.* New York: Anchor Press, 1969.

Riker, William H. *Soldiers of the States: The Role of the National Guard in American Democracy.* Washington: Public Affairs Press, 1957.

Risch, Erna. *Quartermaster Support of the Army: A History of the Corps, 1775–1959.* Washington: GPO, 1962.

Ritter, Gerhard. *The Schlieffen Plan.* New York: Praeger, 1958.

Rizzi, Joseph N. *Joe's War: Memoirs of a Doughboy.* Huntington, W.Va.: Griffin Books, 1984.

Robertson, Sir William. *Soldiers and Statesmen, 1914–1918.* 2 vols. London: Cassell, 1926.

Rommel, Erwin. *Infantry Attacks.* Washington: Combat Forces Press, 1956.

Root, Elihu. *The Military and Colonial Policy of the United States.* Cambridge: Harvard University Press, 1916.

Ropp, Theodore. *War in the Modern World.* Durham, N.C.: Duke University Press, 1959.

Rudin, Harry. *Armistice 1918.* New Haven: Yale University Press, 1944.

Ryan, Garry D. "Disposition of AEF Records of World War I." *Military Affairs* 30 (Winter 1966–1967): 212–219.

Rupprecht, Crown Prince of Bavaria. *Mein Kriegstagebuch.* 3 vols. Berlin: Mittler, 1919.

Russell, Thomas H. *America's War for Humanity.* New York: Walker, 1919.

Sabel, Walter R. "Christmas in the Meuse-Argonne." *National Tribune,* 23 December 1982.

Scott, Hugh L. *Some Memories of a Soldier.* Cincinnati, Ohio: Central Pub., 1919.

Seymour, Charles. *American Diplomacy during the World War.* Baltimore: Johns Hopkins University Press, 1934.

———. *American Neutrality, 1914–1917.* New Haven: Yale University Press, 1935.

Seymour, Charles, ed. *The Intimate Papers of Colonel House.* 4 vols. Boston: Houghton Mifflin, 1926–1928.

Sharp, William Graves. *The War Memoirs of William Graves Sharp, American Ambassador to France, 1914–1919.* London: Constable & Co., 1931.

Slosson, Preston W. *The Great Crusade and After.* New York: Macmillan, 1930.

Smythe, Donald. *Guerrilla Warrior: The Early Life of John J. Pershing.* New York: Scribners, 1973.

———. *Pershing: General of the Armies.* Bloomington: University of Indiana Press, 1986.

———. "The Battle Pershing Almost Lost." *Army* 33 (February 1983): 50–55.

———. "John J. Pershing: A Study in Paradox." *Military Review* 49 (September 1969): 66–72.

———. "The Pershing–March Conflict in World War I." *Parameters* 11 (December 1981): 53–62.

Society of the First Division. *History of the First Division during the World War, 1917–1919.* Philadelphia: Lippincott, 1922.

Spaulding, Oliver. *The United States Army in War and Peace.* New York: G. P. Putnam's Sons, 1937.

Spears, Sir Edward. *Prelude to Victory.* London: Jonathan Cope, 1939.

Spector, Ronald. "'You're Not Going to Send Soldiers Over There Are You?': The American Search for an Alternative to the Western Front." *Military Affairs* 36 (February 1972): 1–4.

Spencer, Samuel R. *Decision for War, 1917.* Ridge, N.H.: Richard Smith Pub.,1953.

Stallings, Laurence. *The Story of the Doughboys: The AEF in World War I.* New York: Harper & Row, 1963.

Stokesbury, James L. *A Short History of World War I.* New York: William Morrow, 1981.

———. "The Aisne-Marne Offensive." *American History Illustrated* (July 1980): 8–17.

Sullivan, Mark. *Our Times: The United States, 1900–1925.* Vol. 5, *Over Here, 1914–1918.* New York: Scribners, 1933.

Sunderman, James F. *Early Air Pioneers, 1862–1935.* New York: Franklin Watts, 1961.

Tansill, Charles C. *America Goes to War.* Boston: Little, Brown, 1938.

Taylor, A. J. P. *History of the First World War.* London: Berkley Press, 1959.

Terraine, John. *The Western Front,* London: Lippincott, 1965.

———. *To Win a War.* London: Sidgwick, 1978.

———. *The Smoke and the Fire.* London: Sidgwick, 1980.

———. "The March Offensive, 1918." *History Today* 18 (April 1968): 234–243.

Toland, John. *No Man's Land: 1918—The Last Year of the Great War.* New York: Doubleday, 1980.

Trask, David F. *The United States and the Supreme War Council: American War Aims and Inter-Allied Strategy, 1917–1918.* Middletown, Conn.: Wesleyan University Press, 1961.

———. *The AEF and Coalition Warmaking.* Lawrence, Kans.: University Press of Kansas, 1993.

———. "Political-Military Consultation among Allies." *Army* (February 1983): 6–9.

Tuchman, Barbara. *The Guns of August.* New York: Macmillan, 1962.

———. *The Zimmerman Telegram.* New York: Dell Books, 1958.

Tucker, George B. et al. *A History of Military Affairs in Western Society since the Eighteenth Century.* Ann Arbor, Mich.: Edwards Brothers, 1952.

Tumulty, Joseph P. *Woodrow Wilson as I Knew Him.* Garden City, N.Y.: Doubleday, Doran, 1954.

United States Army War College, Historical Section. *The Genesis of the American First Army.* Washington: GPO, 1938.

———. *Order of Battle of the United States Land Forces in the World War: American Expeditionary Forces.* Washington: GPO, 1937.

United States Congress. *Congressional Record, 64th Congress, 2d Session; 65th Congress, Special Session, 1st and 2d Sessions; 66th Congress, 1st Session.* Washington: GPO, 1919.

United States Congress, House of Representatives, Military Affairs Committee. *Army Reorganization Hearings, 66th Congress, 1st Session.* Washington: GPO, 1919.

———. *Increasing the Efficiency of the Military Establishment: Hearings, 64th Congress, 2d Session.* Washington: GPO, 1916.

United States Congress, Senate Military Affairs Committee. *Army Reorganization Hearings.* 2 vols. Washington: GPO, 1917.

———. *Increasing the Military Establishment: Hearings, 65th Congress, 1st Session.* Washington: GPO, 1917.

———. *Investigation of the War Department of the United States, December 1917–January 1918 Hearings, 65th Congress, 1st Session.* Washington: GPO, 1918.

———. *Preparedness for National Defense Hearings, 64th Congress, 2d Session.* Washington: GPO, 1916.

U.S. Department of the Air Force. *The U.S. Air Service in World War I.* Edited by M. Maurer. 4 vols. Washington: GPO, 1978.

U.S. Department of the Army. *Army Lineage Book, Volume 2: Infantry.* Washington: GPO, 1953.

———. Historical Division. *United States Army in the World War, 1917–1919.* Washington: GPO, 1948.

U.S. Department of State. *Papers Relating to the Foreign Relations of the United States, 1917.* Washington: GPO, 1926.

———. *Papers Relating to the Foreign Relations of the United States, 1917; Supplement 1, The World War.* Washington: GPO, 1926.

———. *Papers Relating to the Foreign Relations of the United States, 1917; Supplement 2.* 2 vols. Washington: GPO, 1932.

———. *Papers Relating to the Foreign Relations of the United States, 1918.* Washington: GPO, 1933.

———. *Papers Relating to the Foreign Relations of the United States, Supplement 1, The World War.* 2 vols. Washington: GPO, 1933.

United States Military Academy. *The Great War.* West Point: U.S.M.A., 1979.

United States War Department. *Annual Reports: 1917–1919.* Washington: GPO, 1917–1919.

———. *Annual Report of the Secretary of War, 1917, 1918, 1919.* Washington: GPO, 1917–1919.

Upton, Emory. *The Military Policy of the United States from 1775.* Washington: GPO, 1904.

Vagts, Alfred. *A History of Militarism.* New York: Meridian Books, 1959.

Vandiver, Frank E. *Black Jack: The Life and Times of John J. Pershing.* 2 vols. College Station, Tex.: Texas A & M University Press, 1977.

———. *John J. Pershing and the Anatomy of Leadership.* Colorado Springs: United States Air Force Academy, 1963.

Viereck, George, ed. *As They Saw Us.* Garden City, N.Y.: Doubleday, Doran, 1929.

Waite, Robert G. L. *Vanguard of Nazism.* New York: Norton, 1969.

Wallace, E. S., ed. *The Twenty-Eighth Division: Pennsylvania's Guard in the World War.* Pittsburgh, Pa.: 28th Div. Pub. Co., 1923, 1924.

Walworth, Arthur. *Woodrow Wilson.* 2 vols. New York: Longmans, 1958.

Watson, Mark. *Chief of Staff: Prewar Plans and Preparations. Vol. 4 of United States Army in World War II Series.* Washington: GPO, 1950.

Watts, Richard. *Dare Call It Treason.* New York: Simon and Schuster, 1963.

Weigley, Russell F. *The American Way of War: A History of United States Military Strategy and Policy.* New York: Macmillan, 1973.

———. *The History of the United States Army.* New York: Macmillan, 1967.

———. *Towards an American Army: Military Thought from Washington to Marshall.* New York: Columbia University Press, 1962.

Western Front Association. *Stand To: the Journal of the Western Front Association.* Quarterly issues from 1980 to 1986. London: WFA.

Wetzell, George. *From Falkenhayn to Hindenburg-Ludendorff.* Translated by F. W. Merton. Washington: U.S. Army War College, 1935.

Whan, Vorin E., ed. *A Soldier Speaks: Public Papers and Speeches of General of the Army Douglas MacArthur.* New York: Praeger, 1965.

Wilhelm, Crown Prince of Germany. *My War Experiences.* London: Hurst and Blackett, 1923.

Williams, T. Harry. *Americans at War: The Development of the American Military System.* Baton Rouge, La.: University of Louisiana Press, 1960.

Williams, Wythe. *The Tiger of France: Conversations with Clemenceau.* New York: Duell, Sloan and Pearce, 1949.

Willoughby, Charles A. *The Economic and Military Participation of the United States in the World War.* Forth Leavenworth, Kans.: U.S. Army Command and General Staff School Press, 1931.

Woolcott, Alexander. "Them Damned Frogs." *North American* 210 (October 1919): 490–498.

Wolff, Leon. *In Flanders Field: The 1917 Campaign.* New York: Viking Press, 1958.

Wynne, Graeme C. *If Germany Attacks: The Battle in Depth in the West.* London: Faber and Faber, 1940.

———. "The Development of the German Defensive Battles in 1917, and Its Influence on British Defence Tactics." *Army Quarterly.* Pts. 1 and 2, 34 (April–July 1937): pt. 3, 35 (October 1937).

———. "The Hindenburg Line," *Army Quarterly,* 37 (October 1938–January 1939).

Yardley, Herbert O. *The American Black Chamber.* Indianapolis, Ind.: Bobbs-Merrill, 1931.

Young, Peter, ed. *The British Army, 1642–1970.* London: Kimber, 1967.

INDEX

October's Game

Paul Adomites

A
REDEFINITION
BOOK

October's Game

UNDER DIFFICULTY

Fans of all loyalties join together each October to celebrate the World Series, and not only because it crowns the season's champion. It offers one last opportunity to embrace the game of baseball, one last crescendo of sharply hit line drives and 90-mile-per-hour fastballs before the game disappears into the cold silence of winter. Before television drove the Series into prime time, transistor radios hid inside the desks of schoolchildren and office workers, as they strained to hear the muffled play-by-play. Nowadays, the games are scheduled for maximum exposure, but unlike most championship events, the World Series remains largely free of pageantry, sporting only the traditional tricolor bunting on the facade of each ballpark deck. It needs nothing more; the event is majestic enough.

The Clutch

t's called "the clutch" because of the feeling you get in the pit of your stomach, a cold grip on your insides that makes even the most instinctive act—like breathing—intrusive. Your muscles can't relax, and moves you've made thousands of times before seem confused and unfamiliar. Baseball, as every schoolkid knows, is a game of percentages: a batter who hits safely three times out of ten, week after week, is a star. But baseball is also a game of pressure. Some ballplayers are percentage players—day-in, day-out cool and consistent. And some are clutch players. When the situation is tense and the stakes are high, that steady .300 hitter may not rise to the occasion. High stakes call for players who can perform under pressure. And the stakes are never higher than in the white heat of the contest that decides the "World Champions of Baseball"—October's Game, the World Series.

Take Mickey Mantle, for example. Mantle played in a dozen World Series and still holds lifetime Series records for home runs, runs scored and runs batted in. Yet his greatest clutch performance in a Series may have been a 15-foot run—backwards.

Mantle's run is not on anyone's list of legendary Series performances. It came in 1960, in a World Series loaded with the bizarre; one that was an abomination for Yankee fans and a triumph for almost everyone else. The Yankees had brutally outslugged the Pirates with Whitey Ford's shutouts of 10–0 and 12–0 and a 16–3 shellacking. Sportswriter Red Smith called it "a

First baseman Kent Hrbek (14, opposite) was 1 for 13 against Cardinal lefties in the 1987 World Series until he hit a sixth-inning grand slam off Ken Dayley in Game 6 to spark the Twins to an 11–5 win. "I wanted to circle the bases twice," he said.

A remarkable piece of Game 7 baserunning by Mickey Mantle (above) prevented a game-ending double play in the 1960 World Series. With the tying run on third in the ninth, Yogi Berra grounded sharply to Pirate first baseman Rocky Nelson, who stepped on first, then took a few steps away from the bag to get a better angle to throw Mantle out at second. Alertly, Mantle turned and dived back to first ahead of the startled Nelson.

grisly parody of sport." But dogged Pirate defense, clutch pitching by Cy Young winner Vernon Law and reliever Elroy Face, and a few timely hits brought the Pirates to Game 7, the final game—where pressure is at its most numbingly intense.

The Pirates, who were tickled to still be in the Series after having been outscored 46–17 in the first six games, came out loose in Game 7 and held a 4–0 lead after just two innings. But the Yankee scoring machine kept humming, and seven unanswered runs dropped the Pirates down by three as they came to bat in the eighth. Pinch hitter Gino Cimoli led off with a single to right. Bill Virdon followed with a bouncing ball to Tony Kubek at short—a sure double play. But the tricky infield at Forbes Field betrayed Kubek and the Yankees. The ball took a wicked hop, hitting Kubek in the throat and knocking him out of the game. The play left two on and none out. A Dick Groat single made it 7–5.

Two outs later Pittsburgh's Roberto Clemente chopped a Jim Coates pitch down the first-base line. As Bill Skowron made the play behind first, it looked again as though the Pirate rally was history. But while Clemente hustled, Coates dawdled, and the Buc right fielder beat the Yankee pitcher to the bag, and another run scored: 7–6. Ironically, Coates had come in two outs earlier to relieve Bobby Shantz, one of the game's best fielding pitchers.

Veteran catcher Hal Smith, the next man up, checked his swing on a 1–2 pitch from Coates, then hit the next pitch over the left center field wall. The Pirates had exploded for five runs in the bottom of the eighth for a 9–7 lead.

Bob Friend, an 18-game winner during the season, was entrusted to hold the Yanks in the ninth. The New Yorkers liked the idea; Friend had been one of their favorite victims in the Series, lasting only six innings in two starts

and giving up eight runs and 11 hits. This time the Yankees didn't notice anything different; they rapped two quick singles and he was gone. Then Mantle, hitting .375 in the Series with ten RBI and eight runs scored, lined an RBI single to right off Harvey Haddix, bringing the Yanks to within one run.

With one out and the tying run on third, Mantle took his lead off first, knowing that a double play would end the Series and that it was his job to make sure it didn't happen. Yogi Berra, the next man up, scorched a two-hopper over first that Rocky Nelson gloved eye-high. Nelson stepped on first, took a step to his right to get clear of the baserunner, and cocked his arm to throw to second, where a tag on Mantle would end the Series.

But Mickey wasn't going to second. Realizing that Nelson's putout at first had removed the potential force play at second, Mantle reversed course and dived back to the bag, spinning in front of Nelson to elude the tag, sprawling on the ground facing right field. Nelson was flat out, too, reaching in vain for a Mantle who wasn't there. The ninth Yankee run scored, the game was tied, and Mantle had kept Yankee hopes alive.

The rest of the game became legend—Pirate second baseman Bill Mazeroski led off the bottom of the ninth with a home run that gave the Pirates the victory. In a World Series that was full of surprises, his was the crowning blow. But Mantle's baserunning was pure clutch—a game-saving performance made not with bat or glove, but with the brain.

Failure under pressure lives in World Series legend as well. Even if you missed the 1912 Series, you may know the story of "Snodgrass' muff." Like Mantle's baserunning gem, it came in a World Series full of twists and turns. "Never was there a series with so many breaks and bones," said sportswriter William A. Phelon. "Any man who saw those eight games from start to finish

Among the most storied swings of all time, Bill Mazeroski's 1960 Series-winning home run in the ninth inning of Game 7 turned the tables on the home run-happy Yankees. The Yankees outhomered the Pirates 193–120 during the regular season and 10–4 in the Series.

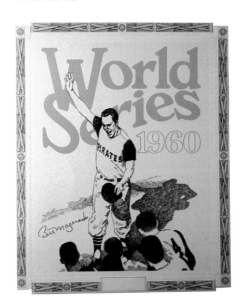

5′ 9½″ 176 lbs.   b 7/31/1892
BL TL   d 12/18/1960

ART NEHF
Pitcher

Lots of players never get any closer to the World Series than reading about it in the newspaper. Others appear so often they seem to be regulars in baseball's greatest drama. Art Nehf, who pitched in the majors for 15 years, spent the first half of his career as one of the former, but wound up as one of the latter.

Nehf picked up his nickname, "the Terre Haute Terror," as a minor leaguer with a 1.38 ERA, and he joined the Boston Braves in 1915. In his first four years with the Braves, he was 44–32 and never went above a 2.69 ERA, but his team just wasn't World Series material. Nehf's fortunes changed dramatically in 1919 when he was traded to a powerhouse—the New York Giants. From 1920 through 1924, Nehf won 87 games and helped the Giants into World Series in 1921, 1922, 1923 and 1924.

In the 1921 Series Nehf came back after two losses to shut out the Yankees in Game 8 and clinch the title for the Giants. *The Sporting News* featured Nehf on its front page and wrote, "Many pitchers, beaten twice, would have been shaken in such a third trial— Nehf stood the supreme test like a hero." The next year—1922—Nehf again won the deciding game in the Series. He shut out the Yankees once more in 1923. And in 1924 Nehf posted his fourth Series win—against the Senators' Walter Johnson.

Nehf pitched in 12 World Series games, placing him seventh on the all-time list, and he ranks fourth all-time with two Series shutouts.

After losing four World Series to the Yankees in eight years, the Brooklyn Dodgers turned to 23-year-old southpaw Johnny Podres to pitch Game 7 in 1955. Podres blanked the Yanks, then went for a ride courtesy of catcher Roy Campanella (39).

has nothing in this life to kick about." Well, any man with the possible exception of Fred Snodgrass.

It started simply enough, with the Red Sox beating the Giants in Game 1, 4–3. Game 2 was called after 11 innings because of darkness, tied 6–6. The tying run scored in the bottom of the tenth when Boston center fielder Tris Speaker, who set an American League record with 53 doubles that season, tripled and kept on running. New York shortstop Tillie Shafer bobbled the relay, but composed himself enough to throw a strike to catcher Art Wilson. Wilson wasn't so composed; he couldn't find the handle, and Speaker scored.

The great Christy Mathewson pitched all of the unfinished Game 2 for the Giants, then, with New York trailing two games to one, came back with a five-hit gem in Game 5. Unfortunately, two of the hits were back-to-back triples by Harry Hooper and Steve Yerkes, followed by an error by second baseman Larry Doyle. Mathewson and the Giants lost to Hugh Bedient and the Red Sox, 2–1.

Down three games to one, the Giants sent 26-game winner Rube Marquard to the Polo Grounds mound in Game 5, while Sox manager Jake Stahl was ordered by owner Jim McAleer to start Buck O'Brien in favor of staff ace Smoky Joe Wood. O'Brien was no pushover; he'd gone 20–13 during the season and had lost a tough 2–1 decision to Marquard in Game 3. But Wood had been nearly unbeatable that season—34–5 with ten shutouts, a 1.91 ERA and 16 wins in a row at one point—and had already beaten the Giants twice in the Series. McAleer, playing the odds, knew he could make more money if the Series went back to Boston for Game 7, where he was sure Wood would clinch the Series. O'Brien cooperated, giving up five first-inning runs for a

GIANTS

Fred C Snodgrass

OF THE
NEW YORK NATIONALS

TURKEY RED CIGARETTES

Official Score Card.
New York Giants vs. Boston Red Sox

A fly ball dropped by Giants center fielder Fred Snodgrass (left) helped the Red Sox score twice in the tenth inning of Game 7 of the 1912 World Series. But it wasn't the only Giant muff that inning. Tris Speaker (below) hit an easy foul pop between first and home that wasn't caught, then singled home the tying run.

5–2 Giants win, but back in Boston, Wood didn't. A delay, caused by angry Boston fans before the game, cooled him off, and a two-run double by Snodgrass sparked a six-run first inning as the Giants tied the Series, 11–4.

Mathewson and Bedient locked up in another pitchers' duel in the eighth and deciding game. The Giants led 1–0 in the fifth when Boston's Harry Hooper raced to the right center field fence after a drive by Larry Doyle, leaped, had the ball pop out of his mitt, then miraculously snatched the ball out of the air with his bare hand as he tumbled into the stands. "I'll never figure out quite how he caught the ball," said Wood. "It was almost impossible to believe even when you saw it." Boston tied the score in the seventh on a pinch-hit double by Swede Henriksen, and Wood came on in relief. The long season had come down to a few white-knuckled innings, and as if scripted in Hollywood, each team had its ace on the mound; Wood and Mathewson faced off for the first time in the Series. The pressure was on—and no one was immune.

In the top of the tenth, Boston's Tris Speaker—a brilliant center fielder who, in Game 7, had become the first and only outfielder in Series history to turn an unassisted double play—juggled a base hit that let Red Murray score the go-ahead run. In the bottom of the tenth, Red Sox pinch hitter Clyde Engle lofted a short fly to the usually reliable Fred Snodgrass. Snodgrass dropped it, and Engle reached second. One sportswriter claimed that a pop bottle thrown from the stands distracted Snodgrass; Snodgrass said no. His mother was watching the game on an electronic scoreboard in a Los Angeles movie theater. When the error was posted, she did what any mom would do. She fainted. Afterwards, Wood was more forgiving: "Maybe once a year a man would drop a ball like that. I'd seen it happen to Speaker, to Hooper, to

Series Firsts

The first official World Series —1903— saw such Series landmarks as the first shutout and inside-the-park home run. Other milestones, like the first no-hitter and Series-winning home run, didn't occur for half a century.

HITTING	PLAYER/TEAM	YEAR	STADIUM	FIELDING	PLAYER/TEAM	YEAR	STADIUM
Inside-the-park home run	Patsy Dougherty, Boston (AL)	1903 Game 2	Huntington Avenue Grounds, Boston	Unassisted double play	Hobe Ferris, Boston (AL)	1903 Game 2	Huntington Avenue Grounds, Boston
Home run	Jimmy Sebring, Pittsburgh (NL)	1903 Game 1	Huntington Avenue Grounds, Boston	Unassisted triple play	Bill Wambsganss, Cleveland (AL)	1920 Game 5	League Park, Cleveland
Pinch-hit home run	George Shuba, Brooklyn (NL)	1953 Game 1	Yankee Stadium, New York	Errorless Series by a team	New York (AL)	1937 5 games	Yankee Stadium, Polo Grounds, NYC
Grand slam	Elmer Smith, Cleveland (AL)	1920 Game 5	League Park, Cleveland				
Series-clinching home run	Bill Mazeroski, Pittsburgh (NL)	1960 Game 7	Forbes Field, Pittsburgh	**MISCELLANEOUS**	**PLAYER/TEAM**	**YEAR**	**STADIUM**
				Steal of home	Bill Dahlen, New York (NL)	1905 Game 3	Columbia Park, Philadelphia
PITCHING	**PLAYER/TEAM**	**YEAR**	**STADIUM**	Radio broadcast	New York (AL) at New York (NL)	1921 Game 1	Polo Grounds, New York
Shutout game	Bill Dinneen, Boston (AL)	1903 Game 2	Huntington Avenue Grounds, Boston	Television broadcast	Brooklyn (NL) at New York (AL)	1947 Game 1	Yankee Stadium, New York
Save	Doc White, Chicago (AL)	1906 Game 5	West Side Park, Chicago	Four-game sweep	Boston (NL) over Philadelphia (AL)	1914	Shibe Park, Philadelphia
No-hitter (perfect game)	Don Larsen, New York (AL)	1956 Game 5	Yankee Stadium, New York	Night game	Baltimore (AL) at Pittsburgh (NL)	1971 Game 4	Three Rivers Stadium, Pittsburgh

all of them. No reason—it just happens." In any case, the term "Snodgrass' muff" entered the baseball lexicon, though it took a few more lapses in the clutch to get the Giants in serious trouble. In fact, Snodgrass made a sensational running catch the very next play on a drive by Harry Hooper. "Ninety-nine times out of a hundred no outfielder could possibly have come close to that ball," said Hooper, a great defensive outfielder in his own right. "I think he *outran* the ball." But Snodgrass' strong throw wasn't enough to keep Engle from moving to third, nor was the catch enough to wipe out the muff. "They always forget about that play when they write about that inning," Snodgrass said years later.

Mathewson, who walked just 34 batters in 310 innings that season, then walked Steve Yerkes. With two on and none out, to the plate came Speaker, a .383 hitter during the regular season made more dangerous by his determination to avenge the error he committed in the top half of the inning. One of Mathewson's famous "fadeaways"—the forerunner of the screwball—fooled Speaker, and all he could do with it was pop an easy foul between home and first. "Any high school player could have caught it," sportswriter Fred Lieb said. Catcher Chief Meyers and first baseman Fred Merkle—whose nickname was "Bonehead" because he had failed to touch second in a game that helped give the Cubs the 1908 pennant—both went toward it. Some accounts say either man could have caught the ball; others claim only Merkle had a chance. But somebody was shouting "Chief! Chief!" for Meyers to take charge. It could have been Mathewson, but more likely it was the savvy Speaker who was shouting Meyers' name, in hopes that Merkle would back off and the ball might drop. If Mathewson was calling the play, he made the wrong call; if it was Speaker, he made the right one. Merkle

stopped; Meyers couldn't make the catch, and Speaker was still alive. According to Hooper, Speaker went back to the batter's box and yelled out to Mathewson, "Well, you just called for the wrong man. It's gonna cost you this ball game." Then he lined a prophetic single over Merkle's head to tie the game. Larry Gardner followed with a sacrifice fly that won the Series for the Red Sox and sent the Giants back to New York wondering how they managed to lose it.

The third time was indeed the charm for Giants southpaw Art Nehf in the 1921 Series. After being beaten in Games 2 and 5 by the Yankees' Waite Hoyt, Nehf twirled a four-hit shutout in Game 8 to beat Hoyt and clinch the Series. It was the first of four straight years in which Nehf pitched in the final game of the World Series; he had two wins, one loss and one no decision.

There have been single plays in the World Series that absolutely crackled with clutch performance. The 1921 Series was the first for the New York Yankees, a best-of-nine test against their hometown rivals, the New York Giants. Since 1913 the Yankees had shared the Giants' home stadium, the Polo Grounds, which played host to the entire Series.

In 1921 the Yanks were far from being the legendary team that made 32 more Series appearances in the next 57 years. New York had joined the American League in 1903 as the Highlanders and hovered around the second division for a decade or more. In 1920 the Yanks had acquired a kid named Babe Ruth and finished only three games out of first place. But in the 1921 World Series they were still just upstarts, while John McGraw's Giants had already appeared in five postseason championships.

Ruth scraped open his arm stealing third base in Game 2, and although he played gamely and well in Games 3, 4 and 5, the wound became infected and he was forced to sit out the next two games. The Giants won both to take a 4–3 lead into Game 8, which matched 20-game winner Art Nehf for the Giants against Waite Hoyt, a 19-game winner for the Yankees. Nehf and Hoyt had dueled in Games 2 and 5, with Hoyt winning both times.

6' 186 lbs.
BL TR

b 2/9/1925
d 7/7/1983

VIC WERTZ
Outfield, First Base

From 1947 through 1951, his first five seasons in the majors, Vic Wertz posted some impressive statistics with the Detroit Tigers. Twice he batted over .300, hit 27 home runs and drove in more than 120 runs. But his production began to fade, and in the early 1950s he was traded several times. He arrived at Cleveland early in the 1954 season with a .202 batting average and was considered a has-been.

But 1954 was a charmed year for the Indians, and Wertz was touched by the magic. He hit .275 for Cleveland, which won an AL-record 111 regular season games and was favored over the New York Giants in the World Series. Wertz went 8 for 16 in the Series—no other regular player hit better than .250. But ironically, he is remembered for a hit he didn't get.

It came late in Game 1—the eighth inning, with the score tied 2–2 and two on. No one, least of all Wertz, thought Willie Mays had a chance to catch up with his vicious shot deep to center in the Polo Grounds. When Mays did, grabbing it like a football receiver catching a long bomb, the Series turned. It was a blow from which the Indians never recovered; the Giants swept the Series. "I wish I had the 1954 World Series film here," Wertz told a dinner audience after the season. "I'd run it over and over until Willie Mays dropped that ball."

Wertz finished his 17-year career with Minnesota in 1963. But in World Series lore, the names Wertz and Mays will be linked forever.

Enos Slaughter's daring Game 7 run from first to home on a single made him the hero of the 1946 World Series as his Cardinals beat the Red Sox, 4–3. Ted Williams turned out to be the goat; the Boston star hit just .200 in his only World Series.

A first-inning error by Yankee shortstop Roger Peckinpaugh—who four years later committed eight errors in a single World Series—allowed Giant shortstop Dave Bancroft to score, giving his team the 1–0 lead it took into the bottom of the ninth. Pinch hitter Ruth led off with a ground out. Second baseman Aaron Ward coaxed a walk from Nehf, bringing up third baseman Frank Baker, whose slugging heroics in the 1911 World Series had earned him the nickname "Home Run." Baker lined a shot toward right field, but second baseman Johnny Rawlings made a sensational stop, diving to knock it down and then throwing to first in time to catch the slow-footed Baker for the second out. Ward, meanwhile, decided to force the action and hustled on toward third. It was a calculated risk, and a questionable one, considering that he was already in scoring position and Yankee catcher Wally Schang, who hit .316 that season, was up next. What Ward failed to factor into his aggressive decision was that George Kelly was playing first base, and that besides having a great arm, Kelly had a history of making clutch plays at the plate and in the field. True to form, Kelly kept his head and whipped a perfect throw to third baseman Frankie Frisch, who slapped the tag on Ward, and the Series was over. The Giants had taken it all on an unorthodox double play—the result of a baserunner hustling in the clutch and the opposition playing heads-up defensive baseball to cancel it out.

Art Nehf played a big role in another World Series pressure performance. In Game 6 of the 1923 Series, Nehf was trying to get his Giants back into a tie with the Yankees. This was the third consecutive year the two titans of New York had met; after winning five games to three in 1921, the last year of the best-of-nine World Series initiated in 1919, the Giants swept the Yankees four straight in 1922.

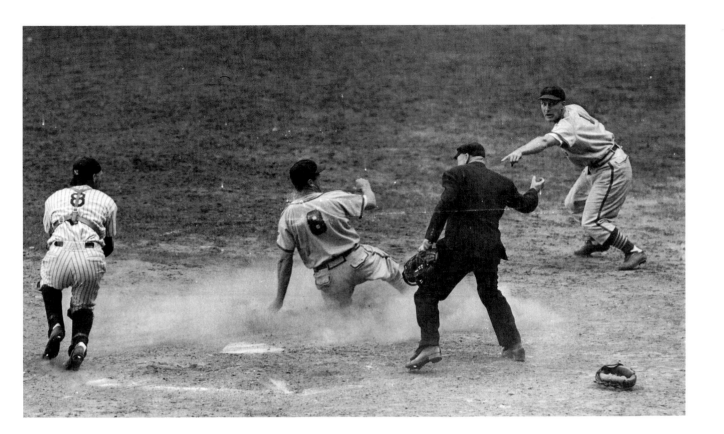

Nehf had hurled a six-hit shutout win for the Giants in Game 3, winning 1–0 over Sad Sam Jones, thanks to a seventh-inning homer by Casey Stengel. In Game 6 Nehf led 4–1 going into the eighth and had given up just two hits. Then the roof caved in. With one out, Schang singled. Shortstop Everett Scott, who had played in World Series for the Red Sox in 1915, 1916 and 1918, singled into the right field corner, sending Schang to third. Huggins then went to his bench for two right-handed pinch hitters in a row to face the Giants' southpaw. Nehf walked the first one, Fred Hofmann, on just four pitches, loading the bases. Next up was "Bullet Joe" Bush, a pitcher who was also a good hitter. Nehf committed an unpardonable pitching sin: he was again unable to throw a strike. A run was in, the bases were still loaded, and Nehf's day was done. Giant reliever Rosy Ryan couldn't stop the tide; the Yanks pushed four more runs across and won their first World Series.

Cardinal third baseman Whitey Kurowski (above, far right) tried to help umpire George Barr with a call in the ninth inning of Game 3 of the 1942 World Series against the Yankees, but Barr called St. Louis outfielder Terry Moore out at home. Kurowski later decided the Series with a two-run homer in the ninth inning of Game 5 that gave the Cardinals a Series-clinching 4–2 win.

T he ability to perform in the clutch is often demonstrated on the basepaths, because baserunning combines both speed and good judgment. In the fourth inning of Game 1 of the 1946 Series between St. Louis and Boston, Cardinal right fielder Enos Slaughter smashed a two-out triple that he wanted to turn into an inside-the-park home run, but he was held up at third by coach Mike Gonzalez. Slaughter was left stranded, and the Red Sox won, 3–2. One of the game's most aggressive players, Slaughter complained to manager Eddie Dyer, who responded, "All right, all right. If it happens again and you think you can make it, go ahead." The result of that advice has gone down in history as Slaughter's mad dash, which made all the difference in the Series.

Reggie Jackson loved nothing more—and did nothing better—than filling the October sky with home runs. He hit ten Series homers in just 98 at-bats, including a record five as a Yankee in 1977 (left). In that Series he earned his nickname, "Mr. October" with three homers on three consecutive swings in Game 6. Jackson warmed up his Series swing with the 1973–1974 Oakland A's (above), hitting one homer in each Series.

White Sox speedster Eddie Collins (above) slid in with the first run of Game 6 in the 1917 World Series when no one covered home during a rundown. New York third baseman Heinie Zimmerman couldn't catch Collins. "Who was I supposed to throw the ball to—myself?" he said. The play led to two more runs, and Chicago clinched the Series with a 4–2 win.

Slaughter had speed—and smarts. Regular Red Sox center fielder Dom DiMaggio had injured his ankle on the basepaths after driving in the tying runs with two outs in the eighth. His replacement, Leon Culberson, didn't have DiMaggio's arm, and everybody—including Slaughter—knew it. In the bottom of the inning, Slaughter was on first with two outs and was off with the pitch as Harry Walker lofted a looping fly over the shortstop's head and into left center field. Rounding second, Slaughter saw that Culberson was going to cut the ball off, but, with Dyer's words in mind, Slaughter wasn't about to stop at third. This time, Gonzalez just watched. "I think he was flabbergasted," Slaughter said.

At this point, the myth takes over. Red Sox fans, seeking a goat, blamed shortstop and cut-off man Johnny Pesky for not making the relay throw to home fast enough. Newsreel films later indicated that Pesky threw home as soon as Culberson's throw reached him, but that his throw was wide. Slaughter rounded third, kept on pounding, and scored on the play. Pesky saw it this way: "I would have needed a rifle to nail Slaughter." The Sox didn't score in the top of the ninth, and so lost a World Series for the first time; they haven't won one since. After it was all over, Cub general manager Jim Gallagher said of Slaughter: "That big-rumped baboon goes into the Army, drinks beer for three years and comes out running faster than before."

The final game of the 1917 World Series also hung on a dramatic piece of baserunning. The Series featured the potent New York Giants, who won the National League flag by ten games, and the Chicago White Sox—considered by many baseball historians one of the great teams of all time.

Chicago led the Series 3–2 going into the top of the fourth inning of a scoreless Game 6. The Giants' third baseman was Heinie Zimmerman. A

1912 Triple Crown winner, he was expelled from baseball for throwing games in 1919. The White Sox' Eddie Collins hit a grounder to Zimmerman, who threw wildly to first, allowing Collins to advance to second. Joe Jackson followed with a fly to right that Dave Robertson dropped, putting runners on first and third with none out. When "Happy" Felsch slapped a comebacker to the mound, Collins was trapped off third, and the rundown—a play major leaguers practice over and over every spring—commenced. Pitcher Rube Benton threw to Zimmerman; Collins headed toward the plate, knowing that if he could prolong the rundown, Jackson and Felsch could advance to third and second. Zimmerman threw to catcher Bill Rariden, moving Collins back toward third, but when Rariden returned the throw to Zimmerman, Collins shifted gears and sped past the catcher. This wouldn't have been such a brilliant piece of baserunning if either Benton or first baseman Walter Holke had covered the plate the way they'd been taught. But in the heat of the moment, both became transfixed spectators. Collins headed home, and Zimmerman chased him all the way across the plate. "Chick" Gandil then singled home two more runs; the Giants scored only two for the game, and Collins' heads-up footwork most likely made the difference in the Series.

Certain players have had good World Series careers, while others have had to settle for great—but fleeting—moments. Detroit's Kirk Gibson has never led the league in anything, yet his ability to perform in the clutch has fashioned some of the most remarkable Series moments in recent memory.

Gibson's raw power and daring baserunning in Game 5 of the 1984 Series put a winning flourish on the Tigers' amazing season. Detroit had been a juggernaut all year, winning 35 of its first 40 games and the AL East by a whopping 15 games, then sweeping the Royals in the American League

Dusty Rhodes (below) hit .333 as a pinch hitter in 1954, then sent the first World Series pitch he saw into the history books. His three-run shot into the right field bleachers at the Polo Grounds traveled only about 260 feet, but cleared the glove of Cleveland's Dave Pope (above), won the game for the Giants and sparked a Series sweep. Rhodes had seven RBI in just six at-bats in the Series.

Going into Game 5 of the 1984 World Series, relief pitcher Goose Gossage (right) hadn't given up a run in 12 innings of World Series action. But the Tigers tagged the San Diego right-hander for four runs in 1⅔ innings, three on Kirk Gibson's eighth-inning homer.

During the 1980s Kirk Gibson authored some of the most dramatic moments in World Series history. In Game 5 of the 1984 World Series (above), his two homers and five RBI led the Tigers to a Series-clinching 8–4 win over San Diego.

Championship Series. Their unlikely World Series opponent, the San Diego Padres, had come back from a 2–0 deficit to beat the Chicago Cubs in the NLCS. Detroit led the Series 3–1 going into Game 5, and Gibson's two-run homer sparked a three-run Tiger rally in the first inning. The Padres battled back to tie the score, giving Gibson another chance to be a hero. He led off the fifth inning with a single. On a long fly ball to left field by Lance Parrish, he tagged up and hustled to second—a play fans might see two or three times a season—and went to third on back-to-back walks. Then, with the bases loaded, pinch hitter Rusty Kuntz popped a fly to right. Padre right fielder Tony Gwynn lost the ball in the lights, so second baseman Alan Wiggins had to make the play, snaring it with his back to the infield. Gibson saw that he had the advantage, tagged up and flew home to give the lead back to the Tigers.

Going into the bottom half of the eighth, the Tigers' lead was still one run. Flamethrower Rich "Goose" Gossage was on the mound for the Padres when the Tigers put men on second and third with one out. With Gibson at the plate and the slow-footed Lance Parrish on deck, Padre manager Dick Williams called for an intentional walk to Gibson to set up the double play. But the confident Goose called Williams out to the mound to try to change his mind. Gossage's persuasion was successful; his pitching was not. The ball Gibson hit landed 20 rows back in the right field stands. Writer Roger Angell recalled that Gibson's memory was a key motivator—Gibson had never forgotten or forgiven Gossage for fanning him in his first major league at-bat.

In 1988 Gibson again had an October power surge. His home run in the top of the 12th won Game 4 of the NLCS for the Dodgers, and his three-run homer in Game 5 was key to another Dodger win. But his biggest clutch homer—and the most dramatic World Series homer of the decade—came a

few days later in Game 1, against Oakland. The Dodgers, down 4–3 in the ninth with two outs and a man on base, called on Gibson to pinch-hit against A's star reliever Dennis Eckersley. It looked like a mismatch, as Gibson— hobbled by a strained hamstring and injured knee—faced Eckersley, whose 45 saves in the regular season were just one shy of the major league record. Twenty minutes earlier, Gibson had been sitting in the trainers' room listening to broadcaster Vin Scully say the Dodger hero "will not see any action tonight." That was too great a challenge for Gibson to ignore, so he jammed an ice pack on his knee and headed for a practice batting tee in the clubhouse runway to take a few swings. He limped to the plate, but Eckersley quickly got ahead, 0–2. Gibson fouled off a few pitches, took a pitch that just missed, and managed to work the count full. Then Eckersley made a mistake, getting a slider down, but not far enough away. Gibson reached down and got it, pulling it into the right field seats. He watched the ball's flight, raised his arm in triumph, and then, according to *Sports Illustrated's* Peter Gammons, "limped around the bases as if he were staggering home from the Russian front." Eckersley was more succinct: "He hit the dogmeat out of it."

Gibson's intensity in the clutch, his sheer refusal to lose, gave the Dodgers more than just a win. As the A's watched Gibson stagger around the bases in pain and in joy, they seemed to sense that the underdog Dodgers had decided to be the better team. Even though he did not play again in the Series, Gibson had set a tone for clutch performance that let the Dodgers live on. Manager Tom Lasorda made all the right moves; unexpected heroes like Mickey Hatcher and Mike Davis came through when they had to. The A's never recovered and managed just one win in the Series. "I live for these moments," Gibson said. ◗

In Game 1 of the 1988 World Series, Kirk Gibson—by that time a Dodger—came up with his biggest postseason blast. Facing Oakland's Dennis Eckersley, that season's most dominant relief pitcher, Gibson limped to the plate on injured legs and golfed a game-winning two-run homer into the right field stands at Dodger Stadium.

Yogi Berra

It's hard to imagine a more unlikely hero than Yogi Berra. To say he was neither handsome nor suave is like saying George Steinbrenner isn't subtle. Yogi was coarse and clownish, his passion was comic books, and he had a way of contorting phrases and misusing words that made him sound as if he didn't quite have the hang of the English language. Yet out on the field, none of this mattered, because Berra was one of best catchers of all time and the man who carried the Yankees in the years between the twilight of Joe DiMaggio and the dawning of Mickey Mantle. Even after Mantle became the latest Yankee legend, Yogi led the supporting cast of players on the team that dominated baseball during the 1950s.

Berra had a knack for becoming a part of World Series lore as hero, victim or clown. In 1947, his rookie year, Berra slugged the first pinch-hit homer in Series history. The next day, with Yankee Bill Bevens pitching a no-hitter and two out in the ninth, Yogi was unable to throw out Brooklyn's Al Gionfriddo as he stole second. Then when Cookie Lavagetto doubled, Bevens lost both the game and a place in the record books. In Game 7 of the 1955 World Series, Yogi hit the fly ball that Dodger left fielder Sandy Amoros snagged as he ran to the stands, saving Brooklyn's first world championship. A year later, Berra created the image that baseball fans always associate with Don Larsen's perfect World Series game when he leapt into the pitcher's arms after the game-ending strikeout. Larsen's first words after his masterpiece were, "Damn Yogi, you're heavy." And

in 1960, when the Pirates' Bill Mazeroski hit the stunning ninth-inning homer that won the Series, it was Yogi, then playing left field, who stood helplessly and watched the ball sail over the brick wall.

His role in key Series plays wasn't an accident. From the late 1940s through the early 1960s, Berra was a Series fixture, playing in a record 75 games. He still holds the World Series records for at-bats (259) and hits (71), and he shares the record for doubles with Frankie Frisch (10). Only Mantle has scored more World Series runs—42 to Berra's 41—and has more World Series RBI—40 to 39. Five times Yogi batted over .300 in the Series, his most productive performance coming in 1956, when he had ten RBI and three homers, including a grand slam in Game 2.

Berra never had problems with hitting. His bat and his strong arm attracted Yankee scouts, and after a stint in the Navy and two years in the minors, he was called up to the big club. But he didn't receive a warm welcome. The veterans took one look at the crude and strange-looking rookie and couldn't resist sharpening their needles. When Berra walked by, they would hang from the dugout roof by one arm and make grunting sounds. Manager Bucky Harris didn't make things easier; he called Yogi "Nature Boy" and "the Ape." Opposing bench jockeys were less subtle. After one told Yogi that he had never seen an uglier face, Berra lashed back, "So I'm ugly. So what? I never saw anyone hit with his face." That was true, but it didn't stop the local sportswriters from joining the chorus, including one who questioned Harris'

With 12 World Series homers, Yogi Berra ranks third all time behind Mickey Mantle and Babe Ruth. Berra's last Series blast came in Game 2 in 1961, and earned him congratulations from teammates Johnny Blanchard (38, below) and Roger Maris.

Although he had to work hard to become a good defensive catcher, Berra was born to hit. And he didn't wait for strikes. "If he could reach it, he could hit it," said Yankee pitcher Allie Reynolds. "His only problem was he swung at some he couldn't reach." Berra's World Series magic eluded him as manager of the 1973 Mets (opposite), who lost to the Oakland A's in seven games.

keeping Berra on the team, pointing out that "he doesn't even look like a Yankee."

Yogi's torment ended in 1949, when Casey Stengel took over the club. He ordered an end to the taunting, adding, "Stop feeding him peanuts." More important, he made Berra, who had been a part-time outfielder, a full-time catcher and brought in Bill Dickey, the great Yankee catcher of the 1930s, to work with him. Despite his squat build, Berra was a quick, natural athlete, but his technique behind the plate was rough and awkward. Dickey drilled him on throwing to second and chasing foul pops and built up his confidence. He made the AL All-Star team in 1949, the first of 14 consecutive seasons he was named to the team.

Berra's batting took care of itself. He had a simple philosophy: "If I can see it, I can hit it," and he made a career of hitting bad pitches all over Yankee Stadium, particularly over the right field fence. Few batters were more feared in the clutch. "When it gets around the seventh inning," said White Sox manager Paul Richards, "Berra is the most dangerous hitter in baseball." For six straight seasons, beginning in 1950, he led the hard-hitting Yankees in RBI, and in 1951, 1954 and 1955, he was the AL's Most Valuable Player. His record of 313 home runs for a catcher seemed unbreakable until Johnny Bench topped the mark late in the 1980 season. Berra said, "I always thought the record would stand until it was broken."

It was a classic Berra comment, one of many that became part of his legend. There was the fa-

mous, "I want to thank you for making this night necessary," when he was honored before a game in St. Louis during his rookie year. There was the time someone suggested they dine at Toots Shor's and Yogi responded, "Nobody goes there any more. You can't hardly get a seat." Or the time that he was asked what he would do if he found a million dollars on the street. "I'd see if I could find the guy who lost it," he said, "and if he was poor, I'd give it back to him." When he became a manager, he didn't lose his touch. "You give 100 percent in the first half of the game," he said during a clubhouse pep talk, "and if that isn't enough, in the second half, you give what's left."

In spite of his problems with English, Berra had a very sharp baseball mind. Stengel recognized this and referred to Berra as an unofficial assistant coach. Yogi, he saw, had a rare talent for gauging his pitchers and an uncanny memory for the strengths and weaknesses of opposing batters. Those qualities, plus his patience, played big roles in Berra's becoming the second manager ever to win the pennant in both leagues—in 1964, with the Yankees, and in 1973, with the Mets. But even then, because he was neither fiery nor eloquent, or perhaps simply because he was Yogi, he was not taken seriously as a leader.

Sometimes it seems only Stengel truly appreciated Berra's gifts, and it was he who best captured him in words. As Casey put it: "He was a peculiar fellow with amazing ability."

YOGI BERRA

Catcher
New York Yankees 1946–1963
New York Mets 1965
Hall of Fame 1972

GAMES	2,120
AT-BATS	7,555
BATTING AVERAGE	
Career	.285
Season High	.322
SLUGGING AVERAGE	
Career	.482
Season High	.534
HITS	
Career	2,150
Season High	192
DOUBLES	
Career	321
Season High	30
TRIPLES	
Career	49
Season High	10
HOME RUNS	
Career	358
Season High	30
TOTAL BASES	3,643
EXTRA-BASE HITS	728
RUNS BATTED IN	
Career	1,430
Season High	125
RUNS	
Career	1,175
Season High	116
WORLD SERIES	1947, 1949–1953, 1955–1958, 1960–1963
MOST VALUABLE PLAYER	1951, 1954, 1955

Jimmy Sebring

Little Guys

In the first modern World Series, the 1903 Pittsburgh Pirates lined up an impressive array of sluggers against the Boston Pilgrims. The Pirates' hitters led the National League in just about everything— triples, homers, runs scored and slugging percentage. Their team batting average of .287 was second—by one point—to Cincinnati's. Shortstop Honus Wagner led the league with a .355 batting average and drove in 101 runs. Left fielder-manager Fred Clarke hit .351, center fielder Ginger Beaumont—who had won the batting title the year before—.341. Although they couldn't have imagined such a thing at the time, both Wagner and Clarke were headed for the Hall of Fame. And then there was Jimmy Sebring. The 21-year-old Pittsburgh right fielder hit .277, next-to-last among the team's starters. But in the 1903 Series, hitting seventh in the order, he was the dominant Pirate. Sebring smacked the first home run in a modern World Series and ten more hits, more than any other player; his .367 average was nearly a hundred points over other Pirate regulars'. Sebring's career lasted only three more years, and he left the majors with a .261 life- time average, but in the 1903 World Series he established a tradition that other forgettable players have since mirrored: for a brief moment he starred.

Baseball is a game of streaks and slumps. Batters get hot, then sud- denly can't buy a hit. Pitchers dominate, then can't find home plate. Over the course of a season, teams win by keeping streaks long and slumps short. But in a short series, anyone can get hot long enough to be a star.

In 1947 Cookie Lavagetto (opposite, center) managed just 18 hits all season, but his two-out, ninth-inning pinch-hit double broke up Yankee pitcher Bill Bevens' no-hitter and won Game 4 of the World Series.

Mets utility infielder Al Weis (above), who hit just seven home runs during ten years in the majors, picked a nice spot to show off his power in the 1969 World Series. His seventh-inning blast in Game 5 helped the Mets clinch the Series over Baltimore.

Al Weis, a spindly utility infielder for the Mets, is a legendary example of the less-than-average player—.219 lifetime—who found World Series pressure to his liking. The Amazin' Mets of 1969 weren't supposed to win *anything*. In their eight-year history they had never finished higher than ninth place, and they began the season as 100–1 long shots. But with intelligent managing by Gil Hodges and a crisp, young pitching staff, they got hot in August and zipped past a slumping bunch of Cubs. They didn't give the Braves a chance to get started in the National League Championship Series, sweeping them behind unlikely batting heroes like Art Shamsky and Wayne Garrett. Second baseman Ken Boswell, who hit just three homers all season, hit two in three games against Atlanta.

Beating the Braves was one thing; beating the mighty Orioles was something else entirely. This was essentially the same Oriole team that had stunned the baseball world by sweeping the Dodgers in the 1966 Series, using only four pitchers and allowing only two runs and 17 hits. These were the Orioles of pitching aces Jim Palmer, Mike Cuellar and Dave McNally; of legends Brooks Robinson and Frank Robinson at third and in right; of powerful Boog Powell at first, smooth-as-silk Mark Belanger at short. The 1969 Orioles won 109 regular-season games; only four teams in major league history ever won more in a season. Nobody expected the Mets' miracle to continue.

In Game 1 Oriole left fielder Don Buford slugged Tom Seaver's second pitch into the Memorial Stadium stands; Mike Cuellar tossed a six-hitter and struck out eight, and the Birds took an effortless 4–1 win.

Lefties Jerry Koosman and Dave McNally squared off in Game 2, and Donn Clendenon got the Mets started with a homer in the fourth. The Orioles didn't get a hit off Koosman until Paul Blair's single in the bottom of the

The Mets' Miracle of 1969, truly a team effort, had as its foundation a brilliant young pitching staff. Jerry Koosman was on the mound to finish off the Orioles in Game 5 of the World Series, but former Met manager Casey Stengel put the feat in focus. "You can't get lucky every day," Stengel said. "But you can if you get good pitching."

October 20, 1969, was Mets Day in New York City, and the unlikely heroes were honored with a ticker-tape parade. Mayor John Lindsay called the team "a modern miracle," but manager Gil Hodges, who had been there from the start, took a different view. "There's nothing miraculous about us," he said.

seventh, but they quickly capitalized when Blair stole second and scored on a single by Brooks Robinson to tie the game. With two outs and none on in the top of the ninth, the Mets' magic kicked back in. Ed Charles and Jerry Grote—.207 and .252 hitters, respectively—smacked back-to-back singles to left, bringing up Weis. The left-handed hitting Boswell had starred in the NLCS, but since the Oriole rotation was dominated by southpaws, the switch-hitting Weis, batting right-handed, was the Mets' second baseman for most of the Series. Although he had just 23 RBI all season, he drove in the Mets' only run in Game 1 with a sacrifice fly. Hodges could have gone to the bench for Art Shamsky, who was 5 for 13 as a pinch hitter that season, but he decided to let Weis hit, and Weis made the Met manager look brilliant by delivering a line single to left, knocking in the go-ahead run. Baltimore put two runners on in its half of the ninth, but reliever Ron Taylor came on to shut the door, and the Mets, amazingly, had tied the Series.

At home in Shea Stadium, the Mets surprised Jim Palmer to win Game 3, 5–0, as Gary Gentry and Nolan Ryan combined on a four-hitter, while Tommie Agee homered and saved at least five runs with two great catches in center field. Baltimore starter Mike Cuellar and reliever Eddie Watt battled the Mets' Tom Seaver to a 1–1 tie through the first nine innings of Game 4, but in the tenth Grote led off with a double and Weis walked. J. C. Martin, pinch-hitting for Tom Seaver, laid down a sacrifice bunt that was fielded along the first-base line by pitcher Pete Richert. Richert's throw hit Martin on the wrist and rolled down the right field line, allowing pinch runner Rod Gaspar to score from second with the winning run. A typical Mets finish. They were now one game from winning the World Series and *everyone* was amazed.

5' 9" 170 lbs.   b 11/25/1951
BR TR

BUCKY DENT
Shortstop

Sportswriters, when they wrote about him at all, usually called him "Little Bucky." But after his clutch performance for the Yankees in the 1978 World Series, he was known as "Mister Dent."

Russell Earl "Bucky" Dent came out of Savannah, Georgia, with a gift for scooping up grounders. No one who saw the plucky shortstop dominate the infield doubted he was destined for the big leagues. Sure enough, he signed with the White Sox in 1970 and walked into Comiskey Park as Chicago's starting shortstop just four years later. He finished second in Rookie of the Year voting and was a member of the 1975 AL All-Star team.

Although Dent was Gold Glove material, his hitting was nothing to rave about. His lifetime average was only .247, with a measly 40 homers over 12 years. When Dent was traded to the Yankees in 1977, little did anyone expect that he'd soon make headlines with his hitting, especially since he was overshadowed by such sluggers as Reggie Jackson, Thurman Munson and Lou Piniella.

But Dent exploded in the 1978 World Series, batting .417, driving in game-winning runs in Games 3 and 6, and earning World Series MVP honors. Basking in the unaccustomed limelight, Dent confessed that the Dodger pitchers had underestimated him: "They were throwing me 'Here, hit this, kid' pitches." So he did. One headline summed it up: "Little Bucky is Yanks' Mr. Big in Clutch."

Pitching was the key to the Braves' miracle in 1914, as they swept the A's in the Series. Boston mayor John "Honey Fitz" Fitzgerald (far left) posed with—from left—pitchers Lefty Tyler, Bill James and Dick Rudolph and manager George Stallings.

Two third-inning homers gave Baltimore a 3–0 lead in Game 5, but a two-run belt by Clendenon—his third homer of the Series—made it 3–2 in the sixth. Weis, already hitting .444 in the Series, led off for the Mets in the seventh, but this time there was no one on base for him to drive home. Although his only two 1969 homers had been big ones—driving in crucial runs in back-to-back games against the first-place Cubs in July—Weis had never homered at Shea Stadium in two seasons as a Met. All four of his Series hits so far were singles. So naturally the 31-year-old veteran blasted an 0–1 fastball over the 371-foot sign in left center field to tie the game. The victim, again, was 20-game winner Dave McNally. The Mets took the lead in the eighth, the Series an inning later, and Al Weis—who hit seven home runs in 800 career games—came from nowhere to become the outstanding hitter of the Series.

Joining Weis on the list of unlikely World Series superstars is a motley crew of oldsters with undistinguished careers, kids still fresh from the farms, squatty catchers and lanky infielders. Perhaps the oddest of all was George Whiteman. Whiteman's moment of glory came in the 1918 September World Series, the earliest one ever played. The Series started early for the same reason that Whiteman was playing in it: the United States had gone to war in Europe. A government-issued "work or fight" order declared that all able-bodied young men had either to go to battle or work in essential occupations, which baseball was not. Many players were already fighting overseas, the season had been abbreviated by executive order, and the Series began on September 5. Among Boston's replacements was the 35-year-old Whiteman. He arrived with only 14 major league games under his

belt, then played in 71 games for the Red Sox, hitting a respectable .266. *Baseball Magazine* called him "a veteran player whom unkind fate has exiled for years to a minor role in obscure leagues."

But when the pressure was on in the 1918 Series between the Red Sox and the Chicago Cubs, George Whiteman was in the middle of it. Looking more like a pulling guard on a sandlot football team than a left fielder, he made sizzling catches when they mattered most and smacked key hits. In Game 1 Boston's young ace, Babe Ruth, threw a shutout as Whiteman's single moved the game's only run into scoring position. He drove in Boston's only run in a 3–1 loss in Game 2. In Game 3 he scored one of the Red Sox' two runs, and in the fourth inning Chicago's Dode Paskert tagged Carl Mays for what looked like a game-tying home run until Whiteman came along and beat the ball to the left-field bleachers. According to *Baseball Magazine*, "Whiteman ran, and galloped, and when tired of galloping, ran some more."

Whiteman walked and scored as the Red Sox took a 3–1 Series lead with a 3–2 win in Game 4. The Cubs put runners on second and third with one out in the first inning of Game 5, when Whiteman made another great catch on a liner by Paskert, then fired a strike to double Charlie Hollocher off second. Whiteman made Hollocher pay again in the sixth, as he nailed the Cub shortstop trying to score from second on a single by Fred Merkle. Whiteman's great defense couldn't prevent a 3–0 loss in Game 5, but with two on and two out in the third inning of a scoreless Game 6, he smacked a line drive that right fielder Max Flack charged but couldn't handle. Two runs scored. In the top of the eighth, with Boston clinging to a 2–1 lead, Cubs pinch hitter Turner Barber looped a Texas leaguer into left field. Even though a miss would put the tying run in scoring position, Whiteman charged in recklessly,

The 1914 Philadelphia A's "$100,000 infield" featured Hall of Famers Eddie Collins at second and Home Run Baker at third, but it was the Boston Braves who went home with the World Series winners' share—$2,812 a man. And Boston's infield wasn't exactly minor league, as the A's Eddie Murphy found out when he was nailed at third (above) on a throw from first baseman Butch Schmidt to Charlie Deal.

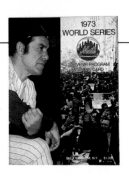

The Overachievers

I f the World Series has a basement, the 1973 New York Mets and the 1987 Minnesota Twins will spend an eternity there. Although the Mets stretched a great Oakland team to seven games before losing the Series, and the Twins actually beat the injury-wracked Cardinals in seven, purists will remember 1973 and 1987 as the years the divisional playoff system allowed two mediocre teams to play in baseball's ultimate contest.

One of the six teams in the National League East had to win the divisional title in 1973. But as late as the final day of the regular season schedule, statisticians announced that a five-way tie for first was one of 23 possibilities for the division's final standings. It wasn't until three rained-out games were made up following the regular schedule that the Mets emerged the victors: the division's only team with a winning percentage over .500.

Just six weeks earlier, on August 26, the overachieving Mets were in last place, 12 games under .500. But thanks to the incompetence of the other teams in the division, last was just six and a half games away from first. By mid-September, all New York had joined reliever Tug McGraw in shouting "You Gotta Believe!" as the Mets moved from fifth to fourth to third. The pitching of McGraw, Cy Young winner Tom Seaver, Jon Matlack, Jerry Koosman and Harry Parker helped the Mets to a 19–7 finish, good enough to take the division, nicknamed "the NL Least."

The feisty Mets, with their 82–79 record and .509 winning percentage, continued their unlikely road to the Series by defeating the 99–63 Cincinnati Reds for the pennant. In the Series, the Oakland A's finally sent the Mets back to Queens, but only after the seventh game of a hard-fought contest. "You

Gotta Believe!" entered the baseball lexicon, and the Mets entered history as the losingest team ever to reach the Series.

In 1987, 14 years after the Mets stumbled into the Series, the Minnesota Twins, nicknamed "the Twinkies," compiled one of the most statistically skewed seasons in baseball history." Even though they had three hitters with 30 homers, the Twins scored just 786 runs and allowed 806. The difference of 20 runs was the worst ever recorded by a division-winning team. And while the Twins were 56–25 at home, they won only 29 on the road to finish 85–77 overall. In the AL East, that would have earned them fifth place; in the West, it gave them the division title.

Once in the playoffs, Twins Manager Tom Kelly disguised the shallowness of his starting rotation by using just three starters, and the Twins tamed the favored Detroit Tigers in five. Detroit's loss gave Tiger skipper Sparky Anderson, who had also managed the Reds in the 1973 playoffs against the Mets, the distinction of losing pennants to the two teams with the worst records ever to reach the World Series.

Minnesota brought its lopsided season to a predictable conclusion, losing all three games at Busch Stadium in St. Louis to a Cardinals team playing without slugger Jack Clark and with an injured Terry Pendleton at third base. The Twins sandwiched those three defeats between four victories at the Metrodome to become the first team in Series history to win it all without a victory on the road, and the only team to win indoors. When it was all over, second baseman Steve Lombardozzi proclaimed, "We are no longer the Twinkies. We are the World Champion Minnesota Twins." Let the purists writhe.

The Minnesota Twins lost 91 games and finished sixth in the AL West in 1986, but a year later they were world champs. The core of the Twins' hard-hitting lineup included (at right, from left to right) outfielders Kirby Puckett and Tom Brunansky and first baseman Kent Hrbek.

Tug McGraw (left) was the most overworked of the overachieving Mets in the 1973 World Series against Oakland. The southpaw relief ace pitched a total of 13⅔ innings in five appearances and racked up one win and one save.

Yankee legend Joe DiMaggio retired after the 1951 season, so in 1952 he was a spectator as the Yankees met the Dodgers in the World Series. DiMaggio played center field in ten Series for the Yankees—they won nine of them. But they didn't seem to miss him in 1952, as they beat Brooklyn for the third time in six years.

Babe Adams' 12 wins ranked fifth on the Pirate staff in 1909, but manager Fred Clarke decided to start the rookie in Game 1 of the World Series against Detroit. Adams responded with three complete-game wins, including a shutout in Game 7, and held Tiger great Ty Cobb to just one hit in 11 at-bats.

made a diving shoestring catch, and saved the game for Boston. In the process, he turned a full somersault, wrenched his shoulder, and had to leave the game, replaced by young Babe Ruth. Whiteman's catch was the last he ever made in the major leagues. By the following summer the war was over, the regulars returned, and George Whiteman went back to the minors. He probably didn't have many great moments of major league-caliber baseball in him, but there's no question he had them at the best possible time.

The Pittsburgh Pirates threw a surprise opening-game starter at the Detroit Tigers in the 1909 Series, and got the idea from an unlikely source: a scouting report from the president of the National League. Before Game 1, NL President John Heydler went to Pirate skipper Fred Clarke and asked, "Why don't you start Babe Adams?" Adams, a rookie, had started only a dozen games that year, the fewest among the Pittsburgh rotation. And even though he went 12–3 with a 1.11 ERA, he wouldn't have been Clarke's first choice. But Heydler mentioned that late in the season he had seen Dolly Gray of the Senators beat the Tigers handily, and he thought Adams' delivery was similar to Gray's.

The president turned out to be a promising scout: the Pirates won 4–1, and Adams won two more games in the Series, including a six-hit shutout in Game 7 to clinch the Series for Pittsburgh. Nowadays, opportunities for managers to start an unexpected pitcher have just about disappeared. Since the introduction of the League Championship Series in 1969 and its expansion to World Series length in 1985, managers have had to use their best hurlers in tight rotation just to get into the Series; in most years, they haven't had the luxury of setting up their favorite rotation for the World Series.

One pitcher whose World Series performances stood in marked contrast to his mediocre career was Yankee left-handed reliever Bob Kuzava. In 1951 Kuzava, who had pitched in just 23 games for the Yankees, wasn't called on until Game 6, and he couldn't have been put in a tougher situation. The Yanks led the Subway Series 3–2, and took a 4–1 lead into the ninth inning of Game 6. But the Giants—fresh from Bobby Thomson's pennant-winning home run in the NL playoff against the Dodgers—wouldn't go down quietly. Three singles loaded the bases, and Johnny Sain's relief stint was over.

Kuzava's nickname was Sarge, and at 6′ 2″ and more than 200 pounds, he was an imposing figure on the mound. But the first batter he faced, Monte Irvin, was a big man himself and belted a long fly to left fielder Gene Woodling that scored Eddie Stanky from third and advanced the other runners. Bobby Thomson then hit another long fly to Woodling, scoring Alvin Dark to make the score 4–3. Giants manager Leo Durocher then went to his bench for little-used catcher Sal Yvars, who pinch-hit for Hank Thompson. Yvars had only batted 41 times in the regular season but hit .317. In his only career World Series at-bat, he hit a low line drive to right that, but for the quick hands and feet of Yankee right fielder Hank Bauer, could have made him a hero. Bauer made a diving catch to end the Giants' hopes. It wasn't pretty, but Kuzava got the job done.

In 1952 Casey Stengel again called on Kuzava only once in the World Series but, again, when the situation was tightest. Facing the Dodgers in Game 7, the Yankees held a 4–2 lead, but with one out in the bottom of the seventh the Dodgers loaded the bases. Kuzava was summoned. Under normal circumstances, bringing in a lefty to face left-handed center fielder Duke

With the bases loaded in the seventh and the Yankees clinging to a 4–2 lead over Brooklyn in Game 7 of the 1952 World Series, manager Casey Stengel (above, center) played an unlikely hunch and brought in Bob Kuzava (right) to relieve Vic Raschi (17). Kuzava—wild during the season with 63 walks in just 133 innings—pitched the rest of the game without allowing a hit.

Yankee catcher Yogi Berra played on ten world champions, and as a result got to perform his celebratory leap on a bunch of different pitchers. In 1952 Berra, who homered twice in the Series, was carried by Bob Kuzava.

The Yankees' fourth straight world title might not have happened if second baseman Billy Martin (above, center) hadn't alertly dashed in to catch Jackie Robinson's bases-loaded pop-up with two outs in the seventh of Game 7 in 1952. "If he hadn't caught it," said Dodger catcher Roy Campanella, "everybody would have scored."

Snider would have been playing the odds. But this game was in Ebbets Field, a park that was considered death to southpaws, and besides, Snider was one of only two left-handers in the Dodger lineup. Brooklyn pitcher Carl Erskine called Stengel's decision an "absolute, unbelievable mystery." But it worked, as Snider popped a 3–2 fastball to third. Kuzava stayed in, against the odds, to face right-handed Jackie Robinson. Kuzava got a fastball in on Robinson's fists, and the great Dodger second baseman popped the ball up to the right side. In the late afternoon sun, Yankee first baseman Joe Collins couldn't track it, and Kuzava himself didn't move off the mound. Bauer watched in horror from right field. "There were four Dodgers tearing around the bases and nobody was close enough to the ball to wave hello to it," he said. It was Yankee second baseman Billy Martin who charged the arcing fly ball, ducking around the baserunner heading for second. When Martin caught it, knee high and about eight feet to the right side of the mound, the tying run had already crossed the plate, to no avail. "I still don't know how Billy got there that fast," Bauer said. "But we knew that nothing the Dodgers did after that could keep us from winning." Kuzava breezed through the eighth and ninth. The Yankees had appeared in four consecutive Series and won them all.

Thanks to the new broadcasting medium called television, the 1947 World Series was the first to top the $2 million mark in earnings. For the Yankees, left fielder Johnny Lindell was their money man. Lindell had nine hits, three doubles, a .500 average and a team-leading seven RBI in just six games—all while playing with a fractured rib. After Game 6, Yankee President Larry MacPhail benched him. "You're not doing the ball club any

It was a long walk to the clubhouse for Yankee pitcher Bill Bevens (above, left) when he lost Game 4 of the 1947 Series, 3–2, after coming within one out of a no-hitter. Two days later, center fielder Joe DiMaggio (right) got robbed on a great catch by Brooklyn's Al Gionfriddo.

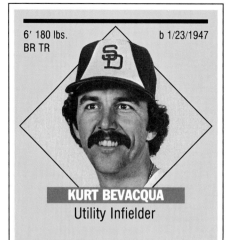

6' 180 lbs.
BR TR

b 1/23/1947

KURT BEVACQUA
Utility Infielder

During his 15-year career with six clubs, utility man Kurt Bevacqua was a team clown and his own chief publicist. For charity, he caught several balls dropped from a 390-foot tower, and missed one when he tried to backhand it. He won a major league bubblegum blowing contest. "I'll do anything to get in the newspaper," declared Bevacqua. He needed to do something. He wound up with an undistinguished .236 career batting average and 27 career home runs.

Bevacqua's most unlikely stunt was becoming a World Series hero with San Diego in 1984 after batting .200 and hitting only one homer during the regular season. In Game 2 against Detroit, with the Padres missing slugger Kevin McReynolds, designated hitter Bevacqua singled and scored in the fourth. In the fifth, he hit a three-run, game-winning homer. As the blast cleared the fence, Bevacqua's trip around the bases included a shuffle that exploded into a vertical leap, a 360-degree pirouette, a cha-cha step over first base, a high-five for coach Ozzie Virgil, and a two-handed kiss blown to his wife Carrie in the stands. When asked if he was anxious to reach the dugout to be with his teammates, Bevacqua said, "Naw. I really wanted to run around the bases again."

The Padres lost the next three games, but Bevacqua, who hit a team high .412 with two homers, finally had his moment in the sun.

good if you're out there not physically fit to play." Lindell must have wondered what fitness was all about.

But the indelible memories of 1947 hang on the image of two players who turned one pitch into baseball history. Neither was a star, and neither ever played in the major leagues again. The first three games of the Yankees-Dodgers Series were characterized by Louis Effrat of *The New York Times* as "the most drab, inept and colorless of all time." But Game 4, played in Ebbets Field, more than made up for the preliminaries. Fred Lieb—scorekeeper, sportswriter and baseball historian—called it "a contest that made the 33,443 crowd stark mad. It was the kind of game that makes the World Series the event it is and explains its hold on the American public." *Baseball Magazine* was less lyrical but no less enthusiastic: "If a guy smoked an opium pipe all day he couldn't dream up such a fantastic finish."

This was the first World Series the Yankees had appeared in since 1928 without the services of Hall of Fame catcher Bill Dickey, who played in eight fall classics before retiring after the 1946 season. Catching chores were being handled by an inexperienced threesome: Yogi Berra, Aaron Robinson and Sherm Lollar. Berra was having his problems behind the plate; no less an expert than Connie Mack said, "Never in a World Series have I seen such awful ketchin' "—and it cost the Yankees dearly.

Starting for the Dodgers was Harry Taylor. He didn't last long. Bill Bevens, the Yankee starter, did. All the way to the bitterest of ends. In the first inning, the Yanks loaded the bases with none out. A walk produced one run, but Dodger reliever Hal Gregg appeared and induced George McQuinn to pop up and Billy Johnson to ground into a double play.

One More Good Game

At the start of the 1929 World Series, 35-year-old pitcher Howard Ehmke was at the end of his career. He had pitched with dull consistency in the majors for 14 years and had compiled a 166–165 career record. He won 20 games in 1923 and 19 in 1924 with the Boston Red Sox, but he also lost 17 games in each of those seasons. He pitched a no-hitter against Philadelphia in 1923, and led the league in complete games in 1925, but his record for the year was only 9–20. When he was traded to the Philadelphia Athletics in 1926, the best that could be said of him was that he was a workhorse.

On September 12, 1929, with a Philadelphia pennant a certainty, manager Connie Mack told Ehmke his pitching days with the A's were over. Ehmke took the news graciously. According to baseball historian Joseph Reichler, Ehmke said, "All right, Mr. Mack, if that's the way you want it. But I've always had the ambition to pitch in a World Series. My arm is not what it once was, but I honestly feel there's one more good game in it. I'd like a chance to prove it to you."

Ehmke's reply gave Mack an idea. He saw the chance to surprise the NL champion Chicago Cubs, who would not be expecting Ehmke to appear in the Series. Mack told Ehmke he would pitch Game 1 of the Series, but Ehmke was not to tell anyone, not even his wife. Mack sent Ehmke to scout the Cubs, and according to Mack's plan, Ehmke didn't return to the clubhouse until the day before the Series.

Philadelphia players, believing Ehmke had been released, were amused to see him get into uniform. But Mack wasn't tipping his hand, even to his own team. He cagily had both Lefty Grove and Ehmke warm up before the game.

Ehmke took the mound. His curve was sweeping and his fastball sneaky. The first Cub batter fouled out, the second singled and the next two flied out. Kiki Cuyler and Riggs Stephenson took called third strikes in the second inning. In the third, Ehmke sandwiched three strikeouts around a single and a double, and Cuyler whiffed again in the fourth. Ehmke got some help; a great diving catch by third baseman Jimmy Dykes in the fourth inning and a stunning one-handed grab by left fielder Al Simmons in the fifth kept the game scoreless. Ehmke threw third strikes past the last two men in the fifth and to all three in the sixth.

In the top of the seventh, the A's took a 1–0 lead on a Jimmie Foxx homer. In the bottom of the inning, with two out and runners on second and third, Ehmke struck out pinch hitter Gabby Hartnett and tied Ed Walsh's 1906 record of 12 strikeouts in a World Series game.

Two fly outs and a ground out closed down the Cubs in the eighth. In the ninth, the A's added two more runs with the help of two Cub errors. But in the bottom of the inning, Ehmke got in a jam. With one out, Cuyler scored on a single by Stephenson, and a single by Charlie Grimm put the tying run on first. Then Footsie Blair's grounder forced Grimm out at second, and Stephenson advanced to third. With two out, pinch hitter Chuck Tolson worked the count full. Ehmke called catcher Mickey Cochrane to the mound and said, "I want to keep this guy guessing. I'll pretend to shake you off on the fastball signal." Ehmke shook his head on cue, then fired his hummer. Tolson swung and missed. The A's won 3–1, and Ehmke set a World Series strikeout record. Connie Mack's ploy had worked, the A's went on to win the Series, and Ehmke had pitched one more good game.

ABOVE THE CROWD By Stookie Allen

COURAGE!

EHMKE HAD PLENTY OF IT IN THE 1929 WORLD SERIES. — BEFORE THE FIRST GAME THE CUBS WHISPERED THAT HE WAS A QUITTER, AND ALL WERE ASTONISHED WHEN CONNIE MACK SELECTED HIM TO PITCH OVER GROVE AND EARNSHAW.

— HOWARD — EHMKE FANNED 13! (A WORLD SERIES RECORD).

SOMETHING FOR DIZZY AND DAFFY TO SHOOT AT.

EHMKE MADE GOATS OF THE CUBS. HE STRUCKOUT HORNSBY AND HACK WILSON TWICE IN TOUGH SPOTS, AND GOT CUYLER ONCE. GOING INTO THE NINTH, AFTER HE HAD FANNED 12, A LINE DRIVE STRUCK HIM IN THE GROIN...

BEFORE FALLING HE THREW TO FIRST — THEN, THOUGH SUFFERING IN-TENSELY, HE STRUCKOUT THE LAST MAN AND SET A RECORD!

Howard Ehmke is best remembered for his surprising 3–1 win and record 13 strikeouts for the Athletics in Game 1 of the 1929 Series. But he came within a debatable scorer's call of pitching two no-hitters in a row in 1923. With the Red Sox, Ehmke no-hit the A's, then in his next start retired 27 Yankees in a row after leadoff hitter Whitey Witt rapped a grounder that bounced off third baseman Howard Shanks' chest. It was scored a hit.

Minnesota's Randy Bush—known more for his power than his speed—gave Cardinal catcher Tony Pena almost nothing to tag as he slid home during Game 2 of the 1987 World Series. Bush's slide (above, with Dan Gladden, 32) capped a six-run rally and the Twins went on to beat St. Louis, 8–4.

Bevens, 7–13 in the season, walked two men in the first, one in the second and one in the third, but did not allow any hits. The Yankees added another run in the fourth, but squandered several other scoring chances. In the fifth the Dodgers pushed a run home on two walks, a sacrifice and a fielder's choice. The Yankees loaded the bases with one out in the top of the ninth, but reliever Hugh Casey came on to throw one pitch—a double-play grounder. The Yanks clung to a 2–1 lead into the bottom of the ninth, and Bevens still hadn't allowed a hit.

Dodger catcher Bruce Edwards led off against Bevens in the ninth, sending Johnny Lindell to the left field fence to haul in his drive. Carl Furillo received Bevens' ninth walk, but Spider Jorgensen fouled out to bring Bevens to within one out of the first no-hitter in World Series history. Al Gionfriddo went in to run for Furillo, and Pete Reiser was sent up to hit for Hugh Casey. Although far below his batting-title form of 1941, Reiser was still a dangerous hitter, batting .309 in 110 games before his season was interrupted by a collision with the center-field wall in Ebbets Field. In what turned out to be a crucial play, Gionfriddo stole second on the inexperienced Berra. The count on Reiser was 3–1 when Yankee manager Bucky Harris decided to have Bevens finish the walk intentionally. In the stands, dubious Yankee fans must have muttered the famous baseball adage: "Never put the winning run on base."

Eddie Miksis went in to run for Reiser, and Cookie Lavagetto was summoned to hit for Eddie Stanky. Lavagetto had been in the majors for ten years —he lost four seasons to service in World War II—and had been a steady if not sensational infielder for the Pirates and the Dodgers. He was hitless in two previous at-bats in the Series. But this was Cookie's moment, and he

delivered a liner that ricocheted high off the right-field wall past Yankee outfielder Tommy Henrich, driving in both runners. With one cut, Cookie Lavagetto had taken away Bill Bevens' no-hitter, given the Dodgers the victory, and sent the Ebbets Field faithful into an unprecedented frenzy. Miksis, who had turned 21 just a few weeks earlier, slid across the plate with the winning run, and stayed awhile to savor the moment. "For what seemed like much more than the three or four actual seconds," wrote Dick Young of the *New York Daily News,* "Miksis just sat there, looked up at his mates gathered around the plate, and laughed insanely." It was Bill Bevens' last major league pitch. For Cookie Lavagetto, it was the only ball he hit to right all year, his final major league hit, and one of the most dramatic moments in World Series history.

When Cookie Lavagetto's game-winning double tied the 1947 World Series at two games each, joy reigned in Brooklyn. "We just went crazy," said Al Gionfriddo, who scored on Lavagetto's hit. "With the fans swarming on the field, it was all we could do to get to the clubhouse."

Catchers seem to have had more than their share of World Series stardom—and shame. Rick Dempsey spent time in both the Minnesota and the Yankee organizations, but never played in a World Series until he became a Baltimore Oriole. Dempsey was known as a solid defensive player and a fine handler of pitchers, but hardly as an offensive threat. In 1983 the Orioles led the league in home runs but Dempsey had little to do with it. In fact, second baseman Rich Dauer, third baseman Todd Cruz and Dempsey, the seventh through ninth batters in the order, were known as "the Three Stooges" for their lack of punch. In Game 2 of the 1983 Series against the Phillies, however, they sparked a three-run rally in the fifth that led to a 4–1 Oriole win. After a solo homer by outfielder John Lowenstein, Dauer singled, Cruz beat out a bunt, and Dempsey belted the first of four doubles he hit in the Series. Oriole pitcher Mike Boddicker, in just his

5' 10" 155 lbs.
BR TR

b 9/6/1903
d 7/29/1957

TOMMY THEVENOW
Shortstop

They were the most unevenly matched opponents when they met in the 1926 World Series: Yankee legend Babe Ruth, who hit a record three homers in Game 4 of the Series, and the Cardinals' Tommy Thevenow, who never hit a ball out of the park in his entire 15-year career.

A quiet sort of man who did his job, Thevenow started with St. Louis in 1924. He didn't call attention to himself, but the skinny shortstop could be dangerous in the field. In 1926 he racked up 597 assists—100 more than any other shortstop in the majors. But his hitting was another story. His method: slap the ball into play and try to beat it to first. His career average: a measly .247.

But Thevenow had the uncanny ability to come through in the clutch. And he was at his career best against Ruth in the 1926 World Series, a struggle that went to seven games. It was no surprise that Thevenow scooped up ball after ball in the field, but his Series batting average of .417—the highest of any player—shocked everyone. It was Thevenow who brought in the winning run in Game 7. Even more bizarre was the inside-the-park homer Thevenow got when center fielder Ruth dropped his fly ball in Game 2.

While Ruth went on to set a record with 714 career homers, Thevenow set a home run record of his own: in 3,347 regular-season at-bats, he never got one.

All season long catcher Rick Dempsey (far left) was the number-nine hitter in the Orioles' lineup, but in the 1983 World Series he became their number-one slugger, with four doubles, a .385 batting average and a .923 slugging percentage.

second major league at-bat, lined a sacrifice fly to left to score Cruz and finish the rally. In Baltimore's Game 3 victory, Dempsey doubled off Steve Carlton and scored the tying run on a single by Benny Ayala, who soon scored the winning run. Dempsey was treated to an intentional walk in Game 4, before being removed for a pinch hitter in the sixth. In Game 5, the final contest, he cracked another double and drove in another run as Scott McGregor shut out the Phillies. For good reason Dempsey was selected the Series' MVP.

After having tasted World Series glory, Dempsey continued his career with moderate success. But another catcher has a double slot in World Series history: hero *and* goat. Hank Gowdy was the starting catcher for the 1914 Boston Braves, who, on July 15, were in a familiar place—last. Then behind a trio of young pitchers—Dick Rudolph, Bill James and Lefty Tyler—the Braves went on an incredible tear, winning 61 of their last 77 games. They passed the NL defending champion Giants for good on September 8, beating them into submission with a 17-game winning streak, and won the pennant by 10½ games. The "Miracle Braves" had fans rooting for them across the country, but they would need another miracle, it seemed, to beat the powerful, highly favored Philadelphia Athletics in the World Series. Connie Mack's Athletics had won the Series in 1910, 1911 and 1913 and had three future Hall of Famers on the pitching staff alone—Eddie Plank, Chief Bender and Herb Pennock. The A's scored 134 more runs than any other AL team, and they placed three of their stars—first baseman Stuffy McInnis, second baseman Eddie Collins and third baseman Home Run Baker—among the top five in RBI for the season. The Braves' roster, meanwhile, was a cut-and-paste hodgepodge—a load of untried kids and cranky veterans from the NL's discard pile. Second baseman Johnny Evers was in his 13th big-league season;

shortstop Rabbit Maranville was in his third. Seven men shared outfield jobs, and the team's best hitter, third baseman Red Smith, was out with a broken ankle. Experts predicted a lopsided Series.

And then there was Gowdy. Originally a New York Giant first baseman, he was cut by John McGraw for being lazy, so in 1911 the lanky, easygoing Ohioan with the engaging grin was traded to the doormat Braves. Gowdy spent the 1913 season in the International League learning how to be a catcher and came back to Boston in 1914.

The experts were right in one regard: the 1914 Series was lopsided. The Braves swept the mighty Athletics in four games—the first complete Series wipeout. And Gowdy was a demon. A .243 hitter during the season, he blasted Athletics pitching for a single, three doubles, a triple and a homer in just 11 at-bats, for an unbelievable 1.273 Series slugging percentage. "Hankus Pankus was the Series' clouting demon," said Fred Lieb. Gowdy's defensive work and handling of the testy Boston pitching staff received high praise, too, and Philadelphia scored just six runs in the four games. For one winter Gowdy was baseball's greatest hero.

The next year the Braves finished second, and the Miracle had ended. They tumbled to third place, then to sixth, then to seventh. By 1917 Hank Gowdy was a part-time catcher. In 1923 the Giants picked him up for backup catching help, and in 1924 Gowdy found himself once again in a World Series.

The Giants and the Senators had traded wins for six tension-filled games, but Game 7 topped them all. A bad-hop single by Washington player-manager Bucky Harris had tied the game in the eighth, 3–3. Legendary fastballer Walter Johnson had come on in relief in the ninth and

It seemed like a mismatch: Cincinnati's Rawley Eastwick, the NL save leader, against Boston's Bernie Carbo, a part-time outfielder with a .257 average. But Carbo (above, with batting helmet) had power and launched a fastball over the center field wall in Fenway Park to score three runs, tie Game 6 of the 1975 World Series and spread hope throughout New England.

After hitting .218 in 1985, Mets third baseman Ray Knight came back to hit .298 in 1986. But he hit his peak in the World Series, scoring the winning run in the tenth inning of Game 6 (right), then homering in the seventh to win Game 7.

had pitched out of several jams to keep the game tied going into the bottom of the 12th inning. With one out, Senator catcher Muddy Ruel hit a foul pop behind home plate. Gowdy tore off his mask—and promptly stepped in it. He tried to shake the mask off his foot but couldn't, and he dropped the ball. "It hung on like a bear trap," he said later. Ruel made the most of being reprieved by smacking a double and, two batters later, scoring the Series-winning run for the Senators. Ten years after his World Series glory, Gowdy was a World Series goat.

In the annals of unexpected stardom, one Series leads all others. In 1931 one man completely dominated the first five games of the Series with his bat and his baserunning. He went without a hit in the final two games, but it didn't matter, because two of the unlikeliest World Series heroes ever took over for him.

In 1931 Johnny Leonard Roosevelt Martin was, at 27, playing in his first full major league season. Nicknamed "Pepper" for his stylish hustle, he performed well for the Cardinals, stealing 16 bases and hitting .300 in a hitters' year. But no one expected Martin to put on a one-man vaudeville show in the World Series against Connie Mack's Athletics, who won 107 games in the regular season behind all-time greats like first baseman Jimmie Foxx, outfielder Al Simmons, catcher Mickey Cochrane and pitcher Lefty Grove.

Martin stole a base to go with his three hits in Game 1, but he was just warming up. His antics in Game 2 captured the imagination of Depression-era baseball fans. He doubled in the second, stole third and scored on a sacrifice fly. In the seventh he singled, stole second, and scored his—and the team's —second run on a squeeze play. Game 3 saw him add two more hits and two

more runs to his total. An interviewer asked him about his speed. Pepper replied, "Well, sir, I grew up in Oklahoma, and out there, once you start running, there ain't nothing to stop you."

Philadelphia's George Earnshaw shut out the Cards in Game 4, allowing only two hits; both belonged to Martin. Cardinal manager Gabby Street moved Pepper from his usual sixth place in the lineup to the cleanup spot for Game 5. Brilliant managing. With a homer, two singles—one on a bunt—and a sacrifice fly, Martin drove in four runs in a 5–1 St. Louis win. In the first five games, Martin had hit .667 with four doubles, a homer and four stolen bases. He either drove in or scored ten of the 14 St. Louis runs. No wonder the Reach *Guide* that year said he was the "divine spark of genius that rescued the Missourians any time they were lagging."

But Martin managed just a walk in four trips in Game 6, and the Cards were beaten by Lefty Grove, tying the Series at 3–3. In the very first inning of the final game, two new World Series heroes were born. Third baseman Andy High and right fielder George Watkins—a combined 3 for 22 in the first six games—hit back-to-back bloop singles off Earnshaw in the bottom of the first. After Frankie Frisch sacrificed the runners to second and third, Earnshaw uncorked a wild pitch that scored High. Martin walked and stole second, and on a dropped third strike, Watkins rushed home for the Cards' second run. Two innings later High again led off with a single, this one a line drive, and Watkins hit a line drive of his own—into the right field pavilion. Burleigh Grimes held the A's in check, and the Cardinals won 4–2 to take the Series. On that day, no one in a Redbird uniform had a hit, scored or drove in a run except for Andy High and George Watkins—two men who proved that it only takes one day in the sun to become a star. ◗▮

Gene Tenace (38) jumped all over Cincinnati pitching—and home plate—in the 1972 World Series. The Oakland catcher, who had homered just five times during the regular season, launched four home runs in the Series, driving in nine of the A's 16 runs in their seven-game win over the Reds.

The Big Catch

nticipation is what fielding is all about—for both the player and the fan. The fielder anticipates all possibilities in order to put himself in the best position to make a play. For the spectator, those few moments between the crack of the bat and the thump in the glove provide that gasp of anticipation which is at the heart of baseball's drama. Every day of the season, ballplayers from the littlest leagues to the majors demonstrate the fine art of fielding. Even in the most lopsided ballgame, a great catch is still a great catch. But grabbing headlines with a glove means making great plays in big games. Few players did it better, or bigger, than Yankee third baseman Graig Nettles.

In 1978 the Yankees and the Dodgers were going head-to-head in the World Series for the second year in a row and the tenth time in history. The Dodgers had pocketed the first two games with relative ease. Ron Guidry, who had startled baseball with a 25–3 record that year, was starting the third game in a last-chance try to get the Yanks back on track. A 2–0 Series deficit had never been overcome.

But the usually dominant Guidry didn't have his best stuff that night. Two Dodgers reached base in the first; in the second Graig Nettles started a double play that squelched a potential Dodger threat. With a run in, one on and two out in the third, Nettles grabbed a Reggie Smith smash on his knees, then scrambled to his feet and threw Smith out.

Yankee third baseman Graig Nettles (opposite) hit just .160 in the 1978 World Series against the Dodgers but turned the Series around with his glove. Nettles' fielding, said Dodger pitcher Tommy John, "took all the starch out of us."

In his first World Series, in 1975 Boston right fielder Dwight Evans came within one putout of tying the major league record for a seven-game Series with 23. In his second, in 1986, he had just 16 putouts, but one in Game 2 (above) was a typically spectacular play, and it derailed a Mets' rally in a 9–3 Red Sox win.

The Yanks were holding on to a 2–1 lead, but just barely, when with two out and two on in the fifth, Nettles dived to his right and got a glove on another Reggie Smith wallop, holding it to a base-loading infield single instead of a run-producing double. Steve Garvey then tested Nettles again, drilling a shot down the line. The two-time Gold Glover snatched it, spun all the way around, and fired a strike that forced the runner at second to end the inning. No runs in and at least two saved.

The Dodgers had the bases loaded in the sixth when Davey Lopes also made the mistake of hitting the ball in Nettles' direction. Again a backhanded stop, again a full pivot and a powerful throw to second for the inning-ending force-out. Another two runs saved. The Dodgers got a man to third in the seventh and put runners on base again in the eighth and ninth, but the defensive damage had been done. Nettles provided the classic understatement: "It takes a little steam out of them when they hit the ball hard and they get nothing." Dodger manager Tommy Lasorda called it "the greatest exhibition of fielding I've ever seen."

You could add up the possibilities and claim that Graig Nettles had single-handedly kept seven potential Dodger runs off the scoreboard. Counting the imaginary doesn't diminish the reality: Graig Nettles made sure the Dodgers scored only once. The Yankees won the game 5–1, and Nettles sparked a comeback that netted them the Series in six games. Just as he had so often stopped the ball from where it was heading and sent it elsewhere, his glove and his arm had changed the direction of the Series itself.

The 1970 Series between the Reds and the Orioles was another dominated by the superb fielding of one man—Oriole third baseman Brooks Robinson. While Nettles had established himself as a good fielder before his

Series outburst, Robinson was already acknowledged as the best at the position of his time, if not all time. But that year he gave a clinic on how to play "the Hot Corner." Here's a scorecard of Brooks Robinson's defensive gems in that Series.

Game 1: Sixth inning, score tied 3–3. Leadoff hitter Lee May smashes what looks certain to be a double deep over the third-base bag. Robinson not only backhands the ball, but in one motion wheels around and throws from deep in foul territory in time to nail May. The Reds put three more runners on in the inning, but don't score, and the Orioles win, 4–3.

Game 2: First inning, runner on first. Robinson makes a diving stop to turn Bobby Tolan's smash into a force-out, helping to hold the Reds' rally to three runs. In the third he has to dive again to reach a Lee May shot and starts a rapid-fire double play to end the inning. Orioles win, 6–5.

Game 3: First inning, men on first and second, none out. A high bouncer by Tony Perez becomes another Robinson-started double play, as he leaps to snag the ball, steps on third, and throws across the infield. In the second, he makes a textbook barehanded pickup and toss on a swinging bunt by Tommy Helms. "He plays like his car has just been repossessed," says Helms. In the sixth inning, he shows he can go to his left as well as to his right—and up, and in—diving to spear a Johnny Bench line drive. Orioles win, 9–3.

Game 5: The icing on the cake. The Orioles are winning handily, 9–3, and on the brink of a world title, but, as *The Sporting News* said, "The game would not have been complete without another fielding 'miracle' by Brooks Robinson, and the hot-sack Houdini did not disappoint." It came in the ninth, on another Bench line drive, this time to Robinson's right. Another div-

In 1970 Baltimore third baseman Brooks Robinson set the standard for World Series wizardry that Graig Nettles challenged eight years later. Time after time, Robinson robbed the hard-hitting Reds, saving runs and sapping their spirit. "He played third like he came down from a higher league," said former umpire Ed Hurley.

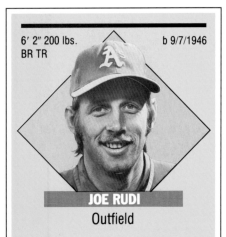

6' 2" 200 lbs.   b 9/7/1946
BR TR

JOE RUDI
Outfield

In 1972, his sixth year in the majors, Joe Rudi ripened into an All-Star, and his team, the Athletics, made its first trip to the World Series since 1931. It was only his second season as the A's regular left fielder, and Rudi led the AL in hits and triples. For an encore, he made the most spectacular World Series catch of the decade.

Rudi was a hero by the third inning of Game 2. He slugged a solo homer that extended Oakland's lead to 2–0, a score that held through the top of the ninth. Leading off the bottom of the ninth, Cincinnati's Tony Perez singled off tiring A's starter Catfish Hunter. Denis Menke hammered Hunter's next pitch, a fastball, toward the left field stands. "When he first hit the ball, I thought it was out," recalled Rudi. Fighting the late-afternoon sun, Rudi sprinted back to the 12-foot fence, leaping as he hit the barrier with his back to the plate. Bracing himself with his right hand on the wall to prevent an impact that might dislodge the ball, Rudi made a backhand grab splayed against the fence like a spider, snaring the drive in the web of his glove.

The grab robbed Menke of at least a double and stemmed the Reds' last-gasp rally, stranding the potential tying run at first base. The A's went on to win the Series.

Rudi was a solid, no-nonsense player throughout his 16-year career with four teams. He explained, "I just try to keep my mouth shut, do my job, and keep out of people's way."

Red Sox shortstop Everett Scott threw out a five-game record 25 runners in the 1916 World Series, including Brooklyn's Jake Daubert (above) at home in Game 3. Two years later, Scott handled 36 chances without an error—another Series record.

ing grasp, another out. Two outs later, as if scripted, the final out comes on a grounder to third. The Orioles win the Series easily, and fielding is suddenly sexy.

Of course, defensive excellence wasn't new to Robinson. His consistency was remarkable. He had just finished winning his 11th consecutive Gold Glove; he won five more in the next five years, too, to retire with 16—a record he shares with pitcher Jim Kaat.

Consistency was shortstop Everett Scott's strength, as well. He played in 1,307 consecutive games, setting a record that lasted until Lou Gehrig came along. Scott's consistency in the field peaked in the 1916 World Series and had the opposition manager moaning.

In Game 1, Brooklyn was losing 6–1 to Scott and the Red Sox going into the top of the ninth. But three singles, two walks, a hit batsman and an error pulled the Robins to within one run. Jake Daubert, a .316 hitter batting for the second time in the inning, pounded a Carl Mays pitch deep in the hole at short. Scott snagged it and fired to first. Daubert slid headfirst, but too late, and the game was over.

Game 2 was tied at one in the top of the eighth, when Scott made another super play—catching Mike Mowrey in a rundown between third and home. Red Sox pitcher Babe Ruth made the putout, and the run he saved was crucial, as the Red Sox won, 2–1, in 14 innings. Everett made three more good plays in the third game, including one as middleman on a relay from left to short to home to nab fleet-footed Jake Daubert. Everett didn't let up in Game 4, throwing out Fred Merkle in the eighth on a grounder that got by third baseman Larry Gardner. Scott ranged far to his right behind Gardner

and made a remarkable play. All in all, Scott's 25 assists by a shortstop in a five-game Series set a record that has yet to be broken. The Red Sox won in five, and Brooklyn manager Wilbert Robinson had had enough of Scott's unerring throws. "I'm tired of that trolley line—Scott to first," he said.

During the regular season, some defensive plays are memorable simply because of their sheer excellence, their sensational beauty. But in postseason play, the vise grip of pressure is so tight that the truly memorable plays are those that both are lovely to look at and affect the score. In the 1965 Series Minnesota left fielder Bob Allison made such a play. Southpaws Jim Kaat and Sandy Koufax matched shutouts for four innings in Game 2, then Dodger right fielder Ron Fairly led off the fifth with a single off Kaat. Second baseman Jim Lefebvre then hit a liner that was hooking into the left field corner. Allison made a lunging, one-handed catch, then slid for 30 feet or more on the wet turf. A first-rate play and a clutch one as well, as it kept the game scoreless. Kaat went on for a 5–1 win. The Twins met Koufax twice more in the Series and came away with no runs, seven hits and 20 strikeouts in 18 innings, and they lost the Series in seven games. Allison struck out to end Game 7, but his catch still ranks as one of the Series' finest.

In the final game of the 1912 Series, Red Sox Harry Hooper's diving, barehanded catch in the right field stands at Fenway Park took a home run away from the Giants' Larry Doyle and set a standard by which all World Series defensive plays are still judged. Dodger-Yankee clashes provided many memorable Series moments: motion pictures let us relive Al Gionfriddo's 1947 dash to the left field corner that left Joe DiMaggio kicking dirt, and Sandy Amoros' carbon copy eight years later that finally took the "World Series Losers" label off the backs of the Dodgers. One of the most striking was

Al Gionfriddo's career with the Brooklyn Dodgers consisted of 41 games—and one great catch. Gionfriddo's dash to the left field fence in Yankee Stadium robbed Joe DiMaggio of a game-tying, three-run homer and saved Game 6 for Brooklyn in the 1947 Series.

Graig Nettles

In 1970, while Orioles third baseman Brooks Robinson was making headlines for his spectacular fielding in the World Series, Cleveland's third baseman, Graig Nettles, was at home. Nettles, at 26, had just completed his first full season in the majors, and it was he, not the Orioles' Series hero, who had led AL third basemen in fielding. A year later Nettles set major league records at the position for assists with 412 and double plays with 54, and his 159 putouts led the league. But in Nettles' own words, "If you don't do it in the Series, you don't get recognition."

Nettles didn't get that recognition until his stunning World Series performance with the Yankees in 1978. The Yankees lost the first two games of the 1978 Series to Los Angeles, and Yankee ace Ron Guidry was struggling to hold a 2–1 lead in Game 3. In the third inning with two out, Nettles made a diving stop of a Reggie Smith smash down the third-base line and recovered in time to throw Smith out at first. In the fifth inning, Nettles repeated the feat with two out and Dodgers on first and second; he knocked down another Smith drive to prevent an extra-base hit, setting up a bases-loaded force-out on the next play. Again in the sixth inning, with the bases loaded and two out, Nettles made a great stop of a Davey Lopes shot down the line and got the force at second. Nettles was credited with saving at least five runs. The Yankees won 5–1, and went on to take the Series 4–2, becoming the first team in history to lose the opening two games and win in six.

"There's no way to beat him," said Dodger center fielder Rick Monday. "We could handcuff his right arm to his left leg and his left arm to his right leg, put a ball and chain around his neck and a blindfold around his eyes, and he would still make the play."

Graig Nettles, born August 20, 1944, in San Diego, attended San Diego State University on a basketball scholarship, but started playing semipro baseball while he was still in school. He also studied that other great third baseman. When he saw that Brooks Robinson practiced throwing while he was moving and off-balance, Nettles said, "I added that to my practices. . . . While it may not come up in the games very often, at least you've worked on it and it won't feel so awkward."

Nettles played smoothly for six teams over 22 years, reaching the playoffs seven times and the World Series five times. In 1976 he led the AL in home runs with 32, and in 1980 passed Robinson as the all-time home run leader among AL third basemen. In 1981 Nettles played his usual splendid game in the field in the ALCS against Oakland, but he was also a star at the plate, going 6 for 12 and driving in nine runs to set a championship series record in the Yankees' three-game sweep.

Not only could he play well, Nettles could be playful, too. In summing up his career with the Yankees during the George Steinbrenner-Billy Martin-Reggie Jackson years, Nettles said, "Some kids dream of growing up to be ballplayers. Others want to run away with the circus. I feel lucky. I got to do both."

Nettles will be remembered for his glove, and for his magnificent effort in Game 3 of the 1978 World Series. After the Series, Robinson—the third baseman whose glovework stole the show back in 1970—sent Nettles a telegram that said, "Thanks for putting a little defense back in the game."

The Dodgers won the first two games of the 1978 World Series, but then Yankee Graig Nettles warmed up his glove. His four great plays—including a diving stop off second baseman Davey Lopes (bottom)—made the difference, as the Yanks won Game 3, then swept the rest of the Series.

GRAIG NETTLES

Third Base
Minnesota Twins 1967–1969
Cleveland Indians 1970–1972
New York Yankees 1973–1983
San Diego Padres 1984–1986
Atlanta Braves 1987
Montreal Expos 1988

GAMES	**2,700**
AT-BATS	**8,986**
BATTING AVERAGE	
Career	**.248**
Season High	**.276**
SLUGGING AVERAGE	
Career	**.421**
Season High	**.496**
HITS	
Career	**2,225**
Season High	**162**
DOUBLES	
Career	**328**
Season High	**29**
TRIPLES	
Career	**28**
Season High	**4**
HOME RUNS	
Career	**390**
Season High	**37**
TOTAL BASES	**3,779**
EXTRA-BASE HITS	**746**
RUNS BATTED IN	
Career	**1,314**
Season High	**107**
RUNS	
Career	**1,193**
Season High	**99**
WORLD SERIES	**1976–1978, 1981, 1984**

Had Giant center fielder Willie Mays not made a spectacular over-the-shoulder catch (right) of Vic Wertz's drive with two on and the scored tied in the eighth inning of Game 1, the Indians might have won a game in the 1954 Series. Instead they got swept. Mays' glove, said Dodger scout Fresco Thompson, "was where triples go to die."

WILTSE-NEWYORK-NAT.

Curveball specialist Hooks Wiltse compiled a horrid 18.90 ERA for the Giants in the 1911 World Series, so manager John McGraw didn't give him a chance to pitch in either the 1912 or 1913 World Series. But as an emergency first baseman in Game 2 in 1913, however, he twice threw out the potential winning run.

the catch by Willie Mays on a drive by Vic Wertz with two men on in the first game of the 1954 Series between the Giants and the Indians. It became an instant legend—a legend of exaggeration. Writers said Mays caught the ball anywhere from 460 to 505 feet from home plate, which would have put him halfway up the Knickerbocker Beer sign in the center field stands. The catch was not in dead center field, but in front of the right center field stands, which are only 450 feet from home. Actually, the key to the Mays play wasn't the catch, which was merely excellent, but his miraculous, immediate turn-and-fire throw that kept the runners from advancing more than one base. Mays' throw kept the game tied; the Giants went on to win Game 1 in the tenth and swept the next three games. In fact, despite the drama of Mays' catch, and the undeniably demoralizing effect it had on the Indians, another Giant center fielder made a World Series catch in the Polo Grounds that *was* more like 460 feet from home: in the Subway Series of 1922 Bill Cunningham raced behind the Eddie Grant Memorial in dead center in Game 4 to take an extra-base hit and two RBI away from—who else—Babe Ruth.

For back-to-back clutch throws, no one has ever done what the Giants' pitcher-turned-first baseman Hooks Wiltse did in Game 2 of the 1913 Series against the Athletics. Fred Merkle had played almost every Giant game at first that year, but at Series time he was hobbled by a bad leg, limping through Game 1, unable to play in Game 2. Fred Snodgrass started Game 2 at first, but came up with a charley horse after going from first to third on a Christy Mathewson single in the third. Wiltse went in to run for Snodgrass, and manager John McGraw left him in to play first.

The Giants' Mathewson and the A's Eddie Plank were locked in a scoreless duel going into the bottom of the ninth. The A's Amos Strunk opened the

bottom of the ninth with a single, and a wild throw by second baseman Larry Doyle on a bunt put men on second and third with none out. Then Wiltse took charge. Jack Lapp smacked a grounder toward first. Wiltse not only made a great stop, but fired home in time for catcher Larry McLean to put the tag on Strunk. Plank, a .107 hitter during the season, was allowed to hit for himself and delivered an instant replay, grounding sharply to first. Wiltse came through again, fielding the ball cleanly and throwing a strike to McLean to nail hard-charging Jack Barry at the plate. Wiltse, nicknamed "Hooks" for his outstanding curveball as well as for his profile, had twice snuffed out the winning run with hard fastballs home. A ground out ended the inning, and the Giants, helped by a Wiltse sacrifice, scored three runs in the tenth. But Wiltse wasn't done. With two outs in the bottom of the tenth, he performed a rare feat—he got an assist and a putout on a play that netted just one out. Home Run Baker bounced to first, and the ball bounced off Wiltse right to Doyle, who caught it and threw it back to Wiltse to end the game.

In the sensational sixth game of the 1975 Series, the Reds' George Foster took a page from Wiltse's book. Foster turned a ninth-inning fly ball down the left-field line into a double play by nailing Denny Doyle of Boston with a true peg to home, wiping out the potential winning run. Most people have forgotten that after Dodger Sandy Amoros made his super catch in 1955, he made an excellent throw to shortstop Pee Wee Reese, who then doubled up Yankee runner Gil McDougald at first. In 1987 the Cardinals' Vince Coleman, known primarily as a base-stealing genius, gunned down *two* Minnesota Twins trying to score in Game 7.

With the bases loaded in the seventh inning, Mets center fielder Tommie Agee (above, left) made his second rally-shattering, two-out catch of Game 3 in the 1969 World Series. Agee's catches saved five runs, and the Mets won, 5–0. Asked after the game if he thought the Mets were a team of destiny, Baltimore manager Earl Weaver replied, "No. I believe they are a team with some fine outfielders."

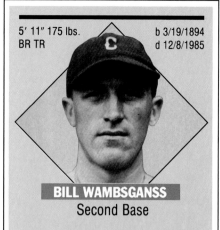

5' 11" 175 lbs.   b 3/19/1894
BR TR   d 12/8/1985

BILL WAMBSGANSS
Second Base

"You'd think I was born the day before and died the day after," Bill Wambsganss complained 45 years after making the only unassisted triple play in World Series history.

Actually, Wambsganss was born in Cleveland, the son of a clergyman, and was expected to follow his father's calling. He played shortstop in college, then attended a seminary. In 1914 he joined the Cleveland Indians, his father's favorite team, and plans for a career in the ministry were dropped. Wambsganss started at shortstop, then became a second baseman.

In 1920 the Indians captured the pennant and met the Brooklyn Dodgers in the World Series. On October 10, with the Series tied 2–2, Cleveland led 7–0 after four innings. Pete Kilduff and Otto Miller began the Brooklyn fifth with singles, putting runners at first and second. Wambsganss shaded the next batter, left-handed Clarence Mitchell, deep and toward the middle. Mitchell slammed a liner toward right center field, and the runners took off. Wambsganss made a leaping grab, tagged second, then turned and tagged Miller, who stood stunned just steps from second. Three outs, end of inning. The Indians went on to win the game and the Series, five games to two.

Wambsganss batted .259 over his 13-year major league career, but never played in another World Series. He spent six more seasons as a player and coach in the minors before retiring near Cleveland.

If not for Wes Covington's brilliant catch off Yankee Gil McDougald, Braves pitcher Lew Burdette might not have been the star of the 1957 Series. Covington's catch set up a 1–0 win in Game 5, and Burdette blanked New York again in Game 7.

Bill Virdon, Tommie Agee, Ron Swoboda, Wes Covington, Carl Furillo, Jungle Jim Rivera, Elston Howard and Dwight Evans all enter the pantheon of great defensive outfield achievers in World Series play. But who can forget Sam Rice of the Washington Senators? In the eighth inning of Game 3 in the 1925 Series, Rice chased what looked like a homer by Pirate catcher Earl Smith into Griffith Stadium's temporary center field bleachers. As he reached the bleacher rail, Rice leaped, the ball hit his mitt, and both he and the ball tumbled out of sight into the highly partisan crowd. Rice didn't reappear for several moments. When he stood up with the ball in his glove, umpire Cy Rigler called Smith out. The Pirates went crazy. Buc manager Bill McKechnie even took his case to Commissioner Kenesaw Mountain Landis, who was sitting in the box seats, but Landis staunchly refused to rule on a judgment call. The Pirates were so flustered they failed to notice that the Senators' relief pitcher Firpo Marberry batted out of turn in the next inning.

After the Series, Landis received letters from fans who claimed they saw Rice miss the ball but had it handed to him by Washington rooters. For years afterward, Sam Rice enjoyed his Series secret. When he was asked if he caught the ball, he replied with a grin, "The umpire said I did, didn't he?" He always refused to comment further but, on the urging of baseball historian Lee Allen, he agreed to write a letter telling the true story—to be opened after his death. Rice died in 1974, 49 years and three days after he made—or didn't make—the catch. His letter was discovered and opened the following year. In it, Rice spoke once and for all, with a heavily ironic twist: he had made the catch cleanly. In fact, he wrote, "I had a death grip on it."

Oakland's Joe Rudi came face-to-face with the left field wall at Riverfront Stadium in the ninth inning of Game 2 in the 1972 Series. Rudi's twisting, back-to-the-plate catch saved a run and probably the game for A's starter Catfish Hunter.

Some other big leaguers were accused of putting a death grip on the ball when they should have been throwing it. In Game 7 of the 1946 Series between the Red Sox and the Cardinals, Boston's Johnny Pesky made his relay with reasonable speed, given how long it took the ball to get to him. It was Enos Slaughter's hustle that made the difference, yet Pesky—who led the league in hits his first three seasons—is remembered as a World Series goat.

Three other shortstops were guilty of doing what Pesky is falsely accused of: failing to make a throw soon enough to prevent a run. In Game 7 of the 1940 Series, Cincinnati trailed the Tigers 1–0 in the seventh. The Reds' Frank McCormick doubled off the left field wall, then Jimmy Ripple lined a shot off the top of the right field screen in Crosley Field. Tiger shortstop Dick Bartell went out to take the relay throw from Bruce Campbell but figured he had no chance to get McCormick at home, even though McCormick was a slow runner. What Bartell didn't see was that McCormick hesitated as he rounded third, and what he didn't hear were the voices of his teammates and Reds' fans yelling at him to throw the ball home. "It was bedlam," Bartell recalled. "If I'd heard anybody yelling at me, I would have turned and thrown home in one motion. I'm standing with my back to the infield with the ball in my hand for I guess what must have seemed like a day and a half to everybody else. By the time I did turn around McCormick still hadn't scored. He must have gone by way of left field or stopped in the dugout for a drink on the way or something. But it was clearly too late to get him by then." McCormick's score tied the game, and when Ripple came home to score on a sacrifice fly, the Reds had taken a 2–1 lead that won them the Series.

In 1972 Oakland shortstop Bert Campaneris held on to the ball long enough to hand Game 3 to the Reds. Cincinnati pitcher Jack Billingham was

Washington right fielder Sam Rice got a record 12 hits in the 1925 World Series against Pittsburgh but is remembered best for his defensive disappearing act in Game 3. Rice leaped into the stands in pursuit of Earl Smith's drive, vanished for about ten seconds, then reappeared—with the ball. The Senators held on for a 4–3 win.

Veterans Stadium

From 1883 through 1970, the Philadelphia Phillies played their home games in six different stadiums—and never won a World Series. In 1971 the team moved to Veterans Stadium, and Phillies baseball hasn't been the same since.

Attendance skyrocketed—up from 708,247 in 1970 to a team-record 1,511,233 in 1971—even though the team slid into last place in the NL East. The fans kept coming, and by 1973 the Phillies had the nucleus of a team that was to become one of baseball's best. Third baseman Mike Schmidt and catcher Bob Boone were rookies in 1973. Slugger Greg Luzinski—who in 1972 slammed a 500-foot homer off a replica of the Liberty Bell that hung from the stadium rafters—was settled in left field and defensive star Larry Bowa was in place at shortstop. Pitching ace Steve Carlton—a 27-game winner in 1972—was in his prime, a prime that lasted a dozen years.

And baseball at the Vet, as it came to be known, was fun from the start. Although it was another in a series of cookie-cutter NL stadiums—multipurpose parks marked by unremitting symmetry and plastic grass—and took 3½ years and almost twice its original budget of $25 million to build, the Vet offered a lively atmosphere, an appealing cast of characters, and the occasional circus act. On Opening Day in 1971, the ceremonial first ball was dropped from a helicopter. Since then Opening Day balls have arrived via hang glider, human cannonball, trapeze artist and the U.S. Army Parachute Team. Philadelphia's historic status as the cradle of American democracy was honored in 1976 when a Paul Revere look-alike brought the first ball on horseback from Boston.

Located in South Philadelphia in a complex that includes John F. Kennedy Stadium for football and the Spectrum—an indoor arena for hockey and basketball—the Vet is the NL's biggest park, with a capacity of 62,382. The stadium's original artificial surface was among the game's fastest and springiest, and after its inaugural season, the outfield fences were raised from eight to 12 feet because so many balls were bouncing into the stands.

Jim Bunning beat Montreal 4–1 on Opening Day in 1971, but Bunning represented the old, hapless Phillies. He retired at the end of the season, and by 1976, the Phillies were division champs. Led by the power of Schmidt and Luzinski, the speed and defense of Bowa and center fielder Garry Maddox, and the pitching of Carlton and relief aces Ron Reed and Tug McGraw, Philadelphia won three straight division titles—and lost three straight NL Championship Series. Still, the Phillies were a great home team, winning 63.7 percent of their games from 1976 through 1980 and the fans flocked to the Vet at an average of over 2.5 million a year during that period.

In 1979 free agent Pete Rose arrived and gave the Phillies the spark they needed. The following year the Phillies beat Houston in the NLCS, then went 3–0 at home in a six-game Series win over Kansas City. McGraw, the Phillies' head cheerleader and most outrageous personality, kept things interesting in Game 6 by loading the bases in both the eighth and ninth. But when McGraw struck out Willie Wilson to end the game, the City of Brotherly Love at last had a world champion.

On August 10, 1981, Rose gave the Vet its second most memorable moment, when he got his 3,631st career hit, breaking the NL record set by Stan Musial.

While Veterans Stadium is one of several symmetrical, multiple-use stadiums built in the 1970s, it did retain a link to the Phillies' past—the home plate from Shibe Park, the team's home from 1938 to 1970.

Veterans Stadium

Broad Street and
 Pattison Avenue
Philadelphia, Pennsylvania

Completed 1971

Philadelphia Phillies, NL
 1971–present

Seating Capacity 62,382

Style
Multipurpose, symmetrical,
 artificial surface

Height of Outfield Fences
12 feet

Dugouts
Home: 1st base
Visitors: 3rd base

Bullpens
Foul territory
Home: right field
Visitors: left field

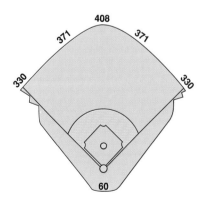

FLAWLESS IN THE FIELD

It's only happened twice. In 1937 the Yankees were the first team to play in a World Series without making a single error. The feat wasn't repeated for nearly three decades, when the 1966 Baltimore Orioles took the Series in a four-game sweep without an error.

The 1937 Series between the Yankees and the New York Giants was remarkable for two reasons. First, it produced Lou Gehrig's last Series homer and Joe DiMaggio's first. Second, the Yankees, in the midst of their four-year string of world championships, played all five games without an error. Their 1.000 fielding percentage broke the record of .996 set by the Boston Red Sox in 1918.

Statistically, the Yankees had not been the most precise fielding team; their 170 regular-season errors ranked third in the league. After the Yankees won Game 3, 5–1, *The New York Times* stated, "the Yanks, who supposedly had entered this series with nothing but power, again did powerfully well on defense."

The 1966 Orioles, however, had been consistently excellent on defense. Their 115 regular-season errors were the league's fewest, and their .981 fielding average was the league's best.

The Yankees' feat is the more impressive for two reasons. First, they played five games; the Orioles played only four against the Los Angeles Dodgers. Second, errors were more common in the 1930s than in the 1960s. In 1937 AL teams averaged 1.1 errors per game in the regular season, and by 1966, the average was .89.

When left-handed pull hitter Yogi Berra hit a fly ball down the left field line with two on in the sixth inning of Game 7, the Yankees felt sure they'd tie the score at 2–2. But Sandy Amoros made the catch, and the Dodgers went on to win the 1955 Series.

locked in a scoreless struggle with Oakland's Blue Moon Odom until the top of the seventh, when, with Tony Perez on second, Cesar Geronimo singled. Campy took the relay, and Perez made the turn for home, but fell down. The crowd was screaming wildly, so Campy couldn't hear third baseman Sal Bando hollering for him to make a peg to the plate. Perez got up and scored the only run of the game.

Even great fielders like Johnny Evers can get cold hands when the heat is on. Evers, playing second base for the Boston Braves, admitted he made a bonehead play by holding the ball in the classic David vs. Goliath 1914 Series between the "Miracle" Braves and the vaunted Philadelphia Athletics. As *Baseball Magazine* described the situation, "Imagine this great captain standing with the ball in his hands, one run galloping over the plate, the other thudding along only a few feet away, and not a movement, not even an attempt at throwing home. It was as though a trance had suddenly come upon the slender leader—as if brain and arm were paralyzed together."

Both Campaneris and Evers can be forgiven, of course. Despite Campy's blunder, the A's still won the 1972 Series. And Evers' "paralysis" didn't hurt the Miracle Braves at all; they swept the favored Athletics. But for all the men who allowed runs by holding on to the ball, many more made their mistakes by letting go when they should have held on. A defensive misplay has been the turning point for many Series games; what is more interesting is how frequently the error snapped a team's confidence. More often than not, teams that make crucial errors never recover; the next time a player makes a major World Series defensive blunder, watch his team lose the Series.

Just as outfielders gain legendary status by making game-saving grabs, catchers are frequently the ones whose bobbles put them in the Hall of Infamy. If an outfielder doesn't catch the ball that's headed into home run territory, well, it's a home run. If a catcher drops a third strike, or muffs a pop-up, the doors can open to a whole slew of misfortune.

Take, for example, poor Boss Schmidt. Charles "Boss" Schmidt was in his second year in the majors when his Detroit Tigers faced the Chicago Cubs in 1907. The Boss was a typical backstop in the game's early decades: rough-hewn and rugged, strong enough to "drive rivets into the clubhouse floor with his fists," someone said. But being tough wasn't enough when the scampering Cubs showed up. The boys from Chicago had swiped 235 bases that season, and they hit the West Side Park ground running in Game 1 of the Series. No one seemed worried that the Cubs had stolen three bases against the Boss as the game entered the ninth. After all, Detroit led 3–1. But a rally begun with a single; a hit batsman and an error loaded the bases with one out. A run scored on Wildfire Schulte's ground out to first; but the Tigers appeared to have escaped when pinch hitter Del Howard missed an outside pitch from Wild Bill Donovan for strike three. But Schmidt couldn't hold the ball, then couldn't find it, and the tying run scored. After three more innings—and four more stolen bases—the game was called because of darkness. In the next four games the Cubs stole 11 more bases for a Series record of 18. No team has ever stolen more in a Series, and the Tigers never won a game in the 1907 World Series.

Just as "to do a Merkle-Meyers" means letting a foul pop drop, one man—Mickey Owen—gave his name to fumbling a third strike. In Brooklyn his name is still spoken with disdain. The year was 1941, a year with much to

By 1958 the Yankees' Elston Howard was primarily a catcher, but he was moved back to left field for the World Series against the Braves. His diving catch of a liner by the Braves' Red Schoendienst in the sixth inning of Game 5 snuffed out a potential rally and preserved a 1–0 Yankee lead. New York then exploded for six runs in the bottom of the inning for a 7–0 win.

Catcher Mickey Owen let a third strike—and the game—slip by him with two outs in the ninth inning of Game 4 of the 1941 World Series. Owen's Dodgers lost their chance to even the Series with the Yankees, and didn't win another game.

write about for baseball historians: Ted Williams hit .406 with a last-day kick that defied belief and just missed winning the Triple Crown; Joe DiMaggio had a reasonable season himself, hitting .357, with a record-setting stretch in which he hit safely in 56 consecutive games. The Series was the first ever between the Dodgers and the Yanks, and it was a tough one.

Games 1, 2 and 3 were close; the teams split the first two by 3–2 scores, the Yankees won the third, 2–1, with all three runs coming in the eighth inning. In Game 4, the Dodgers were set to tie the Series at two games each. They led 4–3 going into the top of the ninth. Dodger reliever Hugh Casey got two quick outs, and with a 3–2 count, Tommy Henrich swung and missed a Casey curve, but Dodger catcher Mickey Owen couldn't hold on to it and Henrich reached first. Joe DiMaggio followed with a single, Charlie Keller fouled off half a dozen balls, then slammed a double off the right field wall. The floodgates were open. Bill Dickey walked, Joe Gordon doubled, and the Yankees, on the brink of defeat, had scored four runs to win the game, 7–4. They won the next day, too, and the first Dodgers-Yankees Series turned from a taut battle into a mismatch on the error of one man. Owen made no excuses, but maybe DiMaggio said it best: "Well, they say everything happens in Brooklyn."

E ven though outfielders seem to have the longest list of Series defensive greats, two outfielders made bad plays that couldn't have been more dramatic. In Game 4 of the 1929 Series, the Cubs were on their way to tying the Series at two games each, and they were having fun doing it. The Philadelphia Athletics had tried three pitchers—Jack Quinn, Rube Walberg and Eddie Rommel—and Chicago had beaten up on all of them.

The bottom of the seventh began with the Cubs holding an 8–0 lead. Al Simmons led off for Philadelphia with a homer, but the Cubs still felt secure.

Jimmie Foxx followed with a seemingly inconsequential single, as did Bing Miller when Chicago center fielder Hack Wilson—a man with a great bat and an iron glove—misplayed his fly ball. Jimmie Dykes tagged Cub starter Charlie Root for another single, scoring Foxx. A's manager Connie Mack told Joe Boley, the next batter, "I think he's losing his stuff. Just swing at the first pitch." Boley did, and he got Philadelphia's fourth straight single. One out later, Max Bishop hit the fifth single of the inning and Art Nehf came on in relief of Root. Then Mule Haas screamed a line drive into center and Wilson froze. He lost the ball in the sun, it sailed over his head to the center field fence, and three more runs scored, making it 8–7. Before the dust settled, Simmons, Foxx and Dykes each had collected their second hit of the inning, and the Athletics had taken a 10–8 lead. The game ended that way, and the Series ended the next day, as Philadelphia's right fielder Bing Miller doubled home the winning run with two outs in the last of the ninth.

There have been other memorable mistakes that cost teams World Series games. Ten years after his "mad dash" won the 1946 Series, Enos Slaughter—now a Yankee—couldn't leap high enough to correct his mistake of coming in too far on a Jackie Robinson single that won Game 6 for the Dodgers. In 1963's October classic, Yankee first baseman Joe Pepitone lost a throw "in the shirts" and cost his team the final game of a Series. It was Game 4, Dodgers leading the Yankees three games to none. With the score tied at one in the bottom of the seventh, Dodger leadoff batter Jim Gilliam got all the way to third on a routine grounder. Pepitone couldn't see Clete Boyer's throw from third because of all the white shirts on the fans in the stands. He

Even in big games, it's the little things that count. Giants second baseman Eddie Stanky was out by a mile trying to steal in the fifth inning of Game 3 in 1951, but he managed to kick the ball out of Yankee shortstop Phil Rizzuto's glove. The Giants went on to score five times in the inning on the way to a 6–2 win.

Cardinal Vince Coleman's blazing speed helped him get to this ball in the 1987 World Series against Minnesota, but in Game 7 it was his arm that mattered. Coleman threw out two Twins at the plate—Don Baylor in the second inning and Gary Gaetti in the fifth—to keep the Cards close. Still, the Twins won, 4–2, to take the Series.

got his wrist on the throw, but not his glove. Willie Davis' sacrifice fly ended the scoring, and the Yanks were swept by the Dodgers.

In the Game 4 of the 1982 Series, a 5–1 Cardinal lead in the bottom of the seventh was blown away when pitcher Dave LaPoint dropped a toss from first baseman Keith Hernandez, leading to six Brewer runs.

And then there's Bill Buckner. Buckner, who was a goat of the 1974 Series because of his bad baserunning, doubled his disgrace in 1986 against the Mets. The memory is an especially bitter one for the Boston fans, and Buckner's nonplay ranks among the most infamous of all time.

In truth, the whole Red Sox team dug their own grave; Buckner only threw in the last shovelful of dirt. Here's how it went:

The Red Sox were leading the Mets 3–2 in the bottom of the eighth of Game 6, and they led the Series by the same amount. A win would give them their first world championship since 1918. But the 131 pitches Cy Young winner Roger Clemens had thrown raised a blister on his pitching hand. His replacement, former Met Calvin Schiraldi, entered the game and gave up a quick Met run to tie the game.

In the top of the tenth, Dave Henderson, whose remarkable clutch hitting saved the American League Championship Series for the Sox, led off with a home run. The citizens of Boston were beginning to celebrate. The celebration got louder when an insurance run came home on a double by Wade Boggs and a single by Marty Barrett. Perhaps the Red Sox *could* win a World Series after all, people were saying. Maybe the difficult seven-game losses in 1946, 1967 and 1975 were not signs of a perennial jinx. In the bottom of the inning, up by two runs, Schiraldi disposed of the first two hitters on easy fly balls. The champagne was ready to be uncorked. But veteran Met catcher

Gary Carter lofted a single to left, Kevin Mitchell slapped a pinch-hit single, and, on a 0–2 pitch, Ray Knight did the same. Carter scored, Mitchell reached third, and the Mets were 90 feet from a tie. You could almost feel the ancient grip of Boston baseball history tightening around the throats of the eager young Red Sox. Everyone—fans included—was having trouble swallowing.

Longtime Boston bullpen ace Bob Stanley was brought in to face Mookie Wilson. A ten-pitch battle ensued, one of the greatest World Series at-bats. The count reached 2–2, and Wilson fouled off two pitches. On the seventh pitch, Stanley threw the ball wild inside, and Mitchell scored the tying run, with Knight going to second. Wilson fouled off two more pitches, then smacked a grounder toward Buckner. In his prime Buckner was a fine defensive first baseman, but he was now 36 and had been replaced dozens of times in the late innings for defensive reasons. By the end of the grueling season, he was hampered by a pair of banged-up legs that made it difficult to run or bend. So with a game, a World Series, and a career on the line, he reached down for Wilson's grounder. The ball went under his glove and through his legs, and the Red Sox were denied a world championship once again. The single error gave the Mets what they needed and took away what the Sox had to have to win the Series in the seventh game. And Bill Buckner, owner of seven .300-plus seasons, became the subject of a very painful joke: What do Bill Buckner and Michael Jackson have in common? They both wear a glove on one hand for no apparent reason. ❿

In 1985 first baseman Bill Buckner set a major league record with 184 assists, but he would gladly have given them all back for a second chance at Mookie Wilson's grounder in the tenth inning of Game 6 of the 1986 Series against the Mets. Buckner's boot capped a nightmare inning for the Red Sox, as they came within one strike of a world title, then lost the Series two days later.

In the Beginning

"SEE THE CONQUERING HEROES COME."

The 1883 AA champion Philadelphia Athletics (above) declined a postseason challenge from the powerful NL champion Boston Bean Eaters and instead took on the NL's worst team, the Phillies, in the first Philadelphia City Championship. Naturally, the Phillies took two of three and the championship.

The time-honored postgame tradition of fans storming the field was in place for the first World Series in 1903 (preceding page). A crowd of 18,801 packed the Huntington Avenue Baseball Grounds in Boston for Game 3 and plowed onto the field after Pittsburgh's 4–2 win over Boston.

The first postseason contest between the two major leagues took place in 1903, but what we now call the World Series actually has its origin in the earliest days of baseball. In the 1840s, 1850s and 1860s, before there were organized leagues, teams representing various athletic clubs traveled to nearby towns to engage the locals in a best-of-three match to determine who was best. It was that simple. Even after the Cincinnati Red Stockings established themselves as the first all-professional team in 1869, the format was frequently the same. They'd send a wire daring a local nine to meet them, rules and payments would be arranged, and the duel would be on.

The National Association of Professional Base Ball Players—not an organization of clubs but of individual athletes—formed in 1871 and began playing a regular schedule of games. The Boston Red Stockings, composed of players who had led the Cincinnati team to an undefeated year in 1869, was organized baseball's first great club, dominating the National Association during its five years of existence. In those days, after the scheduled season was completed, Association players continued to barnstorm, forming makeshift teams and traveling around the countryside to play whoever would take them on, with the winner getting most of the gate receipts.

The National League of Professional Base Ball Clubs replaced the Players' Association in 1876 as an answer to the evils of rowdiness, gambling and inconsistent scheduling that plagued the Association. The real difference, of course, was that the players were no longer in charge of their fate. Now they were hired employees, contracted to teams that were owned by men of power and wealth. It was the nation's first "major league."

The first challenger to the National League was the American Association, founded with six teams in 1882. If the National League represented slick East Coast business and style, the American Association was the embodiment of cruder, tougher Midwestern attitudes. The NL charged 50 cents a ticket and prohibited sales of alcohol at its parks. The AA charged half the NL's admission price, and several teams were owned by breweries and distilleries. With proper haughtiness and with reasonable accuracy, NL moguls called the AA the "two-bit beer-and-whiskey league."

The battle for players was fierce, and the two leagues locked in a bitter war over franchises and players. But after the 1882 season, the AA champion Cincinnati Reds arranged a series of exhibition games against the Chicago White Stockings, the NL winners, plus teams from Providence and Cleveland. Chicago had replaced Boston as the NL's dominant team, winning NL pennants from 1880 to 1882, and was led by manager-captain-first baseman Adrian "Cap" Anson, one of baseball's fiercest competitors. Playing beside the Captain was the legendary Mike "King" Kelly, a great hitter and baserunner who could play any position, and a host of supporting stars: George Gore, Larry Corcoran, Abner Dalrymple, Ned Williamson—a husky infielder who held the record for homers in a season until someone named Babe Ruth broke it—and a lanky blond catcher called Silver Flint. When team captains Anson and Chick Fulmer announced they were playing for the "championship of the world," they could hardly have imagined what they had started.

In Game 1 the men from Chicago were daunted by the seven-hit pitching of Will White and lost, 4–0. Larry Corcoran turned things around for the White Stockings the next day by hurling a three-hitter for a 2–0 win. But that was the end of the first "World's Series." Bad blood between owners in the

In 1886 power was hardly the name of the game and outfielders still played pretty shallow, as shown in the lithograph above. But in the Championship Series that year, Tip O'Neill hit two home runs in Game 2 to help St. Louis of the American Association rout Chicago of the National League, 12–0. St. Louis won the series in six games.

GEO. F. GORE,
CENTER FIELD.
FRANK S. FLINT,
CATCHER.
A. C. ANSON,
CAPTAIN AND 1ST BASE.
JAS. H. McCORMICK,
PITCHER.
M. J. KELLY,
RIGHT FIELD AND CATCHER.
FRED. H. PFEFFER.
2D BASE.

EDWARD N. WILLIAMSON,
3D BASE.
A. DALRYMPLE,
LEFT FIELD.
THOS. E. BURNS,
SHORT STOP.
JOHN G. CLARKSON,
PITCHER.
W. A. SUNDAY,
RIGHT FIELD.

The 1884 Chicago White Stockings featured some of the biggest names of the 19th century—catcher-outfielder King Kelly, first baseman Cap Anson and third baseman Ned Williamson. But it wasn't until the following year that they won the NL pennant, then battled the AA champion St. Louis Browns to a 3–3–1 tie in their postseason series.

two leagues came to a head when H.D. "Denny" McKnight, AA president and chief officer of the Pittsburgh club, threatened the Cincinnati team with expulsion if they continued the series. The teams took the safe way out.

The problem wasn't so much with teams from the two leagues playing each other. After all, in the tradition of postseason barnstorming, the Cleveland Nationals had just beaten Cincinnati in a best-of-three "Ohio State Championship" and did it again in 1883. The NL Phillies played the city's athletic club team for the "Philadelphia City Championship" from 1883 through 1890. Other city championships were played in New York, St. Louis and Chicago. No, the real problem lay in the captains' preseries proclamation. President McKnight didn't like the implication that this series actually *meant* something.

By 1884 the leagues' war had cooled somewhat. During the season, Jim Mutrie, manager of the AA New York Metropolitans, challenged the Providence Grays of the NL to a single championship game and was rebuffed. He tried again, proposing a two-game series, and was refused once more. Mutrie went to the press, charging that Providence was afraid of his New Yorkers. The ploy worked, and a best-of-five postseason series was arranged. Two games were to be played by NL rules, two by AA rules, the fifth to be decided later. Each club put up $500, winner take all.

The starters for Game 1 were Providence's Charles "Hoss" Radbourn and New York's Tim Keefe. In those days, before multiplayer pitching staffs, both had hurled the majority of their team's games. Radbourn had compiled a gaudy 60–12–1 record with 73 complete games. Keefe was slightly less impressive, at 37–17. Because Game 1 was played under AA rules, a hit batsman took first base; he wouldn't have under NL rules. Keefe started the

The NL champion Chicago White Stockings and the AA champion St. Louis Browns made pretty good money from their 1886 postseason series, so they printed up programs (above) and embarked on a preseason barnstorming series the following spring.

game with a wild streak, hitting two men and throwing two wild pitches. Without giving up a hit, Keefe was down 2–0 after one inning. Radbourn, in response, threw a two-hitter, and the Grays won, 6–0. Cold weather ended the second game early, but not before Radbourn fired a three-hitter for a 3–1 win. Providence third baseman Jerry Denny homered to drive in all three Gray runs. And for the record, Denny's clout was the first home run in a major league postseason game.

The weather stayed rotten for the third game, and Radbourn was expected to work his magic again, so only a few hundred fans showed up, and Providence was ready to declare themselves victors and go home without playing. Mutrie asked them to stay and play, even offering to let them choose the umpire. They sensibly chose Tim Keefe, which meant the Mets had to put Buck Becannon in the pitcher's box. Providence battered the young hurler to a 12–2 score after six innings. Umpire Keefe called the deciding game of the series because of cold, darkness and inevitable defeat.

The *Spalding Guide* of 1886 stated that the previous year's postseason series between the NL Chicago White Stockings and AA St. Louis Browns had been for "the Championship of America," the first formal declaration of such a title. Before then, play between the two leagues was considered "exhibition play" and the Spalding and Reach *Guides* routinely listed the October contests along with preseason interleague games. But if the 1885 matchup had a championship title, the play was scarcely of championship caliber. The Browns-White Stockings barnstorming series is described by historian Jerry Lansche as "one of the worst shows of post-season baseball." The teams made over 100 errors in seven "official" games. Each

BAD HANDS

Some World Series are remembered for fielding gems that highlight the excitement of defense and the grace of individual players. The 1885 championship was not one of these.

It was not an official World Series, but a loosely structured, best-of-seven contest that featured two of the most combative teams of the 19th century, the National League's Chicago White Stockings and the American Association's St. Louis Browns. The Browns had stars like Charlie Comiskey, Arlie Latham and Tip O'Neill; Chicago was led by future Hall of Famers Cap Anson, King Kelly and John Clarkson. But in the series, none of them could field. Together, the teams committed 102 errors.

The low standards of play were set in the first game, which was called because of darkness after eight innings. Each team had five runs, but Chicago streaked ahead in the error derby, 11 to 4. In the second game, at St. Louis, the clubs piled on nine more miscues before fans rioted, and the Browns forfeited the game to Chicago. Thanks to 12 Chicago errors, St. Louis won Game 3, described in a Chicago paper as "a miserable exhibition of ball-playing." But both teams were just warming up—ten more errors in the fourth game, eight in the fifth, 17 in the sixth. The bumbling came to a climax in Game 7. Chicago booted 17 balls, and St. Louis, dazzling by comparison, bobbled only ten. The series wound up 3–3 with one tie, but Chicago won the errors race, committing 59 to St. Louis' 43.

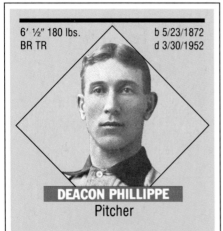

6' ½" 180 lbs.　　　b 5/23/1872
BR TR　　　　　　d 3/30/1952

DEACON PHILLIPPE
Pitcher

In 1903, as the Pittsburgh Pirates prepared to take on the Boston Pilgrims
of the fledgling AL in the first official World Series, Buc manager Fred
Clarke was confronted with a pitching
staff in crisis. Sam Leever, the ace, had
a sore arm, and southpaw Ed Doheny
was in the process of being committed
to an asylum. Standing alone in the
breech was a 31-year-old from Rural
Retreat, Virginia, Charles "Deacon"
Phillippe.

Phillippe, who started in the majors
in 1899, had just completed his fourth
20-win season in five years, and was
ready for the Series. In the course of
six days, he racked up three wins for
Pittsburgh against Boston, beating Cy
Young in Game 1, Long Tom Hughes in
Game 3, and Bill Dinneen in Game 4.
But the rest of the Pirate pitching staff
lost as many games as Deacon won to
keep the Series even.

By the time Game 7 started, Boston
had figured Phillippe out and defeated
him soundly. Down four games to three
in the best-of-nine affair, Clarke decided to go with Phillippe in Game 8 and
told him, "You're our only hope. But if
you pitch as well as you have done, I'm
sure the boys will start hitting behind
you." It was wishful thinking. Poor
fielding and silent bats allowed the
pitcher's solid eight-hit performance to
go to waste. But even in defeat Phillippe had set a record which will never
be matched: throwing five complete
games in a Series.

St. Louis Browns owner Chris Von der Ahe
was among the most flamboyant figures in
19th-century baseball. He often ferried his
players to the ballpark in open carriages
pulled by white horses, and each day took the
game's receipts to the bank via wheelbarrow.

club won three games, one game was a tie, and one ended in a forfeit to
Chicago when team captain Charlie Comiskey took his St. Louis Browns off
the field. One game was played in Chicago, three in St. Louis, one in Pittsburgh, and two in Cincinnati. Both teams took time off to play other exhibition
games. It was a mess.

Before the 1886 season ended, a challenge was issued by the voluble
and colorful saloonkeeper Chris Von der Ahe, owner of the St. Louis
Browns. With his fractured English and dapper goofiness, Von der Ahe
epitomized how different AA owners were from their stuffy NL counterparts.
He wrote to Al Spalding, president of the NL Chicago White Stockings and
baseball's original blueblood patriarch, proposing a "series of contests to be
known as the 'World's Championship Series.'" He negotiated a best-of-
seven series, all games to be played in St. Louis or Chicago, winner take all.

The teams split the first four games, but St. Louis bombed Chicago
pitcher Ned Williamson in Game 5, 10–3, and won Game 6, 4–3, coming from
three runs down to tie the game in the eighth, and winning in dramatic fashion
in the last of the tenth, when Browns outfielder Curt Welch stole home. The
play has gone down in history as "Welch's $15,000 slide," because the
Browns took home nearly that much in receipts for their victory. Von der Ahe
took half; the players each got $580. The "World's Series" seemed to be
growing into a more sensible postseason spectacle: better organized, with
better, more serious play.

Until 1887, that is. Actress Helen Dauvray, wife of New York Giant star
John Montgomery Ward, decided that a mere championship title wasn't
enough. She sold Von der Ahe and Fred Stearn, owners of the AA St. Louis
Browns and NL champion Detroit Wolverines, respectively, on the idea of a

championship cup from Tiffany's, the famous jewelry emporium. To claim the Dauvray Cup, a team had to win three postseason championships in a row. Von der Ahe and Stearn agreed to a 15-game postseason series in ten different cities. The teams traveled together on a special train, and the trip was more like barnstorming than anything else. Detroit won ten of the 15 games, then went to Chicago to play three games with the White Stockings. But Von der Ahe was furious at his team for losing, blaming it on card playing and carousing, and he refused his players any of the Series earnings. He sold the players he thought were most guilty—pitchers Bob Caruthers and Dave Foutz and catcher Doc Bushong—to the Brooklyn Bridegrooms. Then the Wolverines and the Browns met again for a 13-game tour of the South and three games in San Francisco. The St. Louis players, who had won no money from the original 15-game battle, were perfectly happy to play more exhibition games on the West Coast.

The Spalding *Guide* of 1891 claimed that the 1887 curtain call "fully established the world's series as a regular closing campaign for the United States championship, and now the world's series is regarded not only as the most interesting portion of the annual campaign, but as an additional incentive to the clubs of the League and the Association to strive for their respective championship honors."

In spite of such praise, the 1887 "World's Series" was a full-scale fiasco. The flaw in the concept of the Dauvray Cup was the three-year consecutive-wins requirement, so beginning in 1888 the Hall Cup was awarded to each year's winner. But the format of the Series was still confusing. In 1888 the NL New York Giants played the AA Browns in a ten-game Series. Eight games were played at the two home parks; two at neutral

The 1886 St. Louis Browns could get along without catcher Doc Bushong (right) and pitcher-right fielder Bob Caruthers (center), but they needed pitcher Dave Foutz (left). Foutz went 41–16 for the AA champion Browns and helped the team beat Chicago in the championship series, 4–2.

Pittsburgh's Forbes Field and the World Series go back a long way together. The year it opened, 1909, the Pirates made Forbes the site of the Series and home to a world champion. In 1960 University of Pittsburgh students cheered Forbes' last world championship, as Bill Mazeroski's Game 7 homer made the grand old ballpark host to the Series' most dramatic moment.

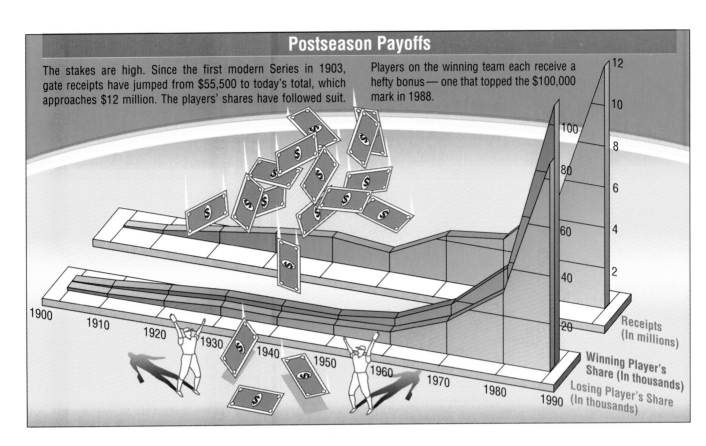

The stakes are high. Since the first modern Series in 1903, gate receipts have jumped from $55,500 to today's total, which approaches $12 million. The players' shares have followed suit.

Players on the winning team each receive a hefty bonus — one that topped the $100,000 mark in 1988.

Receipts (In millions)

Winning Player's Share (In thousands)

Losing Player's Share (In thousands)

In 1888 the Hall Cup (above)—valued at $1,000—went to the NL's New York Giants for their 6–4 series win over the St. Louis Browns of the AA.

sites. The Series encouraged heavy betting, and at a stopover in Pittsburgh between Games 6 and 7, former Brown Curt Welch accused umpire John Kelly of betting against St. Louis. Von der Ahe claimed *both* the umps—Kelly and John Gaffney—were cheating. The umpires threatened to quit, and the Series looked to be over. But Von der Ahe pulled a familiar ploy, claiming he had been misquoted by the press. Things cooled down enough for the Series to continue. When the Giants took their sixth win in Game 8, they had won the Series. But the teams kept on playing, and the championship again became an exhibition. Only 711 people attended Game 9; 412 saw Game 10. Undaunted, the teams played an additional contest, called a "players' game." The championship didn't interfere with barnstorming tradition.

The World's Series took a step toward coherence and success in 1889 with a battle between the NL New York Giants and the AA Brooklyn Bridegrooms. New York and Brooklyn had played each other in postseason "City Championships" twice before, but the 1889 Series sparked a long-standing rivalry that crossed the continent. Brooklyn had won the AA pennant by two games, largely because of a sensational year by Bob Caruthers, who went 40–11. The champion of this prototype Subway Series was to be the first team to win six games. Fans turned out in a big way — 47,256 baseball "cranks" showed up to watch the Giants take the Bridegrooms in nine games.

Upset by a salary cap, a reserve clause that prevented players from changing teams voluntarily and other restrictive management-installed rules, John Montgomery Ward led the players to form their own league in 1890. More than half the NL players and a third of the AA's left their teams to join the new league, which immediately dominated baseball. Albert Spalding, the power behind the NL, went to work. He raided the AA for players, paid

bribes to players to leave Ward and his Players' League, and threatened not to advertise his sporting goods company in newspapers reporting Players' League scores. When Spalding's efforts succeeded, Players' League owners sued for reconciliation. Battles raged over the return of players and geographical rights. Spalding won everything he wanted, destroyed the Players' League for good, and in the process weakened the AA as well.

The World's Series that year was, almost fittingly, a tie. Brooklyn, which had jumped from the AA to the NL, and the AA champion Louisville Cyclones each won three games, with Game 3 called because of darkness at 7–7 after eight innings.

With Spalding flexing his muscles, and warfare once again between the two leagues, there was no championship in 1891. In fact, there were no city or state championships, either. At the end of the 1891 season, the AA disbanded; its four strongest teams—Louisville, Washington, St. Louis and Baltimore—asked, and were allowed, to join the National League. The others closed their doors. With only one major league, of course, there was no postseason play. But NL owners hit on a bright idea: the 1892 season was split into halves, the two winners played each other for the championship. The Cleveland Spiders lost to the Bean Eaters of Boston, five games to none, with one tie. The Spalding *Guide* proudly harrumphed that baseball was saved—proof being that the series, scheduled for best-of-nine, ended after five wins. After all, if there had ever been an occasion when the teams could throw a couple of games to make more money, this was it.

In 1894 the National League tried a postseason series called "the Temple Cup," in which the two top teams played in a best-of-seven series. The Baltimore Orioles lost the first two Temple Cups, to the Giants and to Cleve-

The Boston Bean Eaters, champs of the NL in 1883, slipped quickly into the league's second division. But by 1888 they had acquired the star battery of the Chicago White Stockings—catcher King Kelly (second row, third from left) and pitcher John Clarkson (second row, far right). By 1891 they were league champs again.

It may have been the World Series, but in 1903 dugout conditions were Spartan for the Pittsburgh Pirates as they faced Boston. An intrepid photographer used the sagging dugout roof for a floor to get a good shot, while star Pirate shortstop Honus Wagner (seated to the right of the man not in uniform) looked on.

land, and then won the next two, beating Cleveland and Boston handily. No one mistook these cup contests for what the World's Championship Series had been. The Spalding *Guides*, the official word of baseball, barely mentioned them. They were seen as a bonus, a way for winning clubs to put some more money in their pockets, not as a test of champions.

A poor American economy and war with Spain in 1898 put an end to the Temple Cup. The National League, which had enjoyed the power that came from having the only games in town, began to lose attendance and interest among the fans. In 1899 the four weakest franchises —Cleveland, and three of the AA transfers, Washington, Baltimore, Louisville—were dropped from the league and Ban Johnson saw his chance.

Johnson was president of the Western League, a high minor league that had to fight to keep its players from being seduced away by the AA and NL. Johnson had tried without success to gain major league status for the WL, until the NL's ouster of four teams provided a good supply of major league talent. In 1900 Johnson changed his league's name to the American League, and it had a great year. In 1901 Johnson declared that his was a major league, on a par with the NL, which was by then a quarter century old. The league war was on again, and for two years the rivals fought for players and territories. By early 1903, they had reached an agreement. One of the biggest winners in the deal, besides Johnson himself, was Pirates owner Barney Dreyfuss. In exchange for being allowed to put a team in New York, the AL promised to stay out of Pittsburgh.

The World Series, as we have come to know it, was conceived in August 1903. Dreyfuss wrote to Henry Killilea, owner of the AL Boston Pilgrims:

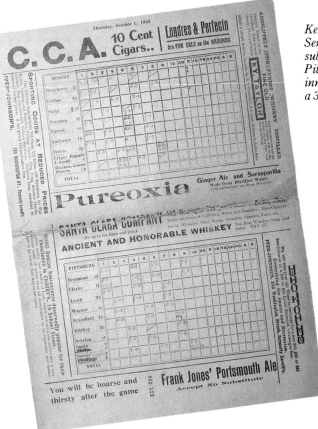

Keeping a scorecard in the 1903 World Series (left) wasn't too tough, as substitutions were few. But in Game 2, Pittsburgh starter Sam Leever lasted just one inning, as Boston scored twice on the way to a 3–0 win.

"The time has come for the National League and the American League to organize a World Series. It is my belief that if our clubs played a series on a best-of-nine basis, we would create great interest in baseball, in our leagues, and in our players. I also believe it would be a financial success." This letter is the first time the term "World Series" instead of "World's Series" was used.

Killilea went to ask Ban Johnson his opinion. But Johnson asked a more important question: Can you beat them? Killilea said Boston manager Jimmy Collins felt that Boston's Cy Young and Bill Dinneen would stop Pittsburgh's Honus Wagner, Fred Clarke and "those other batters." Johnson replied, "Then play them! By all means, play them!"

Dreyfuss and Killilea met to outline rules: best-of-nine, over when one team won five; they also settled on dates, umpires and expenses. Minimum admission was set at 50 cents, twice the regular charge, with the visiting club to get half. A handwritten note stipulated that "No player [shall] participate who was not a regular member of [the] team September 1, 1903." This rule, a logical way to avoid stacking the deck at the last minute, has been in place for every World Series since.

Dreyfuss offered his players half of the team's share. Killilea didn't. And the first modern World Series was almost canceled before it got started, because of the Boston players' demands. But two days later, Killilea settled with his players and the Series was set. Pre-Series chatter was very much like what fills today's sports pages in October. A poll of Cleveland players picked Boston to win. A few days later, NL president Harry Pulliam picked the Pirates. The oddsmakers favored the Pilgrims 10–9.

The World Series began in Boston on October 1, 1903. No matter that the Ohio, St. Louis, Philadelphia and Chicago city championships were going

AL president Ban Johnson (above) didn't like the rowdy nature of NL play, and made it tough on Baltimore manager John McGraw, who played NL-style ball in the AL in 1901. So McGraw jumped leagues in 1902 and led his NL New York Giants to a world championship in 1905, beating the Athletics in the second World Series.

Tim Keefe

They don't make pitchers like this anymore. On July 4, 1883, Timothy John Keefe, a soft-spoken right-hander for the New York Metropolitans of the American Association, pitched a one-hitter against the Columbus Colts. Thanks to Keefe's powerful arm, the Metropolitans won the first game of their Independence Day doubleheader, 9–1. After a short break, Keefe amazed the holiday crowd when he trotted out to the mound *again*—to start the second game of the doubleheader. This time he gave up two hits as his team won 3–0, and earned himself a place in the record books alongside the handful of pitchers who have won two games on the same day.

As his Fourth of July endurance test proved, Tim Keefe was apparently made of solid stuff. In 1883 he went on to win a remarkable 41 games and led the league in innings pitched, strikeouts and complete games. During his 14-year career, from 1880 through 1893, Keefe won a total of 344 games, eighth on the all-time list. He pitched at least 30 victories six times for second place on the all-time list, and 20 or more wins eight times for eighth place. After his 41 wins in 1883 he went 37–17, 32–13, 42–20, 35–19, 35–12, before "tailing off" to a 28–13 season in 1889. Keefe added another record to his collection in 1888 when he won 19 *consecutive* games in one season for the New York Giants; only one other pitcher, Rube Marquard, has matched this record.

By all accounts, Keefe was modest about his prodigious pitching talent. Nicknamed "Sir Timothy" by his teammates, this mild-mannered son of Irish immigrants spent his free time studying shorthand instead of bellying up to the bar with his fellow players. He explained that he wanted to ensure he'd have a career should his arm fail him.

Keefe needn't have bothered; as the record books attest, his arm never failed him. Keefe had both a powerful fastball and an exquisite curve but is best remembered as a pioneer of the change-of-pace pitch. His "slow ball" was a sort of palmball that he controlled through pressure from the base of his thumb. Not only did he have an array of pitches, he knew when to use them. His teammate, pitcher "Smiling Mickey" Welch once explained, "I never saw a pitcher better than Keefe . . . He was a master strategist, and knew the weakness of every batter in the league."

Keefe ended his career with the Philadelphia Phillies in 1893. Then he decided to call strikes rather than throw them and became a National League umpire. However, after making a few unpopular calls during a game at the Polo Grounds—the scene of his greatest triumphs—he was pelted with dirt and pebbles by enraged fans and had to be escorted from the field by a cordon of police. That was too much for Keefe, who'd never even raised his voice to an umpire. That night he telegraphed his resignation to league headquarters.

On May 22, 1880, two and a half months before his major league debut, the *New York Clipper* ran a profile on the 23-year-old Keefe. In it a sportswriter noted, "He combines in a remarkable degree all the needed qualifications to excel in his chosen position, having wonderful speed, a troublesome curve and great command of the ball." Keefe lived up to—and surpassed—his early promise, and became one of the greatest hurlers of the 19th century. Timothy John Keefe was elected to the Hall of Fame in 1964.

Tim Keefe was by all accounts one of baseball's most modest heroes, though in 1889 his income was anything but. On the strength of six straight seasons of at least 32 wins, Keefe earned $5,000 in 1889, the highest salary in the NL.

TIM KEEFE

Right-Handed Pitcher
Troy Trojans 1880–1882
New York Metropolitans 1883–1884
New York Giants 1885–1889, 1891
New York Giants (Players' League)
 1890
Philadelphia Phillies 1891–1893
Hall of Fame 1964

GAMES	**601**
INNINGS	
Career	**5,072⅓**
Season High	**619**
WINS	
Career *(8th all time)*	**344**
Season High	**42**
LOSSES	
Career	**225**
Season High	**27**
WINNING PERCENTAGE	
Career	**.605**
Season High	**.745**
ERA	
Career	**2.62**
Season Low *(1st all time)**	**0.86**
GAMES STARTED	
Career	**595**
Season High	**68**
COMPLETE GAMES	
Career *(3rd all time)*	**558**
Season High *(7th all time)**	**68**
SHUTOUTS	
Career	**40**
Season High	**8**
STRIKEOUTS	
Career	**2,533**
Season High *(10th all time)**	**361**
WALKS	
Career	**1,231**
Season High	**151**

* Among pitchers before 1893, when the distance between the mound and the plate changed.

GREETINGS · FROM · THE

GIANTS

BOWERMAN   AMES   MERTES   MATHEWSON   M'GINNITY   TAYLOR

NEW YORK

COPYRIGHT BY J.T.DYE. 1905   PUB. BY SOUVENIR POST CARD CO. N.Y.

1045

The 1905 New York Giants led the NL in runs scored, batting average, slugging percentage and home runs, but they managed just seven earned runs and 32 hits in five games against Philadelphia in the World Series. Still, it was more than enough, as the Athletics scored in only one of the five games.

on at the same time. The new interleague Series was a success in every way. Attendance topped 100,000 for the eight games played, bringing in $55,000. Jimmy Sebring hit a homer for Pittsburgh. Boston came back from a 3–1 deficit to take the first world championship. The fans loved it. Boston's famous Royal Rooters rode the train to Pittsburgh, marched through the streets, and sang their theme song, "Tessie," over and over again. Not to be outdone, the Pickerings of the Pittsburgh furniture business took a load of rooters to Boston.

The world apart from the Series was turning, too. On the day Game 5 was played, Samuel Langley tried to sail a 60-foot steel airship, which crashed, "a total wreck," into the Potomac River near Washington, D.C. Two months and four days after the Series ended, the Wright brothers successfully flew an airplane at Kitty Hawk, North Carolina. America—and the world—entered a new age.

The Pirates took home $1,316 each, because the magnanimous Dreyfuss gave his players *his* share of the gate as well. The winning Boston team got just $1,181 a man, so the losers took home more than the winners—a World Series record that will *never* be broken.

Barney Dreyfuss had benefited from the agreement between the two leagues, but Giant owner John T. Brush hated the new arrangement, especially having an AL team in New York. The Giants were winning the NL pennant handily in 1904 when they were challenged by the then league-leading AL New York Highlanders to play a series for the world's championship.

New York fans loved the idea of a "Nickel Series" in which the Giants' young Christy Mathewson would go head-to-head with Highlander ace Jack

One of the reasons John McGraw (near left) was such a great manager was that he put Christy Mathewson (far left) on the mound regularly. He also designed special black uniforms for the 1905 World Series. Mathewson was great no matter what color he wore, and his career World Series totals include a record ten complete games and four shutouts, as well as a 1.15 ERA.

Chesbro. But Giant management wanted no part of it. As manager John McGraw explained, "When I came to New York, three years ago, the team was in last place. Since that time I have worked to bring the pennant to New York. Now that the New York team has won this honor I for one will not stand to see it tossed away like a rag. The pennant means something to me. It means something to our players, and they are with me in my stand."

The 1904 NL champion Giants went on a barnstorming tour, and Brush added $5,000 to their take, but contrary to McGraw's claims, the players were not pleased at missing out on the bigger payday of a World Series. Joe McGinnity was quoted as being "sore to the core." Brush was stubborn but not stupid. The next year he proposed a code called the John T. Brush rules, many of which are still followed today. The World Series would be a compulsory, best-of-seven contest, with 60 percent of the first four games' receipts going to the players, split 75–25 between winner and loser. As in 1903, only players on their club rosters by September 1 would be eligible.

The Highlanders fell off the pace in 1905, leaving the Philadelphia Athletics to challenge the Giants in the World Series. Every game was a shutout—Mathewson threw three of them and allowed only 14 hits—and McGraw's Giants reigned triumphant. The World Series had come of age. ◑

Christy Mathewson's performance in the 1905 World Series was—and probably will remain—incomparable. Not only did he pitch three complete-game shutouts against Philadelphia in six days, he walked only one and allowed just one runner to advance to third base.

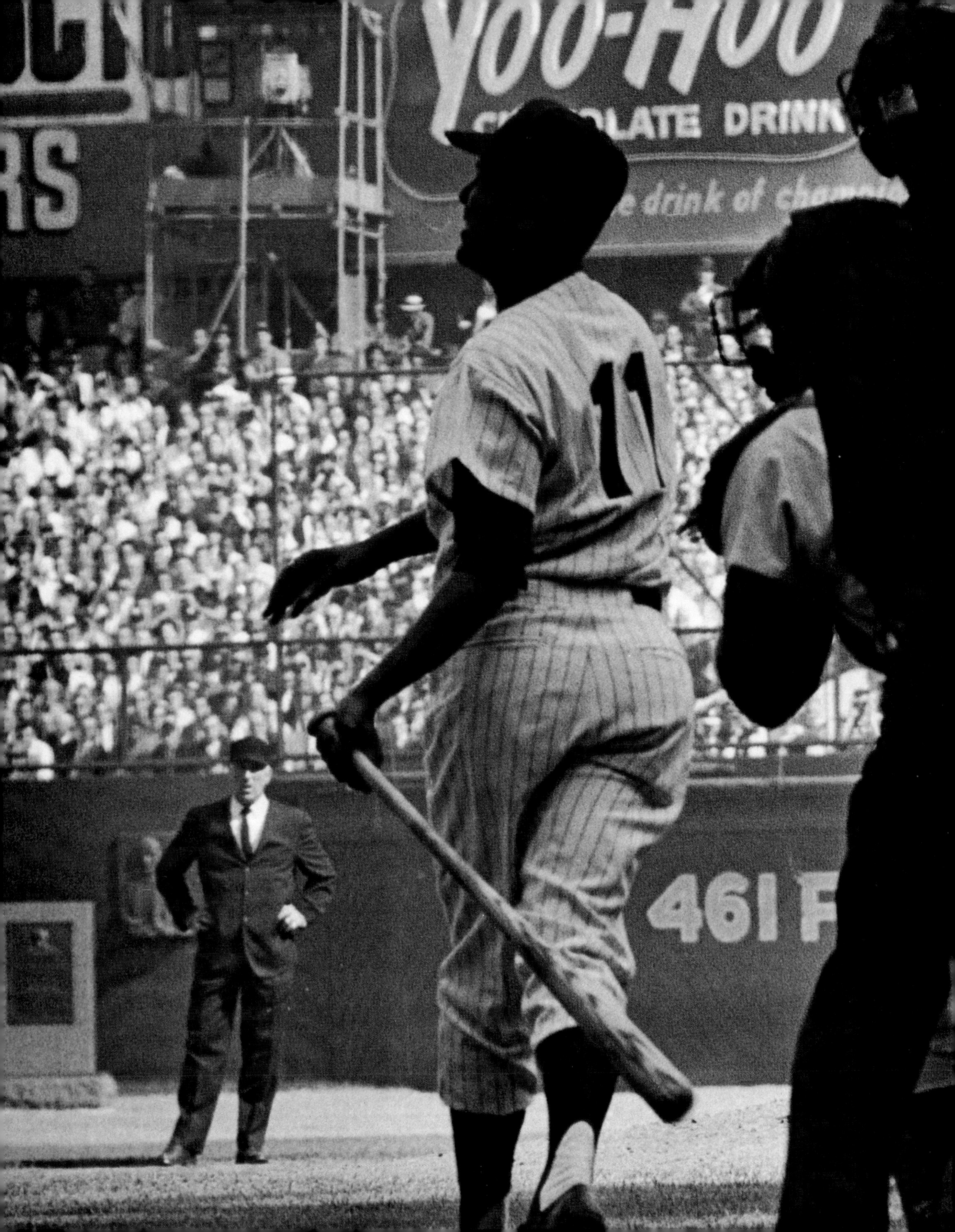
YOO-HOO
461

The Pitcher's Edge

Frank Viola provided bookend beauties for Minnesota in the 1987 Series against St. Louis. Viola allowed five hits and one run in Game 1, and six hits and two runs in Game 7. The Twins won both games, and the Series, and Viola was named MVP.

In his 14-inning marathon in Game 2 of the 1916 World Series, Red Sox starter Babe Ruth got better as the game wore on. After giving up a run in the first, Ruth pitched 13 scoreless innings, the last six of them hitless. Ruth went 0 for 5 at the plate, but the Red Sox won, 2–1.

Sandy Koufax (preceding page) did more than blunt the powerful Yankee attack in Game 1 of the 1963 World Series. He buried it. Of the first 14 batters he faced, ten struck out and only one hit the ball in fair territory. Koufax finished things off by fanning Harry Bright to set a new Series record of 15 strikeouts.

Batters can thrill, fielders can dazzle, but only a pitcher can dominate. When pitchers are "on," they can make even the game's finest hitters look overmatched and out of sync. Pitchers initiate baseball's action, and are the only ones who can take and keep total control over it. Although perfection was achieved just once in postseason play—by the Yankees' Don Larsen in 1956—the World Series has seen more than its share of awe-inspiring pitching. From 1903 through 1989, there have been 97 World Series shutouts, roughly one every six games. During the 1988 regular season, in contrast, shutouts averaged one every 12 games, and even in a dead-ball season like 1903, just one every seven games.

Pitchers start out the World Series with a built-in advantage: many of the batters they face have never hit against them before, and scouting reports can tell a hitter only so much. But the grace period for pitchers is short, and the names of the Series' greatest performers tend to be the same as those in Cooperstown. The great—and near great—have combined over the years to provide fans with some memorable pitching duels. But one stands above the rest.

It happened in 1916, and was the World Series pitching debut of a 21-year-old kid from Baltimore, Babe Ruth. Ruth had won 23 games for the Red Sox that season, and led the AL with a 1.75 ERA. Pitching against Ruth was Brooklyn's Sherrod Malone "Sherry" Smith. Described as a "big-chested Georgian," the left-handed, red-headed Smith had just finished his second full season in the majors, winning 14 games for the second time. Smith was the third starter on a remarkably balanced pitching staff for manager Wilbert Robinson, from whom the team took its name, the Robins.

The Red Sox won the first game, 6–5, despite a four-run Robin rally in the top of the ninth.

Baseball Magazine called Game 2 "a battle of giants." Ruth disposed of the first two batters in the first inning, then Brooklyn center fielder Hy Myers "smote the ball full on the muzzle" over center fielder Tilly Walker's head and scampered around the bases for an inside-the-park homer.

Smith was tough, too. Everett Scott led off the bottom of the third with a triple, but held at third when catcher Pinch Thomas grounded out to second baseman George Cutshaw. When Ruth hit a grounder to the same spot, Scott headed home, and Cutshaw, trying to throw the ball home before he had it, lost the handle. Scott scored, and the game was tied. Clutch pitching and defense took over.

Smith, a .273 hitter during the regular season, had run himself out of a possible lead in the top of the third when he was thrown out trying to stretch a one-out double into a triple. Myers made a rolling somersault of a catch to rob Boston's Harry Hooper of a hit in the sixth. In the ninth, with Boston runners on first and third with none out, Myers waved Zack Wheat off a fly ball, snagged it, and threw home in time to nail Hal Janvrin. Boston had another chance in the tenth when, with Scott on second and two out, Hooper bounced a slow grounder to Mike Mowrey at third. Sensing he was too late to get the speedy Hooper, Mowrey instead wheeled around and threw to third, where shortstop Ivy Olson caught Scott off the base to end the threat.

As they began the 14th, darkness had fallen. Ruth had allowed only five hits since Myers' homer, Smith just six. Off-duty umpire Bill Klem, watching the game from the stands, maintained that the 14th should never have been

Yankee pitcher Ralph Terry got a rare shot at redemption in Game 7 of the 1962 World Series, and he didn't waste it. Terry, who gave up Bill Mazeroski's Series-winning homer in 1960, outdueled the Giants' Jack Sanford in a 1–0 thriller.

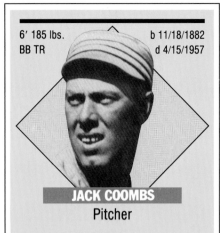

6' 185 lbs. b 11/18/1882
BB TR d 4/15/1957

JACK COOMBS
Pitcher

Philadelphia's Jack Coombs struggled through Game 2 of the 1910 World Series. The Athletics won 9–3 over the Chicago Cubs, but Coombs gave up eight hits and nine walks. So Athletics owner Connie Mack startled fans when he picked Coombs to start Game 3.

Mack's choice was the result of Coombs' steadiness and endurance. On September 1, 1906, barely two months after Coombs signed with the Athletics, he set an AL record, pitching 24 innings for a 4–1 victory over Boston. And Mack had noticed a sharper break in Coombs' curve when the pitcher's arm was tired.

By 1910 Coombs was Philadelphia's ace. He went 31–9 with a 1.30 ERA, pitched 52 consecutive scoreless innings, and posted a league-leading 13 shutouts. After his Game 2 victory in the 1910 Series, Coombs returned to the mound for Game 3 and for the Game 5 finale. Not only did Coombs tie Christy Mathewson's 1905 feat of three complete-game wins in a five-game Series—still the record—he also batted .385 to help give the Athletics their first world title.

Coombs was 49–22 for 1911 and 1912, and he chalked up another Series victory in 1911. In early 1913 Coombs nearly died of typhoid fever. He was able to pitch only a few innings in 1913 and 1914. But Coombs returned to the mound full-time with Brooklyn in 1915, and in the 1916 Series, he pitched the Robins' lone win, earning a 5–0 Series record and first place on the all-time Series percentage list with 1.000.

Dodger rookie Bob Welch starred in Game 2 of the 1978 Series, as he fanned Yankee slugger Reggie Jackson in a nine-pitch duel of power against power. But Welch gave up the winning hit in Game 4, and a Series-clinching homer to Jackson in Game 6.

played. But it was, and Ruth put the Robins away in the top half on two grounders and a fly out.

Leading off the bottom of the inning, Red Sox first baseman Dick Hoblitzell walked for the fourth time in the game. Bunted to second, he was then replaced by pinch runner Mike McNally. Fans could barely see the ball when pinch hitter Del Gainer cracked a hit over Mowrey's head, and the winning run crossed the plate in the longest, and definitely the closest, World Series game of all time. The Red Sox went on to win the Series in five games, and after Myers' home run, Ruth settled down to pitch almost 30 more World Series innings before allowing another run. Two years later Ruth won two more games in Boston's six-game Series win over the Cubs. Smith, meanwhile, found more hard luck in the 1920 Series, losing 1–0 to Cleveland's Duster Mails in Game 6. Brooklyn, as usual, came up empty.

Sometimes a World Series rides on a single at-bat—one face-to-face confrontation between a pitcher and a hitter. Many fans remember the epic battle between Yankee slugger Reggie Jackson and Dodger rookie Bob Welch in Game 2 of the 1978 Series. With two on and two out and the Yankees trailing 4–3 in the ninth, Jackson and Welch staged a duel that had most of America on the edge of their couches. Jackson loved fastballs, and Welch had a great one. Jackson got behind 1–2, then fouled off two pitches, took one for a ball, fouled off another, then ran the count full. All Jackson needed to tie the game was a single, but each of his five swings was for the cheap seats, swings that made Jackson "resemble a dangerously defective drilling machine," as Roger Angell wrote. "I had been secretly hoping that Welch would attempt a change-up, because it seemed possible that

the Jackson machinery would break into several pieces when he swung at it, but Bob Welch, too, wanted this entertainment pure." Welch threw one more high fastball, and Jackson missed it, ending the game with a trademark whiff. "The kid beat me," Jackson said later. The Dodgers had taken a 2–0 Series lead, but it was their last win, and Jackson got his revenge six days later by slugging a homer off Welch to put the Dodgers away in the sixth and final game.

Another legendary World Series whiff happened in 1926, in another battle between a rookie and a seasoned veteran. This time, however, the rookie was the hitter, young Yankee Tony Lazzeri, and the veteran was St. Louis' Grover Cleveland "Pete" Alexander. With 373 career wins, Alexander trails only Cy Young and Walter Johnson. He won 20 or more games nine times, and at least 30 games three years in a row. He threw 90 shutouts, more than anyone else except Johnson. But by 1926, Alexander was a grizzled 39 years old and nearing the end of his Hall of Fame career. His face did a poor job of hiding the rough life he had led. An alcoholic and an epileptic, Pete had a jowly visage surrounded by deep, distanced eyes. He was famous for being "missing" for days at a time, going on drinking binges that ended in the gutter.

No one expected Alexander to appear in Game 7 that year. He already had two complete-game victories, one in Game 6. Baseball lore has it that he had celebrated heavily after the previous day's win, and was in no shape to pitch. But with the bases loaded and two outs in the seventh, and the dangerous Lazzeri coming up, Cardinal manager Rogers Hornsby called for Old Pete. The story says that Hornsby met him at deep short as he trudged in from the bullpen and stared into his eyes to see if he could handle the situa-

The 1926 Yankees (above) averaged almost 5½ runs a game during the regular season and led the AL in runs scored, homers and slugging percentage. But in the World Series they were tamed by 39-year-old Grover Cleveland Alexander (below), who pitched two complete-game wins for St. Louis, then saved Game 7 with 2⅓ innings of scoreless relief.

Boston's Jim Lonborg was nearly perfect in Game 2 of the 1967 Series against St. Louis—he gave up just one hit and one walk in a 5–0 win—then tossed a three-hitter in Game 5. But pitching on two days' rest in Game 7 he was tagged for all seven runs in a 7–2 loss to Bob Gibson and the Cardinals.

CARL ERSKINE

BROOKLYN DODGERS

With two outs in the ninth inning of Game 3 of the 1953 Series, Dodger ace Carl Erskine had a record 14 strikeouts, but he faced the potential winning run at the plate in the person of Yankee first baseman Joe Collins. Collins, who had already struck out four times in the game, tapped back to Erskine and the Dodgers escaped with a 3–2 win.

tion. Alexander denied that he was hung over, and said that he was ready, although he hadn't thrown a single warm-up pitch. "I've got just so many throws left in this arm. If you want me, I'll take my warm-up pitches on the mound." And eight was all he needed.

The year before, Lazzeri had smacked 60 home runs and driven in an amazing 222 runs in the Pacific Coast League. He hit just .275 in his first major league season, but his 114 RBI were second in the American League to teammate Babe Ruth's 145. His sacrifice fly in the tenth inning had won Game 5 for the Yanks.

On a 1–1 count, Lazzeri lined a fastball into the left field seats that was foul by a few feet. Alexander's fourth pitch was a curve low and outside, and Lazzeri swung and missed, ending the inning. The incident was told and retold so many times that years later, when Alexander ran across Lazzeri in San Francisco, he said, "Tony, I'm getting tired of fanning you." "Maybe you think I'm not?" Lazzeri replied.

Alexander stayed perfect through the eighth, and retired the first two men in the ninth as well. His 3–2 pitch to Babe Ruth was called ball four, and Old Pete ambled toward home plate umpire George Hildebrand. "I've been around for twenty years; I'd think you'd give an old fellow like me a close one like that." But then, with .315 hitter Bob Meusel at the plate, Ruth ruined another potentially dramatic confrontation by trying to steal second. Cardinal catcher Bob O'Farrell threw him out to end the Series.

The strikeout, of course, is the ultimate domination of a single at-bat. When a hurler fans a dozen or more, he is dominating the whole team.

Howard Ehmke, the surprise starter for the Philadelphia Athletics in Game 1 of the 1929 Series, beat the Cubs 3–1 and fanned 13 of them, his

sidearm delivery coming by way of the left field bleachers in Wrigley Field. His record stood until 1953, when Carl Erskine of the Dodgers whiffed 14 Yanks in Game 3, including two ninth-inning pinch hitters, Don Bollweg and Johnny Mize. "Oisk" won the game, 3–2, thanks to a Roy Campanella homer in the last of the eighth.

Ten years later the Yanks and Dodgers met again in the Series. The Dodgers had managed to beat their crosstown rivals only once in seven tries. But by 1963 the boys from Brooklyn were the men from Los Angeles, and it was a much different story. That year, Sandy Koufax started Game 1 for the Dodgers in Yankee Stadium against Whitey Ford. In the eighth inning, Koufax tied Erskine's mark by fanning Phil Linz and Bobby Richardson. With two out in the ninth and the Dodgers leading, 5–2, pinch hitter Harry Bright swung and missed, and Koufax had broken Erskine's record. Yogi Berra summed up how the Yankees felt about the brilliant left-hander. "I see how Koufax won twenty-five games," Berra said of Koufax's regular-season record. "What I don't understand is how he lost five."

Bob Gibson broke Koufax's record five years later with a 17-strikeout performance against the Tigers in Game 1 of the 1968 Series. Gibson's ferocity on the mound, his glowering countenance and his speedy delivery were truly intimidating. Facing 31-game winner Denny McLain, Gibson shut out the Tigers on only five hits. He was coming off an incredible regular season in which he posted a 1.12 ERA, the fourth lowest of all time, and tossed 13 shutouts. He fanned seven of the first nine Tigers to face him, and he closed the game in fierce fashion by striking out the side in the ninth. The Tigers were awestruck.

Phillies screwball artist Tug McGraw was on the mound at the end of four of the six games in the 1980 Series against Kansas City. He lost one, but finished three with a flourish—striking out Willie Wilson to end Game 1, Jose Cardenal to end Game 5 (above), and Wilson again in Game 6.

Nearly Perfect

Don Larsen was not a great pitcher. He started in the majors in 1953, and after two seasons, his record stood at 10–33, including a league-high 21 losses in 1954 for the Orioles. In 1955 Larsen became a Yankee and rebounded with a 9–2 record. He made one miserable appearance in the World Series, starting Game 4 but lasting just four innings. He gave up five hits, five earned runs and two walks, and recorded an 11.25 ERA.

Larsen had a reputation as a carouser; in the wee hours of one spring-training morning in 1956 the rented car he was driving ran into a telephone pole. Despite his off-field antics, his 1956 season record was 11–5, and Larsen was back in another World Series for the Yankees, starting Game 2 against the Dodgers. The pregame headline said, "Larsen Shrugs Off Prestige of Series Start."

Apparently Larsen kept shrugging. Although a Yogi Berra grand slam helped the Yanks grab a 6–0 lead after an inning and a half, Larsen and his defense couldn't hold the lead. Before the second inning was over, the Dodgers had put six runs on the board and Larsen was gone. The Yankees lost 13–8, and Larsen's Series record was awful.

With the Series tied 2–2, Larsen took the mound for Game 5. His opponent was Sal "The Barber" Maglie, nicknamed for his tendency to give hitters close shaves with his fastball. And Maglie liked to follow his close-shave fastballs with low outside curves. To gain every advantage, Maglie's start was delayed one day in order to have NL umpire Babe Pinelli, known as a low-ball ump, behind the plate.

Larsen struck out the first two batters he faced. The second, Pee Wee Reese, took strike three on a 3–2 count, and became the only Dodger to see a three-ball count that day. Maglie sailed through the first three Yanks. Leading off in the second for the Dodgers, Jackie Robinson smashed a liner off Andy Carey's glove at third, but hustling shortstop Gil McDougald grabbed the loose ball and threw hard to first. Robinson was called out on a close play. Then Gil Hodges fanned and Sandy Amoros popped out. Maglie had less trouble—a pop-up, a fly out and a strikeout.

Larsen breezed through the third, needing only seven pitches to ring up three outs, and then he struck out Duke Snider to end a 1–2–3 fourth. Maglie was rolling, too, and got the first two hitters out. In four innings, Maglie faced just one batter more than the minimum—but that batter was Mickey Mantle, who homered just inside the right field foul pole to give the Yankees a 1–0 lead.

Larsen faced his toughest challenge in the top of the fifth. Robinson, leading off again, flied deep to right. Hodges crashed a liner into left center that Mantle ran down to make a smooth backhanded catch. Amoros hit a drive toward the right field stands, but at the last second it curved foul, according to Hank Bauer, the Yankee closest to the ball, "by inches." Then Amoros grounded to second.

Maglie wasn't letting up. A leadoff walk in the fifth was erased by a force-out, and the Dodgers closed the inning with a double play. Two short flies and a strikeout got Larsen through the sixth. In the bottom half, Maglie had his only bad inning. A single, a sacrifice and two more singles got another Yankee run in and put runners at the corners with one out. But Mantle tapped a ground ball to Hodges, who turned it into a double play, throwing home to trap Bauer coming in from third.

Larsen was perfect again in the seventh, and the 64,519 fans in Yankee Stadium knew they were watching a potential no-hitter—and a possible perfect game. Maglie was still tough; a single and a walk by

Game 5 in 1956 was the last World Series appearance for the Dodgers' Sal Maglie (above), and just happened to come on a day when the Yankees' Don Larsen was perfect. Less than two weeks earlier, Maglie had pitched a no-hitter against the Phillies.

According to sportswriter Shirley Povich, Larsen earned his perfect game in the 1956 World Series "with a tremendous assortment of pitches that seemed to have five forward speeds, including a slow one that ought to have been equipped with backup lights."

the Yankees in the seventh produced no runs. In the eighth, Robinson grounded back to Larsen, Hodges lined to Carey, and Amoros hit the second pitch directly to Mickey Mantle. Maglie replied by striking out the side. He had given up just five hits and two runs. But Larsen had it all—even umpire Pinelli's help—in the ninth.

Leadoff hitter Carl Furillo fouled off four pitches before he flied out. Larsen said later, "I was so weak in the knees out there in the ninth inning, I thought I was going to faint." Campanella headed to the plate, hearing the words of Dodger publicity head Irving Rudd: "To hell with history, Roy. Let's get on base and *start* something." Campanella grounded out to Billy Martin.

Dale Mitchell, the first substitute by either side in the game, came up to pinch-hit for Maglie. The first pitch was away, ball one. Then Larsen threw a strike. Mitchell swung and missed the third pitch, strike two. He fouled off the next pitch. Larsen mumbled a prayer and threw his 97th pitch of the game. The fastball appeared to be high and outside, but Pinelli shot his right arm into the air. Larsen had pitched the first perfect game in the majors in 34 years, and the only no-hit game in World Series history. Sal Maglie had nothing to show for his excellent work but a loss.

After the game a reporter asked Casey Stengel, "Was this the best game you ever saw Larsen pitch?" Casey had a ready answer, "So far."

The Cardinals' Bob Gibson (45) made things easy on infielders like third baseman Mike Shannon (18) and first baseman Orlando Cepeda (far right) in the 1968 Series. He struck out 35 Tigers in 27 innings, walked just four, but lost Game 7 when center fielder Curt Flood misjudged a fly ball that led to three runs.

Gibson won Game 4 with another five-hitter, and while he struck out only ten, he became the only pitcher to fan ten or more batters five times in World Series play. Only Koufax, Bob Turley and Walter Johnson had managed the feat more than once. In Game 7, Gibson was working on a one-hit shutout going into the seventh, but with two on and two out, center fielder Curt Flood misjudged a Jim Northrup line drive, allowing two runs to score. Gibson and the Cardinals lost, 4–1. It was only his second loss in nine Series starts, and it kept him from achieving what no other pitcher has ever done—winning three games in two separate Series.

Since only four victories are needed to win a world championship— with the exception of best-of-nine Series in 1903 and 1919 through 1921—any pitcher who wins three games in a single Series is clearly its most dominant player. In 1964 Gibson had lost to the Yankees in Game 2, then defeated them in Games 5 and 7. In 1967 he was undefeated, giving the Bosox only three earned runs in three complete-game victories, thereby becoming the 11th pitcher to win three games in a World Series.

When Gibson squared off against Mickey Lolich in the final game of the 1968 Series, both starters had won two games in the Series already. Lolich, pitching on just two days' rest, tossed a five-hitter and became the 12th pitcher—and only the second left-hander—to win three games in one World Series.

The first southpaw to turn the three-victory trick was the Cards' Harry "The Cat" Brecheen in 1946, although his third victory came in relief against the Red Sox. That was the game in which teammate Enos Slaughter's hustling gallop from first scored the winning run. Brecheen had pitched a

When 31-game winner Denny McLain faltered in the 1968 World Series, southpaw Mickey Lolich stepped in and assumed the star's role. He won three games, had a 1.67 ERA, and in Game 2 hit his first major league home run.

Even the brilliance of Jim Konstanty—the first relief pitcher ever to win the Most Valuable Player Award—couldn't save the Phillies in the 1950 Series. Konstanty started Game 1 and allowed just one run on four hits, but Vic Raschi pitched a shutout that sparked a Yankee sweep.

complete-game win in Game 6, but a rain-out day gave his arm enough time to rest, and he was able to throw the final two innings in Game 7.

In 1903 the ultimate rarity occurred: two pitchers each won three games for their teams. Boston's Bill Dinneen started the second, fourth, sixth and eighth games. He lost Game 4, but won the other three. Luckily, Dinneen had Cy Young as his mound partner. Young pitched in Games 1, 3, 5 and 7, and earned a record of 2–1.

Deacon Phillippe had no such help. The Pirates, whose great pitching staff netted them pennants in 1901 and 1902, had been hurt by the defection of Jack Chesbro and Jesse Tannehill to the American League. Steady Sam Leever had injured his arm and tossed a mere ten innings in two Series games. Ed Doheny, who had won 16 games, suffered a mental breakdown shortly before the Series, attacking and almost killing a faith healer and a nurse with a piece of cast iron; he spent the rest of his life in an insane asylum. It was clear Phillippe couldn't win the Series on his own, although he gave it a noble effort.

In the early days of the 20th century, teams relied on fewer pitchers than they do today, so sending a pitcher out every other day was no surprise. In fact, for the entire eight-game Series in 1903, Boston used only three pitchers, one of whom threw only two innings. Dinneen hurled 35 frames, Young 34. But poor Phillippe. He set Series records for starts, complete games, innings pitched, hits, runs and earned runs—records that still stand.

Connie Mack's Athletics used just two pitchers against the Cubs in the 1910 Series—Jack Coombs and Chief Bender. Coombs pitched three complete-game wins, and Bender split two complete games, earning Philadelphia a world title.

6′ 1″ 170 lbs. **b 9/12/1940**
BB TL

MICKEY LOLICH
Pitcher

Although Mickey Lolich ranks 12th among all-time strikeout leaders, the Detroit pitcher traded power for finesse in order to win the 1968 World Series final against St. Louis.

Lolich had pitched complete-game victories in Games 2 and 5 for the Tigers. After just two days' rest, he took the mound against Cardinal ace Bob Gibson for Game 7.

"My arm was dead," he recalled. "When I warmed up I could see I didn't have a live fastball. I began to turn the ball over and the ball started to sink good. I thought, 'I'll nip the corners here, I'll nip the corners there.' "

He pitched without his notorious fastball. Detroit won, 4–1, and Lolich became the 12th pitcher to win three games in a single Series.

Lolich went on to post two seasons, 1971 and 1972, with more than 20 wins. He flourished despite his build, which by 1971 incorporated 210 pounds and a potbelly. He thought fans identified with him. "Some fat guy in front of the TV set at home in his T-shirt and shorts . . . looks at me and says, 'Mabel, that guy's fat just like me. Now get me another beer, will ya?' "

Lolich's best year was 1971, when he had a 2.92 ERA and led the AL with 25 wins, 376 innings pitched and 308 strikeouts. When customers at the Mickey Lolich Donut Shop in Lake Orion, Michigan, mention the great 1968 Series, Lolich reminds them of "the greatest year of my life. . . . The 1971 season was more satisfying than the World Series."

Ty Cobb called Chief Bender (above) the "brainiest pitcher" he ever saw, and Bender got especially smart in the postseason. His totals from five World Series with the Athletics include a 6–4 record, 2.44 ERA, 9 complete games and 59 strikeouts.

Babe Adams, inserted as the Pittsburgh starter for Game 1 in 1909 on a suggestion from National League president John Heydler, baffled the Tigers in that game and two more. Smoky Joe Wood grabbed his third win in the 1912 Series—to go with one loss—when he came in to relieve in the eighth inning of the final game, and stayed around through the tenth-inning finish that was marked by Snodgrass' muff, the Merkle-Meyers confusion, and Larry Gardner's Series-ending sacrifice fly.

Hall of Famer Red Faber was 1–1 in his first two White Sox starts in the 1917 Series, but he picked up a win in relief in Game 5 when notorious errors by Buck Herzog and Heinie Zimmerman helped the Sox erase a 5–2 deficit against the New York Giants' Slim Sallee. Faber was then the recipient of some good luck in Game 6: teammate Eddie Collins outraced Zimmerman to the plate on a misplayed rundown, and Faber won his third game.

Spitballer Stan Coveleski was a three-time winner in the 1920 Series for the Indians. Coveleski's remarkable performance—he threw three five-hit games and allowed only two runs—was overshadowed by the litany of other ills that befell the Brooklyn team that year: Cleveland's Elmer Smith was the first man to slug a grand slam in a World Series, Jim Bagby became the first pitcher to hit a Series homer, and Brooklyn castoff Duster Mails, a man with an immense ego and a big mouth, backed up his bragging by tossing a three-hit shutout against his former mates. To add ignominy to insult, Clarence Mitchell lined into Bill Wambsganss' unassisted triple play and followed it up by grounding into a 3–6–3 double play, setting the unlikely record of making five outs in two at-bats.

The 1920 meeting was a best-of-nine Series, although the Indians were able to dismantle Brooklyn in seven games. For that reason, Coveleski's

effort ranks a little lower than the others mentioned. He did win three games, but his team had to win five to capture the championship.

After Coveleski's three complete-game wins, the feat wasn't achieved again for 37 years. It took Milwaukee's Lew Burdette to match the performance, and he did it against the "unbeatable" Yankees in 1957. The Yankees had lost only one World Series in nine appearances since 1943. For those who didn't follow baseball during the 1940s and 1950s, it's hard to explain how dominant the Yankees were. Everyone in America seemed to cheer the Dodgers' upset of the Yanks in 1955, but the Yanks silenced the cheering by slapping the Dodgers down in 1956.

Burdette was the difference in 1957. The Yanks opened the Series by toppling 21-game winner Warren Spahn, outdueled by the equally crafty Whitey Ford. It was Ford's fifth Series win.

While Spahn was being beaten, 3–1, Burdette watched the Yanks from the bench and decided they were not invincible. "They're a good team, but they can be pitched to," he thought. Burdette won the second game, 4–2, as the Yankees appeared to be sleeping. Acting as though beating the ace Spahn would guarantee a sweep, the men from New York played poorly. One writer said, "Of the four Braves runs, only Johnny Logan's home run didn't smell of limburger."

The Yanks woke up in the first Series game played in Milwaukee, battering Bob Buhl and five other Braves pitchers in a 12–3 Game 3 win. Native Milwaukeean and Yankee left fielder Tony Kubek said hello to his old friends by belting two homers and driving in four runs. Eddie Mathews' two-run homer in the tenth won Game 4 for Milwaukee, and with the Series tied 2–2, Burdette got the ball for Game 5 and turned in one of the great World

At the tender age of 21, Bret Saberhagen pitched the Kansas City Royals to their first world championship. With his team behind the St. Louis Cardinals two games to none, Saberhagen scattered six hits in Game 3, then came back with a five-hit shutout in Game 7.

The Dominators

Only 12 pitchers have ever won three games in a single World Series, and it's an increasingly rare feat. It's happened just four times since 1920, and not at all since Detroit's Mickey Lolich turned the trick in 1968. All but three of them pitched complete games in all of their wins, and the others—Harry Brecheen, Red Faber and Smoky Joe Wood—pitched two complete games. Below is a comparison of their individual records for the Series in which they won three games.

Name	Year	Team	W–L	IP	H	BB	SO	ERA
Deacon Phillippe	1903	Pirates	3-2	44	38	3	20	3.27
Bill Dinneen	1903	Red Sox	3-1	35	29	8	28	2.06
Christy Mathewson	1905	Giants	3-0	27	14	1	18	0.00
Babe Adams	1909	Pirates	3-0	27	18	6	11	1.33
Jack Coombs	1910	Athletics	3-0	27	23	14	17	3.33
Smoky Joe Wood	1912	Red Sox	3-1	22	27	3	21	3.68
Red Faber	1917	White Sox	3-1	27	21	3	9	2.33
Stan Coveleski	1920	Indians	3-0	27	15	2	8	0.67
Harry Brecheen	1946	Cardinals	3-0	20	14	5	11	0.45
Lew Burdette	1957	Braves	3-0	27	21	4	13	0.67
Bob Gibson	1967	Cardinals	3-0	27	14	5	26	1.00
Mickey Lolich	1968	Tigers	3-0	27	20	6	21	1.67

Series single-game pitching efforts. He won 1–0, allowing seven singles and walking none. The only run came with two out in the sixth when Jerry Coleman was slow to charge Mathews' slow hopper to second, and Hank Aaron and Joe Adcock followed with singles. A sensational running, leaping-at-the-fence catch by Wes Covington in the fourth inning helped Burdette's cause. Yankee second baseman Jerry Coleman alluded to Burdette's reputation for wetting one up now and then: "There isn't anyone in our league who pitches like Burdette." Others openly accused "Nitro Lew" of throwing a spitter.

Manager Fred Haney called on Burdette to pitch Game 7 on two days' rest, and he delivered another shutout and a world championship for the folks from Milwaukee. The final score was 5–0, with four of the runs scoring in the top of the third when a bad throw by Kubek opened the floodgates.

The Yankees made a strong comeback in the last of the ninth. They loaded the bases with two outs, and Moose Skowron slammed a shot down the third-base line. Mathews made an excellent backhanded stop and rushed to the bag to force Gil McDougald. Of his final swing, Skowron said, "I don't know what I hit, but whatever it was, I hit the ——— out of it." Still, Burdette was the Series hero, having closed out the Yankees—who averaged almost five runs a game during the regular season—with 24 straight scoreless innings.

Of all the great hurlers who have dominated their opponents—for a single at-bat, for a game, or for a Series—no one was ever so completely in charge as Christy Mathewson in 1905. He threw three complete-game shutouts in the space of six days, struck out 18, allowed just 14 hits, and walked one.

Of course, the shutout was standard operating procedure that year. All five games were whitewashes; the only game the Giants dropped to the Athletics they lost 3–0 on three unearned runs. Joe McGinnity pitched a 1–0 shutout—also an unearned run—for the Giants' only non-Mathewson win. The Athletics could have used the help of their wacky but brilliant pitcher Rube Waddell, but he wasn't available. Allegedly, Waddell had injured his shoulder in a train scuffle over teammate Andy Coakley's new straw hat. Some thought otherwise. Joe Vila suspected the gamblers had gotten to him. Bob Callahan wrote, "Wiser men had him holed up in a lush Manhattan apartment with a group of Broadway showgirls, his expenses paid by a New York betting crowd."

The stunning pitching in 1905 was America's introduction to an uninterrupted string of World Series that still runs. What a beginning. ◗▯

Lew Burdette's 17 wins ranked third on the Braves' staff in 1957, but in the Series against the Yankees he was the undisputed ace, winning three games. After Burdette's 5–0 win in Game 7, Braves manager Fred Haney said, "If Lew could cook, I'd marry him."

Bob Gibson

Nineteen sixty-eight was a lousy year for the Democrats and for any hitter who had to face Bob Gibson. The Cardinal right-hander blew away the National League in '68, putting up numbers that hadn't been seen since the dead-ball era. His 1.12 ERA was the best since Dutch Leonard's 1.01 in 1914—and the best ever for a pitcher with more than 300 innings; his 13 shutouts were second only to Grover Cleveland Alexander's 16 in 1916. He allowed an average of just under six hits per nine innings, struck out more than four hitters for every one he walked, won 15 straight games and put together a string of 47 consecutive scoreless innings.

Then he turned his attention to the World Series and the Detroit Tigers. Gibson was the defending Series MVP, coming off a three-win, 26-strikeout performance in 1967 against Boston. He capped it with a three-hitter in Game 7, striking out ten and hitting a home run. And while Gibson had the mound's most glowering expression and glittering stats in 1968, the most ballyhooed number going into the Series was 31—the number of games Detroit's Denny McLain had won in the regular season; McLain was baseball's first 30-game winner since 1934. The pair of aces faced off in Game 1, and Gibson had something to prove.

Nine innings later, the Tiger lineup lay in ruins. Gibson had thrown a five-hit shutout, walked just one and struck out a Series-record 17. Al Kaline, who was in his 16th year in the majors, said, "I've never seen such overpowering pitching."

Gibson pitched another five-hitter in Game 4, but lost his chance to become the first pitcher ever to win three games in two separate Series when Curt Flood misjudged a fly ball in Game 7 and helped Detroit win the Series. Still, Gibson ranks second all-time with seven Series wins and 92 strikeouts—the strikeouts came in just 81 innings, while all-time leader Whitey Ford took 146 innings to fan 94.

Gibson cared about just one thing—winning. He is acknowledged as one of the fiercest competitors ever to play the game. He threw the ball as hard as he could for as long as he could. With every pitch, Gibson flung his 6' 1", 189-pound frame at the hitter, as his follow-through sent him falling off the mound toward first base.

He was a magnificent athlete, but his early life gave no indication of an athletic future. Gibson grew up in the black ghetto of Omaha, Nebraska, and his youth was racked with illness, including rickets, pneumonia, asthma and a rheumatic heart. He became a healthy teenager, played baseball and basketball in high school, and won a basketball scholarship to Creighton University, where he was the team's star and its first black player. In college, and early in his pro career, Gibson felt the sting of racial prejudice, which he carried throughout his career. After receiving a hero's welcome in Omaha following his 1967 Series performance, Gibson remembered being refused a hotel room or restaurant table in towns like Tulsa and St. Petersburg. "I wasn't particularly touched by all this," he said. "All they're saying is I'm a 'special' Negro. That's the only reason some neighbors accept me. It makes me want to vomit."

His fierce independence earned him few friends among sportswriters, but won the respect and admiration of teammates and opponents. "No one ever had more pride than Bob Gibson," said Joe Torre,

Bob Gibson held nothing back when on the mound. "He can reach back anytime and burn your bat," said Felipe Alou.

a teammate of Gibson's from 1969 to 1974. "He does it all—Cy Young, 20 games, World Series—then works as hard as anyone, if not more. Just personal pride. And you've got to respect a man like that."

Signed by the Cardinals in 1957, Gibson struggled with his control in the minors. That fall, he played basketball with the Harlem Globetrotters, but wasn't suited to play with any team that put entertainment ahead of winning. He feuded with Cardinal manager Solly Hemus in 1959 and 1960, winning just six games as a reliever and spot starter. But when

Johnny Keane took over midway through the 1961 season, Gibson got his chance. On Keane's first day as manager, he handed a ball to Gibson and said, "Here. You pitch." Gibson hit a home run and beat the Dodgers that day, and his win total increased every year for the next five years, from 13 in 1961 to 21 in 1966.

Gibson's first World Series action came in 1964 against the Yankees, and he quickly showed that he was at his best in big games. After taking a loss in Game 2, he came back to strike out 13 in a ten-inning

Gibson's gutty win in Game 7 won the 1964 Series for St. Louis and primed him for greatness. Manager Johnny Keane saw it coming. "You're on your way, Hoot," Keane told Gibson. "Nothing can stop you now."

win in Game 5. In that game Gibson showed why he is considered one of the finest fielding pitchers ever. Leading 2–0 with one on and one out in the ninth, Gibson was hit on the right hip by a line drive off the bat of Joe Pepitone. The ball bounced toward third, but Gibson recovered, scooped up the ball and threw Pepitone out all in one motion. Tom Tresh then blasted a home run to right, which would have won the game had Gibson not made the play on Pepitone. Catcher Tim McCarver won the game for St. Louis with a homer in the tenth. "I don't know of any other pitcher in baseball who could have made that play," Keane said. Gibson came back for Game 7, and led 7–3 going into the ninth when he gave up two homers. Keane stuck with Gibson. "I had a commitment to his heart," Keane said. Gibson got the next batter, and the Cards were world champs.

Gibson had a change-up, but rarely used it, relying instead on two fastballs—one that sailed and one that sank—a devastating slider, and a hard curve. His brushback was one of the game's most effective pitches. "A brushback is not to scare a hitter or to hit him," he said. "It is to make him think."

Despite an arthritic elbow and injuries that ranged from a broken leg in 1967 to a torn thigh mus-

cle in 1971, Gibson continued to pitch well into his midthirties. In 1970, at the age of 34, he went 23–7 and won his second Cy Young Award. A knee injury ended Gibson's career after the 1975 season, but not before he had won 251 games, struck out ten or more in a game 72 times, won nine Gold Gloves and hit 24 career homers, eighth on the all-time list among pitchers. His hitting was remarkable, and in 1962 he drove in 20 runs, more than any other entire pitching *staff* in baseball.

Gibson's numbers were enough to earn him election to the Hall of Fame by an overwhelming margin in 1981, but to really understand what kind of a pitcher he was, you've got to talk to the hitters that had to face him. Former Dodger Tommy Davis called Gibson's fastball "the radio ball; you hear it but you don't see it." Former Yankee and Brave third baseman Clete Boyer said, "Gibson has such a great arm, such great motion, and such complete command of his situation that all we opposing batters can do is admire him and maybe wait for him to hang a pitch."

Perhaps it was former Dodger Ron Fairly who best captured the Gibson approach: "I'm Bob Gibson, and brother, if you don't know what that means, I'm going to teach you."

BOB
GIBSON

Right-Handed Pitcher
St. Louis Cardinals 1959–1975
Hall of Fame 1981

GAMES	**528**
INNINGS	
Career	**3,884⅔**
Season High	**314**
WINS	
Career	**251**
Season High	**23**
LOSSES	
Career	**174**
Season High	**13**
WINNING PERCENTAGE	
Career	**.591**
Season High	**.767**
ERA	
Career	**2.91**
Season High *(4th all time)*	**1.12**
GAMES STARTED	
Career	**482**
Season High	**36**
COMPLETE GAMES	
Career	**255**
Season High	**28**
SHUTOUTS	
Career	**56**
Season High *(2nd all time)*	**13**
STRIKEOUTS	
Career *(10th all time)*	**3,117**
Season High	**274**
WALKS	
Career	**1,336**
Season High	**119**
NO-HITTER	**1971**
WORLD SERIES	**1964, 1967, 1968**
MOST VALUABLE PLAYER	**1968**
CY YOUNG AWARD	**1968, 1970**

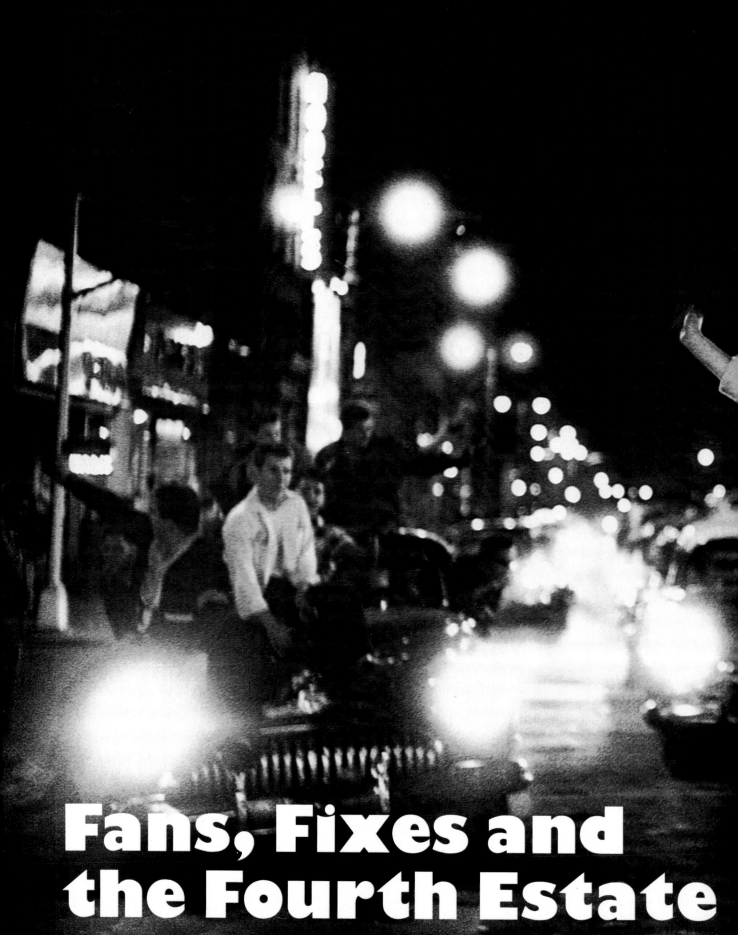

Fans, Fixes and the Fourth Estate

Dodger outfielder and chief flake Mickey Hatcher hit just one homer during the regular season in 1988, then hit two in the World Series as L.A. beat the favored A's in five games. Asked why he ran around the bases so fast after his Game 1 homer, Hatcher replied, "Basic lack of experience."

After losing seven straight World Series, the Brooklyn Dodgers won their first world championship in 1955, when Johnny Podres shut out the Yankees in Game 7. Long-suffering fans filled the streets of Brooklyn (preceding page). "I never in my life ever seen a town go so wild," said right fielder Carl Furillo.

The moments of World Series history that stick in our memories are the diving catches, the clutch homers and the key strikeouts. Whether we saw them on television, film, in photographs, or heard them on radio, the images are indelible. Yet some of the most memorable events affecting World Series play have taken place *off* the field. Owners have meddled, gamblers have manipulated, fans have protested, players have threatened to strike. Sportswriters have coaxed quotes from players that incensed the opposition. As recently as 1988, NBC TV announcer Bob Costas stated during a pregame show that the Dodgers were fielding what might be the worst nine ever to start a Series game. Dodger skipper Tommy Lasorda heard the remark and made sure his team did, too. On the field, the motivated Dodgers had little trouble disposing of the heavily favored Oakland A's.

Long before baseball went professional, players figured out how to make a few extra dollars by pleasing gamblers. "So common has betting become at baseball matches, that the most respectable clubs in the country indulge in it to a highly culpable degree," said *Harper's Weekly* in 1867. By the 1870s, at-the-park betting had become more professional than casual. A section at the Brooklyn Atlantics' park was called the Gold Board, "where activity rivaled that of the stock exchange," according to historian Lee Allen.

Powerful men who loved baseball—men like ace pitcher and businessman Al Spalding, writer Henry Chadwick, and financier William Hulbert—realized that baseball would never become America's game, and that decent men like themselves would never realize the relatively honest financial gain it could provide them, if gambling were not controlled.

OUR WHITE SOX

The Black Sox Scandal—in which eight Chicago White Sox players were banned from baseball for their role in a gambling scheme to throw the 1919 World Series—ended baseball's age of innocence. The story blared in newspaper headlines and on editorial cartoons nationwide. "I've lived a thousand years in the last 12 months," said pitcher Eddie Cicotte, a prime figure in the scandal.

So in early 1876, Hulbert led a group that formed the National League of Professional Base Ball Clubs. Their first set of rules stated: "Any player who shall in any way be interested in any bet or wager on the game in which he takes part . . . shall be dishonorably expelled, both from the club of which he is a member and from the League." They weren't kidding. The following year four players were expelled for life for betting, including Jim Devlin, one of the league's best pitchers. More expulsions were to come.

When gamblers were thrown out of the stands, they went to pool halls, hangouts for both pocket billiards and off-field betting. Baseball pools were big business; prizes could run as high as $1000 a week at a time when the average working man's salary was around $500 a year.

Many of the game's famous players were connected with betting. Late-season games were often "hippodromed," particularly when one team had a chance to finish in the first division and share postseason money. Gamblers and players were no strangers to each other, which is why Chick Gandil was familiar enough with one Sport Sullivan in 1919 to lay plans for throwing the World Series. Even after Commissioner Kenesaw Mountain Landis expelled the eight "Black Sox" for life in 1920, baseball stumbled over gambling scandals for a dozen years or more.

One of the more notorious incidents came to light in 1926, when the Detroit Tigers and the Cleveland Indians summarily released two of the American League's biggest drawing cards, the legendary Ty Cobb and Tris Speaker. The pair were accused of attempting to throw a late-season game between the two AL clubs back in 1919. Commissioner Landis, fed up with gambling allegations following the Black Sox affair, invoked his own five-year

1 JIMMY DYGERT, P.
2 TOPSY HARTSEL, L.F.
3 JACK BARRY, S.S.
4 BRIS. LORD, L.F.
5 CONNIE MACK, MGR.
6 HARRY KRAUSE, P.
7 EDDIE PLANK, P.
8 CHIEF BENDER, P.

9 RUBE OLDRING, C.F.
10 EDDIE COLLINS 2ND B.
11 JACK LAPP, C.
12 PAT DONAHUE, C.
13 JOHN McINNIS, S.S.

14 IRA THOMAS, C.
15 DANNY MURPHY, R.F.
16 BEN HOUSER 1ST B.
17 CAPT. H. DAVIS, 1ST B.
18 PADDY LIVINGSTONE, C.
19 FRANK BAKER, 3RD B.
20 JACK COOMBS, P.
21 TOMMY ATKINS, P.
22 CY MORGAN, P.
23 AMOS STRUNK, L.F.

While the 1910 NL champion Chicago Cubs finished out their regular season—a week longer than the AL's—the Athletics stayed sharp by playing exhibition games against a team of AL All-Stars led by Walter Johnson and Ty Cobb. Philadelphia then beat the Cubs in the World Series in five games.

statute of limitations and reinstated Cobb and Speaker. They each played a few more seasons, but not with Detroit and Cleveland.

Baseball has been free of fixed games for many years. As the sad incident of Pete Rose proved in 1989, baseball is still heavily bet upon, but the Commissioner's office keeps a close eye on gambling. The long season and a guaranteed share of World Series earnings keep players immune from gamblers' solicitations. And today players are paid better than most company presidents, so gambling's impact on the championship of baseball is a matter of history.

The greed of owners has played a role in several Series. In 1910, for one, the National League played a week longer than the American. Powerful Charley Ebbets, boss of the sixth-place Brooklyn Dodgers, loved the large receipts of holiday games, so he "requested" that the NL play through Columbus Day. The league, never eager to miss a good gate, extended the season through October 15.

The Chicago Cubs had clinched the NL pennant weeks earlier, winning the flag by 13 games. So they lolled through extra, meaningless games for a week longer than the AL champion Philadelphia Athletics. The Series was to be a battle of powerhouses, with the Cubs having won 104 games during the regular season to the Athletics' 102.

But while the Cubs relaxed, the Athletics got ready. In 1910 the American League was still young and looked down on as new kids by the old guard of the National. An intense desire to prove themselves made the AL owners especially fierce, so looking to gain an edge in the upcoming Series—to say nothing of a little extra revenue—they conjured up the idea of

the Athletics playing a daily exhibition series against an AL All-Star team. And not a bad bunch it was: Walter Johnson, Ty Cobb, Clyde Milan, George McBride, Tris Speaker and Ed Walsh were among the Athletics' opponents. The All-Stars beat the pennant winners four out of five games. Playing tough against tough opposition got the Athletics rolling.

When the Series began, the Athletics were tested and primed for battle. They dynamited the Cubs in five games, with Chicago's only win coming in the bottom of the tenth of Game 4. The Athletics hit .316 as a team—a record that stood for 50 years. Philadelphia needed only two pitchers to dispose of the overmatched Cubs. Jack Coombs pitched three complete games; Chief Bender pitched the other two. There was another difference between the leagues in 1910. Some claim the use of the new cork-center ball in the Series was what buffaloed the Cubs. But the ball didn't matter; it was lively for both teams. What had mattered was Charley Ebbets' desire for some extra money; it had cost the NL dearly because by mid-October the Athletics were ready for hardball and the Cubs weren't.

Ebbets managed to influence another World Series with his greed. When his Dodgers played the Red Sox in 1916, Ebbets raised the price for Series grandstand seats to $5 each—a remarkable hike, two dollars more than had ever been charged before. Ebbets explained his move with delightfully larcenous logic. Since Brooklyn had only about half the seating capacity of Boston, he *had* to charge more. After all, he said, "Brooklyn has some civic pride in its gate receipts." The crowds were smaller than expected, but it didn't matter. A grandstand 40 percent empty at $5 was just as good as one filled to the brim at $3. So the Series was financially successful.

Maestro Charles O. Finley conducted his Oakland A's to three straight world championships from 1972 to 1974 and left no doubt as to who was in control. "My middle initial stands for Owner," he said.

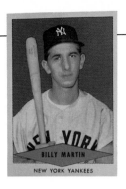

Billy Martin

Before he was a manager with a bad temper, he was a player with an even worse one. Although Billy "The Kid" Martin was a deeply religious man, he never quite mastered the technique of turning the other cheek.

"The way I play the game," the scrappy second baseman explained, "I always get mad. That's what makes me play harder."

It also got him into trouble. The Kid wasn't in the majors long when he started a free-for-all that resulted in a record $850 in fines. The fight began after Martin tagged out St. Louis' Clint Courtney—by hitting him in the mouth with the ball. The Brownie had a reputation for using his spikes, and Martin claimed he was only teaching Courtney a lesson and protecting his teammates.

So he was a hothead; he was a lovable hothead. And his teammates knew that when push came to shove, they could count on Billy. He'd grown up fighting adversity from early on, in a poor family, abandoned by his father when he was just 8 months old. But the skinny kid with the big ears and beaked nose never let up.

"I never felt equal to people," Martin said. "Sports was one way I could even up." By age 15—at 5′ 5″ and 125 pounds—he was playing sandlot ball. He started with the Yankees in 1950, and made his first Series appearance as a pinch runner a year later.

Martin revealed his potential in 1952 when he saved the championship for the Yankees in Game 7 with a shoestring catch of a bases-loaded Jackie Robinson pop-up to end a seventh-inning Dodger rally. Then in 1953, while his personal life fell apart, his championship play came together.

Martin's wife pressed for a divorce, and he made daily trips to church to stave off a nervous breakdown. He took nerve pills for his insomnia. The fans chided him. Yankee general manager George Weiss was looking for any excuse to get the trouble-maker off the team. The press belittled him. But Martin and the Yankees were on their way to another World Series.

"I react to what I read in the papers—especially at World Series time," Martin said. "I always got the feeling I had to show them, all of them." And show them he did. In the 1953 Series, the Kid batted .500 and tied the all-time Series mark with 12 base hits. He broke Babe Ruth's six-game Series record with 23 total bases, tied three other batting records and drove in the winning run in the final game.

In Martin's six and a half years with the Yankees, the team lost the pennant only once: in 1954, the year Martin was in the Army. In five Series, he made 33 hits in 28 games including five homers, three triples and two doubles. But Martin couldn't stay out of trouble. In 1957 a fracas broke out during Martin's birthday party at the Copacabana. Though Martin didn't throw a single punch, the publicity damaged his already battered reputation, and soon afterward, Weiss traded him. Mickey Mantle, his best friend, cried. Casey Stengel, who loved him as a son, called Martin "the smartest little player I ever had."

Martin never played in the World Series again, but he returned to the Series as the Yankees' manager in 1976, and his reputation as a hothead never faded. "Jesus Christ took a whip to the money changers, right? Well, that's a temper, and that's not a bad guy to follow," he said. "The way I see it, my temper is a great ally. It is what has pushed Billy Martin." On Christmas Day of 1989 Martin died in a car accident.

Billy Martin got 33 hits in just 28 World Series games, but perhaps the biggest was his Series-clinching single in the bottom of the ninth inning in Game 6 of the 1953 Series. It gave the Yankees an unprecedented fifth straight world title and earned Martin a hug from coach Frankie Crosetti (above, 2).

BILLY MARTIN

Second Base
New York Yankees 1950–1953, 1955–1957
Kansas City Athletics 1957
Detroit Tigers 1958
Cleveland Indians 1959
Cincinnati Reds 1960
Milwaukee Braves 1961
Minnesota Twins 1961

GAMES	1,021
AT-BATS	3,419
BATTING AVERAGE	
Career	.257
Season High	.267
SLUGGING AVERAGE	
Career	.369
Season High	.401
HITS	
Career	877
Season High	151
DOUBLES	
Career	137
Season High	24
TRIPLES	
Career	28
Season High	6
HOME RUNS	
Career	64
Season High	15
TOTAL BASES	1,262
EXTRA-BASE HITS	229
RUNS BATTED IN	
Career	333
Season High	75
RUNS	
Career	425
Season High	76
WORLD SERIES	1951–1953, 1955–1956

An earthquake that registered 6.9 on the Richter scale stopped Game 3 of the 1989 World Series between San Francisco and Oakland before it got started, and turned what had been a showcase for the Bay Area into what baseball commissioner Fay Vincent called "a modest little sporting event." The quake shook up Giants sluggers past and present, Willie Mays (above, right) and Kevin Mitchell.

And Ebbets' players shared his generous style: they voted all the money to themselves—not a nickel to coaches, clubhouse attendants or anyone else.

Another owner in search of deeper pockets was the Phillies' William F. Baker. Faced with the prospect of playing the Red Sox in 1915 in Boston's new Braves Field, he figured he had to add temporary seats in his tiny Baker Bowl. He squeezed in enough extras by putting up temporary stands in right center to raise the capacity to 20,000. Red Sox outfielder Harry Hooper thanked him by popping two homers into the temporary seats in Game 5. The Sox won the game, 5–4, and in one game Hooper had matched his entire season's home run output.

The 1912 World Series is famous for terrific play on the field, but it had more than its share of off-the-field bobbles, too. The Red Sox led the Giants 3–1—one game had ended in a tie—in a Series that alternated between New York's Polo Grounds and Boston's brand-new Fenway Park. Sox ace Smoky Joe Wood was everyone's expected choice for the possible clincher. Everyone except Boston owner Jim McAleer.

Called "the greatest center fielder that ever was," during his playing days, McAleer was a tough customer who had had more than a few battles with Boston's equally plucky manager, Jake Stahl. Before Game 6, McAleer "suggested" that Stahl pitch Buck O'Brien instead of Wood. According to Fred Lieb, McAleer's logic was that "After O'Brien's fine work in the third game, I think he deserves another shot at the Giants." Stahl disagreed vehemently, but he was overruled.

Before the Series began, it was generally acknowledged that it would be the biggest money-maker of any Series so far. Fenway Park held almost

35,000 fans. The tie in Game 2 had additionally swelled the teams' coffers. Was McAleer already counting the house for a seventh game in Boston? No one knows for sure, but Buck O'Brien started for the Sox, got creamed—five runs in the first inning—and the Series moved back to Boston. Smoky Joe, 34–5 that season, got his chance to end the Series, and McAleer got another stadium full of paying customers.

But then some fans got into the act. A rowdy bunch called the Royal Rooters led Boston fans in cheering, marching and doing all they could to annoy the opposition. The Rooters performed their customary march to the park on the day of Game 7, led by politico "Honey Fitz" Fitzgerald, John F. Kennedy's grandfather, and bartender "Nuf Ced" McGreevey. But when they arrived, they found that the tickets reserved for them had been sold by an unsuspecting ticket clerk. There were no seats for the Rooters.

As Wood began to warm up on the mound, the Rooters outside were already overheated. Breaking through the outfield fence, they marched around the field, letting everyone within earshot know how they felt about McAleer and other Sox officials. The day was cold and windy, and Wood left the mound for the quiet of the dugout. Mounted police took nearly half an hour to clear the field of the irate marchers.

Wood cooled down, and the Giants got a chance they didn't deserve. The New Yorkers tagged him for six runs in the first inning, won 11–4, and the Series was tied at three games apiece. The next day only 17,000 fans showed up, partly because of miserable weather and partly in protest against the shoddy treatment shown the Royal Rooters. The Red Sox did salvage the Series, as Wood won Game 8 in relief.

Boston's Royal Rooters—nearly 500 strong—followed their beloved Red Sox to New York's Polo Grounds (above), where they performed their traditional pregame parade before a 1912 World Series game. But when they arrived at Fenway Park for Game 7 and found their seats had been filled, they kicked up a fuss, and mounted police had to be called in to remove them from the field.

After tussling with Tiger third baseman Marv Owen in St. Louis' 11–0 win in Game 7 of the 1934 Series in Detroit, Cardinal left fielder Joe "Ducky" Medwick was greeted with a shower of produce from Tiger fans. "I know why they threw that stuff at me," Medwick said. "What I don't know is why they brought it to the ball park in the first place."

The behavior of the Royal Rooters certainly didn't help their beloved Bosox. Yet the incident was not the last time that raucous fan behavior nearly resulted in a forfeit against the home team. A similar debacle occurred in the final game of the 1934 Series in Detroit between the Tigers and the Cardinals. Paul Dean had beaten the Tigers twice; his brother Dizzy had beaten them once. But Detroit had also won three games, and Game 7 opened with Tiger fans hoping that their club would clinch its first world championship. But Dizzy proved tougher than Detroit's Eldon Auker and his submarine-style deliveries, and the Cards leaped to a 7–0 lead after three innings.

In the top of the sixth, St. Louis added a run when Joe Medwick tripled home Pepper Martin. Medwick's slide into third was a hard one, and Tiger third baseman Marv Owen was slightly spiked. Radio announcer France Laux called it "a little hard feeling between Medwick and Owen. . . . Several of the players are out. They're still arguing about it down there." The battle was broken up, but the hometown fans, already upset by the score, were not so forgiving. When Medwick headed to his position in left field for the bottom of the sixth, the fans turned him into fruit salad.

It was a riot—with citrus. France Laux continued the play-by-play: "Medwick is really getting a reception from the fans out there in the bleachers. They're throwing oranges, apples and everything else out in the field. . . . Even a few pop bottles have landed on the field . . . Umpires are going out trying to stop them . . . Groundskeepers going out to try and clean up the stuff." Obviously embarrassed by what was going on before his eyes, Laux tried to change the subject but returned to describing the barrage. "All kinds of stuff has been tossed out there, including oranges, bananas, pop bottles and everything else . . . Fans continue to boo Medwick

Irate Tiger fans made Medwick's continued presence in Game 7 in 1934 ill-advised, so he was escorted off the field. Bob Elson called the action. "I gave it to 'em, tomato by tomato, pie by pie, without missing a lemon, banana, cabbage, or whatever."

b 2/14/1913

MEL ALLEN
Broadcaster

While Reggie Jackson was still in diapers, the original Mr. October was already a World Series veteran. Broadcaster Mel Allen, the Voice of the Yankees, covered 20 Series on radio and television between 1940 and 1963, and his expressive Alabama drawl helped make the Yanks larger than life for a whole generation of baseball fans.

Allen was partisan—but never prejudiced, he claimed. In the booth he was always on the edge of his seat, a proxy for the fan at home. When the crowd roared, Allen roared louder, and from his combination of frenzy and wonder came phrases like "Going, going, GONE!" and his trademark, "How about that?"

Allen's dominance of World Series broadcasting was tied to the Yankees' dominance of baseball. They won 14 pennants between 1947 and 1963, and The Voice seldom got to go on vacation before mid-October. But had announcers been assigned to the Series based on talent alone, Allen still would have been there. As telecaster Lindsey Nelson has said: "He was the best *ever* to broadcast the game."

Allen was unceremoniously fired after the 1963 season amid rumors of personal problems. But after more than ten years of being virtually blacklisted, he resurfaced as the voice of "This Week in Baseball," where he is the only broadcaster unashamed to say "gee whiz" on national television.

out in left field . . . The umps are trying to get the fans to quit . . . Here starts more pop bottles and stuff . . . Just the minute Medwick goes back to his position, they start throwing pop bottles and everything at him." When a photographer ran out on the field to take a picture of Medwick, he was narrowly missed by an orange.

During the delay, Cardinal third baseman Pepper Martin and center fielder Ernie Orsatti played catch with a grapefruit. Commissioner Kenesaw Mountain Landis, in his third-base box seat, didn't notice the ruckus immediately, later confiding to J. G. Taylor Spink of *The Sporting News* that he had at that moment mastered the art of spitting tobacco juice.

Landis called the participants in the squabble—Medwick, Owen and the four umpires—to his side and quickly ordered Cardinal manager Frankie Frisch to remove Medwick from the game. Because the score was 9–0, the Commissioner's decision was made easier, and Frisch did not object. Had the game been close, an entirely new riot might have begun over the decision.

Nearly 30 years later, a similar incident occurred in the 1973 NL Championship Series. With the best-of-five playoffs tied at one game each, the hometown Mets had a 9–2 lead in the top of the fifth inning of Game 3. In an unsuccessful attempt to break up a double play, Reds left fielder Pete Rose slid hard into Mets shortstop Bud Harrelson, knocking him down. Harrelson responded by shoving Rose. One push led to another and in moments Rose was on top of the smaller Harrelson, pummeling him. Both benches emptied.

After the fight was stopped, Rose took his position in left field. The fans at Shea Stadium in 1973 were much better armed than the fruit tossers at

The Gang's All Here

From Boston's Royal Rooters to the raucous bleacher bums of Ebbets Field and Wrigley Field, baseball fans have always been a big part of the show. In 1984 fans at Tiger Stadium popularized the now-famous wave, and the Tigers rode it to a world championship. In 1987 Twins fans broke all records for indoor noise and hanky-waving, and the Twins were unbeatable at home on their way to a world title.

It's always been that way. The crowd is the home team's tenth man, and fans come out in force on those rare occasions when the locals make the Series. They line up days before tickets go on sale, camping out in hopes of being on hand when the next Don Larsen or Bill Mazeroski reaches out and stops time.

Art "Happy" Felsch (right) liked being first in line, so much so that in 1940 he camped outside Crosley Field for 11 days before the start of the World Series between Cincinnati and Detroit. But that was nothing compared with 1936, when Felsch arrived 23 days early for the Series between the Giants and the Yanks at the Polo Grounds.

Whether it means waiting all night in Pittsburgh for the few seats left for Game 7 in 1960 (top), a sea of rallying red outside St. Louis' Busch Stadium in 1985 (above), or keeping up in the jungles of Panama via Armed Forces Radio in 1942, the World Series is among the most powerful magnets in sports.

Cincinnati's Pete Rose earned the undying enmity of Mets fans everywhere when he scrapped with 160-pound shortstop Bud Harrelson in Game 3 of the 1973 NLCS. Mets fans in the left field stands pelted him with anything that was handy, but the Mets themselves got the best revenge by winning the series.

Tiger Stadium in 1934. Uneaten lunches, cans, paper cups, and even a whiskey bottle came flying from the stands at Rose. Reds manager Sparky Anderson removed his team from the field, but the New York faithful weren't satisfied. They continued covering the outfield with garbage. NL President Chub Feeney ordered Mets manager Yogi Berra and outfielder Willie Mays—then in his last season—to plead with the fans for order. Feeney felt that those two, as longtime New York favorites, had the best chance of settling the mob down. Tom Seaver, Rusty Staub and Cleon Jones joined them, begging for civility from the mob. Enough calm was restored for the game to continue, but the fans were far from finished. After the Mets won the fifth and deciding game, fans tore the field apart. There was almost no grass left. According to Mets historian Jack Lang, the rowdy fans even dismantled parts of the outfield fence. "Fortunately they [had] a week to get Shea Stadium in shape again" for the World Series.

Boisterous fans affected play in the 1987 World Series as well, when the incredible noise generated by the Minnesota Twins' faithful in the confines of the Metrodome pumped up the home team and shook up the visiting St. Louis Cardinals. Fans watching on TV were treated to a running account of the crowd noise, in decibels, on ABC's sound meter. After Kent Hrbek's Game 6 grand slam broke open a close game, the sound meter broke as the Metrodome shook. The Twins, who combined a miserable 29–52 road record with a league-leading 56–25 at home, obviously preferred the noisy interior. The Cards won the three games on their home turf; the Twins, the four played in the Metrodome, to deliver a Series upset.

All the noise fans have made during World Series competition hasn't matched the impact of an occasional "slip of the lip" by the players

themselves. Twice—43 years apart—an AL champion paid dearly for using the word "bush" in regard to the Braves.

The first time was in 1914, when the "Miracle Braves" of Boston under manager George Stallings turned around a dismal first-half season to win the NL flag going away. When Connie Mack, manager of the AL champion Athletics, ordered pitcher Chief Bender to go to New York to scout the Braves in a late-season game against the Giants, the Chief never left Philadelphia. "What's the use of me wasting a perfectly good afternoon watching those bush-leaguers?" Bender said. All the Miracle Braves did was continue their miracle, becoming the first team to knock Bender out of a Series game, and delivering the first four-game sweep in World Series history.

In 1957 the Braves, now from Milwaukee, were set to face the potent New York Yankees in the World Series. After the Braves and Yanks split the first two games in Yankee Stadium, a giant celebration was roaring in Milwaukee to welcome the NL champs home. After all, it was the first major league pennant ever for the city. The boys from the Big Apple were not impressed with the hoopla. Mickey Mantle—perhaps sour because he was hurt and not able to play much—spoke out of turn. "This is bush league stuff," he said.

Milwaukee fans heard him loud and clear. Large signs saying, "Welcome to Bushville" popped up everywhere. Braves fans were enjoying the putdown; it brought them even closer together. When the Braves, behind Lew Burdette's three complete-game victories, downed the Yanks in seven, Milwaukee became the capital of the baseball world. It was only the second time the Yanks had lost a Series in their last ten appearances, and the first time since 1942 they had been beaten by an opponent not from New York.

The home crowd was never more important than in the 1987 Series, when, for the first time, the home team won every game. Twins fans made headlines by yelling like mad and waving their Homer Hankies, to which at least one Cardinal fan (above) had a stinging response. The Twins won the Series, 4–3.

*Branded as bush league fans by the Yankees'
Mickey Mantle, Braves loyalists poured
into the streets after Milwaukee beat New
York in Game 7 of the 1957 Series. A city
holiday was declared shortly after the
game ended, and Milwaukee hailed its first
world champions.*

*Souvenirs of a miracle don't come around
every day, so fans at Shea Stadium grabbed
handfuls of turf after the Mets—NL doormats
since their debut in 1962—won the 1969
World Series over Baltimore.*

Perhaps the best response to the Yankee charges of "bush" was from the *Milwaukee Journal:* "And behold the bush burned with fire, and the bush was not consumed." (Exodus 3:2.)

Sometimes a player can fire his team up by issuing a public challenge, but it can backfire, too. In 1979 the Orioles faced the Pirates in the Series. The young Bucs, under Chuck Tanner, were famous for stealing bases. They swiped 180 bases that year, succeeding on 73 percent of their attempts—the best rate in baseball. Oriole catcher Rick Dempsey announced that the Bucs wouldn't steal on him. They didn't. Only two Pirates attempted to steal in the entire Series. Dempsey threw out Gary Alexander and Bill Madlock, and Dave Skaggs nailed Madlock in his second attempt. But because fastballs give catchers a better chance to throw out base-stealers, Oriole catchers called for more fastballs than normal. Fastballs are easier to hit, and the Pirates responded mightily to the O's pitch selection. Five Pirates had ten or more hits; Bill Madlock had nine. The team batted .323 and slugged .438. Dempsey's plan had achieved its objective, but it gave the Pirates too much in return. Pittsburgh first baseman Willie Stargell was the most eager recipient. He smashed 12 hits in the Series, including three home runs and four doubles.

Not all pre-Series pronouncements are verbal. Perhaps the most emphatic statement was delivered to the Pittsburgh Pirates in batting practice by the 1927 Yankees, featuring the 107-homer team of Babe Ruth and Lou Gehrig. Even in the immense Forbes Field, Murderers' Row put on a pregame slugging display that—according to legend—shattered the morale of the boys from Steeltown.

Ford Frick, the sportswriter who later became commissioner of baseball, related the party line in *Baseball Magazine*. "As the Pirates sat there in the stands watching, [Yankee manager] Miller Huggins was quick to grasp opportunity. Out to the mound he sent Herbie Pennock and Bob Shawkey, wiliest of wily pitchers. And their instructions were definite. 'Groove everything,' Huggins told them. 'We'll show these chaps some hitting. Let them see a few go over the fence.' " The Yanks then allegedly put on a homer show. Pie Traynor is said to have commented, "That's the greatest exhibition of hitting I've ever seen." Lloyd Waner said to brother Paul, "Gee, those guys are big."

The flaw in the legend is evident, and the story of the Series bears it out. First, what batting practice pitcher *doesn't* "groove everything"? That's their job. Further, Lloyd Waner denied even seeing the Yanks' batting practice that day, and said of his brother Paul, "I don't think Paul ever saw anything on a ballfield that could scare him."

And finally, in the ensuing Series, the Pirates were not pounded into submission by Yankee might. There were only two homers hit in the Series—both by Ruth—and while the Pirates were swept, they lost Game 1 because of a pair of crucial errors, and Game 4 on a ninth-inning wild pitch. So it appears, after all, that it wasn't the batting practice power show that did the Pirates in. As *Baseball Magazine's* Frank Lane pointed out, it was a combination of fate, fielding errors, weak pitching and a batting slump that brought about the downfall of the formidable Pirates. They did it to themselves. ◖

It's bad enough to have to watch helplessly as a home run goes over your head, but White Sox left fielder Al Smith looked up and got a faceful of beer in the fifth in Game 2 of the 1959 World Series against the Dodgers. Chicago lost the game, 4–3, and the Series, 4–2.

Decisions, Decisions

There aren't many jobs where the ultimate goal is to go completely unnoticed: sniper, private detective and baseball umpire. Good umpires are decisive and consistent behind the plate and on the bases, and as a result are largely invisible. Good umpires also make bad calls from time to time, and when they do so in a World Series, people notice. Questionable decisions have created some of the wildest moments in World Series history, but none was wilder than a play in Game 3 of the 1975 Series between the Boston Red Sox and the Cincinnati Reds. The game, which featured three home runs by each team, turned on an umpire's call on a sacrifice bunt. The score was tied at five with none out in the bottom of the tenth when the Reds' Cesar Geronimo singled. Ed Armbrister was sent up to pinch-hit. Armbrister bunted, but it wasn't a good one. The ball bounced high in the air off the Astroturf in front of the plate. Armbrister stepped out of the batter's box, then hesitated. Red Sox catcher Carlton Fisk, rushing out to snare the bunt, collided with Armbrister, retrieved the ball, and shoved Armbrister out of his way. Then, trying to start a double play, Fisk threw wildly to second. Armbrister wound up on second, Geronimo on third, and two batters later, Joe Morgan singled in Geronimo to win the game.

Home plate umpire Larry Barnett made no call. As he saw it, "It was just a collision," and was not intentional on Armbrister's part. The Red Sox couldn't believe it, and tried to document their disbelief. The rule book

When Oriole catcher Elrod Hendricks tried to tag the Reds' Bernie Carbo (25) in Game 1 of the 1970 Series, umpire Ken Burkhart got bowled over. Burkhart made a decisive out call, but replays showed that Hendricks tagged Carbo with an empty mitt.

Sometimes no call is the worst call. In his first World Series, AL umpire Larry Barnett sparked a huge controversy when he didn't call interference on the Reds' Ed Armbrister, who blocked Carlton Fisk's path on a sacrifice bunt in Game 3 of the 1975 Series. The Red Sox catcher got around Armbrister, but rushed his throw to second. The overthrow led to a 6–5 Reds win.

states, "It is interference by a batter or runner when he fails to avoid a fielder who is attempting to field a batted ball." There's no mention of "intention" at all. As Fisk re-created the play, "I'm an infielder. I'm fielding a ball in front of the plate. He can't run into me. Do I have to wait till the ball hits the ground to field it? It's just like a pop-up between the plate and first. I'm an infielder fielding the ball and he stands right in my way. If that's not interference . . ."

The storm raged in the press for days, and statements by the commissioner's office didn't help. John H. Johnson, chairman of the Playing Rules Committee, claimed that another subsection was the applicable rule. Interference, it states, should be called "if in the judgment of the umpire, a batter-runner willfully and deliberately interferes with a batted ball or a fielder with the obvious intent of breaking up a double play." Both the runner and the batter are out when that happens. But famed sportswriter Red Smith answered Johnson by reminding him that the rule he cited was written to deal with Jackie Robinson, who, as a baserunner, had a knack for running in front of obvious double-play grounders, thereby rendering the ball dead and limiting the defense to only one out. So the Johnson rule didn't apply, either.

Several months later, Roger Angell wrote that "the news filtered out of the league offices that the Series umpires had been acting under a prior 'supplemental instruction' to the interference rules." This addendum stated, "When a catcher and a batter-runner going to first have contact while the catcher is fielding the ball, there is generally no violation and nothing should be called." This, of course, explains Barnett's comment, "It was just a collision." But when he was surrounded with people quoting rule books, why didn't he mention to anyone that his call was made with the newly instated World Series addendum? Why didn't the commissioner's office

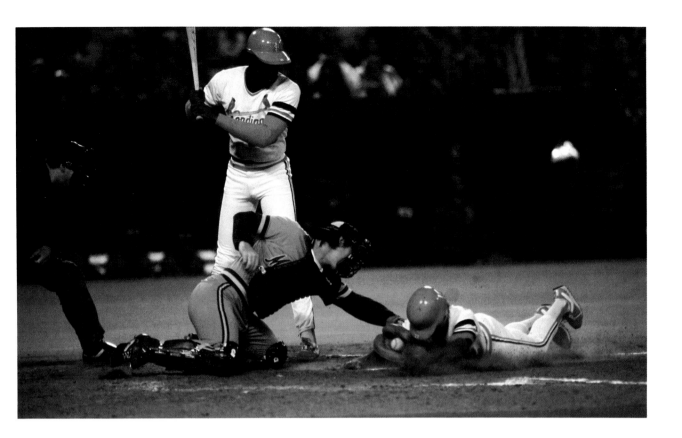

tell everyone it was making some new rules for the Series, and tell the reporters what they were?

Larry Barnett received a harrowing series of death threats, and all the umpires were given round-the-clock protection for the rest of the Series. Red Sox pitcher Bill "Spaceman" Lee offered his own solution: "I'd have bitten Barnett's ear off. I'd have Van Goghed him!"

Then there was the comment from highly respected writer Leonard Koppett: "Not one of the umps had the guts to call the play right," which pointed to a more serious underlying problem. World Series umpires were chosen on merit till 1970, when a union contract settlement established a system of rotation among all experienced umps. Neither Barnett nor any of the five other umpires for the Reds-Red Sox Series had ever worked under the intense pressure of a World Series before.

An almost perfect example of how cooler, wiser heads can prevail occurred in the 1980 NL Championship Series, when an umpire sorted through a pile of confusing options and made the call correctly and fairly. It has gone down in history as the Phantom Triple Play.

The Phillies were playing the Astros in Game 4 of the NLCS. With men on first and second, Phils center fielder Garry Maddox smacked a soft liner back toward Astros pitcher Vern Ruhle, who snagged it and threw to first to double off Manny Trillo. Veteran home plate umpire Doug Harvey ruled that the ball had been trapped, not caught. But the other umpires overruled him. The Phillies came out to beef, and during the turmoil, Astros first baseman Art Howe noticed that Bake McBride had run to third on the play. Howe ran to second, touched the base, and claimed a triple play. The scene was bedlam.

The Cardinals won three NL pennants in the 1980s by playing aggressive baseball, and they didn't slow up in the World Series. Lonnie Smith (above, sliding) was called out trying to steal home by umpire Jim Evans in Game 6 of the 1982 Series against Milwaukee. Ted Simmons applied the tag and George Hendrick held his stance. Replays indicated that Smith was safe, but the Cards went on to batter the Brewers anyway, 13–1.

Bill Klem

He called himself "the Old Arbitrator," but in truth, he was the law. No one sprayed Bill Klem's face with obscenities. No one even dared to think of kicking dirt on him. During the first third of the 20th century, it was a fact of baseball life that you didn't cross Bill Klem unless you had no intention of playing anymore that day.

He did not invent the art of umpiring, but no one did more to polish it, to make it a profession worthy of respect and a decent wage. He was demonstrative without showboating, autocratic without being abusive. Most of all, he was unfailingly fair, which explains why he was chosen to umpire in 18 World Series between 1908 and 1940, a record no one else has come close to matching.

From the start, Klem made it clear that he took his job seriously. Back in 1904, when umpires worked alone and baseball was a game with a high quotient of rowdies on the fields and in the stands, he quickly earned a reputation in the American Association as an umpire with a quick hook and a lot of nerve. That year, a confrontation with a notorious bully laid the foundation for the Klem legend. The player was so incensed by a call Klem made on a close play at second that he charged in from his position in center field. Klem had already started walking back to the plate, but sensing big trouble coming from behind, he paused at the pitcher's mound long enough to draw a line in the dirt. The hotheaded player, snorting and howling, never crossed it. The Klem standard had been set.

He would continue to draw lines in the dirt in the National League, which hired him in 1905. Anyone who crossed one would get thrown out of the game. Naturally, this frustrated managers itching for a fight, particularly John McGraw, the feisty field general of the New York Giants. Klem and McGraw were good friends off the field, but they constantly battled on it. Fittingly, they were adversaries in an incident that became the heart of Bill Klem lore. In a 1911 game at the Polo Grounds, which had just been rebuilt after a grandstand fire, a Giant player powered a fly ball off the scoreboard down the short left field line. This was always a tough call in that park because the scoreboard straddled the foul line without being marked itself. Klem called the ball foul, which sent McGraw into a rage. Afterward, McGraw had the stadium engineer look for the dent in the scoreboard. To McGraw's chagrin, Klem had been right—the ball had been foul by three inches. Two days later, when the engineer congratulated Klem for the correctness of his call, the umpire responded, "I never missed one of those in my life."

McGraw would never let Klem forget that comment, but his attempts to needle the ump only served to enhance his reputation. Klem later amended his comment, saying that what he meant was that he had never missed a call "in my heart," but "I never missed one in my life" became Klem's tag line, a testament to his skill and his integrity. He said he knew it was time to retire in 1941 when a fan called him "Pop," but Klem never really left the game. For another ten years he worked with NL umpires, instilling a new generation of umps with his professionalism and his passion for fairness. When he became the first umpire chosen for the Hall of Fame, no one argued the call.

Bill Klem worked behind the plate in the days when intimidating umpires was just another piece of strategy, and no one enjoyed it more than Giants manager John McGraw. But Klem refused to be intimidated. Once, when McGraw threatened to take Klem's job away, Klem retorted, "If you can get it, I don't want it."

You can't make the right call unless you're in the right position. Umpire John Shulock got the right angle on this play in Game 5 of the 1985 World Series, and despite the pleas of Cardinal catcher Tom Nieto, Shulock called Royals catcher Jim Sundberg safe.

Harvey realized, rightly, that his signal of "no catch" was why Trillo and McBride had not stayed at their respective bases. So he consulted with NL president Chub Feeney and the other umpires for 20 minutes, while the Phils and Astros tried to make their cases.

Harvey explained how he had seen the play go down: "Maddox hit the ball and stepped in front of me. There are runners out there wondering if it's a catch or a trap. My first reaction is no catch and I put my hands down to signal fair ball in play. But I see the pitcher throw to first as if he's going for the double play. I ask for help and they tell me the pitcher caught the ball and that's good enough for me."

In the end, Harvey ruled that Howe's attempt to create the triple play had happened after time was called, so both Maddox and Trillo were out, and McBride was allowed to remain at second. Instead of being intimidated by the players, coaches, managers and fans—and by his own initially mistaken call—Harvey, already a veteran of three NLCS and two World Series, sorted out the options and made a wise choice. Only an umpire who has been through the pressure cooker of postseason play is likely to do that.

Umpire George Hildebrand made a sensationally unpopular choice in Game 2 of the 1922 World Series. Before the 11th inning started, third-base umpire Bill Klem consulted with Hildebrand; he was worried that it would soon be dark, and that at the rate the teams were playing, they might not be able to finish the inning in light. He referred Hildebrand to a 14-inning game in the 1916 Series which ended on a hit that might have been an out if it hadn't been so dark. Apparently, Klem's comments made an impression. At 4:40 p.m., with the score tied after ten innings, Hildebrand

called the game because of "darkness." By all accounts, there was at least half an hour of light left.

The fans didn't like the idea one bit. Because Hildebrand had walked to the commissioner's box before announcing his decision, they accused Judge Landis of being the one who called the game. Landis' salty comment: "I don't pretend to be the smartest person in the United States, but at least I can tell day from night." The thoroughly embarrassed commissioner decided that for the two teams to keep the gate receipts would be cheating the fans, so he turned over all the money, a total of $120,000, to charity.

A questionable umpiring decision in the 1985 Series between the Cardinals and the Royals may well have turned the course of the entire championship. Leading 1–0 going into the ninth inning of Game 6, St. Louis needed just three outs to win its second Series of the decade. Cardinals manager Whitey Herzog called in Todd Worrell and his amazing fastball to shut the door on K.C. In 4⅓ innings of relief earlier in the Series, Worrell had allowed only one hit. Pinch hitter Jorge Orta led off with a bouncer to first baseman Jack Clark. Worrell covered first base to take the throw, and he seemed to catch the ball cleanly and beat Orta to the bag, but umpire Don Denkinger ruled otherwise. Replays showed not only that the throw was there first, but that Orta didn't step on the base at all. He stepped on Worrell's foot.

At this point, the Cards could still have swallowed hard and not let the ump's miscall bother them. But they didn't swallow so well; unspoken outrage was stuck in their throats. Jack Clark immediately misplayed Steve Balboni's foul pop-up, and the K.C. slugger responded with a second-chance single. A sacrifice failed when Orta was forced at third, but with Hal McRae at

Three outs away from a world title, the Cardinals got stung by umpire Don Denkinger in Game 6 of the 1985 Series. Denkinger called the Royals' Jorge Orta safe, though replays indicated that the throw to pitcher Todd Worrell beat Orta to the bag. The Royals went on to score the tying and winning runs, then won Game 7, during which Denkinger, working behind the plate, ejected Cardinal manager Whitey Herzog and pitcher Joaquin Andujar.

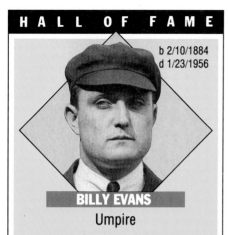

b 2/10/1884
d 1/23/1956

BILLY EVANS
Umpire

In 1904 Billy Evans was working for an Ohio newspaper when he went to report on a minor league game. The umpire failed to show up, and Evans filled in. Two years later, when he was only 22, he was hired as a full-time AL umpire. In those days, umpires announced team batteries. When Evans was to announce the batteries for a Philadelphia-Boston match that included legendary hurlers Rube Waddell and Cy Young, he was overwhelmed. "My lips moved, but no sound came from my throat. I suppose you can say I choked up."

Evans called 40 World Series games from 1909 through 1923. Back in 1909 only two umpires worked each game. But in Game 2 of the Series, Evans and NL ump Bill Klem couldn't see a long fly ball, and the two had to ask spectators if it was fair or foul. Four umpires were used in Game 3, and that later became the standard for all major league games.

Evans wrote on the side. His sports column, "Billy Evans Says," was carried by more than 100 papers, and *The Billy Evans Course on Umpiring* has become a bible for rookie umpires.

Evans became general manager for Cleveland in 1927, and turned the Indians into first-division finishers. Then he shifted sports, and managed the Cleveland Rams football team in 1941. But after one season, he returned to baseball, first as president of the Southern Association, then, in December 1946, as general manager for the Detroit Tigers. He retired in 1951 and was elected to the Hall of Fame in 1973.

Umpires—like everything else on the field—are in play. Reds first baseman Frank McCormick dropped the ball after running into umpire E. Lee Ballanfant in Game 6 of the 1940 Series, and Detroit's Earl Averill was safe at first. The Reds won anyway.

the plate, catcher Darrell Porter let a pitch get past him, and the runners scampered to second and third. McRae was walked intentionally to load the bases, and Dane Iorg—who had been a hero for the Cardinals in the 1982 Series—looped a single to right that scored the tying and go-ahead runs. Naturally, the Cards blamed Denkinger for the loss. The Cardinals couldn't erase the memory of the bad call, nor could they regain their concentration for Game 7; as a result, the Royals won their first World Series with an 11–0 blowout.

Game 3 of the 1935 World Series had both teams furious at the umpires. In the top of the sixth inning, Detroit, behind Chicago 3–0, broke through when a one-out triple by Pete Fox scored Goose Goslin. But savvy Cub catcher Gabby Hartnett picked Fox off third. Tiger third-base coach Del Baker protested so vehemently that umpire Ernest Quigley sent him to the showers.

The second-base umpire, George Moriarty, had once been a Tiger himself—he had played third base in Detroit's seven-game loss to Pittsburgh in the 1909 Series a quarter century earlier—and the Cubs weren't about to let him forget it. Throughout the first two games, the Cubs were constantly provoking Moriarty. When Moriarty called Phil Cavarretta out on an attempted steal in the bottom of the sixth, Cub manager Charlie Grimm gave the ump an earful: so much so that Grimm was also ejected. This only increased the abuse from the Cubs' bench. Infielder Woody English and outfielder Tuck Stainback, both reserves, were kicked out of the game by Moriarty. Manager Grimm, it is said, was directing the assault through a hole in the wall behind the players' bench.

Detroit scored four in the eighth to take the lead, but the Cubs rallied to tie with two runs in the ninth. In the top of the 11th, Jo-Jo White singled in a run, and the Tigers held on to win. They also won Games 4 and 6 to earn their first world championship after Series losses in 1907, 1908, 1909 and 1934.

Most of the people in baseball take a philosophical attitude toward the admittedly rare blatant misses by umpires. Bill Stewart had been an NL arbiter for 16 years when he took up his post at second base for Game 1 of the 1948 Series between the Cleveland Indians and the Boston Braves. He was originally assigned to the plate, but George Barr, a more senior umpire, pulled rank. Stewart's day would have gone a lot better had he been behind the plate.

Cleveland's Bob Feller and Boston's Johnny Sain squared off in one of the finest Game 1 matchups ever. Through 7½ innings, Feller had allowed just one hit and one walk; Sain had given up four singles and had walked none. Catcher Bill Salkeld led off the bottom of the eighth by coaxing a second free pass off Feller. Phil Masi, also a catcher, but nowhere near as slow as Salkeld, ran for him. A bunt moved Masi to second, so Eddie Stanky was walked intentionally. With Sain at the plate, Feller spun and fired to Cleveland player-manager Lou Boudreau at second, who had sneaked in behind Masi. Everyone who saw the play thought Masi had been picked off to end the threat. Everyone, that is, but Bill Stewart, who called Masi safe. The Indians shouted and stomped, and Boudreau was particularly incensed. Feller got Sain on a liner to right for the second out, bringing up the dangerous Tommy Holmes, a .325 hitter during the regular season. Holmes singled, driving in Masi for the game's only run, and Feller lost a two-hitter.

Umpire George Moriarty (above, second from right) had played with the Tigers for seven years, so Cubs manager Charlie Grimm and his players were ready for controversy when they met the Tigers in the 1935 World Series with Moriarity a member of the crew. When Moriarity called Phil Cavarretta out trying to steal in the sixth inning of Game 3, Grimm and a posse of Cubs went out to argue, but to no avail.

Hall of Fame pitcher Bob Feller never won a World Series game, and if you ask former Indians player-manager Lou Boudreau, he'd probably say it was Bill Stewart's fault. Though the Braves' Phil Masi appeared to be out on an eighth-inning pickoff play (shown below and at right) at second in Game 1 of the 1948 Series, Stewart called him safe, and Boudreau—who made the tag—couldn't believe it. One out later, right fielder Tommy Holmes lined a single to score the game's only run.

Although instant replays were several decades away, photographs of the play seemed to indicate that Masi was out. When Indians owner Bill Veeck saw the photos, he said, "Very interesting, but the game is over."

Boudreau said later he had wanted to tip off Stewart that the Indians liked to use the pickoff move at second. Unfortunately, in the pregame meeting between the umps and the managers, Braves manager Billy Southworth was present, so Boudreau kept mum. Why Boudreau kept mum during the seven innings that he and Stewart stood next to each other in the infield is another issue.

For the second game, Stewart moved to first base and caught some more abuse from Indians fans. In the first inning, Boston took a 1–0 lead and had men on first and second when Bob Lemon attempted a pickoff at second on Earl Torgeson. It worked, Lemon settled down, and Cleveland won 4–1. Stewart was behind the plate for Game 3, and everyone found his work satisfactory.

But when he moved to third for Game 4, Stewart was put in a jam almost immediately. With one out in the bottom of the first, Boudreau hit a liner down the first-base line that scored Dale Mitchell, but strong relay throws from right fielder Tommy Holmes and shortstop Alvin Dark caught Boudreau as he tried to stretch his hit to three bases. Boudreau got up to argue once more, and Stewart did what umpires were trained to do; he turned his back and walked away, down the left field line. Boudreau chased him, screaming all the way that he had been safe, but to no avail. Once again, a Cleveland newspaper later produced photographic evidence to demonstrate Stewart's mistake. But the Tribe held no grudges. Bill Stewart ended his baseball career as a scout—for the Cleveland organization.

Everybody performs with a little more flair in the World Series, even the umpires. In Game 3 of the 1986 Series, umpire Harry Wendelstedt had an easy call as the Mets' Lenny Dykstra slid home safely while Red Sox catcher Rich Gedman tried to find the ball; Wendelstedt still gave an extra wide safe sign.

O ver the decades, the men in blue have had to deal with the changes in the game. Perhaps there is no better example of that than two umpiring decisions that displayed totally opposite responses to the same situation. The second game of the 1970 AL Championship Series featured a cold, blustery day in Minnesota's Metropolitan Stadium. Oriole manager Earl Weaver, always looking for an edge, suspected that Twins reliever Ron Perranoski might be using pine tar to get a better grip on the chilly baseball. Umpire Bill Haller checked the hurler's glove. Sure enough, he found the sticky stuff. Haller knew that—unlike a spitter, shiner or even a knuckler —using pine tar to help grip the ball doesn't make the pitch do anything unusual. So he ordered Perranoski to wipe off his glove before he threw a pitch. Perranoski did, and the game continued.

But baseball has since become oversensitized to the idea of "cheating." As a result, the umpires handled things much differently in 1988. On a cold, rainy day in Shea Stadium during that year's NLCS, Mets manager Davey Johnson accused Dodger reliever Jay Howell of pulling the same trick: using pine tar to get a better grip on the ball. Howell was caught, too, but Howell wasn't just asked to clean up his act, er, glove. He was ejected, and suspended for two games. The Dodger pitching coach at the time, by the way, was Ron Perranoski. ◑

Odd Men Out

Ernie Banks was famous for the quote, "Let's play two." But he would have settled for one —any one—if only it had come in the World Series. The man they called "Mr. Cub," who smashed 512 home runs in 19 seasons with Chicago and earned election to the Hall of Fame in his first year of eligibility, never played in a World Series. He wasn't alone.

Some Hall of Famers played before there was a World Series; others, like Philadelphia's Rube Waddell, were injured or unable to play when their teams went to the Series. That leaves nine other major league Hall of Famers—Luke Appling, Rick Ferrell, Harry Heilmann, George Kell, Ralph Kiner, Nap Lajoie, Ted Lyons, George Sisler and Banks' teammate, Billy Williams—on the wrong-place-at-the-wrong-time team. And the odds are that seven-time AL batting champ Rod Carew, and pitchers Ferguson Jenkins (another Cub), Gaylord Perry and Phil Niekro, will join them in Cooperstown.

Six of the ten current Hall of Famers are further linked, having played at least one season in Chicago: Banks, Williams and Kiner were Cubs; Appling, Lyons and Kell were White Sox.

The Cubs, perhaps baseball's most celebrated underachievers—their last Series was in 1945, their last world championship in 1908—seemed to have a shot at the Series in 1969, then endured one of the game's greatest collapses late in the season.

Banks retired two years later. Williams, a left fielder, was with the Cubs from 1959 to 1974. Like Banks, he was an incredibly consistent performer. His streak of 1,117 consecutive games played ranks fifth all-time; he hit over .300 five times and had at least 20 home runs for 13 straight seasons. After the 1974 season Williams was traded to the Oakland A's.

The A's won the AL West in 1975, but lost to the Red Sox in the playoffs, and Williams, denied again, quit a year later.

Luke Appling was a shortstop from 1930 to 1950 with the White Sox. Appling won two batting titles, and hit over .300 fifteen times, but his team never finished higher than third. The same was true for pitcher Ted Lyons, who won 260 games in a career that lasted from 1923 to 1946—less the three years he lost to military service in World War II. He even managed the Sox from 1946 to 1948, but the best he could do was fifth place.

In 1922 Lyons was offered a contract by the Philadelphia Athletics, but he rejected it to sign with the White Sox. Seven years later, just before the A's and the Cubs met in the Series, Lyons ran into Philadelphia manager Connie Mack in a Chicago hotel. "Young man, you see what would have happened if you had signed with us. You'd now be with a championship team," Mack said.

Ralph Kiner, a left fielder who won or shared seven consecutive home run titles, spent most of his ten-year career in Pittsburgh. He was hailed as "the franchise" by Pirates general manager Roy Hamey, but he could hardly carry Pittsburgh to a pennant by himself. From 1946 until he was traded to the Cubs early in 1953, the Pirates finished last or next to last five times.

Kiner often fondly recalls an exchange he had with Pirates vice president Branch Rickey. Kiner wanted more money, and used his home run numbers as ammunition. Rickey shot back: "We finished last with you, we can finish last without you."

Lajoie, a three-time batting champ whose .422 mark in 1901 is second all-time since 1900, was with the A's in 1902—for one game. He was traded to

With Ernie Banks (above), the Cubs never won a pennant and finished second only twice in 19 years. Without him, said Reds' coach Jimmie Dykes, "the Cubs would finish in Albuquerque." The first NL player ever to top 50 home runs in two seasons, Ralph Kiner (left) played the first 7½ years of his career in Pittsburgh, and in that time never got closer than 8½ games to the World Series.

In 1904 Napoleon Lajoie (above) led the American League in batting, slugging, hits, total bases, doubles and RBI, but his Indians finished fourth. Lajoie hit .381, the rest of the team hit .245.

From 1921 to 1929, Detroit's Harry Heilmann never hit lower than .328, and the Tigers never finished closer than six games out of first place.

Cleveland, which went on to finish fifth, while the A's won the pennant. Then, as player-manager with Cleveland in 1908, Lajoie directed the Naps—they were even named for him—to 90 wins, tying them for most wins in the league with Detroit. Unfortunately for Lajoie, the Tigers had one loss fewer because they never made up a game that had been rained out earlier in the season. Had they made the game up and lost, it would have forced a playoff. Cleveland's predicament led to what is known as the 1908 rule, which required teams to make up rain-outs or tie games that can affect a pennant race. The rule came too late for Lajoie, as Cleveland finished one-half game behind Detroit.

George Sisler's 1922 Browns came almost as close, falling one game short of the pennant-winning Yankees. The first baseman—who hit .420 that season—took a 41-game hitting streak into early September, when he suffered a shoulder injury. He missed four games, then his hitting fell off because he was still playing with shoulder pain. The injury likely cost St. Louis a World Series berth.

Catcher Rick Ferrell, who played in the majors from 1929 through 1947, divided his career among St. Louis, Boston and Washington. Although Ferrell hit over .300 for five seasons, his numbers—a career .281 batting average with 28 home runs—aren't Hall of Fame material, but he was elected on the basis of his fine defensive play.

Third baseman George Kell played with five teams in his 15-year career, starting with Philadelphia in 1943. In 1946 the A's traded Kell to Detroit, and he responded with a .322 average; for eight years in a row he hit over .300. And Kell was a solid third baseman who led the league in fielding percentage seven times. But the closest Kell came to postseason play was in 1946 and 1947, when the Tigers finished second.

Then there was the case of Harry Heilmann, who was with the Tigers for all but one season from 1914 through 1929. Although Heilmann won four batting titles in the 1920s, each time hitting at least .393, Detroit mustered only one distant second-place finish while he played there. Heilmann played for Cincinnati in 1930 and 1932, then rejoined the Tigers, just in time for Detroit's two consecutive World Series appearances in 1934 and 1935. But there was just one problem. By the time Heilmann returned to the Tigers, he was no longer their right fielder. He was their broadcaster.

Luke Appling never played in a World Series, but he did create some drama when, at age 73, he homered in a 1982 old-timers' game (above).

Unlike the other nine Hall of Famers who never got in a World Series, Billy Williams (above) did play in postseason. But his experience was pretty bleak, as his 1975 A's lost 3–0 to Boston in the ALCS. George Kell (below) played third base for five teams in 15 years—he hit .306 lifetime—three times finishing second.

George Sisler was a monster talent—a two-time .400 hitter and perhaps the finest fielding first baseman in history. But he played mostly for the St. Louis Browns, who won their only pennant in 1944—14 years after Sisler retired—and then, only because World War II had robbed the majors of most of its talented players.

The Ruling Class

The first modern World Series, in 1903, featured a National League team that had won three consecutive pennants—the Pittsburgh Pirates. But standout starters Jesse Tannehill and Jack Chesbro jumped from the Pirates to the American League New York Highlanders after the 1902 season, and 24-game winner Deacon Phillippe wasn't enough to stop the upstart Boston Pilgrims from winning the Series five games to three. Giants manager John McGraw refused to play the AL champion Pilgrims in 1904 but agreed to a best-of-seven contest against the Philadelphia Athletics in 1905 under the John T. Brush rules, which had stabilized relations between the two leagues. The rest of that decade was dominated by a pair of World Series dynasties.

In 1906 the Chicago Cubs made their first World Series appearance. Managed by first baseman Frank Chance, "the Peerless Leader," the Cubs won 116 and lost only 36 for a .763 winning percentage—an unbreakable record. Their pitching staff was dominant, with Orval Overall, Mordecai Brown, Ed Reulbach and Jack Pfiester, who earned the nickname "Jack the Giant Killer" for his lifetime mastery—15–5—over the Cubs' major rival, the New York Giants. Johnny Kling was an intelligent catcher with a .312 average. The outfielders—Wildfire Schulte in right, Jimmy Slagle in center and Jimmy Sheckard in left—were "fleet-footed gazelles." With third baseman Harry Steinfeldt, the Cubs had power: Steinfeldt led the league in RBI that year.

Only two stadiums fly flags of three or more consecutive world champions—New York's Yankee Stadium and the Oakland Coliseum (opposite). The A's won from 1972 through 1974; the Yanks were champs from 1936 through 1939, and from 1949 through 1953.

Center fielder Ty Cobb (at bat, above) was the cornerstone of an ill-fated Detroit Tiger dynasty in the early 1900s. The Tigers won three straight pennants from 1907 to 1909, then lost three straight World Series, including two to the Chicago Cubs.

The Cubs were pitted against their crosstown AL rivals, the White Sox, and it didn't look as if it would be much of a contest. While the fearsome Cubs had led the league in runs, hits, triples, RBI, batting average and slugging percentage, the Sox had the lowest batting average in the league; despite stalwart pitching—they allowed the fewest runs in the league, had 32 shutouts and allowed the fewest walks—it took a 19-game winning streak in August to get them to the top. The only offensive category they led was walks received, which is how they earned their nickname, "the Hitless Wonders."

Game 1 was a 2–1 pitching duel between the Cubs' Three Finger Brown and the Sox' Nick Altrock, with both Sox runs scoring as a result of misplays by the usually reliable Johnny Kling. The Cubs' Ed Reulbach thought he had put the White Sox in their place when he tossed a one-hitter at them the next day. The pitching-dominated Series continued through Games 3 and 4, as the Sox' Ed Walsh and the Cubs' Brown traded two-hit wins.

But the White Sox' anemic hitting disappeared in Game 5. They exploded for 12 hits—and overcame a record six errors—in an 8–6 win. They continued their solid hitting in the final game, pounding Three Finger Brown —who had allowed only one earned run in 18 innings in the Series—for six earned runs in an inning and two-thirds. The Sox clinched the Series with an 8–3 win, as first baseman Jiggs Donahue and shortstop George Davis each had three RBI. The winningest club in major league history had been defeated by a power outburst from "the Hitless Wonders," in one of the most surprising Series of all time.

But the Cubs were back in 1907. Although they won "only" 107 times, they outdistanced the second-place Pirates by 17 games. The White Sox weren't back, beaten in an exciting pennant race by the fiery Detroit Tigers.

"HUGHIE" AND HIS TIGERS.

PENNANT.

The Tigers were led by rookie manager Hughie Jennings, a spunky, noisy fireplug who played with John McGraw for the old Baltimore Orioles. Jennings' rugged personality was perfect for this team, which included hitting stars Ty Cobb and Sam Crawford and pitchers Wild Bill Donovan, George Mullin, Ed Killian and Ed Siever, all 20-game winners except Siever, who had won a mere 18.

But the Detroit fire cooled quickly in the Series. Game 1 was called a 3–3 tie after 12 innings because of darkness, and the Tigers never got close again. The Cubs smacked them with four straight losses—the first World Series in which the losing team did not win a single game. Ty Cobb managed only four hits for a woeful .200 average.

The same two teams met in 1908, the first time that back-to-back pennant winners faced each other in the Series. The Tigers had shown their toughness, beating the White Sox on the final day of the season to clinch the AL pennant. The NL race was even tighter, arguably the most remarkable pennant race in history. To win it, the Cubs had to defeat the Pirates on the last day of the season, then whip the Giants in a replay of the legendary tie game in which Fred Merkle forgot to step on second base.

Losing 6–5 in Game 1, the Cubs wrapped six consecutive hits around a double steal in the ninth and scored five times. The Tigers, behind Ty Cobb's clutch hitting—in this Series he batted .368—won Game 3, but that was all. Orval Overall and Three Finger Brown each won two games and five Cubs batted over .300. The tempestuous Tigers had lost again.

In 1909 the Cubs' string ended; their 104 wins weren't enough to top the Pirates' 110. But the Tigers returned. The 1909 Series was the first to go seven full games; it was also the first Series in which the two league batting

As player and manager, Hughie Jennings was associated with two early dynasties. He played shortstop in three NL championships with the Baltimore Orioles from 1894 to 1896, then managed the Tigers to three straight AL pennants from 1907 to 1909.

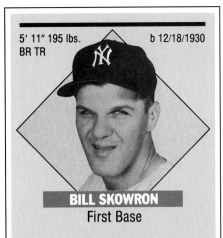

5′ 11″ 195 lbs. b 12/18/1930
BR TR

BILL SKOWRON
First Base

When Bill Skowron was a 21-year-old in the Yankee farm system, his stature and power had scouts comparing him to Rogers Hornsby and Ted Williams. That was the kind of player he was—sometimes. Casey Stengel, who managed Skowron for seven of his nine seasons, described the big first baseman more accurately when he said, "This fella can hit .500 one week and .200 the next. The only trouble is you're never sure what week he's in."

Skowron was full of inconsistencies. Nicknamed "Moose" as a child because he resembled Italian dictator Benito Mussolini, he was known as one of the gentlest men in the game. His swing was so ugly it could make a batting instructor cry, but he sent balls sailing to the reaches of ballparks that only men like Gehrig and Foxx had assaulted before. His muscles had muscles, but he once injured himself stooping to pick up his glove, and virtually never had an injury-free season.

The .500 hitter that Stengel talked about always performed when he was needed most. His World Series batting average was .293, and he homered in a seventh Series game on three separate occasions. His eight Series homers rank seventh on the all-time list.

But Skowron's coolness in the clutch wasn't always a blessing to the Yankees. In 1962 he was traded to Los Angeles, and in the 1963 Series he went 5 for 13 as the Dodgers beat the Yanks in four games.

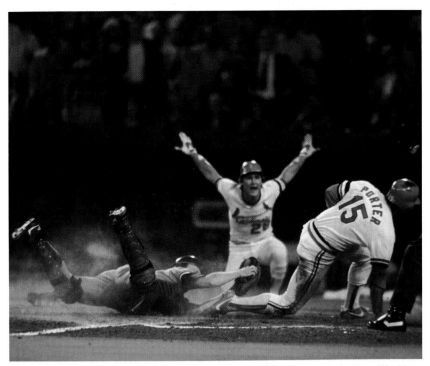

With speed as a primary weapon, the St. Louis Cardinals earned spots in three World Series in the 1980s. Even catchers like Darrell Porter (above, right) ran the bases aggressively. In each of their pennant years, the Cards led the NL in stolen bases.

champions played against each other—Ty Cobb of the Tigers and Honus Wagner of the Bucs. The other batting-champion face-offs occurred in 1931, with the Athletics' Al Simmons facing the Cardinals' Chick Hafey, and in 1954, when the Indians' Bobby Avila challenged the Giants' Willie Mays.

Ty Cobb hit just .231 and stole only two bases, but he electrified the crowd in Game 2 by stealing home on Pirate reliever Vic Willis' first pitch. Wagner hit .333 and swiped six bases in the toughest Series to date. The teams alternated wins, with plenty of aggressive baserunning and spikings. When Pittsburgh rookie Babe Adams completed a six-hit shutout for his third complete-game win in the Series, the Tigers became the only team in history to lose three straight World Series.

For World Series streaks, no team comes close to the sheer domination of the Yankees in the 1920s, 1936 through 1939, and 1949 through 1953. Paced by the young Babe Ruth, the Yankees won their first AL pennant in 1921, lost the Series to the Giants that year and the next and beat them in 1923. The Yankees had another three-year Series cycle starting in 1926, with their legendary Murderers' Row—Ruth, Gehrig, Meusel and Lazzeri. The 1930s Yankee team was full of legendary baseball names: Gehrig, DiMaggio, Lazzeri, Dickey, Keller, Gomez, Ruffing. They won the AL pennant every year from 1936 to 1939, averaging 102 wins a season. In 1936 and 1937, the Yanks battered the Giants, winning the first Series in six games and the second in five, outscoring Bill Terry's men by an amazing 71 runs to 35. Then the Bronx Bombers got serious, sweeping the Cubs in 1938 and the Reds in 1939, making them 16–3 in World Series play over four years.

The Yanks who won five straight series from 1949 through 1953 were no less impressive. Joe DiMaggio still led the offense and played peerless defense through 1951. Aiding him were shortstop Phil Rizzuto, outfielders Hank Bauer and Gene Woodling, catcher Yogi Berra and first baseman Johnny Mize. In 1951 a new face entered the Yankee lineup: a combination of speed and power the like of which no one had ever seen—Oklahoma's own Mickey Mantle. Allie Reynolds, Vic Raschi and Eddie Lopat were the mainstays of the pitching staff, with Joe Page supplying excellent relief. The Dodgers went down in five games in the 1949 Series, while the Phillies scored just five runs in four straight losses in 1950. In 1951 the Yankees faced the amazing New York Giants, who had stormed back from 13½ games out of first to push the Dodgers into a three-game playoff that ended on Bobby Thomson's "Shot Heard 'Round the World." But the Giants didn't have much left for the Series and fell in six.

In 1952 the Yankees were pushed to a seventh game for only the third time in 19 Series. The talented Brooklyn Dodgers were not quite up to victory. In 1953 the Yanks and the Dodgers met again, this time with Billy Martin a batting star. He hit .500 and drove in the Series-clinching run for the Yankees in the ninth inning of Game 6.

It took 111 wins by the Cleveland Indians in 1954 to snap the Yanks' streak of AL pennants, but the Yankees returned in 1955 and—except for 1959—stayed in the World Series through 1964. But in that ten-year span fate wasn't as kind to the Yanks as in their previous Series strings.

In 1955 the Dodgers' World Series record was 0–7, five of which they had lost to the Yankees. But they finally broke through in 1955, behind the left arm of 23-year-old Johnny Podres.

There's one shower no pitcher minds hitting, and Oakland pitchers Catfish Hunter (center) and Rollie Fingers enjoyed three straight from 1972 to 1974. Hunter won 67 games during that period, and when he did need relief, it was usually Fingers—with 61 saves in the three title seasons—who finished up.

Whitey Ford

In 1961 Roger Maris' pursuit of Babe Ruth's home run record almost obscured Whitey Ford's best year. On a four-day rotation with the Yankees, Ford garnered a league-leading 25 wins and an .862 winning percentage. When he pitched his 32nd consecutive scoreless inning in World Series play, Ford, like Maris, broke a record that belonged to Ruth. Typically, Whitey didn't gloat. He quipped, "Poor Babe. This has been a tough year for him."

For 16 seasons the 5' 10", 180-pound pitcher proved to be a fierce competitor with a playful soul. Catcher Johnny Blanchard recalls one time that Ford called him to the mound: "I started thinking that something must be wrong, he must be hurt. Then I started thinking about how much trouble we would be in without Whitey. So I asked, 'Whitey, what's wrong?' 'Nothing.' 'Then why bring me out here?' 'I figured you could use a break.' "

Ford, the blithe spirit, once perched a pet iguana on the bullpen mound, named his pet poodle "Casey" after the Yankee manager, and told Dizzy Dean: "No wonder you won 30 games pitching in that crummy National League. I could win 40 in that league myself."

Ford, the rugged competitor, posted a .690 career winning percentage. Veteran catcher Gus Triandos said, "I don't think I get two hits a year off the son of a gun. I just can't time him. He's got about four speeds and that blankety-blank curve ball. And he never stops working on you. . . . He just battles."

Ford's repertoire included a sneaky, sinking fastball, a slow curve that doubled as a change-up, and, later, a slider that helped him gain a career-high 209 strikeouts in 1961. However, his greatest asset may have been guile. "I saw Whitey get power hitters out by throwing three straight belt-high fastballs," said relief pitcher Ryne Duren. At times he preferred trickery to psychology. Occasionally, he would spit into his glove while the umpire threw out a new ball: instant spitter. A ring he claimed to be his wedding band was actually employed to scrape balls. Even after the umpires caught on, contends Tony Kubek, Ford may have doctored the ball "just to give hitters something else to think about."

Edward Charles Ford grew up in the working-class Astoria section of Queens, New York. He played street stickball until he was old enough to play baseball. In 1946 he tried out for the Yankees as a first baseman. He received no consideration, but a Yankee scout told him, "Stop thinking about first base . . . even when you're just throwing the ball around, you're pitching curves."

Eventually, he signed with the Yankees for $7,000 and made a smashing debut in 1950 with a 9–1 record. Through 1967, Ford set nine Yankee records and 14 World Series marks that still stand. He holds Series records for games started with 22, wins with ten and strikeouts with 94.

One May night in 1967, when he felt he could no longer win, he walked off the mound and cleaned out his locker. The man Yankee Elston Howard called "the Chairman of the Board" retired just like that.

In the mid-1980s, Mickey Mantle remembered flubbing a fly that cost Ford his 20th victory on the last day of the 1956 season. Mantle recalled, "He came up to me and said, 'Ah, Mick, the heck with it. We'll get 'em.' And Whitey meant it; that's why players loved him."

Whitey Ford checked in at just 5' 10", but when October rolled around, he stood taller than any other pitcher in history. His World Series record of 33 consecutive scoreless innings still stands. "Ford had the guts of a burglar," said scout Fresco Thompson.

WHITEY FORD

Left-Handed Pitcher
New York Yankees 1950, 1953–1967
Hall of Fame 1974

GAMES	**498**
INNINGS	
Career	**3,170⅓**
Season High	**283**
WINS	
Career	**236**
Season High	**25**
LOSSES	
Career	**106**
Season High	**13**
WINNING PERCENTAGE	
Career *(3rd all time)*	**.690**
Season High	**.862**
ERA	
Career	**2.75**
Season Low	**2.01**
GAMES STARTED	
Career	**438**
Season High	**39**
COMPLETE GAMES	
Career	**156**
Season High	**18**
SHUTOUTS	
Career	**45**
Season High	**8**
STRIKEOUTS	
Career	**1,956**
Season High	**209**
WALKS	
Career	**1,086**
Season High	**113**
WORLD SERIES	**1950, 1953, 1955–1958, 1960–1964**
CY YOUNG AWARD	**1961**

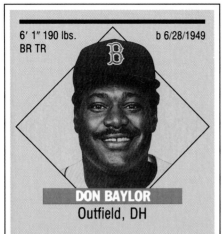

6' 1" 190 lbs.
BR TR

b 6/28/1949

DON BAYLOR
Outfield, DH

Outfielder-turned-designated hitter Don Baylor had played in the major leagues 17 years when he finally made it to the World Series with the Boston Red Sox in 1986. Then he did it as a Minnesota Twin the next year, and again with Oakland in 1988. No one before or since has played in three consecutive World Series on three different teams.

In the mid-1970s Baylor became a high-salaried free agent. He paid off for the Angels with an MVP year in 1979, when he hit 36 homers, scored a league-leading 120 runs and knocked in an AL decade-leading 139 RBI. But Baylor had a problem—a throwing arm described as being "as useful as adenoids."

By the time Baylor made it to the World Series, he was a DH and had distinguished himself as the player hit by more pitches—267—than any other. He had a bull's-eye printed on his T-shirt.

Early in his career, Baylor said, "the single most important thing to me is to win the World Series." The 1986 Bosox and the 1988 A's were Series losers, but Baylor got his glory with the Twins in 1987 against the St. Louis Cardinals. The Cards had a 3–2 Series lead. In the fifth inning of Game 6, with a man on second and the Twins behind by two runs, Baylor sent southpaw John Tudor's first pitch sailing into the left field seats to tie the game. The Twins went on to win, and the following evening they became world champions.

Joe DiMaggio hit his first World Series home run in Game 5 of the 1937 World Series (above) as the Yankees clinched their second straight world title. His last Series homer came 14 years later, in his tenth and final Series.

Podres took an unspectacular 9–10 season into the Series, but he turned the tide in Game 3, giving up seven scattered hits in an 8–3 win, Brooklyn's first of the Series. Homers by Roy Campanella, Gil Hodges and Duke Snider backed an 8–5 Dodger win in Game 4, and another youngster, 24-year-old Roger Craig, outdueled the Yankees' Bob Grim in Game 5 to give the Dodgers a 3–2 edge. But Whitey Ford stopped the Brooklyn offense cold in Game 6, allowing just four hits in a 5–1 win. Podres took the ball again for Game 7 against the Yankees' Tommy Byrne, who went 16–5 during the regular season. Although Byrne, Grim and Bob Turley combined to allow just two runs—one earned—on five hits, Podres was better. He shut out the Yankees on eight hits, with a big hand from Sandy Amoros, whose spectacular catch in the sixth inning of Game 7 finally brought "next year" to Brooklyn.

When the two teams met again in 1956, the Bums took the first two games: one a Sal Maglie win over Whitey Ford, the other a 13–8 thrashing when Don Larsen couldn't hold a six-run lead. Then Yankee pitching took over. Ford beat Roger Craig, 5–3, and Tom Sturdivant tied the Series with a six-hitter in Game 4. Don Larsen's 97-pitch perfect game gave the Yankees a spectacular edge, but the Dodgers won Game 6 when Enos Slaughter misplayed Jackie Robinson's tenth-inning single for the game's only run. The Game 7 scenario was familiar, as a 23-year-old took the mound for the biggest game of his life and was superb. But this time the youngster wore pinstripes, and Johnny Kucks' three-hit shutout gave the Yankees a 9–0 win and their 17th world championship.

Milwaukee's Lew Burdette stopped the Yankees three times in the 1957 Series, including another Game 7 shutout. But revenge came the fol-

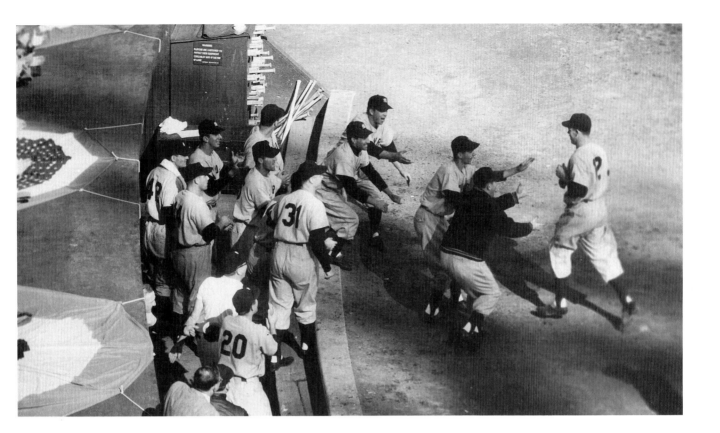

lowing season: the Yankees beat Burdette twice in 1958, including a 6–2 pounding in Game 7 of that year's Series.

The Yankee Series seesaw continued in 1960, when they hit .338 as a team, outscored the Pirates 55–27, and managed to come up empty when Bill Mazeroski's ninth-inning homer in Game 7 brought an improbable Series to an impossible conclusion. Many of the Yankees blamed their loss on poor decisions by manager Casey Stengel, and Stengel "retired" after the Series with a World Series managerial record that will be tough to top: ten appearances, seven wins.

E xpansion came to baseball in 1961, and watered-down pitching staffs livened up the offensive action. The Yankees set a record with 240 home runs, helped by Roger Maris' crowning achievement of 61 and Mantle's 54. The NL winners were the Cincinnati Reds, whose pitching staff, led by Joey Jay, 21–10, Jim O'Toole, 19–9, and Bob Purkey, 16–12, led the league in both shutouts and saves. Some felt the inevitable tide of history at work. The Pirates had avenged their embarrassing four-game 1927 sweep at the hands of the Yanks; now it was the Reds' turn to pay the Yankees in kind for their sweep of the 1939 Series.

It wasn't to be. The Reds couldn't score on Whitey Ford in 14 innings, as the Yankee southpaw ran his World Series shutout string to a record 32 innings. Cincinnati won just one game, and the Yankees had, for the sixth time, rebounded from a Series loss to become world champions the following year. Stengel's replacement, Ralph Houk, became the third rookie manager to win a Series, after Washington's Bucky Harris in 1924 and the Cardinals' Eddie Dyer in 1946.

From 1949 to 1953 the Yankee juggernaut mashed its World Series opponents into pulp. The Yanks won 20 games and lost only eight. One of their most decisive wins was a 13–1 laugher against the Giants in 1951 that featured a grand slam by Gil McDougald (above).

From 1947 through 1953, Jackie Robinson and the Brooklyn Dodgers managed to get into four World Series and managed to lose all four to the Yankees. Two years later, in 1955, Robinson hit just .182 in the Series, but his aggressive baserunning (above, in Game 3) helped the Dodgers end the Yankee jinx in seven games.

Another familiar scenario ushered in the 1962 Series, as the Giants beat the Dodgers in a three-game playoff for the right to meet the Yankees. The teams traded wins for the first six games, setting the stage for a classic Game 7, which 23-game winner Ralph Terry won for the Yanks.

The next year the unthinkable happened. The Yanks weren't just beaten in the Series; they were swept, scoring only four runs in four games against the Los Angeles Dodger pitching machine paced by Sandy Koufax, Don Drysdale and a familiar foe from an earlier era, Johnny Podres.

In 1964 the Yankees made their 15th Series appearance in 18 years, though they barely made it, winning the pennant on the next-to-last day of the season. The Cardinals cut it even closer, clinching the NL pennant in the season's final game. The Series itself was as tight as the pennant races. The Yankees scored one more run and had one less hit than the Cardinals over the seven games, but they lost their second consecutive World Series for the first time in 42 years. It took them 12 years to get back to the Series in 1976, but two years later, the Yankees became the last team to play in three consecutive World Series.

The Philadelphia Athletics, who had been beaten by New York in the all-shutout Series of 1905, returned to the championship in 1910 and whipped the Cubs in five. The Athletics featured great pitchers: Chief Bender and Jack Coombs—16-game winner Eddie Plank wasn't needed. Future Hall of Famers Eddie Collins and Frank Baker manned second and third, and hit .429 and .409 in the Series. In 1911 and 1913, the Athletics met stiffer competition in the Series. The New York Giants players matched the intensity of their manager John McGraw, and the team boasted a pitching

staff led by the inimitable Christy Mathewson and Rube Marquard. The Athletics' manager was a man of a different sort—the genteel, noble Connie Mack, who rarely displayed emotion and never left the bench. In fact, he wouldn't wear a uniform, appearing instead in a business suit.

After Mathewson beat Bender 2–1 in Game 1 in 1911, Frank Baker homered to win Game 2. He homered off Mathewson in the top of the ninth to tie Game 3, and two Giant errors gave the Athletics the win in the 11th. Then it rained for six days, and when the skies cleared, the sufficiently rested Mathewson took the mound again for the Giants in Game 4, and lost again. The Giants had to score two runs in the last of the ninth to tie Game 5, before winning it in the tenth. But Philadelphia pounded Leon Ames, Hooks Wiltse and Rube Marquard for 13 hits and a 13–2 win in the sixth and final game.

McGraw's Giants lost again in 1912—stifled by Snodgrass' muff and Red Sox ace Smoky Joe Wood—then limped into the 1913 Series against Philadelphia. Christy Mathewson, as usual, pitched spectacularly, allowing only two earned runs in 19 innings. But with center fielder Snodgrass, catcher Chief Meyers and first baseman Fred Merkle injured, he managed just one win, and his 3–1 loss in Game 5 clinched the Series for the Athletics. McGraw's fabled Giants had lost three Series in a row. The Athletics went on to win the pennant again in 1914, but they severely underestimated the "Miracle Braves," who then swept them in four Series games.

Philadelphia stayed in the AL cellar for seven years, then began a slow uphill climb, as the unflappable Connie Mack assembled a new team of stars piece by piece. Scrappy Jimmy Dykes became a regular infielder, and Mack's talent hunt turned up three future Hall of Famers: outfielder Al Simmons, who became a regular in 1924 and hit .384 the next year, catcher Mickey

From 1966 to 1983 no team in baseball was as consistently successful as the Baltimore Orioles. They won eight AL East titles, six pennants and three World Series. The third came in 1983, as catcher Rick Dempsey (above) hit .385 and Oriole pitchers allowed just nine runs in five games.

The Big Red Machine was supposed to win the World Series in 1970, but lost to Brooks Robinson and the Orioles. The Reds were supposed to win again in 1972, but lost to Gene Tenace and the A's. The 1975 Series against Boston was an emotional rollercoaster, and when the Reds finally won it, they performed a dance of pure joy across the field at Fenway Park.

6' 192 lbs. b 7/31/1922
BR TR

HANK BAUER
Outfield

Voted by his teammates the "man most likely to succeed in a free-for-all," ex-Marine Hank "the Bruiser" Bauer had more than his share of scraps during his tenure with the Yankee dynasty. The Bruiser started with New York in 1948 and wore pinstripes for the next 12 years, during which he appeared in nine World Series. He clubbed four home runs in the 1958 fall classic, and hit safely in a record 17 consecutive Series games. He played in a total 53 Series games, which ranks him fourth on the all-time Series list.

Bauer's only natural gifts were a body immune to injury and a face that has been described as looking like a clenched fist. Everything else was the product of hard work. Early in his career, Bauer served a lot of bench time —a victim of manager Casey Stengel's platoon system. But the Bruiser began the 1955 season by saying that he was determined to "whack that platoon thing out of whack." Bauer proceeded to hit 20 home runs, and then batted .429 in the seven-game Series against the Brooklyn Dodgers.

In 1959 Bauer was traded to the Kansas City A's, where he became player-manager in 1961 and manager in 1962. Two years later, he became the Baltimore Orioles' pilot and led them to a world championship in 1966. With the arrival of Earl Weaver in 1968, Bauer lost his job, but not his desire to be a winner. An amiable fan once informed him that the law of averages says you have to lose sometimes. "I know that," Bauer shot back, "but there's no law that says you have to like it."

About the only wrong move the Yankees made in 1928 was backing Al Smith for president. With a lineup featuring Lou Gehrig (holding the "R"), Tony Lazzeri ("A"), Earle Combs ("I") and Babe Ruth ("T"), the Yanks swept the Cards in the Series.

Cochrane and pitcher Lefty Grove. George Earnshaw and Rube Walberg joined Grove in the rotation, and the Athletics finished second in 1925, third in 1926, then second again in 1927 and 1928, before unseating the second-place Yanks by 18 games in 1929. That was the year first baseman Jimmie Foxx hit 33 homers and Simmons led the league with 157 RBI. The Athletics were a team of monstrous talent.

Joe McCarthy's 1929 Cubs had power, too: a .303 team batting average. Four Cubs had over 100 RBI, led by Hack Wilson, whose 159 RBI led the majors. Second baseman Rogers Hornsby matched Wilson's 39 homers and batted .380, while left fielder Riggs Stephenson hit .362, and right fielder Kiki Cuyler, .360. But while the Cubs were a very good team, the Athletics were a great one. The Cubs had a chance to tie the Series at two games each when they took an 8–0 lead in Game 4, but collapsed in the seventh as the Athletics scored a Series-record ten runs. Chicago blew another late lead in Game 5, as a two-run homer by Philadelphia's Mule Haas tied the score, and a double by Bing Miller scored teammate Simmons to win the Series.

In 1930 the Athletics topped 100 wins for the second straight year, then dispatched the Cardinals in six games. The big slugging of the 1929 Series was gone—Philadelphia batted just .197—but they had power when they needed it, belting six homers, and pitchers Earnshaw and Grove each won twice. In 1931 the Athletics won 107 games, and only the Cardinals stood between them and an unprecedented third straight world title. But the 1931 Cardinals had something the 1930 Cardinals didn't—Pepper Martin. Martin put on one of the greatest individual shows in World Series history by batting .500 and stealing five bases, and the Athletics ran out of luck in Game 7.

In the late 1960s, a new team arose to play in three consecutive Series—the Baltimore Orioles. The Orioles, whose young and stellar pitching staff had shut down the vaunted Dodgers four straight in the 1966 Series, reappeared in 1969. An injury to the brightest of their young hurlers, Jim Palmer, had kept them out of the running in 1967 and 1968, but when Palmer returned, he joined Mike Cuellar and Dave McNally as baseball's best starting trio. The defense was excellent, with Gold Glovers Davey Johnson, Mark Belanger and Brooks Robinson at second, short and third. The outfield was speedy, with Frank Robinson and Don Buford flanking another Gold Glove winner, Paul Blair. Boog Powell and Frank Robinson provided power: each hit more than thirty homers and drove in at least 100 runs. Manager Earl Weaver's well-balanced, immensely talented team won 109 games during the regular season, then swept Minnesota in the first American League Championship Series. But when the World Series began, the O's faced a team that had destiny sitting on its bench. The New York Mets had surprised everyone, first by winning the NL East, then by sweeping the Braves in the NLCS.

The Mets' "miracle" seemed to have stalled when Cuellar handled them easily in Game 1. But pitcher Jerry Koosman and light-hitting second baseman Al Weis got it going in Game 2, and center fielder Tommie Agee took over in Game 3 with a homer and two amazing catches. The Mets took Game 4, with a 2–1, ten-inning win. The next day the Orioles took their final spill as the Miracle Mets scored five runs in the last three innings to win, 5–3. The amazing New York Mets had toppled the potent Baltimore Orioles.

In 1970 the O's won 108 games and again swept Minnesota in the ALCS. Their World Series opponents were a young Cincinnati Reds team, destined

Power-hitting first baseman Willie McCovey played in just one World Series in 19 years with the San Francisco Giants, but his vicious line drive in the ninth inning of Game 7 almost won it. Unfortunately for the Giants, McCovey's shot was hit right at Yankee second baseman Bobby Richardson, and the Giants lost the 1962 Series by a run.

Almost Champs

Almost doesn't count in the majors, but it does produce some collectors' items. Baseball tradition—and practicality—dictated that as each year's pennant races heated up, teams with reasonable shots at making the World Series printed tickets and programs and stamped out pins in anticipation of a spot in the fall classic. Nowadays, the commissioner's office works with teams to decide when and if to print playoff and World Series tickets, which then go on sale to season ticket holders and the public. If a team doesn't make the playoffs, all ticket holders are entitled to a refund, but some keep the tickets as souvenirs. This provides a hefty profit margin for the teams that sold the tickets, but hardly makes up for the revenue—and excitement—that accompanies a spot in the playoffs and World Series.

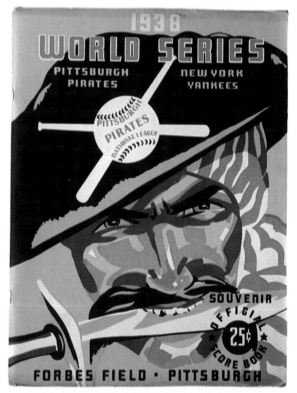

A late-September sweep by the Cubs over the Pirates—including Gabby Hartnett's famous "Homer in the Gloaming"—helped keep the Pirates out of the 1938 World Series and these programs out of circulation.

World Series pins and tickets for teams that don't make the Series find their way into the hands of collectors each season, but not programs anymore. Since the late 1970s, Major League Baseball has printed—during the league championship series—a generic World Series program that features all four division winners.

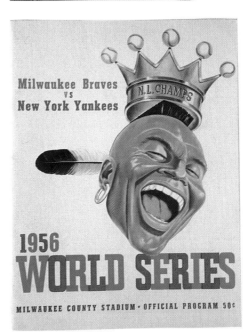

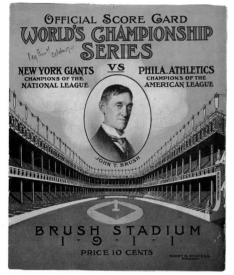

The 1911 World Series featured two powerhouse teams led by two of the game's greatest managers. The Giants' John McGraw led the Athletics' Connie Mack in pennants won, 10–9, but Mack came out a winner in two of their three World Series meetings, beating McGraw's Giants in six games in 1911 and in five in 1913. Instead of featuring a team portrait or logo, the 1911 World Series program honored the man who paid the bills from 1903 to 1912, Giants owner John T. Brush.

Hat Tricks

For a single team to play in three consecutive World Series is rare—it has happened just 16 times in baseball history. The New York Yankees take all-time honors and are the only team to play in five straight Series, which they did twice.

Chicago Cubs	1906–08
Detroit Tigers	1907–09
New York Giants	1911–13, 1921–24
New York Yankees	1921–23, 1926–28, 1936–39, 1941–43, 1949–53, 1955–58, 1960–64, 1976–78
Philadelphia Athletics	1929–31
St. Louis Cardinals	1942–44
Baltimore Orioles	1969–71
Oakland A's	1972–74

There have been a few near misses: the Philadelphia Athletics won four pennants in the five seasons of 1910 through 1914, and the Brooklyn Dodgers played in World Series six times from 1947 through 1956. In the 1970s the Cincinnati Reds played in 1970, 1972, 1975 and 1976. The Oakland A's played in the 1988 and 1989 Series.

to become one of the best teams of the decade. But Reds pitching was slim, Brooks Robinson hit and caught everything in sight, and the Orioles won in five games. In 1971 the Orioles became only the fourth AL team to play in three straight World Series, facing another young and powerful opponent in the Pittsburgh Pirates. The consensus was that Pittsburgh didn't have much of a chance. Dave McNally held the Pirates to three hits in Game 1, and Baltimore's 11–3 win in Game 2 was called by Red Smith "the grisliest parody of sport since the Pirates of 1960 were flogged by the Yankees...and wound up as champions of the world."

But the Pirates counterattacked. Steve Blass three-hit the Orioles in Game 3, and Bruce Kison's 6⅓ innings of one-hit relief sparked a 4–3 comeback win in Game 4, the first night World Series game. Pittsburgh's Nelson Briles threw a two-hitter in Game 5, but the Orioles answered with a 3–2, ten-inning win to force a seventh game. Steve Blass again played the hero for Pittsburgh with a four-hitter behind Roberto Clemente's sparkling play—he hit .414 and slugged .759—for a 2–1 clincher and Blass' second complete World Series-game win. The Orioles dropped to 2–2 in World Series play.

Two more teams managed three straight trips to the Series in the 1970s—the 1972–1974 Oakland A's and the 1976–1978 New York Yankees. The brash A's were unified in their dislike of their overbearing owner, Charles O. Finley. They wore handlebar mustaches and long hair, and when they faced the clean-cut Reds in 1972, Cincinnati manager Sparky Anderson was heard to cluck, "Millions of kids watch these games on television and the players can be a great influence on the kids." But long hair wasn't the point; winning was, and though the A's were outscored 21–16,

The Philadelphia Athletics won three straight pennants from 1929 to 1931 largely on the brilliance of four future Hall of Famers. First baseman Jimmie Foxx (left) and outfielder Al Simmons were run-producing machines—in 1930 they combined for 321 RBI. And the awards never stopped for the battery of catcher Mickey Cochrane (below, left) and pitcher Lefty Grove (below, right). Cochrane won Most Valuable Player awards in 1928 and 1934, while Grove was MVP in 1931.

they won the Series in seven games largely on the strength of Gene Tenace's four home runs and Rollie Fingers' brilliant relief.

The Mets returned to the Series in 1973, having won the NL East with the lowest winning percentage in history—.509. But they outlasted the Reds in the NLCS, then battled Oakland through seven grueling games, with A's reliever Darold Knowles seeing action in each one.

In Game 1, Ken Holtzman outdueled Jon Matlack, 2–1, to give the A's a 1–0 lead. Game 2 was a circus, featuring six errors and 11 pitchers. The Mets came back from a 3–2 deficit with four runs in the sixth, then the A's tied it with two in the ninth, the last on a single by the A's Mr. October, Gene Tenace. A two-out RBI single in the 12th by Willie Mays—his last major league hit—gave the Mets the lead, and two errors by Oakland second baseman Mike Andrews gave them the game. Game 3 also went into extra innings, and Oakland won when Met catcher Jerry Grote reminded historians of Boss Schmidt and Mickey Owen; he dropped a third strike to Angel Mangual, which enabled runner Ted Kubiak to advance to second and then to score on a Bert Campaneris single. The Mets took Games 4 and 5 to go up 3–2 in the Series, but Catfish Hunter outdueled Tom Seaver in Game 6 for Oakland to even the Series. Game 7 was decided early, as both Campaneris and Reggie Jackson hit two-run homers for the A's in the third. The Mets never recovered, and Oakland repeated as world champion.

Quiet, Bible-quoting Alvin Dark replaced fiery Dick Williams as Oakland's manager in 1974, but the A's didn't change. They were still battling each other in the clubhouse and beating the opposition on the field. After beating the Orioles for the second straight time in the ALCS, they turned to the Dodgers and the first all-California World Series. The Dodgers were on

Every aspiring dynasty needs a trademark, and for the 1988–1989 Oakland A's, it was the forearm bash, as practiced at right by catcher Terry Steinbach (36) and center fielder Dave Henderson (42). The A's bashed opponents to the tune of 104 wins in 1988, and 99 in 1989, becoming the first team to win back-to-back pennants since the 1977–1978 Yankees.

The Pittsburgh Pirates won six NL East titles in the 1970s, and Willie Stargell swung a big bat on all of them. Stargell averaged 32 homers during the division title years, and homered three times in the Pirates' 1979 Series win over Baltimore.

the verge of becoming a powerhouse, and made the Series again in 1977 and 1978. In 1974 their infield of Steve Garvey at first, Davey Lopes at second, Bill Russell at short and Ron Cey at third spent the first of eight straight seasons together. Outfielder Jim Wynn hit 32 home runs and, as usual, the Dodgers had great pitching. Andy Messersmith won 20 games, scuffball artist Don Sutton, 19, and reliever Mike Marshall, 15—to go along with his 21 saves and a record-setting 106 appearances.

Still, 1974 turned out to be Oakland's easiest Series victory. Sutton beat Vida Blue 3–2 in Game 2, the first and last game the Dodgers won. Oakland won Games 1, 3 and 5 by the same 3–2 score, a score that had almost become their trademark: of their 12 Series wins in those three years, seven were by 3–2.

The Yankees made good on two of their three World Series appearances in the 1970s, and the A's got going on another possible dynasty with back-to-back trips to the Series in 1988 and 1989. Through the 1970s, baseball's history could be written around the great teams that dominated their leagues year after year. But it's been more than a decade since any team has won back-to-back World Series, and nowadays any team that manages to defend its division title more than one year is considered a powerhouse. Until the 1989 Oakland A's turned the trick in the AL West, it had been four years since any team had won its division two years in a row.

The first reason for the decline of baseball dynasties is structural. Since expansion of the leagues in 1969, a team that outplays its division rivals over 162 games has to win a Championship Series on its way to the World Series. For the first 16 years of the League Championship Series, a best-of-five format was used, which felt like sudden death to many teams. Thirteen of the

first 32 LCS were three-game sweeps. Only two teams, the 1982 Brewers and the 1984 Padres, ever came back from losing the first two games to advance to the World Series. When the LCS was expanded to best-of-seven in 1985, it became like another World Series: some players contended that the LCS games had all the pressure and the World Series was fun in comparison.

There are other reasons for the decline of dominant teams. Baseball has become more specialized: designated hitters, role players and structured bullpens have all helped to diminish the differences between teams. Sophisticated pitching charts, improved defensive alignments and computerized scouting have helped weaker teams to diminish the advantage of more talented teams, and free agency has kept teams from stockpiling quality midlevel players to fill in for injured or slumping stars. For a team to stay on top, it needs much more than consistency; it needs a string of luck that defies the odds. ⚾

No team has, or probably ever will, dominated baseball the way the New York Yankees have in this century. From 1921 through 1981, the Yankees were the AL's representative in the World Series over half the time—33 pennants in 61 years. And they beat their NL opponents 22 times, losing only 11. But their most frustrated foes may have been the Red Sox, who finished second to the Yankees six times from 1938 to 1978, including a one-game divisional playoff loss at Fenway Park (above) in 1978.

Casey Stengel

It was not a happy day when Casey Stengel was named manager of the New York Yankees in October 1948. Not a happy day at all. For starters, he was replacing Bucky Harris, a lively, likable skipper. Harris led the team to a pennant in 1947 and just missed repeating in 1948 but had run afoul of general manager George Weiss by letting his players spend too many nights carousing. Then there was the matter of Stengel's age—he was close to 60—and his reputation. As a player, he had been known as a clown and entertainer. As a manager, he had been known as a clown and a loser. In nine seasons with the Brooklyn Dodgers and the Boston Braves in the 1930s and early 1940s, he had never managed a team to a first-division finish. One year the Dodgers actually paid him not to manage. When he was with the Braves, he sat out two months of the 1943 season after being hit by a taxi, and one acerbic Boston writer voted the cabdriver "the man who did the most for Boston."

Later, Stengel managed several minor league teams and guided one to a championship. But, his detractors argued, this was the big leagues. More important, this was the Yankees. The grizzled Stengel knew all this. "They don't hand out jobs like this just because they like your company," he soberly told the reporters gathered at his coming-out press conference. "I got the job because people think I can produce for them."

No one in the room that day, Stengel included, would have dared to predict just how well he would produce. The Yankees won the World Series that year, and the next, and the year after that, until they had won five straight championships, a record no other manager has come close to matching. Overall, the Yankees won ten AL pennants and seven World Series in the 12 years of the Stengel era. Stengel managed 63 Series games and won 37 of them—more than any other manager. Fans and sportswriters would continue to laugh with Stengel, but never again would they laugh at him.

He had always been fun to watch, from his first playing days as an outfielder with the Dodgers in 1912, and later with a string of teams through the mid-1920s. He was a talented mimic and a hilarious storyteller, and he just couldn't stifle his personality on the field. Once, while playing with the Pittsburgh Pirates, Stengel stood so rigidly still in center field that his manager ran out to see what was wrong, whereupon Casey told him he was too weak to move because he wasn't getting paid enough to eat. In another routine as a Pirate, he responded to the boos of the Brooklyn fans who had once cheered him by bowing low and doffing his cap. When a sparrow flew off his head, the crowd was enthralled. The story goes that Stengel had found the dazed bird lying in the outfield during batting practice, revived it in the dugout, then placed it under his hat as an ideal prop for his sideshow.

The consummate showman, Stengel seemed to play best when lots of people were watching, namely the World Series. His batting average topped .390 in three World Series—with the Dodgers in 1916 and the Giants in 1922 and 1923. The 1923 Series against

the Yankees featured his most inspired performances. In Game 1 he hit a two-out, ninth-inning,
inside-the-park homer, nearly lost his shoe as he ran
and just beat the throw to the plate with a desperate
headfirst dive. In Game 3, he hit a game-winning
homer, and as he rounded the bases, he thumbed his
nose at the entire Yankee bench. Yankee owner
Jacob Ruppert complained to Commissioner Kenesaw Mountain Landis that Stengel's actions were
"not a credit to baseball." Landis replied, "A fellow
who wins two games with home runs has a right to
feel a little playful, especially if he's a Stengel."

Generally, though, Stengel was a slightly
above-average player and throughout his career he
was often benched against left-handed pitchers. He
complained about being platooned, but once he was
managing, he embraced the concept wholeheartedly;
in fact, some writers have mistakenly credited him
with inventing it. In his first season running the
Yankees, he juggled lineups furiously, playing seven
different men at first base and choosing his starting
outfield according to who was pitching for the other
team. Despite an epidemic of sore arms on the pitching staff and the loss of Joe DiMaggio for almost half
the season because of a bone spur in his heel, the

*Casey Stengel was born in Kansas City but New York
was his baseball home. He played 8½ years with
Brooklyn and the Giants, then managed three New York
teams for 19 years.*

Stengel managed the Yankees to seven world championships, and outfielder Hank Bauer (left) played on all of them. Bauer went on to manage the 1966 Baltimore Orioles to a world title.

1949 Yankees stayed in the race, then won the pennant on the last day of the season with a victory over their archrivals, the Red Sox. The Yankees made quick work of the Brooklyn Dodgers in the Series, beating them in five games.

That set the pattern for the Stengel streak. The following year, the team overtook the Tigers for the pennant, then swept the Phillies in the Series. In 1951 they chased down the Indians for the pennant, then beat the Giants in the Series. The next season, the Yankees again battled the Indians to the bitter end and then won the last two games of the Series in the Dodgers' Ebbets Field. The last championship in the string was the easiest—a walk to the pennant ahead of the Indians and a six-game Series win over the Dodgers in 1953. Still Casey had his detractors. "You or I could have managed and gone away for the summer and still won those pennants," Yankee shortstop Phil Rizzuto told an interviewer years later. "That's how good we were."

Stengel, Rizzuto complained, had forced veterans off the club so he could replace them with younger players he could control. He did, in fact, have a preference for young players he could teach and mold. Under his wing, Yogi Berra became a perennial All-Star; Mickey Mantle, a legend; Billy Martin, a spark plug.

The Stengel magic faded a bit in the late 1950s. The Yankees won five more pennants through 1960, but only two more World Series and both were come-from-behind victories—one over the Dodgers in 1956 and the other over the Milwaukee Braves in 1958. When the Yanks lost the 1960 Series to Pittsburgh, Stengel came under fire. He had failed to start Whitey Ford until the third game, and Ford threw shutouts in Game 3 and Game 6. The team's management, convinced that the game had passed by the 71-year-old Stengel, put him out to pasture.

Naturally, Casey didn't stay there very long, coming back in 1962 to run New York's new team, the Mets. During his four years there, they were one of the most inept teams baseball had ever seen, but Stengel, with great fondness, always called them "my amazin' Mets." The team rarely won, but no one

Stengel's fortunes plummeted as manager of the New York Mets—the team finished last in each of his four years—but his sense of humor never faltered. "The only thing worse than a Mets game is a Mets doubleheader," he said.

minded because Stengel made the show so entertaining. In his mid-seventies, he would get down on all fours and imitate the Mets' bumbling first baseman, "Marvelous Marv" Throneberry, once cracking that Marv did not get a cake on his birthday because he would drop it.

He regaled reporters in Stengelese, a form of language void of grammar and characterized by long monologues in which most of the phrases were unrelated to one another. And as he again became a media darling, Stengel stories were traded like valuable icons. He said that Roger Maris "had more power than Stalin," and he gave a monologue on Jackie Robinson that ended with the sentence: "So it's possible a college education doesn't always help you if you can't hit a left-handed change-up as far as the shortstop, but I'm not bragging, you understand, as I don't have a clear notion myself about atomics or physics or a clear idea where China is in relation to Mobile."

That Casey sure could talk. He also sure could win.

CASEY STENGEL

Outfield
Brooklyn Dodgers 1912–1917
Pittsburgh Pirates 1918–1919
Philadelphia Phillies 1920–1921
New York Giants 1921–1923
Boston Braves 1924–1925
Hall of Fame 1966

GAMES	1,277
AT-BATS	4,288

BATTING AVERAGE	
Career	.284
Season High	.316

SLUGGING AVERAGE	
Career	.410
Season High	.436

HITS	
Career	1,219
Season High	141

DOUBLES	
Career	182
Season High	27

TRIPLES	
Career	89
Season High	12

HOME RUNS	
Career	60
Season High	9

TOTAL BASES	1,759
EXTRA-BASE HITS	331

RUNS BATTED IN	
Career	535
Season High	73

RUNS	
Career	575
Season High	69

WORLD SERIES	**1916, 1922–1923**

The Last At-Bat

f the more than 500 World Series games played since 1903, no fewer than 88 have been decided by a run scored in a team's final at-bat. Twelve world championships were won by a team taking its final chances at the plate. In some ways, these are the most memorable plays of World Series history. The men who have won World Series games with one swing of the bat have a special place in the annals of the sport, just as the players whose misplays ended a game share a dark place in the collective memory. The last-crack magic of Cookie Lavagetto, Kirk Gibson, Bill Mazeroski and Carlton Fisk is remembered most vividly for the very sharpness of the thrill or disappointment it brought us.

In World Series history, the final at-bat is full of the bizarre as well as the heroic. Games have ended in fisticuffs as well as glory. There have been big turnarounds, when an unexpected sequence of events produced a pile of runs. There have been single plays that made all the difference.

For sheer improbability, Game 7 of the 1924 Series is without equal. An incredible thing happened to Freddie Lindstrom of the New York Giants in the eighth inning of that game against the Washington Senators. Then it happened again. Lindstrom was only eighteen years and ten months old when the Series began, which made him the youngest person ever to play in the fall classic. He had earned his job at third base because Heinie Groh had an injured knee. During the regular season, Lindstrom played well for a rookie, if

Tim McCarver's biggest at-bat came early in his career, as the 22-year-old Cardinal catcher (opposite) won Game 5 of the 1964 Series with a three-run homer in the tenth inning. McCarver's blast made a winner of Bob Gibson, who struck out 13 Yankees.

There have been few single plays on which entire Series hung, but they represent stories that are retold—and even reenacted. In 1924, when a ground ball hit a pebble and bounced over 18-year-old Freddie Lindstrom's head, it gave the World Series to the Washington Senators. Twenty-seven years later, Lindstrom donned his Giants uniform and reenacted the play, this time with the pebble more visible.

The 1925 World Series was a nightmare for Senators shortstop Roger Peckinpaugh (above, left). He committed eight errors, the last one leading to a Series-winning Pirate rally in the bottom of the eighth in Game 7. Pittsburgh outfielder Max Carey (above, right) had four hits and scored three runs in the game.

not spectacularly, hitting .253 in 52 games on a team that averaged exactly .300. The Series was a different story. Lindstrom finished with ten hits in thirty at-bats and tied for the team lead with four RBI.

The Giants led the seventh game, 3–1, with one out in the bottom of the eighth. New York's third Series victory in four years was only five outs away, and their pitcher, Virgil Barnes, had allowed only three hits. But then Nemo Leibold pinch-hit a double past Lindstrom down the third-base line, and Muddy Ruel singled off the glove of first baseman George Kelly. A walk loaded the bases, but a shallow fly ball to Irish Meusel brought the second out without a run scoring. The Senators were down to just four outs.

The next play might have been the worst of all bad hops. Senators player-manager Bucky Harris tapped a grounder toward third that Lindstrom could only watch: the ball hit a pebble, or a divot, or something, and bounced high over his head. Two runs scored, and the game was tied.

Walter Johnson came in to pitch for the Senators and struggled to hold the game even through the ninth, tenth, eleventh and twelfth. In the last of the twelfth, Muddy Ruel got a second chance when catcher Hank Gowdy stumbled over his mask and couldn't reach an easy foul pop. Ruel cashed in his reprieve with a double. After a Giant error, Washington's Earl McNeely stepped to the plate. Like Lindstrom, McNeely was a rookie, a 26-year-old Californian who had played only 42 games in the Senators' outfield that year. Facing Giant reliever Jack Bentley, McNeely plugged the same kind of shot to third that Harris had in the eighth, with exactly the same result. Unbelievably, the ball bounded over the head of the startled Lindstrom, and Ruel scored on McNeely's only World Series RBI, the run that won the game and the Series for the Nats.

The Yankees weren't on the losing end of a late-inning rally very often, but two future Hall of Famers teamed up to beat them in Game 2 of the 1942 World Series. Enos Slaughter (left) doubled and scored the game-winner on Stan Musial's single as Yankee catcher Bill Dickey (8) looked on. The Cards won the Series in five games.

Banner headlines were in order as the Pirates came back from a 3–1 deficit to beat the Senators in the 1925 World Series. Pittsburgh came from behind in each of the last three games, including a dramatic three-run rally in the eighth inning for a 9–7 win in Game 7.

Walter Johnson chalked up his only World Series victory in 1924 on that grounder McNeely hit past Lindstrom. Until then, playing for the Senators since 1907 had denied "the Big Train" world championship honors, but he had another chance in 1925. Johnson won Games 1 and 4 in that Series against the Pirates, but the day of his third start, for Game 7, he didn't have the stuff that earned him 416 major league victories.

In their first at-bat the Senators jumped all over Pirate starter Vic Aldridge, tallying four times. But by the seventh inning, the game was knotted at six all, helped along by Roger Peckinpaugh's error at shortstop—his seventh of the Series, after he had honored the Senators by winning the American League's MVP award. Peckinpaugh then cracked a solo homer in the eighth to regain the Senators' lead, 7–6, and Johnson disposed of the first two Pirates in the bottom of the eighth with little trouble.

The field that day was in terrible shape. The game had already been postponed by rain once, but Commissioner Landis ordered it continued if at all possible, even in rain—and it proved to be the correct decision: it rained in Pittsburgh for the next 17 days. In the words of sportswriter Fred Lieb, the game "started in a cold drizzle, which turned into a real downpour in the third frame, which continued unabated until the end of nine nerve-wracking innings." Five times Johnson asked for sand to dry up the mound. Five times the Pirate groundskeepers delivered wheelbarrow loads of sand—sand they had kept soaked under a hose. Johnson got no edge from the Pirate grounds crew that day, and the Pirate batters showed no mercy. Earl Smith and pinch hitter Carson Bigbee cracked doubles, and the score was tied. Eddie Moore walked, and Max Carey hit a bouncer to short, but as Peckinpaugh tried to run with the ball to force the man at second, he slipped on the wet ground and

The Reds got used to frantic finishes to World Series games in the 1970s. In 1972 Reds pitcher Clay Carroll (right, 36) had a long walk to the dugout after giving up a game-winning single to Oakland's Angel Mangual in the ninth inning of Game 4. In Game 2 of the 1975 Series, Ken Griffey's double scored Dave Concepcion (below, 13) with the go-ahead run in the ninth as the Reds beat Boston, 3–2.

dropped the ball. Peckinpaugh had committed his eighth error of the Series, the bases were loaded, and weary Walter Johnson faced Pirate right fielder Kiki Cuyler, who had ended the season with a solid .357 batting average and a league-leading 144 runs. It was the moment thousands of sodden Pittsburgh fans had been counting on, and Cuyler was ready. He lined a shot just inside the first-base bag—ruled a ground-rule double—scoring Bigbee and Moore. The Pirates took the lead, 9–7, the first time they had led in the game. No Senator reached base in the ninth, and the Pirate comeback was complete.

Dramatic late-inning turnarounds have been a big part of World Series action from the beginning. In 1908 the Cubs were losing 6–5 in Game 1 as they went to bat in the top of the ninth. But they bunched six singles around a double steal against Tigers reliever Ed Summers to score five runs. The final was 10–6. Detroit had come unglued and won only one game in the Series, their second consecutive Series defeat at the hands of Frank Chance's Cubs.

After a ninth-inning National League Championship Series victory over the Pirates in 1972, the Cincinnati Reds went on to face the Oakland A's in the World Series, where *they* felt the chilling effects of a ninth-inning comeback in Game 4. In the bottom of the fifth, A's Gene Tenace hit a solo homer for the game's first run. In the top of the eighth, the Reds fought back as Bobby Tolan doubled down the right field line to drive in two runs. With one out in the bottom of the ninth, Reds reliever Pedro Borbon gave up a single to Oakland pinch hitter Gonzalo Marquez. When Borbon went to 2–1 on Tenace, Clay Carroll took over on the mound. Tenace singled anyway, and Don Mincher followed suit to tie the game. With one out and runners on first and

third, the next Oakland batter was Angel Mangual, whose fluid and graceful batting style reminded some of Roberto Clemente's. Mangual rapped a single through a drawn-in infield to give the A's a tough 3–2 win.

Kansas City first baseman Willie Mays Aikens (above) performed like his namesake in the 1980 World Series against the Phillies. Aikens smashed four home runs, and drove in the winning run in Game 3 with a two-out, tenth-inning single.

For a final inning full of excitement, the tenth frame of Game 3 between the Athletics and the Giants in 1911 at New York's spanking-new Polo Grounds has to be among the greats. The opposing hurlers were Jack Coombs and Christy Mathewson, both destined for the Hall of Fame. After eight innings, the Giants had only two hits, but they had put them back-to-back in the third inning to produce the game's only run. When Mathewson induced Philadelphia's leadoff batter Eddie Collins to ground out in the top of the ninth, Giants fans began streaming for the exits. The next batter, Frank Baker, took Mathewson to a 2–1 count. Baker had hit a sensational home run off Rube Marquard to win Game 2 in Philadelphia, and the next day's newspapers contained an article ghostwritten for Mathewson disagreeing with Marquard's pitch selection to the Athletics' third sacker.

The time for second-guessing was over. Mathewson's fourth pitch to Baker was a curve that Baker deposited in the right field stands. Suddenly, startlingly, the game was tied. And Frank Baker, after leading the AL in homers for the first of four consecutive years, earned himself one of the most memorable nicknames of the dead-ball era: "Home Run" Baker.

The Giants' Fred Snodgrass led off the last of the tenth with a walk and was sacrificed to second. Athletics catcher Jack Lapp bobbled a pitch, and Snodgrass tried for third. The throw from Lapp to Baker was in time to nail Snodgrass, but he severely spiked Frank Baker. *Baseball Magazine* called it "the worst and most deliberate case of spiking ever seen on any

5' 9" 170 lbs.   b 8/19/1935
BR TR

BOBBY RICHARDSON

Second Base

The publicity spotlight rarely shined on Bobby Richardson, second baseman for the New York Yankees from 1955 through 1966. It's not that he didn't deserve it; he won five Gold Glove Awards, once led the AL in hits, and played in seven All-Star games. But he was overshadowed by such teammates as Mickey Mantle, Roger Maris, Yogi Berra, Elston Howard and Whitey Ford. Richardson didn't seem to mind. "I was an average player on a great team," he once modestly explained.

While Richardson seemed content to stand out of the limelight during the regular season, he had a knack for holding center stage when the World Series rolled around. Consider the 1960 contest between the Yankees and the Pirates. Richardson's regular season stats had been fairly typical; he hit .252 with only 26 RBI and just one home run. But in Game 3 of the Series he slugged a grand slam homer and got six RBI, setting a Series record. Richardson was named Series MVP, the only player on a losing team ever to win the award.

He finished the Series with 12 RBI—another record—and hit .367. Yankee manager Casey Stengel summed up his second baseman's moment of glory: "He was perfection!"

Four years later Richardson again caught fire in the World Series, setting a record with 13 hits in seven games against the Cardinals and going .406 for the Series. When it came to Series play, noted one sportswriter, Richardson "was a David among Goliaths."

Chief Wilson knew how to get to third base—he had 36 triples in 1912. But when he tried to steal third in Game 6 of the 1909 Series, he became the last out for Pittsburgh in a 5–4 loss to Detroit.

ball field," and described the response: "The amount of fiery language that was passed back and forth was something horrible." John McGraw said it was Baker's fault; he was a clumsy third baseman. But the only other person ever to spike Baker was Ty Cobb, who spiked as routinely as most men scratch their noses. After Merkle walked, Jack Lapp then threw him out trying to steal second, the Giants' fourth attempted swipe that Lapp had halted that game.

And then came the Athletics' eleventh. With one out, Eddie Collins singled. Frank Baker slapped a scratch hit to third, and when Bucky Herzog threw wildly, both Collins and Baker moved up a base. Danny Murphy bounced to shortstop Art Fletcher, who bobbled the ball, letting one run score and Baker go to third. Then Harry Davis singled to right field, scoring Baker, but a great throw from Red Murray to Herzog nailed Murphy. Davis tried to pilfer second, but received the same treatment Lapp had given the Giants. He was out. The Athletics took a 3–1 lead into the bottom of the eleventh.

Herzog led off the bottom of the eleventh inning for the Giants with a redeeming double and advanced to third on the second out of the inning, a grounder to second. Pinch hitter Beals Becker also grounded to second, but the usually sure-handed Eddie Collins couldn't come up with it, and the Giants had a run. With Josh Devore at the plate, Becker recklessly tried to do what Jack Lapp had successfully prevented all day. He, too, was caught stealing—Lapp's fifth victim—ending the game. Two stellar pitchers going down to the wire, the tying run scoring on a one-out ninth-inning homer, then three runs scoring in the eleventh on three singles, a double, three errors and three men put out on the basepaths: quite an ending to quite a game.

World Series Clinchers

Bill Mazeroski's bottom-of-the-ninth home run for the Pirates in 1960 is the only one that actually decided a World Series then and there. However, six other world championships have actually been won as a result of timely and decisive home runs.

1915—Game Five.
Harry Hooper's second homer of the game off Phillies pitcher Eppa Rixey in the top of the ninth, gave the Red Sox a 5-4 victory to take the Series 4 games to 1. Both home runs bounced into the stands, but under existing rules, that was enough.

1933—Game Five.
Mel Ott's long fly ball for the New York Giants off Jack Russell in the top of the tenth with the score tied 3–3, fell out of Washington center fielder Fred Schulte's glove into the bleachers. At first the umpires ruled it a double, then changed their minds.

1942—Game Five.
Whitey Kurowski's two-run homer off Red Ruffing in the top of the ninth broke a 2-2 tie, giving the Cards the game and the Series over the Yankees.

1943—Game Five.
Bill Dickey's final World Series hit was a two-out, two-run homer in the sixth inning off Mort Cooper that provided all the runs in a 2–0 Yankee victory over the Cardinals.

1960—Game Seven.
Pirate second baseman Bill Mazeroski led off the bottom of the ninth with a game-and-Series-ending belt off Ralph Terry to break a 9-9 tie with the favored Yankees.

1966—Game Four.
The Orioles won the fourth and final game against the Dodgers, 1–0, on Frank Robinson's fourth-inning homer off Don Drysdale.

1979—Game Seven.
Pirate Willie Stargell's two-run homer in the sixth off Scott McGregor erased the 1–0 lead Rich Dauer's home run had given Baltimore. The Orioles used five pitchers in the top of the ninth, but the Bucs added two more for a 4–1 final.

Heads-up baserunning made the difference in the final at-bat of Game 2 of the 1914 Series between the Athletics and the "Miracle Braves." In the top of the ninth of a scoreless game, Boston third baseman Charlie Deal bopped a fly into center field that Amos Strunk misplayed; it was called a double by the official scorer. Deal took a healthy lead at second, and Athletics catcher Wally Schang thought he could pick him off. When Deal saw the throw leave Schang's hand, he realized he couldn't make it back to second, so he lit out for third, made it safely, and ultimately scored on a two-out single by Les Mann.

Game 6 of the 1909 Series between the Tigers and the Pirates ended with some "heads-down" baserunning, surely the most violent finish a World Series game ever had. Detroit was winning 5–3 when Pirates Dots Miller and Bill Abstein opened the ninth with singles. Owen "Chief" Wilson bunted down the first-base line and fiercely collided with Tiger first baseman Tom Jones, knocking him cold. As Jones lay unconscious, the ball trickled into the outfield, one run scored, and the other runners advanced to second and third.

Jones left the field on a stretcher, and Sam Crawford took his position. George Gibson tested Crawford with a grounder, and Abstein charged home, sliding in with spikes high. Detroit catcher Boss Schmidt took the throw from Crawford, and although Abstein drew blood, Schmidt held the ball. The fans in Detroit's Bennett Park were roaring for more blood, and after two strikes on pinch hitter Ed Abbaticchio, Wilson tried to steal third, spikes flashing. Abbaticchio fanned, and Boss Schmidt's throw to George Moriarty beat Wilson to the bag, saving the game for Detroit. The Chief was out, and the game ended with Moriarty and Wilson on the ground, kicking at each other with their spikes like gamecocks.

Forbes Field

Forbes Field, home to the Pittsburgh Pirates for 61 years, was huge. Built on a cow pasture, Forbes was 376 feet to right field, 360 to left, 462 to center and 110 feet from home plate to the backstop when it opened in 1909. Athletics owners Ben Shibe and Connie Mack had begun work on a steel-and-concrete stadium in Philadelphia late in 1908, and Pirates owner Barney Dreyfuss decided his club deserved a similar home. His timing couldn't have been better, as the Pirates drew more than 80,000 fans to the three World Series games played at Forbes in 1909, a figure greater than the entire attendance at the 1908 Series. With its spacious power alleys, Forbes was a triple hitter's dream and an outfielder's nightmare, and the Pirates wasted no time taking advantage of its dimensions.

They won the pennant in 1909, leading the NL with 92 triples. In that Series, rookie Babe Adams pitched three complete-game wins as the Pirates won their first world title. Three years later they increased that total to 129—led by Owen "Chief" Wilson's 36—and set a modern record that will likely never be challenged. For the next 25 years the Pirates featured some of the game's most famous line-drive hitters, including Hall of Famers Honus Wagner, Pie Traynor, Kiki Cuyler and the Waner brothers—Paul and Lloyd. And they showcased their talents in one of baseball's first true showpieces. The 1910 *Reach Baseball Guide* said that "For architectural beauty, imposing size, solid construction and public comfort and convenience, it has not its superior in the world."

With its impressive scoreboard and ivy-covered brick wall in left field, Forbes remained one of the game's most elegant stadiums into the 1960s, and was the site of numerous landmark events. On October 2, 1920, it hosted the NL's last tripleheader. On August 26, 1926, Paul Waner went 6 for 6, using a different bat for each hit. On May 25, 1935, Babe Ruth hit the last three home runs of his remarkable career, and a year later the Phillies' Chuck Klein blasted four homers in a game. Home runs got easier to come by in 1947, when, in honor of the Pirates' acquisition of slugging first baseman Hank Greenberg, a fence was erected 30 feet in front of the scoreboard in left field. Christened "Greenberg Gardens," the area quickly got a new name: "Kiner's Corner," after outfielder Ralph Kiner, who hit 51 homers in 1947 for the second in a string of seven NL home run titles. On May 28, 1956, Dale Long of the Pirates belted his eighth homer in as many consecutive games, a record tied by the Yankees' Don Mattingly in 1987.

But the most famous date in Forbes Field history is October 13, 1960. On that day, Pirate second baseman Bill Mazeroski etched his name in baseball lore as the only man ever to end an entire World Series with a home run. Mazeroski's blast came in the bottom of the ninth inning, and gave the Pirates a 10–9 win over the Yankees in Game 7.

Forbes Field closed on June 28, 1970, as the Pirates faced the very same team that they had opened against in 1909—the Chicago Cubs. The Pirates lost Forbes' first game, but in its finale they swept a doubleheader from the Cubs. Forbes was demolished in 1971, having played host to just about everything the game has to offer, except one thing—a no-hitter.

Despite its status as a landmark achievement in stadium design and construction, Forbes Field took just four months and $2 million to build. Fifty-one years later, Pirate pitcher Bob Friend (19, right) stranded Gino Cimoli (18) at third and took the loss as the Yankees pounded the Pirates, 16–3, in Game 2 of the 1960 World Series. A week later Bill Mazeroski made Forbes Field home to baseball's most storied swing.

Forbes Field

Boquet Street and
  Sennott Street
Pittsburgh, Pennsylvania

Built 1909
Demolished 1971

Pittsburgh Pirates, NL
  1909–1970

Seating Capacity
35,000

Style
Major league classic

Height of Outfield Fences
Left: 12 feet
Center: 12 feet
Right: 9 feet 6 inches

Dugouts
Home: 1st base
Visitors: 3rd base

Bullpens
Home: left field
Visitors: right field

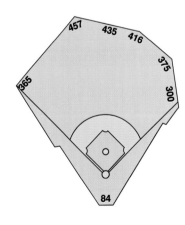

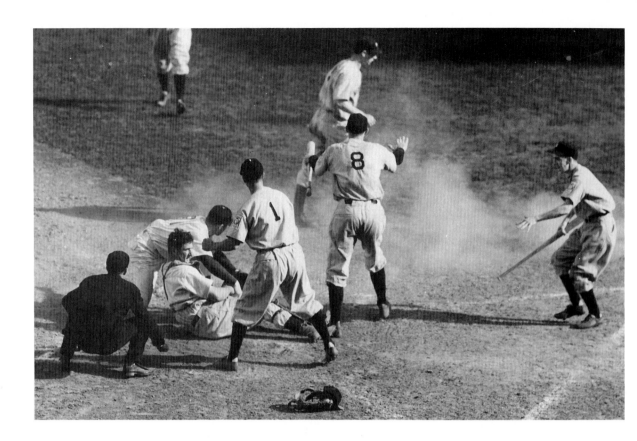

Three runs scored on Joe DiMaggio's tenth-inning single in Game 4 of the 1939 World Series, but Reds catcher Ernie Lombardi probably didn't remember any of them. Frank Crosetti (1) scored the first run, and then Charlie Keller knocked Lombardi flat to score the second. As Lombardi lay dazed, DiMaggio (above, top) came all the way around to score. The play capped the Yankees' four-game sweep.

Baserunning also played a pivotal role in the 1939 Series between the New York Yankees and the Cincinnati Reds. The Yankees took the first three games, but were losing Game 4 in Crosley Field in the top of the ninth. Two runs tied the game at 4, and New York shortstop Frank Crosetti walked to lead off the top of the tenth. One out later, Charlie Keller was safe at first on a Cincinnati error, Crosetti moving to third. Yankee mainstay Joe DiMaggio singled to right, easily scoring Crosetti. When right fielder Ival Goodman didn't come up with the ball cleanly, Keller set out for home, and proved why he held the nickname "King Kong." The throw was late; Keller and catcher Ernie Lombardi collided at the plate. Lombardi lay on the ground, obviously stunned, with the ball lying a few feet away. The fleet-footed DiMaggio never stopped, easily scoring the third run of the play. The Reds couldn't get back on their feet, and the Yankees won the game—and the Series, four straight.

For sheer drama, nothing beats the "Big Bang"—the clutch homer or extra-base hit that sends the game- and sometimes the Series-winning run home. The 1929 Philadelphia Athletics were one of the greatest teams in baseball history. Their starting lineup boasted six .300-plus hitters, from Al Simmons with .365 to Mule Haas with .313. In the World Series they were having little trouble with Joe McCarthy's Cubs. In Game 4, down 8–0, they sent ten runs plateward in the seventh inning to win the game. They were also losing in the bottom of the ninth of Game 5, when, with one out, Max Bishop singled and Haas belted a two-run homer over the center field wall to tie the game. But the flurry of long hits wasn't finished. Simmons doubled off the scoreboard, narrowly missing a homer, and then Bing

Miller repeated the trick, smacking a long shot off the scoreboard that won the game and the Series.

Late-inning homers have provided much drama for World Series contests, and many of them have been slugged by famous hitters. Rudy York belted a solo shot to win the first game of the 1946 Series for the Red Sox. Joe DiMaggio popped up five straight times in the 1950 Series before he homered to break a 1–1 tie in the tenth inning of the second game.

The final game of the 1933 Series between the Giants and the Senators was won in extra innings with a home run in the last at-bat. It wasn't a homer at first, though. In the top of the tenth, Mel Ott poked a long fly to the far reaches of Griffith Stadium. Wildfire Schulte, Senators' center fielder, chased back to the fence and reached up, only to have the ball fall out of his glove into the bleachers. Umpire Charles Pfirman, a National Leaguer, ruled that Ott's hit was only a double. But the Giants argued that the ball had hit Schulte, not the ground, before it fell into the seats. Pfirman then talked with his colleagues and changed his mind. When the Senators left two men stranded on base in the last of the tenth, the Series was over.

Mickey Mantle won the second game of the 1953 Series for Yankee teammate Eddie Lopat with a two-out two-run homer off Brooklyn's Preacher Roe in the bottom of the eighth. Tom Tresh won Game 5 in 1962 with a three-run blast in the same inning. In 1964 Tresh also belted a two-run game-tying shot with two out in the bottom of the ninth in Game 5, but in the top of the tenth, Cardinal catcher Tim McCarver hit the long ball with two men on, and the Redbirds beat the Yankees, 5–2.

In the third game of the 1961 matchup between New York and Cincinnati, Yankee outfielder Johnny Blanchard pinch-hit a blast to

Yankee second basemen—from Tony Lazzeri to Billy Martin to Willie Randolph (above)—have a history of sparking the team's offense, especially in the World Series. In Game 1 in 1977, Randolph doubled in the 12th and then scored the game-winner on Paul Blair's single.

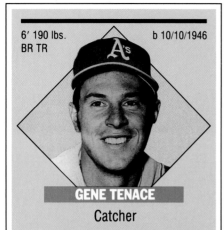

6' 190 lbs.   b 10/10/1946
BR TR

GENE TENACE

Catcher

His first name is Fury—the anglicized form of Fiore Gino Tennaci—and World Series MVP Gene Tenace lived up to his name when the underdog Oakland Athletics unleashed him on Cincinnati in 1972. Tenace became the only player to homer in his first two Series at-bats, on his way to a .348 average for the Series and nine RBI, eight more than any of his teammates. Tenace tied the record for homers in a seven-game Series with four, and he set a seven-game Series record for slugging percentage with .913.

Tenace signed as a shortstop out of Valley Local High in Lucasville, Ohio. During five years in the minors, Tenace learned to catch, but he advanced on the strength of his line-drive swing and discriminating eye at the plate, not his prowess behind it. He made the A's in 1969 as a backup to catcher Dave Duncan. Tenace spent most of his time on the bench until late in the 1972 season, when Duncan fell into a slump, and Tenace was put in the lineup.

Nothing foreshadowed Tenace's outstanding Series performance. He wound up the regular season with a .225 batting average. In the playoffs against Detroit, Tenace was 0 for 16 until his last at-bat in the finale, when he hit an RBI single to give the A's a 2–1 lead that held, and the A's clinched the pennant.

Tenace played in three more World Series during his 15-year career. He logged a total of 201 regular-season home runs, but never hit a Series homer after 1972.

The Braves' Nippy Jones (25) had incontrovertible evidence—a smudge of black shoe polish on the ball—that he had been hit by a pitch in the tenth in Game 4 of the 1957 Series. Then Johnny Logan drove in the tying run with a double.

tie the game in the top of the eighth inning, and Roger Maris finished the scoring with a home run in the top of the ninth. In 1930 Jimmie Foxx slugged a two-run belt in the top of the ninth of Game 5 to provide the winning margin. Two famous Dodgers delivered out-of-the-park game winners: Roy Campanella in 1953 and Gil Hodges in 1959. The Cardinals won the fifth and final game of the 1942 Series on a two-run ninth-inning smash by Whitey Kurowski.

The big blow of the 1947 Series between the Yanks and the Dodgers was Cookie Lavagetto's ending both Yankee Bill Bevens' no-hit try and the game with his two-out ninth-inning double in Game 4. The Yanks came back to take the Series in seven, but a third-place finish in 1948 cost manager Bucky Harris his job. His replacement was the man who managed the Yanks for the next decade, the man who had beaten them in Game 1 of the 1923 Series with an inside-the-park home run in Yankee Stadium: Casey Stengel. All the Case did in his first year was to win the pennant in thrilling style. The 1949 Series between the same two teams was the first in which a game actually ended with a homer.

Game 1 was a masterful pitchers' duel. Yankee Allie Reynolds allowed only two hits; his Dodger opponent, Don Newcombe, permitted just five and fanned 11 Yanks in the process. Six men reached second in the game; one made it to third. In the bottom of the ninth, the first two pitches from Newk to the Yank leadoff hitter, Tommy Henrich, were balls. Henrich turned the third pitch into a low liner that cleared the right field fence for the win. The next day Yank Vic Raschi lost a 1–0 game to Preacher Roe, but it was the only Dodger victory in a five-game Series.

The first game of the 1954 World Series also ended on a dramatic home run—a three-run pinch-hit clout into the right field stands of the Polo Grounds by Dusty Rhodes of the Giants to beat the Indians. Rhodes' winning the game was made possible by New York Giant center fielder Willie Mays' memorable catch of Vic Wertz's drive deep to right center in the eighth. The irony was that Wertz smashed a 400-foot out, and Rhodes, a 260-foot game-winning fly.

Most critical World Series plays come from a big bat or a hot glove, but occasionally a player has to do next to nothing. By Game 4 in 1957, the Yanks had a two-games-to-one lead over the challengers from Milwaukee. Warren Spahn's six-hitter had the Braves in front, 4–1, as he coasted into the ninth inning. But with two out, New York's Yogi Berra and Gil McDougald singled, and first baseman Elston Howard smashed a Spahn pitch into the left field stands to tie the game in dramatic fashion. When the Yankees added another run off Spahn in the top of the tenth, the situation looked sour for the Braves.

Nippy Jones was sent in to pinch-hit for Spahn to lead off the last of the tenth. Jones had played his first World Series 11 years earlier with the Cardinals, with one empty pinch-hit appearance. Winding up a career plagued with injury, he had come up from a Braves farm team a month before. But Nippy had his shoes well shined—after all, he was in the *World Series*—and 11 years of baseball and nine and a half innings of sitting on the bench hadn't diminished the luster. On the first pitch, Yank pitcher Tommy Byrne tried to get Jones to chase a low-inside curve. Jones claimed the ball hit his shoe. Home plate umpire Augie Donatelli disagreed, until Jones showed him the fresh mark of black shoe polish on the ball. Donatelli told Jones to take his base, and after a double by Johnny Logan scored Jones' pinch runner, Eddie Mathews ended the contest with a monstrous two-run homer to right.

Braves third baseman Eddie Mathews hit 512 homers in his Hall of Fame career, but none was bigger than his game-winning two-run shot in Game 4 of the 1957 Series against the Yankees. It made a winner of another Hall of Famer—Warren Spahn.

Yankee reliever Joe Page (above, left of Johnny Mize, 36, after the last out of the Series) made the last at-bat fruitless for the Dodgers in the 1949 Series. Page won Game 3 with 5⅔ innings of strong relief, then finished out the Series with 2⅓ scoreless innings in Game 5.

Game 3, 1964, was another World Series classic pitching duel broken wide open by one of baseball's most enduring batters. Curt Simmons of the Cardinals and Jim Bouton of the Yanks had each allowed just one run through eight innings. St. Louis manager Johnny Keane ordered in his bullpen ace, knuckleballer Barney Schultz, to pitch the last of the ninth. Mickey Mantle, playing his 12th and last World Series for New York, was tired of waiting. Mantle timed Schultz's first pitch perfectly and sent it screaming deep into the right field stands. The game was over in a flash.

Other World Series games that ended with home runs are the stuff of baseball legend: Bill Mazeroski's ninth-inning belt over Forbes Field's ivied wall that finished the 1960 Series; Carlton Fisk's late-night smash over the Green Monster in Fenway Park in the sixth game of 1975. Kirk Gibson achieved special World Series historical recognition for taking the Dodgers from a run down to a victory with his homer that ended Game 1 in 1988. And in Game 3 of that year, Mark McGwire of the Oakland A's ended a 1–1 tie with a shot out of the park off Dodger reliever Jay Howell.

Perhaps the most pulse-pounding World Series home run was belted in the opening game of the 1923 Series between the Yankees and the Giants by a man who—as player and manager—saw more World Series action than any other. In the first World Series game to be played in Yankee Stadium, a game tied at four with two out in the top of the ninth, the talented but erratic Giant outfielder Casey Stengel came to the plate. Casey was known as a cutup, but his antics hid the fact that he was a talented, hard-working player. A decade earlier he had smacked the first home run out of the brand-new Ebbets Field in Brooklyn, and he had just finished his 12th major league season with a .339 average and a .395 on-base percentage. Not bad for an old gaffer of 34 years.

On a three-and-two count, the Yankee outfield swung to the right on the pull hitter. Casey didn't quite get around on a Joe Bush change-up, but he still cracked it into deep left center, the deepest part of cavernous Yankee Stadium. Stengel had injured his heel late in the season and was wearing a protective cushion inside his shoe. As he took off on his gallop around the bases, the pad slipped. Casey thought his shoe was coming off, and tried to run and keep his shoe on at the same time. Sportswriter Grantland Rice stood up to watch along with thousands of screaming fans: "The dust flew as Casey tossed one loose foot after another, identified each one and picked it up again." Casey's all-out hustle beat the relay throw home with the game-winning inside-the-park home run, the first Series home run ever in Yankee Stadium. The Giants poured off the bench to engulf the breathless Stengel, and no World Series crowd was ever more ecstatic.

When Casey hit a second home run that broke up a 0–0 tie in the seventh inning of Game 3, it left the park, and Case was able to amble around the bags instead. But it couldn't put the lid on his effervescence. As the ball reached the stands, he held up two fingers to indicate how many homers he had hit. Then he thumbed his nose at the Yankee bench and blew them a large kiss. He had earned the privilege. ◗

Baltimore's Brooks Robinson is best remembered for his performance in the 1970 World Series against the Reds—he hit .429 and made a slew of spectacular plays at third base—but he followed it up with another solid Series in 1971. He drove in Frank Robinson with a sacrifice fly in the tenth to win Game 6, one of five RBI in the Series. This time the Orioles lost in seven games to Pittsburgh.

Every world championship is special, but none so much as the first. The Phillies had been in Philadelphia since 1883, but went nearly a century before their first World Series win. It happened in 1980 and touched off a wild celebration in the City of Brotherly Love.

World Series Results

Year	Winner	Loser	Year	Winner	Loser
1903	Boston (AL) 5	Pittsburgh (NL) 3	1947	New York (AL) 4	Brooklyn (NL) 3
1904	No Series		1948	Cleveland (AL) 4	Boston (NL) 2
1905	New York (NL) 4	Philadelphia (AL) 1	1949	New York (AL) 4	Brooklyn (NL) 1
1906	Chicago (AL) 4	Chicago (NL) 2	1950	New York (AL) 4	Philadelphia (NL) 0
1907	Chicago (NL) 4	Detroit (AL) 0; 1 tie	1951	New York (AL) 4	New York (NL) 2
1908	Chicago (NL) 4	Detroit (AL) 1	1952	New York (AL) 4	Brooklyn (NL) 3
1909	Pittsburgh (NL) 4	Detroit (AL) 3	1953	New York (AL) 4	Brooklyn (NL) 2
1910	Philadelphia (AL) 4	Chicago (NL) 1	1954	New York (NL) 4	Cleveland (AL) 0
1911	Philadelphia (AL) 4	New York (NL) 2	1955	Brooklyn (NL) 4	New York (AL) 3
1912	Boston (AL) 4	New York (NL) 3; 1 tie	1956	New York (AL) 4	Brooklyn (NL) 3
1913	Philadelphia (AL) 4	New York (NL) 1	1957	Milwaukee (NL) 4	New York (AL) 3
1914	Boston (NL) 4	Philadelphia (AL) 0	1958	New York (AL) 4	Milwaukee (NL) 3
1915	Boston (AL) 4	Philadelphia (NL) 1	1959	Los Angeles (NL) 4	Chicago (AL) 2
1916	Boston (AL) 4	Brooklyn (NL) 1	1960	Pittsburgh (NL) 4	New York (AL) 3
1917	Chicago (AL) 4	New York (NL) 2	1961	New York (AL) 4	Cincinnati (NL) 1
1918	Boston (AL) 4	Chicago (NL) 2	1962	New York (AL) 4	San Francisco (NL) 3
1919	Cincinnati (NL) 5	Chicago (AL) 3	1963	Los Angeles (NL) 4	New York (AL) 0
1920	Cleveland (AL) 5	Brooklyn (NL) 2	1964	St. Louis (NL) 4	New York (AL) 3
1921	New York (NL) 5	New York (AL) 3	1965	Los Angeles (NL) 4	Minnesota (AL) 3
1922	New York (NL) 4	New York (AL) 0; 1 tie	1966	Baltimore (AL) 4	Los Angeles (NL) 0
1923	New York (AL) 4	New York (NL) 2	1967	St. Louis (NL) 4	Boston (AL) 3
1924	Washington (AL) 4	New York (NL) 3	1968	Detroit (AL) 4	St. Louis (NL) 3
1925	Pittsburgh (NL) 4	Washington (AL) 3	1969	New York (NL) 4	Baltimore (AL) 1
1926	St. Louis (NL) 4	New York (AL) 3	1970	Baltimore (AL) 4	Cincinnati (NL) 1
1927	New York (AL) 4	Pittsburgh (NL) 0	1971	Pittsburgh (NL) 4	Baltimore (AL) 3
1928	New York (AL) 4	St. Louis (NL) 0	1972	Oakland (AL) 4	Cincinnati (NL) 3
1929	Philadelphia (AL) 4	Chicago (NL) 1	1973	Oakland (AL) 4	New York (NL) 3
1930	Philadelphia (AL) 4	St. Louis (NL) 2	1974	Oakland (AL) 4	Los Angeles (NL) 1
1931	St. Louis (NL) 4	Philadelphia (AL) 3	1975	Cincinnati (NL) 4	Boston (AL) 3
1932	New York (AL) 4	Chicago (NL) 0	1976	Cincinnati (NL) 4	New York (AL) 0
1933	New York (NL) 4	Washington (AL) 1	1977	New York (AL) 4	Los Angeles (NL) 2
1934	St. Louis (NL) 4	Detroit (AL) 3	1978	New York (AL) 4	Los Angeles (NL) 2
1935	Detroit (AL) 4	Chicago (NL) 2	1979	Pittsburgh (NL) 4	Baltimore (AL) 3
1936	New York (AL) 4	New York (NL) 2	1980	Philadelphia (NL) 4	Kansas City (AL) 2
1937	New York (AL) 4	New York (NL) 1	1981	Los Angeles (NL) 4	New York (AL) 2
1938	New York (AL) 4	Chicago (NL) 0	1982	St. Louis (NL) 4	Milwaukee (AL) 3
1939	New York (AL) 4	Cincinnati (NL) 0	1983	Baltimore (AL) 4	Philadelphia (NL) 1
1940	Cincinnati (NL) 4	Detroit (AL) 3	1984	Detroit (AL) 4	San Diego (NL) 1
1941	New York (AL) 4	Brooklyn (NL) 1	1985	Kansas City (AL) 4	St. Louis (NL) 3
1942	St. Louis (NL) 4	New York (AL) 1	1986	New York (NL) 4	Boston (AL) 3
1943	New York (AL) 4	St. Louis (NL) 1	1987	Minnesota (AL) 4	St. Louis (AL) 3
1944	St. Louis (NL) 4	St. Louis (AL) 2	1988	Los Angeles (NL) 4	Oakland (AL) 1
1945	Detroit (AL) 4	Chicago (NL) 3	1989	Oakland (AL) 4	San Francisco (NL) 0
1946	St. Louis (NL) 4	Boston (AL) 3			

Performance Leaders: Batting

4-Game Series	5-Game Series	6-Game Series	7-Game Series	8-Game Series

At-Bats:

19
Mark Koenig, NY (AL), 1928
Rickey Henderson, OAK (AL), 1989

23
Hal Janvrin, BOS (AL), 1916
Joe Moore, NY (NL), 1937
Bobby Richardson, NY (AL), 1961

28
Joe Moore, NY (NL), 1936

33
Bucky Harris, WAS (AL), 1924
Sam Rice, WAS (AL), 1925
Omar Moreno, PIT (NL), 1979

36
Jimmy Collins, BOS (AL), 1903

Hits:

10
Babe Ruth, NY (AL), 1928

9
Frank Baker, PHI (AL), 1910
Eddie Collins, PHI (AL), 1910
Frank Baker, PHI (AL), 1913
Heinie Groh, NY (NL), 1922
Joe Moore, NY (NL), 1937
Bobby Richardson, NY (AL), 1961
Paul Blair, BAL (AL), 1970
Brooks Robinson, BAL (AL), 1970
Alan Trammell, DET (AL), 1984

12
Billy Martin, NY (AL), 1953

13
Bobby Richardson, NY (AL), 1964
Lou Brock, StL (NL), 1968
Marty Barrett, BOS (AL), 1986

12
Buck Herzog, NY (NL), 1912
Joe Jackson, CHI (AL), 1919

Batting Average:

.625
Babe Ruth, NY (AL), 1928

.500
Larry McLean, NY (NL), 1913
Joe Gordon, NY (AL), 1941

.500
Dave Robertson, NY (NL), 1917
Billy Martin, NY (AL), 1953

.500
Pepper Martin, StL (NL), 1931
Johnny Lindell, NY (AL), 1947 (played in six games)
Phil Garner, PIT (NL), 1979

.400
Buck Herzog, NY (NL), 1912

Slugging Average:

1.727
Lou Gehrig, NY (AL), 1928

.929
Joe Gordon, NY (AL), 1941
(Donn Clendenon, NY [NL], 1969, had S.A. of 1.071 but played only four games)

1.250
Reggie Jackson, NY (AL), 1977

.913
Gene Tenace, OAK (AL), 1972

.600
Buck Herzog, NY (NL), 1912

Runs Scored:

9
Babe Ruth, NY (AL), 1928
Lou Gehrig, NY (AL), 1932

6
Frank Baker, PHI (AL), 1910
Danny Murphy, PHI (AL), 1910
Harry Hooper, BOS (AL), 1916
Al Simmons, PHI (AL), 1929
Lee May, CIN (NL), 1970
Boog Powell, BAL (AL), 1970
Lou Whitaker, DET (AL), 1984

10
Reggie Jackson, NY (AL), 1977

8
Tommy Leach, PIT (NL), 1909
Pepper Martin, StL (NL), 1934
Billy Johnson, NY (AL), 1947
Mickey Mantle, NY (AL), 1960
Bobby Richardson, NY (AL), 1960
Mickey Mantle, NY (AL), 1964
Lou Brock, StL (NL), 1967

8
Freddy Parent, BOS (AL), 1903

RBI:

9
Lou Gehrig, NY (AL), 1928

8
Danny Murphy, PHI (AL), 1910
Lee May, CIN (NL), 1970

10
Ted Kluszewski, CHI (AL), 1959

12
Bobby Richardson, NY (AL), 1960

8
Tommy Leach, PIT (NL), 1903
Pat Duncan, CIN (NL), 1919

Performance Leaders: Batting

4-Game Series	5-Game Series	6-Game Series	7-Game Series	8-Game Series

Total Bases:

4-Game Series	5-Game Series	6-Game Series	7-Game Series	8-Game Series
22 Babe Ruth, NY (AL), 1928	**17** Brooks Robinson, BAL (AL), 1970	**25** Reggie Jackson, NY (AL), 1977	**25** Willie Stargell, PIT (NL), 1979	**18** Buck Herzog, NY (NL), 1912 Joe Jackson, CHI (AL), 1919

Home Runs:

4-Game Series	5-Game Series	6-Game Series	7-Game Series	8-Game Series
4 Lou Gehrig, NY (AL), 1928	**3** Donn Clendenon, NY (NL), 1969	**5** Reggie Jackson, NY (AL), 1977	**4** Babe Ruth, NY (AL), 1926 Duke Snider, BKN (NL), 1952 Duke Snider, BKN (NL), 1955 Hank Bauer, NY (AL), 1958 Gene Tenace, OAK (AL), 1972	**2** Patsy Dougherty, BOS (AL), 1903

Strikeouts:

4-Game Series	5-Game Series	6-Game Series	7-Game Series	8-Game Series
7 Bob Meusel, NY (AL), 1927	**9** Carmelo Martinez, SD (NL), 1984	**12** Willie Wilson, KC (AL), 1980	**11** Eddie Mathews, MIL (NL), 1958 Wayne Garrett, NY (NL), 1973	**10** George Kelly, NY (NL), 1921

Stolen Bases:

4-Game Series	5-Game Series	6-Game Series	7-Game Series	8-Game Series
3 Rickey Henderson, OAK (AL), 1989	**6** Jimmy Slagle, CHI (NL), 1907	**4** Davey Lopes, LA (NL), 1981	**7** Lou Brock, StL (NL), 1967 Lou Brock, StL (NL), 1968	**4** Josh DeVore, NY (NL), 1912

Performance Leaders: Pitching

4-Game Series	5-Game Series	6-Game Series	7-Game Series	8-Game Series

Innings Pitched:

4-Game Series	5-Game Series	6-Game Series	7-Game Series	8-Game Series
18 Dick Rudolph, BOS (NL), 1914 Waite Hoyt, NY (AL), 1928 Red Ruffing, NY (AL), 1938 Sandy Koufax, LA (NL), 1963	**27** Christy Mathewson, NY (NL), 1905 Jack Coombs, PHI (AL), 1910	**27** Christy Mathewson, NY (NL), 1911 Red Faber, CHI (AL), 1917 Hippo Vaughn, CHI (NL), 1918	**32** George Mullin, DET (AL), 1909	**44** Deacon Phillippe, PIT (NL), 1903

Complete Games:

4-Game Series	5-Game Series	6-Game Series	7-Game Series	8-Game Series
2 Dick Rudolph, BOS (NL), 1914 Waite Hoyt, NY (AL), 1928 Red Ruffing, NY (AL), 1938 Sandy Koufax, LA (NL), 1963	**3** Christy Mathewson, NY (NL), 1905 Jack Coombs, PHI (AL), 1910	**3** Chief Bender, PHI (AL), 1911 Hippo Vaughn, CHI (NL), 1918	**3** Babe Adams, PIT (NL), 1909 George Mullin, DET (AL), 1909 Stan Coveleski, CLE (AL), 1920 Walter Johnson, WAS (AL), 1925 Bobo Newsom, DET (AL), 1940 Lew Burdette, MIL (NL), 1957 Bob Gibson, StL (NL), 1967 Bob Gibson, StL (NL), 1968 Mickey Lolich, DET (AL), 1968	**5** Deacon Phillippe, PIT (NL), 1903

Performance Leaders: Pitching

4-Game Series	5-Game Series	6-Game Series	7-Game Series	8-Game Series

Games Won:

2
Dick Rudolph, BOS (NL), 1914
Bill James, BOS (NL), 1914
Waite Hoyt, NY (AL), 1928
Red Ruffing, NY (AL), 1938
Sandy Koufax, LA (NL), 1963

3
Christy Mathewson, NY (NL), 1905
Jack Coombs, PHI (AL), 1910

3
Red Faber, CHI (AL), 1917

3
Babe Adams, PIT (NL), 1909
Stan Coveleski, CLE (AL), 1920
Harry Brecheen, StL (NL), 1946
Lew Burdette, MIL (NL), 1957
Bob Gibson, StL (NL), 1967
Mickey Lolich, DET (AL), 1968

3
Bill Dinneen, BOS (AL), 1903
Deacon Phillippe, PIT (NL), 1903
Joe Wood, BOS (AL), 1912

Saves (since 1969):

2
Will McEnaney, CIN (NL), 1976

2
Rollie Fingers, OAK (AL), 1974
Tippy Martinez, BAL (AL), 1983
Willie Hernandez, DET (AL), 1984

2
Tug McGraw, PHI (NL), 1980
Goose Gossage, NY (AL), 1981

3
Kent Tekulve, PIT (NL), 1979

Most Runs Allowed:

11
Grover Alexander, StL (NL), 1928
Bob Lemon, CLE (AL), 1954

16
Three Finger Brown, CHI (NL), 1910

10
Slim Sallee, NY (NL), 1917
Red Ruffing, NY (AL), 1936
Don Gullett, NY (AL), 1977
Don Sutton, LA (NL), 1978

17
Lew Burdette, MIL (NL), 1958

19
Deacon Phillippe, PIT (NL), 1903

Most Hits Allowed:

17
Red Ruffing, NY (AL), 1938

23
Jack Coombs, PHI (AL), 1910
Three Finger Brown, CHI (NL), 1910

25
Christy Mathewson, NY (NL), 1911

30
Walter Johnson, WAS (AL), 1924

38
Deacon Phillippe, PIT (NL), 1903

Most Walks Allowed:

8
Bob Lemon, CLE (AL), 1954

14
Jack Coombs, PHI (AL), 1910

11
Lefty Tyler, CHI (NL), 1918
Lefty Gomez, NY (AL), 1936
Allie Reynolds, NY (AL), 1951

11
Walter Johnson, WAS (AL), 1924
Bill Bevens, NY (AL), 1947

13
Art Nehf, NY (NL), 1921

Strikeouts:

23
Sandy Koufax, LA (NL), 1963

18
Christy Mathewson, NY (NL), 1905

20
Chief Bender, PHI (AL), 1911

35
Bob Gibson, StL (NL), 1968

28
Bill Dinneen, BOS (AL), 1903

INDEX

FOR FURTHER READING

Craig Carter, ed., *The Series,* The Sporting News, 1988.

Richard M. Cohen & David S. Neft, *The World Series,* MacMillan, 1986.

Donald Honig, *The World Series,* Crown Publishers, 1986.

Jerry Lausche, *The Forgotten Championship,* MacFarland Publishing, 1989.

David Quentin Voigt, *American Baseball: From the Gentleman's Sport to the Commissioner System,* The Pennsylvania State University Press, 1983.

PICTURE CREDITS

Front cover: 1984 Detroit Tigers by John W. McDonough

Back cover: Game 6, 1986 World Series by Robert Riger

Opening spread: 4-5 Marvin E. Newman; 5 Culver Pictures

The Clutch
6 Tony Tomsic/*Sports Illustrated;* 7 Ron Menchine Collection/Renée Comet Photography; 8 AP/Wide World Photos; 9 (top) Marvin E. Newman; 9 (bottom) Ron Menchine Collection/Renée Comet Photography; 10 (left) National Baseball Library, Cooperstown, New York; 10 (right) AP/Wide World Photos; 11 (top left) Ron Menchine Collection/Renée Comet Photography; 11 (top right) National Baseball Library, Cooperstown, New York; 11 (bottom) Ron Menchine Collection/Renée Comet Photography; 13 (left) UPI/Bettmann Newsphotos; 13 (right) *The Sporting News;* 14 (left) AP/Wide World Photos; 14 (right) UPI/Bettmann Newsphotos; 15 AP/Wide World Photos; 16-17 Sportschrome East/West; 17 Walter Iooss, Jr./*Sports Illustrated;* 18 *The Sporting News;* 19 (top) AP/Wide World Photos; 19 (bottom) AP/Wide World Photos; 20 (left) UPI/Bettmann Newsphotos; 20 (right) John W. McDonough; 21 Focus on Sports, Inc.; 22 Ron Menchine Collection/Renée Comet Photography; 23 (top) Richard Darcey; 23 (bottom) AP/Wide World Photos; 24 (left) Robert Riger; 24 (right) AP/Wide World Photos; 25 Walter Iooss, Jr.

Little Guys
26 Hy Peskin/*LIFE* Magazine © 1947 Time Inc.; 27 National Baseball Library, Cooperstown, New York; 28 *The New York Times;* 29 (left) Louis Requena; 29 (right) Herb Scharfman/*Sports Illustrated;* 30 (left) National Baseball Library, Cooperstown, New York; 30 (right) Dennis Goldstein Collection; 31 National Baseball Library, Cooperstown, New York; 32 Ron Menchine Collection/Renée Comet Photography; 33 (top) David Walberg; 33 (bottom left) Walter Iooss, Jr./*Sports Illustrated;* 33 (bottom right) Ron Menchine Collection/Renée Comet Photography;

34 (left) National Baseball Library, Cooperstown, New York; 34 (right) Mark Kauffman/*LIFE* Magazine © 1952 Time Inc.; 35 Mark Kauffman/*LIFE* Magazine © 1952 Time Inc.; 36 (left) AP/Wide World Photos; 36 (right) AP/Wide World Photos; 37 (left) AP/Wide World Photos; 37 (right) National Baseball Library, Cooperstown, New York; 38 Dennis Goldstein Collection; 39 (left) Mark Rucker; 39 (right) Mark Rucker; 40 David Walberg; 41 Hy Peskin/*LIFE* Magazine © 1947 Time Inc.; 42 (left) UPI/Bettmann Newsphotos; 42 (right) Heinz Kluetmeier/*Sports Illustrated;* 43 AP/Wide World Photos; 44 George Tiedemann/*Sports Illustrated;* 45 Walter Iooss, Jr./*Sports Illustrated.*

The Big Catch
46 James Drake/*Sports Illustrated;* 47 Focus on Sports, Inc.; 48 Walter Iooss, Jr./*Sports Illustrated;* 49 Dick Raphael; 50 (left) National Baseball Library, Cooperstown, New York; 50 (right) UPI/Bettmann Newsphotos; 51 UPI/Bettmann Newsphotos; 52 Janet Pooley Collection; 53 (top) Nancy Hogue; 53 (bottom) AP/Wide World Photos; 54 (top) AP/Wide World Photos; 54 (bottom) Library of Congress; 55 AP/Wide World Photos; 56 (left) National Baseball Library, Cooperstown, New York; 56 (right) AP/Wide World Photos; 57 (left) Tony Triolo/*Sports Illustrated;* 57 (right) National Baseball Library, Cooperstown, New York; 58 Al Tielemans; 59 (top) Lewis Portnoy/Spectra-Action, Inc.; 59 (bottom) Al Tielemans/Phillies; 60 (left) National Baseball Library, Cooperstown, New York; 60 (right) Culver Pictures; 61 AP/Wide World Photos; 62 Grey Villet/*LIFE* Magazine © 1955 Time Inc.; 63 UPI/Bettmann Newsphotos; 64 John Iacono/*Sports Illustrated;* 65 Mickey Pfleger.

In the Beginning
66-67 Courtesy of the Boston Public Library; 68 Mark Rucker; 69 Mark Rucker; 70 National Baseball Library, Cooperstown, New York; 71 (left) Dennis Goldstein Collection; 71 (right) Museum of the City of New York; 72 (left) National Baseball Library, Cooperstown, New York; 72 (right) Courtesy of the Missouri Historical Society; 73 (all) Ron Menchine Collection/Renée Comet Photography; 74-75 George Silk/*LIFE* Magazine ©

1960 Time Inc.; 76 National Baseball Library, Cooperstown, New York; 77 Courtesy of the Boston Public Library; 78 Courtesy of the Boston Public Library; 79 (left) Mark Rucker; 79 (right) National Baseball Library, Cooperstown, New York; 80 Ron Menchine Collection/Renée Comet Photography; 81 North Wind Picture Archives; 82 Ron Menchine Collection/Renée Comet Photography; 83 (left) Library of Congress; 83 (right) Brown Brothers.

The Pitcher's Edge
84-85 Robert Riger; 86 (left) Brown Brothers; 86 (right) John Iacono/*Sports Illustrated;* 87 UPI/Bettmann Newsphotos; 88 (left) National Baseball Library, Cooperstown, New York; 88 (right) Nancy Hogue; 89 (top) Brown Brothers; 89 (bottom) National Baseball Library, Cooperstown, New York; 90 (left) Ron Menchine Collection/Renée Comet Photography; 90 (right) Marvin E. Newman; 91 Walter Iooss, Jr./*Sports Illustrated;* 92 Ron Menchine Collection/Renée Comet Photography; 93 (top both) AP/Wide World Photos; 93 (bottom) George Silk/*LIFE* Magazine © 1956 Time Inc.; 94 Malcolm W. Emmons; 95 (left) Marvin E. Newman; 95 (right) AP/Wide World Photos; 96 (left) National Baseball Library, Cooperstown, New York; 96 (right) Library of Congress; 97 Ronald C. Modra; 99 (left) Garibaldi Studios; 99 (right) AP/Wide World Photos; 100 Ron Menchine Collection/Renée Comet Photography; 101 Walter Iooss, Jr./*Sports Illustrated;* 102 Marvin E. Newman; 103 Marvin E. Newman.

Fans, Fixes and the Fourth Estate
104-105 Martha Holmes/*LIFE* Magazine © 1955 Time Inc.; 106 John Iacono/*Sports Illustrated;* 107 (top) New England Sports Museum; 107 (bottom) Richard C. Crepeau Collection; 108 Ron Menchine Collection/Renée Comet Photography; 109 Walter Iooss, Jr.; 110 Ron Menchine Collection/Renée Comet Photography; 111 (top) AP/Wide World Photos; 111 (bottom) Marvin E. Newman; 112 Otto Greule/Allsport USA; 113 Thomas Carwile Collection/Renée Comet Photography; 114 AP/Wide World Photos; 115 (left) UPI/Bettmann Newsphotos; 115 (right) AP/Wide World Photos; 116 (top) Jeffrey E. Blackman; 116 (bottom) Culver Pictures; 117 (top) Robert

Riger; 117 (bottom left) Lewis Portnoy/Spectra-Action, Inc.; 117 (bottom right) UPI/Bettmann Newsphotos; 118 (left) John Iacomo/*Sports Illustrated;* 118 (right) Heinz Kluetmeier/*Sports Illustrated;* 119 Ron Vesely; 120 (left) UPI/Bettmann Newsphotos; 120 (right) Photo Courtesy of Milwaukee County Historical Society; 121 (all) AP/Wide World Photos.

Decisions, Decisions
122 Focus on Sports, Inc.; 123 National Baseball Library, Cooperstown, New York; 124 National Baseball Library, Cooperstown, New York; 125 John Iacono/*Sports Illustrated;* 126 Smithsonian Institution; 127 (top) UPI/Bettmann Newsphotos; 127 (bottom) National Baseball Library, Cooperstown, New York; 128 Lewis Portnoy/Spectra-Action, Inc.; 129 Ronald C. Modra/*Sports Illustrated;* 130 (left) UPI/Bettmann Newsphotos; 130 (right) UPI/Bettmann Newsphotos; 131 UPI/Bettmann Newsphotos; 132 (left) AP/Wide World Photos; 132 (right) UPI/Bettmann Newsphotos; 133 Ronald C. Modra/*Sports Illustrated;* 134 Ron Menchine Collection/Renée Comet Photography; 135 (top) Malcolm W. Emmons; 135 (bottom) AP/Wide World Photos; 135 (right) Culver Pictures; 136 UPI/Bettmann Newsphotos; 137 (top left) Kevin Fitzgerald; 137 (top right) AP/Wide World Photos; 137 (bottom left) Brown Brothers; 137 (bottom right) UPI/Bettmann Newsphotos.

The Ruling Class
138 Bill Eppridge/*Sports Illustrated;* 139 Ron Menchine Collection/Renée Comet Photography; 140 Mark Rucker; 141 Ron Menchine Collection/Renée Comet Photography; 142 (left) National Baseball Library, Cooperstown, New York; 142 (right) Lewis Portnoy/ Spectra-Action, Inc.; 143 Fred Kaplan; 144 AP/Wide World Photos; 145 (top) Marvin E. Newman; 145 (bottom) Richard Darcey; 146 (left) National Baseball Library, Cooperstown, New York; 146 (right) AP/Wide World Photos; 147 AP/Wide World Photos; 148 Hy Peskin/*Sports Illustrated;* 149 John Iacono/*Sports Illustrated;* 150-151 Walter Iooss, Jr.; 152 (left) National Baseball Library, Cooperstown, New York; 152 (right) National Baseball Library, Cooperstown, New York; 153 Lee Balterman; 154-155 (all) Ron

Menchine Collection/Renée Comet Photography; 156 Smithsonian Institution; 157 (left) National Baseball Library, Cooperstown, New York; 157 (right) UPI/Bettmann Newsphotos, courtesy of the Cleveland Public Library; 158 (left) AP/Wide World Photos; 158 (right) Garibaldi Studios; 159 Walter Iooss, Jr./*Sports Illustrated;* 160 (both) Ron Menchine Collection/ Renée Comet Photography; 161 (left) National Baseball Library, Cooperstown, New York; 161 (right) Library of Congress; 162 Dennis Goldstein Collection; 163 Fred Kaplan.

The Last At-Bat
164 UPI/Bettmann Newsphotos; 165 Anthony Neste; 166 (left) UPI/Bettmann Newsphotos; 166 (right) *The Sporting News;* 167 (left) AP/Wide World Photos; 167 (right) Carnegie Library, Pittsburgh, Pennsylvania; 168 (left) John Iacono/*Sports Illustrated;* 168 (right) AP/Wide World Photos; 169 Richard Mackson/*Sports Illustrated;* 170 (left) National Baseball Library, Cooperstown, New York; 170 (right) National Baseball Library, Cooperstown, New York; 172 National Baseball Library, Cooperstown, New York; 173 (left) Library of Congress; 173 (right) Marvin E. Newman; 174 AP/Wide World Photos; 175 Dick Raphael; 176 National Baseball Library, Cooperstown, New York; 176 (right) AP/Wide World Photos; 177 Mark Kauffman/*Sports Illustrated;* 178 AP/Wide World Photos; 179 Fred Kaplan/Black Star; 180-181 Lewis Portnoy/Spectra-Action, Inc. 183 (both) Ron Menchine Collection/Renée Comet Photography.

ACKNOWLEDGMENTS

The author and editors wish to thank:

Peter P. Clark, Tom Heitz, Bill Deane, Patricia Kelly, Dan Bennett, Frank Rollins and the staffs of the National Baseball Library, Cooperstown, New York; Helen Bowie Campbell and Gregory J. Schwalenberg, Babe Ruth Museum, Baltimore, Maryland; Ellen Hughes, National Museum of American History, Smithsonian Institution, Washington, D.C.; George Hobart and Mary Ison, Prints and Photographs Division, Library of Congress, Washington, D.C.; Dennis Goldstein, Atlanta, Georgia; Thomas Carwile, Petersburg, Virginia; Mark Rucker, Saratoga Springs, New York; Clarence "Lefty" Blasco, Van Nuys, California; Richard C. Crepeau, Orlando, Florida; Bob Davids, Washington, D.C.; Adrienne Aurichio, New York, New York; Lillian Clark, Cleveland Public Library, Cleveland, Ohio; Deborah Cohen, *LIFE* Picture Service, New York, New York; Renée Comet, Renée Comet Photography, Washington, D.C.; Maggie Hearn, UPI/Bettmann Newsphotos, New York, New York; Mrs. Meredith Collins, Brown Brothers, Sterling, Pennsylvania; Tom Logan, Culver Pictures, New York, New York; Stephen P. Gietschier, *The Sporting News,* St. Louis, Missouri; Karen Carpenter and Sunny Smith, *Sports Illustrated,* New York, New York; Nat Andriani, AP/Wide World Photos, New York, New York; Joe Borras, Accokeek, Maryland; Dave Kelly, Library of Congress, Washington, D.C.; Elizabeth McLean, Decatur, Georgia; Julie Harris, Arlington, Virginia; Maria F. Negron, Falls Church, Virginia; Jayne E. Rohrich, Alexandria, Virginia; Phil Walklet, Branford, Connecticut; Nick Cappetta, Alexandria, Virginia.

World of Baseball is produced and
published by Redefinition, Inc.

WORLD OF BASEBALL

Editor	Glen B. Ruh
Design Director	Robert Barkin
Production Director	Irv Garfield
Senior Writer	Jonathan Kronstadt
Text Editor	Sharon Cygan
Picture Editing	Rebecca Hirsh
	Louis P. Plummer
Picture Research	Catherine M. Chase
Design	Edwina Smith
	Sue Pratt
	Collette Conconi
	Monique Strawderman
Copy Editing	Ginette Gauldfeldt
	Carol Gardner
Copy Preparation	Anthony K. Pordes
Production Assistant	Kimberly Fornshill Holmlund
Editorial Research	Janet Pooley
	Mark Lazen
	Ed Dixon
Illustrations	Dale Glasgow
Index	Lee McKee

REDEFINITION

Administration	Margaret M. Higgins
	June M. Nolan
Fulfillment Manager	Karen DeLisser
Marketing Director	Harry Sailer
Finance Director	Vaughn A. Meglan
PRESIDENT	Edward Brash

Library of Congress Cataloging-in-Publication Data
Adomites, Paul D.
October's game: the World Series/Paul D.
Adomites
p. cm.— (World of Baseball)
includes index.
1. World Series (Baseball)—History.
I. Title. II. Series.
GV878.4.A33 1990 89–77288
796.357'646—dc20
ISBN 0–924588–06–3

Printed in the U.S.A.
10 9 8 7 6 5 4 3 2 1

CONTRIBUTORS

Paul D. Adomites is a Pittsburgh-based writer
specializing in travel, food and sports. He is
editor of the *SABR Review of Books,* published
each year by the Society for American Baseball
Research. As a player, he helped his Little
League team to an unblemished 0–27 record.

Henry Staat is Series Consultant for World of
Baseball. A member of the Society for American
Baseball Research since 1982, he helped initiate
the concept for the series. He is an editor
with Wadsworth, Inc., a publisher of college
textbooks.

Ron Menchine, an advisor and sports
collector, shared baseball materials he has been
collecting for 40 years. A sportscaster and sports
director for numerous radio stations, he
announced the last three seasons played by the
Washington Senators.

The editors also wish to thank the following
writers for their contributions to this book:
Robert Kiener, Washington, D.C.; Leonard
Hochberg, Falls Church, VA; David Rice,
Washington, D.C.; Eliot Cohen, Washington,
D.C.; Regina Demris, Alexandria, VA; Randy
Rieland, Washington, D.C.; Michael Leccese,
Washington, D.C.

This book is one of a series that celebrates
America's national pastime.

Redefinition also offers World of Baseball Top
Ten Stat Finders.

For subscription information and prices, write:
Customer Service, Redefinition, Inc.,
P.O. Box 25336,
Alexandria, Virginia 22313

The text of this book is set in Century Old
Style; display type is Helvetica and Gill Sans. The
paper is 70 pound Warrenflo Gloss supplied by
Stanford Paper Company. Typesetting by
Intergraphics, Inc., Alexandria, Virginia. Color
separation by Lanman Progressive, Washington,
D.C. Printed and bound by Ringier America, New
Berlin, Wisconsin.